Behind Closed Doors

Behind Closed Doors

THE SECRET HISTORY OF THE COLD WAR

BY REAR ADMIRAL

Ellis M. Zacharias U.S. NAVY (ret.)

IN COLLABORATION WITH LADISLAS FARAGO

FOUNDED 1838

GPPS

G. P. PUTNAM'S SONS   NEW YORK

MANUFACTURED IN THE UNITED STATES OF AMERICA

H. WOLFF, NEW YORK

TO THE PEOPLE OF AMERICA

Contents

Part Four:

AT BATTLE STATIONS

Part Five:

COLD WAR ON THE AMERICAN PLAN

Part Six:

CONCLUSIONS AND RECOMMENDATIONS

Those who compare the age in which their lot has fallen with a golden age which exists only in imagination, may talk of degeneracy and decay; but no man who is correctly informed as to the past, will be disposed to take a morose or desponding view of the present.

MACAULAY in *History of England*

There is a mysterious cycle in human events. To some generations much is given. Of other generations much is expected. This generation of Americans has a rendezvous with destiny.

In this world of ours in other lands, there are some people, who, in times past, have lived and fought for freedom, and seem to have grown weary to carry on the fight. They have sold their heritage of freedom for the illusion of living. They have yielded their democracy.

I believe in my heart that only our success can stir their ancient hope. They begin to know that here in America we are waging a great and successful war. It is not alone a war against want and destitution and economic demoralization. It is more than that; it is a war for the survival of democracy.

We are fighting to save a great and precious form of government for ourselves and for the world.

FRANKLIN DELANO ROOSEVELT
in Philadelphia on June 27, 1936

Part One

THE ISSUE OF WAR OR PEACE

1.

D-DAY IN THE
RUSSO-AMERICAN
WAR

And so we shall go to war, Glaucon. Shall we not?
Most certainly, he replied.

PLATO's Republic, *Book Two*

THE UNCERTAIN days of the precarious peace that we call the cold war are numbered.

War between the United States and the Union of Soviet Socialist Republics, which would be the third and probably decisive world war in the life of this tragic, unruly generation, is likely to materialize some time between the summer of 1952 and the fall of 1956.

War may come in response to a series of aggressive Soviet moves, which the Kremlin will regard as essential to Russian security but to which we shall react violently and with determination.

Or it may come, as Soviet experts now say it will, as a move of desperation on the part of the United States to stave off an "inevitable" depression or, better still, to turn depression into prosperity.

On the other side of the Atlantic, and especially behind the iron curtain, abundant and tangible evidence [1] reveals that the U.S.S.R. has definitely decided to abandon the prolonged shadow boxing of the cold war.

This decision was reached on the basis of an "Estimate of the Situation," prepared in the fall of 1948 at the specific request of Generalissimo Stalin by a select group of top-ranking Soviet spe-

3

cialists—military experts, economists, political observers, diplomats, and spies.

Upon that estimate, the Politburo unanimously agreed, in
extraordinary session on January 28, 1949, to accept as immediately valid Lenin's thesis that war between capitalism-imperialism and communism is inevitable. At once they ordered the
whole vast Soviet state to gird itself for the showdown between
the United States and the U.S.S.R.

Today everything in the huge Soviet empire is geared to the
estimate of the experts and the decision of the Politburo. They
dominate—indeed, predetermine—every decree and development
from Berlin to Vladivostok, from such a seemingly innocuous
move as the curtailment of curricula in grammar schools to the
explosive decision to revive Russia's claims to the Dardanelles
in Turkey and Spitsbergen in the Arctic Ocean.

Over and above the stepped-up propaganda of Russia's shrewd
global peace campaign, designed to weaken us through disunity
and disarmament, the U.S.S.R. is strengthening herself by lavish
and ruthless expenditures on armament and by efforts to tighten
national unity by persuasion or compulsion.

We seem to be blind to these realities, even though they are
evident in innumerable documents reaching us, from articles in
Pravda and *Bolshevik* to highly classified intelligence reports.
The latter describe proceedings even behind the closed doors of
the Kremlin.

Despite the convincing argument of these reports, we are told
by Secretary of Defense Louis Johnson that "we have good reason to believe the prospects of averting another world conflict
are steadily improving," [2] by General Walter Bedell Smith that
"the Soviet Union's present line of internal and external policies seems to be based on the expectations of peace for several
years," [3] and by General of the Army Dwight D. Eisenhower
that the Russians "are too logical and too sensible to deliberately start a war at this time . . . [or] in the near future." [4]

There is much, both deliberate and unwitting, in the Soviet
master plan that seems to justify such optimistic prognostications.

The war, when and if it comes, will be a new kind of conflict.
It will come upon us in stages. In fact, some of its stages are

already upon us. Others will be hardly recognizable as such. Still others will defy description under the conventional nomenclature that still dominates thinking in the Western world.

Despite the cataclysmic consequences of the ultimate blow, its *initial* moves will not have the sly and vicious impact of the Japanese attack on Pearl Harbor. Rather they will form part of an intricate operation, composed of manifold strokes, gradually developing in sound and fury—a desperate tour de force in a new kind of warfare. The moves will be painstakingly designed and executed so as to place the entire onus of the new war on the United States. All the drums of Soviet propaganda will be beating full blast, to protest the "innocence" of the U.S.S.R. and to "expose" the "criminal conspiracy" of the "warmongering imperialists of the West."

The U.S.S.R. will be in an excellent position to put the onus on us, if only because its initial moves will be covert, circumspect, frequently ambiguous, and diffuse—whereas our response to them will be by necessity overt, straightforward, plainly severe, and—alas!—unimaginative.

To the Soviet Union's new kind of war we shall oppose a traditional form of campaign, bigger and better than any of our previous wars by essentially the same strategy and tactics.

The U.S.S.R. anticipates exactly such a response and bases its expectation of ultimate victory on it.

THE TIME

There are available to us several convincing clues as to the date the U.S.S.R. regards as most likely to be the D-day of a shooting war.

The years 1952, 1954, and 1956 are regarded as crucial in the calculations of the Kremlin.

It is no mere coincidence that the year 1952 was the only future date explicitly mentioned in the recent Russo-Chinese treaty between Moscow and the Communist regime in Peiping.

The same year, accepted by Soviet analysts as the last tranquil year of the cold war, also recurs in the secret protocols of the treaties and military alliances Moscow concluded with its satellites in Warsaw, Prague, Budapest, Bucharest, and Sofia. It is frequently mentioned in Cominform documents as a "year of decision"—the outside date at which certain plans have to be concluded, quotas reached—"the end of an era and the beginning of a new epoch." [5]

By 1952, the first postwar Five-Year Plan of the Soviet Union will be concluded. A new plan, adapted to the demands of a new situation, will be well under way.

Events in Western Europe and the United States focus the Kremlin's expectant interest on this year. In 1952 Marshall Plan aid to Europe is expected to end, its conclusion creating conditions of uncertainty and possibly economic chaos. It is the year of presidential election in the United States when preoccupation with domestic issues and the opportunism of campaign necessities will most likely emphasize the short-range needs of political parties rather than the long-range interests of the nation.

The year 1952 is, therefore, accepted in the U.S.S.R. as the first of three decisive years—the turning point in Russo-American relations, in American relations with Western Europe, and in the Soviet Union's position in the world order. It is regarded as the beginning of the end of what Stalin called the "epoch of world revolution." [6] According to Bolshevik dogma that epoch will end with the collapse of the United States as the last bulwark of imperialist capitalism.

Between now and 1952 the U.S.S.R. will deploy its forces to occupy positions of strategic importance for carefully planned tactical moves. Then in 1954 the United States is expected to oblige Bolshevik planners with the fulfillment of still another one of their prognostications. In that year, the economic recession of the United States, supposedly begun in 1946, is expected to reach its first climactic stage with a depression of major proportions. In that year, too, the number of unemployed in the United States is expected to reach the critical figure of 12 million, forcing the government to desperate emergency measures and ushering in a period of crises that will, in the calculations of Soviet planners, reach a definite climax in 1956, the last of these years of decision.

When we thus give the world but another five years of peace, we reflect the estimate of a group of top-ranking Soviet planners, informed Bolshevik representatives both within and without the U.S.S.R., and several official spokesmen of the Soviet empire.

Such a spokesman is Rear Admiral Eugeni Georgievich Glinkov, until recently (1950) naval attaché of the U.S.S.R. Embassy in Washington, D. C., who stated in so many words that war would break out "within five years." [7]

This was as explicit a pronouncement as may be expected from a high Soviet official. It was made on the record by a responsible soldier diplomat who is himself one of the planners of war and who has access to the highly classified plans of others. It cannot be accepted as an inadvertent slip of the tongue. Rather the authors are inclined to regard it as a calculated indiscretion.

It goes without saying that Admiral Glinkov described the United States as the aggressor. He gave depression in the United States as *casus belli*. This, too, was the recurrent theme of a series of informal interviews we conducted in an atmosphere of off-the-record intimacy with a number of Communist leaders in Europe, in the Delegates' Lounge at Lake Success, during the Paris session of the UN General Assembly, in the drawing rooms of satellite embassies and UN delegations in Washington and New York, and with Soviet members of the Military Staff Committee of the United Nations. [8]

Typical of such talks were those we had with the two foremost Communists of Western Europe's strategic North—Norway's Axel Wahl of Hammerfest and Gottfred Hoelvold of Kirkenes. [9]

In Oslo everyone warned against both men: "They are exceptionally dangerous." But up north, where the West physically borders upon Russia, they are generally viewed with friendship, understanding, respect, and, insofar as Hoelvold is concerned, even admiration.

Wahl is a theoretical Communist, secretary of the Party, and a full-time politician, whose allegiance to communism may not, in the final analysis, prove identical with allegiance to the U.S.S.R.

Hoelvold is the enigma of the North. He is a little man, the kind of labor leader Upton Sinclair used to portray, with searching eyes under a low forehead, his black hair turning an uncertain gray. He wears a gray sweater and trousers with gray stripes.

Only his eyes betray his fervor, although they display some disillusionment as well.

Against the visitor "from the States," he turns an angry barrage of propaganda. He sputters all the familiar words of Radio Moscow: "Finance capital, Yankee dollar, neo-Fascism of the Truman Doctrine, world domination by Wall Street."

In the course of our conversation we asked Hoelvold the question foremost in the minds of Norwegians there in the Far North, "Do you regard war between the U.S. and the U.S.S.R. as imminent or inevitable?"

The rapid flow of Hoelvold's studied answers suddenly stopped, and he pondered the answer to this particular question for an unusually long time. Finally he said, "The war between the U.S. and the U.S.S.R. is inevitable—but it is not imminent. It will come as America's answer to its depression, which is also inevitable. When depression comes to America, America will go to war."

"When do you think this will happen?"

The Norwegian Communist leader shrugged his shoulders. "What difference does it make whether it comes sooner or later?"

He thought again, then he said, "It will come within the next five or ten years."

Prior to leaving Moscow, late in 1948, General Walter Bedell Smith decided to conduct an informal poll among the foreign diplomats accredited to the Soviet Government to ascertain as best as he could, "the probabilities of future peace or war between the Soviet orbit and the West." He was most interested in the views of envoys representing the satellites in Moscow, and properly so since Soviet policies and intentions can now be gauged with approximate accuracy in their deliberate or unwitting indiscretions.

"While the opinions of Westerners varied," General Smith reports, "those of the Communist satellite diplomats were practically unanimous. They all expressed the opinion that it was impossible for the two systems to live together in peace and that a clash was inevitable. . . . Some said war would come 'when the Soviet Union is prepared.' Others estimated that hostilities might be expected in five, ten or fifteen years. . . . All gave the impression of believing that the initiative would rest with the

Soviet Union, thus paying an unintentional tribute to the basically pacific policy of the United States and the other Western democracies." [10]

The opinions expressed by these Communist statesmen, some of them privy to the innermost secrets of the Kremlin, reflect Stalin's own opinion as communicated to us by several of his closest advisers on foreign policy. One of these was Andrei A. Gromyko, then Soviet delegate at the UN, now first deputy foreign minister of the U.S.S.R. He made his disclosure to several important American business leaders in the course of his efforts to bring about rapprochement between the United States and the U.S.S.R., on Generalissimo Stalin's terms. [11]

According to Gromyko, and certain other informants, Stalin's views on this score were expressed informally in a letter he was said to have written to President Truman some time in 1948.

The Russians insist that the letter was dispatched through diplomatic channels via Ambassador Panyushkin, who, so they say, delivered it to the White House in person.

In the letter, Stalin presumably outlined in as convincing terms as he could his desire for world peace and his opposition to the war mongers, who "professionally and habitually poison the wells of international collaboration." Stalin invited Truman to join him in a declaration expressing devotion to peace. He then proceeded to develop the idea which is today the recurrent theme of Soviet propaganda.

"I am aware of the fact," Stalin is said to have written, "that some people in the United States regard war as the sole alternative to depression. But the alternative with which we are confronted is not war or depression. The alternative is war or peace."

There is some slight circumstantial evidence to indicate that an exchange of views along these lines did occur between the White House and the Kremlin. At just about the date of Stalin's alleged letter to Truman, the Chief Executive was quoted by White House correspondents as expressing almost identical views. He, too, was represented as speaking of the two alternatives—war or depression and war or peace. He, too, was said to have expressed unqualified determination to choose the second alternative. The informed few with whom we discussed the mystery of Stalin's phantom letter to Truman inclined to attribute Mr. Truman's mood of 1947-1948, as well as his famous remarks about "good old Joe in the Kremlin," to a deep impression that Stalin's letter seemed to have created in him.[12]

But even if Stalin's letter was never written or if written never delivered, the fact that the Russians are still spreading the rumor of its existence goes far to expose Stalin's attitude toward the issue of war and peace. Reduced to its simplest terms, his formula of war between the United States and the U.S.S.R. revolves around the equation in which $X = $ Depression.

According to the authoritative Soviet "Estimate of the Situation," (1) *the United States of America will experience a depression of major proportions between 1954 and 1956,* and (2) *the United States will then go to war to stave off the cataclysmic effects of depression on her national economy and morale.*

To forestall this American move, the U.S.S.R. is determined to move first, between now and 1956, to occupy all positions from which a physical attack against the U.S.S.R. could be launched without actually engaging in open hostilities. The U.S.S.R., so the Kremlin's planners calculate, could then lure the United States into a conventional land war at the end of an immensely long supply line, across dangerous waters. In other words, Russia plans to compel the United States to wage war on Soviet terms, in the manner most advantageous to the U.S.S.R. Such a war if started by us would have to be a total war and is expected to be a protracted one, leading to an eventual application of Stalin's favorite military theory: "Victory through the strategic counteroffensive."

This means a final, cumulative, massive counteroffensive against a militarily, morally, and economically exhausted foe. The theory, developed by Stalin while reading Clausewitz's and Shaposhnikov's erudite treatises on war, was tested in World War II and worked to the Generalissimo's complete satisfaction.[13]

Thus the Soviet Union expects the war of the future to be started by the United States in a move of desperation for its own economic survival and not as a response to a long series of insidious Soviet provocations. This Soviet conception is remote from the American, which sees the Soviet Union as the aggressor in a possible or probable Russo-American war, expected to follow established conventional lines in all its phases and manifestations.

IMAGES OF A NEW WAR

The fact-minded, antimystic Anglo-Saxon can scarcely visualize the kind of campaign Stalin has in store for him. We depict the opening hours of the coming Russo-American war in images of our past experience.

The simplest is the Defense Department's concept, outlined by Secretary Johnson when he spoke of the possibility of an attack "from the opposite hemisphere without warning and with unpredictable fury"—an image suggested by the experience of Pearl Harbor.[14]

A second image reduces the invading force to the forlorn person of a single commercial traveler with a hydrogen bomb in his luggage, smuggling it into a vacant lot in Detroit or Pittsburgh or Oak Ridge. A third image envisions the arrival of a squad of Typhoid Mary's attended by clandestine bacteriologists from, say, the Krasnodarsk Institute of Red Army Medicine, poisoning our wells, our major sources of food, and other points susceptible to such assault.

And carrying this Wellsian phantasmagoria to the absurd extreme, a fourth image expects a lone submarine surfacing off the Virginia coast, releasing a mysterious guided missile from its catapult. The weapon would race at supersonic speed to a celestial point miles above the geographical center of the United States, exploding there only to release some chemical that would eliminate the oxygen from the air and kill all beings dependent on that element in their daily diet.

These are, all of them, images of an old and outdated war or the martial apparition of an unlikely doomsday. The layman seems to be most fascinated by the mechanized monsters of a push-button war, while our professional military men seem to be tied to the obsolescent image of the archaic campaigns they themselves used to study in stale texts when they sat at the desks of their military schools.

This was alarmingly demonstrated by Colonel Louis B. Ely of

the United States Army, West Point 1919, an officer "engaged in directing important intelligence activities for the past decade." In recent months he published a book entitled *The Red Army Today,* purporting to be a reliable exposé of its branches, tactical abilities, command echelons—and possible objectives.[15]

But the image of war that Colonel Ely attributes to the Soviet General Staff is the image of an old war—the conventional movement of troops on the checkerboards of old-fashioned battlefields, the image foremost in the ballasted minds of our own intelligence experts rather than in the operations plan of the Red Army General Staff. If our military leaders look for the Russian advances only in places where Colonel Ely expects them to occur, they will be sorely disappointed. In his imaginary counterattack, just three paragraphs from the concluding sentence of his last chapter, Colonel Ely places the Allies "still 1,200 miles from the Soviet border." Three paragraphs later the war is over: "The fate of the Red Empire was sealed."

It is, therefore, important to state that Stalin has no conventional imperialist or military designs on America. He prepares no expeditionary forces to conquer or subjugate it by means of an old-fashioned assault across the broad expanses of the Atlantic and Pacific Oceans.

What Stalin has in mind for the United States is a fate worse than military defeat in war, subjugation in armed truce, or "liberation" in communism.

Stalin's war against the United States, which is already on, is a subtle campaign aimed at the complete obliteration of this country as a potent opponent of Russian-Bolshevik aspirations, first, by isolating it within its oceanic borders, and, then, by disorganizing and disintegrating it to prevent it from ever breaking out of its degrading, decaying, impotent isolation.

Stalin recognizes in the United States the only potent obstacle to his aims. He is determined to remove this obstacle from his path by demolishing the stones of which it is built, one by one.[16]

FIELDS OF BATTLE

In order to accomplish this *strategic* aim, the Soviet Union will strike major operational but not necessarily military blows at the overseas tentacles of what Russian propaganda calls the

American octopus. It is possible, on the basis of reliable intelligence, to trace the projected course of Soviet expansion:

In *Northern Europe* it will move into the strategic Baltic area via Finland, to engulf Sweden and Spitsbergen in the Arctic Ocean. It will come to a halt at the water's edge, whence it can still control the Skagerrak and the Kattegat, the narrow passages from the Baltic to the open sea.

In *Southern Europe* it will move into Yugoslavia but will probably bypass Greece, isolating it like a barked branch left to wither on a live tree.

In *Western Europe* it will continue to harass Italy and France, awaiting the time when they will fall helplessly into "the orbit" because of progressive inner paralyzation, aggravated by the terrorism of Communist activists and Red Guard saboteurs.

In the *Euro-Asia borderland* it will move across the Black Sea into Turkey, again stopping at the water's edge, and via Iran to the Persian Gulf area. The Near Eastern area is regarded as a land bridge across which Russia can always pass to the African continent.

In *Central Asia* it will engulf Afghanistan and the Asiatic Highlands, including the Northwest Frontier region.

In *Southern Asia* it will harass Hongkong, Viet Nam, Burma, the Malay Peninsula, India and Pakistan, Indonesia and the Philippines, awaiting their revolutions by internal forces.

In the *Far East* it will overflow into Japan eventually allocating preponderant influence to it in the Bolshevik organization of the Far East.

Left to stew in their own juice in what Stalin himself called "a helpless position of isolation" will be England and her remote peripheral commonwealth. The United States will be confined to her "Monroe area," with the southern part of the Western Hemisphere, the whole of Latin America, moving restlessly like a feverish bosom and contaminating the entire continent with a progressive disease of anarchy, nihilism, and corruption.

This is the total plan, or what Bolshevik terminology calls the maximum objective. It is an important element of Soviet strength that the leaders of the U.S.S.R. rarely indulge in illusions—or at least try to guard themselves against them. Such an illusion would be that the maximum objective can ever be accomplished in the face of an alerted and nervous opponent.[17]

What we may expect to see, and for what we must prepare ourselves, is the gradual achievement of lesser goals—what Bolsheviks call the minimum objective.

There are in the world today five major danger points where Soviet aggression, without armed warfare, may be expected between now and 1954. They are:

(1) *Yugoslavia.* The grand strategic plan of the U.S.S.R. cannot succeed unless this vital Adriatic beachhead is regained from its present Titoist rulers—dissident, unreliable Bolsheviks.

(2) *Iran.* The Soviet Union is determined to regain control over Iranian Azerbeijan in the near future. The occupation of Iranian Azerbeijan is regarded as essential to Soviet security from the point of view of its fuel supplies. First, it is regarded as vital for the strategic protection of the Baku-Batum oil area, and of the Soviet Union's exposed "soft underbelly," extending from 30 degrees to 60 degrees eastern longitude, from the Ukraine to Turkmenia, more than 1,400 miles. There seems to be another reason. According to the geologists of the Soviet Academy of Sciences, subterranean deposits in Iranian Azerbeijan are draining off immense quantities of oil from the Baku-Batum fields of the U.S.S.R., resulting in a gradual but lately rapid reduction of output and representing the danger of premature exhaustion of the vital Soviet fields. For a time the Kremlin seemed to be satisfied to prevent the acquisition of concessions in northern Iran by foreign interests. But now the Soviet Union may be expected to insist upon gaining those concessions for herself—and she is determined to gain them even by means of armed pressure on Iran.[18]

(3) *Turkey.* A century and a half ago Napoleon was told by the Tsar's representative that Russia wanted control over Constantinople. Russia's claim to the Dardanelles has never been abandoned either by Tsarist or by Communist Russia. It will be revived again in the near future with the threat of armed pressure, similar to the decision Stalin suggested to Hitler in 1940 in Berlin.[19]

(4) *Sweden.* The precarious neutrality of the leading Scandinavian country is less impressive to Soviet strategists than the availability of her rolling farmland, tundra, and ice-covered

lakes as landing fields and deployment areas to the Western allies. Satisfactory guarantees are regarded as essential to Soviet security, and the Kremlin is now determined to gain such guarantees from Sweden, even by means of armed pressure. (For further details, see Chapter 14.)

(5) *Southeast Asia.* The area represents no immediate danger to Soviet security. But it provides one of the great opportunities to advance the Soviet orbit to unexpected outposts, not by the strength of the U.S.S.R. but by the weakness of its adversaries. (See Chapter 11 for further details.)

How was the decision reached in the immense privacy of the Kremlin to increase the intensity of the cold war?

On what exactly was that decision based?

What master plan was drafted on the basis of that decision?

And how could a bold American plan still prevent the execution of the Soviet plan?

To these questions the chapters that follow will seek to provide answers.

2. THE HISTORIC POLITBURO MEETING

IT WAS almost five o'clock in the morning of a new day—Friday, January 28, 1949. Georgi Maximilianovich Malenkov, presiding over the regular weekly meeting, leaned forward in his chair and adjourned an abnormally protracted session of the Politburo.

Stalin had gone to his private quarters a few hours earlier, when the trend of debate indicated to him the inevitable decision. The few dozen men he left behind in the paneled conference room of the Politburo—members, alternates, specialists, and secretaries—were too exhausted to appreciate the historic significance of this particular session. There had been great tension in the room. Now it was relaxed as Malenkov announced the vote and the decision.

The men gathered their scattered papers, moving jerkily like automatons, and prepared to leave quickly. There seemed to be no elation, no thrill, either on their faces or in their hearts. Too tired to judge even their own part in this historic meeting, they descended the broad eighteenth-century stairway of the rambling Kremlin palace, originally designed by the architect Kasakov for the Moscow Senate. Their waiting cars, lined up on Kalyayev Square in front of the ornate Arsenal, alongside cannons captured from Napoleon, now came rolling forward one by one, preceded and followed by their regular MVD escorts, to pick up their distinguished passengers.

The clock bell in Spasskiye Gate, masterpiece of a forgotten English craftsman, was striking five in its ponderous metallic baritone. Moscow was sleeping soundly through this historic dawn. But the snow-covered Arbat was alive with scores of militiamen on extraordinary duty and with special squads of the MVD's Kremlin branch, guarding the safe passage of their charges. Bundled in clumsy winter attire these high officials sat almost unconscious with weariness behind the bullet-proof windows of their curtained cars.

Then the cavalcade sped out through the Troitzky Gate of the Kremlin, across the bridge over what once was the Neglinka, past the white Kutafia Tower—both mementos of a Tsarist past —toward their country homes.

A few minutes later an unusual quiet settled on this restricted part of the Kremlin as, silently, invisible guards switched off the searchlights that had illuminated the huge red flag with golden Sickle and Hammer fluttering boastfully from the dome of Kasakov's palace. The square was suddenly dark; the shadowy figures disappeared like so many ghosts recalled to their shady pits below by the first morning crow of a rooster.

This strange nocturnal drama was described in a special intelligence report,[1] to which we gained access, by one of the men who were present: a young colonel of the Guards, staff member of Marshal Voroshilov's Special Military Subcommittee within the Politburo. He alone seemed to feel, to realize the thrill of the historic night he had just lived through.

The Politburo session he had just witnessed from the chair directly behind that of Voroshilov, and whose minutes he had kept for the secret archives of his chief, had been called to decide on the showdown with the West. But it went beyond that mere decision. It actually drafted a timetable and fixed the flexible D-day for the showdown, sometime between 1952 and 1956.

A few weeks later, Colonel Khralov, the confidential informant, was sent as a special officer courier to Marshal Konstantin K. Rokossovsky's headquarters at Liegnitz in Silesia. He carried documents and instructions containing the first concrete implementation of the decision. The issue of war and peace was no academic matter to the young colonel. It was a living operations plan, elaborated in explicit detail, resting in a sturdy leather briefcase fastened to his wrist by a long thin stainless-steel chain.

It was the secret of a few men who expected him to protect it with his life.

His grave responsibility was to arouse in Colonel Khralov a first groping desire to escape somehow from the captivity of his momentous secret. He wanted to share it with the world, in a single-handed effort, to prevent it from doing the ruinous harm for which the plan had been specifically designed.

Such a radical solution for his dilemma was slow in formulating in the Colonel's tormented mind. From Liegnitz he returned to Moscow, to Marshal Voroshilov's office in the Kremlin, to the frightening chores of his new assignments. Then, toward the end of August, 1949, he was called upon to attend still another extraordinary meeting, in Generalissimo Stalin's private quarters, to review the January decision of the Politburo, as they said, "in the light of certain new factors."

Foremost among those new factors was the achievement by the U.S.S.R. of an atomic explosion. This was a gain, a credit entry on the Russian ledger of war.

On the debit side was Yugoslavia's departure from the orbit. One of the bastions, on which a major part of the Politburo's ambitious plan was supposed to be resting firmly, had been demolished by the unpardonable truculence of a "chauvinistic turncoat." [2]

While the January meeting had been preoccupied with the broad policy questions and long-range plans whose gradual maturation was left to several years, this particular session in August was devoted to immediate problems requiring prompt and direct action and to the drafting of a short-range program for the showdown with Tito.

The session was not confined to the usual Thursday conclave. It spread over three busy days with but little sleep allowed to its participants during two work-filled nights. Again the Colonel was sitting behind Voroshilov, again he was recording the proceedings in minute detail, again he was to go to Liegnitz with urgent instructions to Rokossovsky. Those instructions included the Marshal's recall to Moscow preparatory to his assignment to Poland as minister of defense and commander-in-chief of the Polish Army. [3]

War again was the dominant theme of this Politburo session—

a subsidiary to the impending greater conflict but one that the Politburo realized could if imprudently handled unleash the showdown planned for 1954–56. Even in the face of this calculated risk the decision was made to eliminate Tito by all means fair or foul and to recapture for the greater plan the indispensable bastion of Yugoslavia.

It was the cynicism of these calculations that started Colonel Khralov on his road to treason. By the time he reached Liegnitz on his second courier trip, his mind was made up. From Rokossovsky's GHQ he continued his journey to Berlin. There he crossed the flimsy demarcation line into the British zone, surrendered to a bored intelligence officer, and disappeared from the grip of the MVD with the full story of the great decision.

Presumably both the British and the American authorities have the man's voluminous report on file. If they were impressed by the intelligence he brought, they did not show enthusiasm or gratification. After a few sessions with the Colonel they abandoned him to an uncertain fate. It seems that the strategic material failed to impress his Western interrogators. They occupied far too low positions in the Berlin intelligence hierarchy to comprehend implications beyond the tactical sphere. The tactical material, especially information concerning the Soviet atom bomb and the plan for the showdown with Tito, met with some understanding. It seems it did reach higher echelons in our own government. Shortly afterward it was announced in Washington that our own National Security Council had decided to go to Yugoslavia's aid in case of a Russian attack.[4]

The hapless Russian was not rewarded for his own great decision. His story was not allowed to gain the publicity he himself deemed necessary to frustrate the long-range Soviet plan. He was dropped by his new friends in Western intelligence and told to try to carve out a future for himself. Russian friends who had preceded him into exile saved him from starvation. They paved his way out of Berlin, to Belgium, where he stayed for a few weeks in a run-down family hotel. It was by certain Belgian contacts that his material was brought to our attention. He is no longer in Brussels—should the Foreign Branch of the MVD regard this account as a clue to his whereabouts.[5]

We are describing the Khralov incident in some detail because it has a significance far greater than its mere importance as an intelligence scoop. Our experience with him is no isolated case. We have, either ourselves or through several trusted contacts, been in touch with more than two hundred self-exiled Soviet officials of substantial standing who left Moscow in much the same manner as Khralov's sudden departure. Most of them held positions of importance, material and moral security never enjoyed by the rank and file of Bolsheviki. Their lives were in no immediate danger. Their everyday comforts were assured. They hobnobbed with the great and belonged to that privileged class which Vishinsky likes to describe as "no mere shopkeepers."

And yet they decided to exchange the comforts of Soviet high officialdom for the discomforts of exile, their security on the privileged list of the MVD for the insecurity of its blacklist.

Some of them made the break for selfish reasons—including the expectation of money, "up to a million dollars," for the voluntary and expedient transfer of their loyalties. But the vast majority expected no material benefits from their action. Even today and especially in Russia there are men of the Swiftian mold who prefer to "suffer death, rather than submit to break their eggs at the smaller end." [6]

THE EXPERTS ARE CALLED TO THE KREMLIN

The January, 1949, conference of the Politburo at which the crucial decision for a third world war was reached concluded a series of sessions held week after week for several months, between September, 1948, and January, 1949. To the outsider the atmosphere of these special meetings revealed little unusual, certainly nothing of the momentousness of the issues discussed. For many years, under Stalin's leadership, the Politburo has been holding its meetings customarily on Thursdays. Its deliberations often extend far into the next morning. Usually attended by all members, Politburo meetings also frequently bring to the Kremlin the best brains of the Soviet Union.

Thus the parade of distinguished specialists who had been summoned to the Kremlin from all parts of the Soviet Union appeared merely as a routine procedure.

Some of these specialists were officials of the Minindel (Ministry of Foreign Affairs), others professors of Moscow University's

College of Diplomacy. Included in this group were Andrei A. Gromyko, deputy foreign minister; Boris Krylov, the U.S.S.R.'s representative at the Hague Court of International Justice; Professor Boris Stein, a veteran diplomat, at one time the Kremlin's ambassador to Mussolini; Arkady A. Sobolev, then one of the UN's assistant secretaries general; and many others of similar stature.

The cavalcade of military scientists included strategists and students of military history like Generals Sarayev, Yarchevski, Kostin, Subbotin, Vechny, Talenski, Samsonov, Broneski, Shilovski, Solodovnik, Cheprakov, Voronin, Zamyatin, Panfilov, Korkodinov, and Ionov; Admirals Belli, Shner, and Alafuzov.[7]

Among the economists, the reappearance of academician Eugene S. Varga created a mild sensation. The stormy petrel and independent thinker of the defunct Institute of World Economics and World Politics appeared with his chief accuser Kuzminov, author in 1947 of the original *Bolshevik* article that had chastized Varga for his "un-Marxian" prediction "of an inevitable upward swing in production in the U.S.A. and some other capitalist countries in the wake of the war." Also present were Alexander Trakhtenberg, an economic conformist of the Academy of Sciences, and Lev Mendelsohn, who shared with Varga temporary ostracism and then gained with him readmission into the Politburo's inner sanctum.

Other *rapporteurs* advised the Politburo on collaboration within the Soviet orbit and on the state of the Cominform, on the Communist parties in the world, on the help Russia could expect from sympathizers throughout Europe and Asia, and on questions of propaganda and agitation. Among these specialists were Pavel Yudin, administrative head of the Cominform, and General Yevgeni Zhukov. The latter had been but recently released from Yugoslav captivity, where he had been held for months for his activities as chief of the anti-Tito Russian espionage network. Zhukov is an archaic creature of Russian conspiracy, a living link between Tsarist plots and Bolshevik schemes. We shall meet him again.

When this particular series of sessions was decided upon, the Politburo formed five subcommittees, an unusual occurrence since the questions to be dealt with by these new and temporary agencies had been fully reviewed by the permanent administrative branches of the Communist party's Central Executive Committee. But the exceptionally high rank of the specialists called in and the degree of secrecy of their deliberations raised this brain trust from the level of the Central Committee to the sublime level of the Politburo itself.

Each subcommittee was headed by a Politburo member or alternate: the Foreign Affairs Subcommittee by V. M. Molotov; the Military Affairs Subcommittee by Voroshilov, who despite his advanced age was thus returned to influence from temporary sinecure; the Economic Affairs Subcommittee by Saburov, a comparative newcomer to the Politburo. The Cominform Subcommittee was headed by Nikolai A. Bulganin, then recently transferred from the Ministry of the Armed Forces to a top-level liaison office supervising with an iron hand members of the Soviet commonwealth; and, finally, a Propaganda Subcommittee was assigned to Suslov, who was shortly to be relieved of his duties as chief of the Agitprop (the Propaganda Administration of the Executive Committee) to concentrate on the gigantic task of mobilizing world opinion for Russia in preparation of the showdown.

The five subcommittees were co-ordinated by Malenkov, top-ranking secretary of the Communist party. He also shared with Bulganin the supervision of the Cominform Subcommittee and was in complete charge of a collegium dealing with the specific and ticklish problem of Yugoslavia. He, too, kept Stalin posted on the progress of these subcommittees while the Generalissimo was resting in Sochi.

The task assigned to these *ad hoc* subcommittees of the Politburo was threefold: (1) The preparation of a broad and comprehensive survey of Russo-American relations. (2) An investigation into the respective and relative positions of the United States and the U.S.S.R. in the new world order. (3) The drafting of recommendations for the Politburo to aid it in the solution of the long-range and short-range problems this ambitious review was expected to bring to light.

3. WHAT THE EXPERTS TOLD STALIN

Were half the power, that fills the world with terror,
Were half the wealth, bestowed on camps and courts,
Given to redeem the human mind from error,
There were no need for arsenals or forts...
        LONGFELLOW: The Arsenal at Springfield

THE "Estimate of the Situation" that the Politburo's experts drafted contained both lights and shadows and thereby gave the impression of objectivity. To one unaffected by those influences to which totalitarian scholars are subjected, its objectivity seems to be full of holes. However, we do not intend to argue with that estimate—"fight the problem," as they say in the War College. We shall merely report upon it. Perhaps we would regard the errors with somewhat greater compassion were reason left free in the U.S.S.R. to combat them. As it is, the world may be moving toward grave and perilous times as a result of the work of erring men.

The estimate, as reconstructed for us by Colonel Khralov and others, follows the conventional pattern of such documents. It is based upon verified information, fair assumptions, and, to a somewhat greater degree than our own similar estimates on analyses, in this case invariably inspired by dogmatic, often anachronistic, quotations from Lenin and Stalin.

The document, although comprising five sections, falls into two major parts: an Estimate of the Economic Situation and an Estimate of the Military Situation. While perfunctory references are made to other countries, the estimates are preoccupied with the United States and Great Britain.

Both estimates emphasize weaknesses, representing these as far outweighing the indisputable strength of the two countries. The Economic Estimate thus speaks of the economic crisis in the United States as already existing, while the Military Estimate discounts the strategic value of absolute weapons and places undue emphasis on an alleged disorganization within the armed forces in the United States.

These estimates were drafted in the Kremlin between December 20, 1948, and January 25, 1949. Their drafting coincided with a series of significant events in the United States, which need to be enumerated since they had, according to trustworthy informants, an immediate bearing on the conclusions themselves.

(1) General of the Army George C. Marshall was replaced at the head of the State Department by Dean G. Acheson.

(2) President Truman submitted to Congress the largest budget in the peacetime history of the United States. It included $15,900,000,000 for national defense and $6,700,000,000 for foreign aid—a total of $22,600,000,000 or more than 50 per cent of the whole budget.

(3) The Air Force announced an appropriation of $300,-000,000 to purchase B-36's and B-50's, described by an official spokesman as planes "capable of carrying an A-bomb to any target within Russia and returning to their bases in the United States."

(4) Secretary of State Dean G. Acheson assured a senatorial committee of investigators that he would refrain from a policy of appeasement vis-à-vis Russia.

(5) The trial of eleven Communist leaders before Federal Judge Harold R. Medina was moving toward its opening, the Supreme Court having refused to intervene.

(6) In his inaugural speech, President Truman pledged American economic and diplomatic support to all battling against "the forces and false philosophies of Communism," and American military aid and other assistance "to freedom loving nations against the dangers of aggression."

(7) The collapse of the Nationalist forces in China was continuing at a mounting rate.

(8) Negotiations for the conclusion of a North Atlantic Defense Pact were progressing in Washington and in the capitals of prospective member countries. Though talks aimed at a Scandinavian defense alliance collapsed and Sweden subsequently removed herself from the proposed union, twelve other Western countries appeared to be making rapid progress toward the drafting of an all-inclusive defense pact.

In the light of these events, the subcommittees of the Politburo accelerated their efforts and reported that they would be ready to present a report at the January 28 meeting of the Politburo.

The development that did more than anything else to bring about the speed-up was the democratic West's rapid move toward the North Atlantic Defense Pact. The Kremlin was fully informed by its intelligence services of the details of these negotiations then progressing behind closed doors—including certain difficulties and disagreements. But judging the United States by their own standards, the leaders of the U.S.S.R. looked forward to the conclusion of the pact, if only because they expected the United States to demand adherence to it and the eleven others to succumb to our pressure without alternative.

THE MILITARY ESTIMATE OF THE SITUATION

In a very careful analysis of available information, we extracted twelve major items in which the Military Estimate of the Situation recognized certain weaknesses and acknowledged definite strength in our war-making capacity.

(1) Our great strength was recognized as the immense industrial base of our military establishment and our ability to organize for war on a lavish scale, although not as fast as the innate speed of a new conflict would require.

(2) Our second strength was acknowledged to be the potential war-making capacity of Western Europe as a whole. The estimate pointed out that if and when we should succeed in coordinating, reorganizing, and consolidating the member countries of the North Atlantic Defense Pact and in equipping them with weapons, a vigorous ideology, a high-minded and efficient

officers' corps, and an effective military theory, the United States would have gained a formidable coalition, strong enough to vanquish a coalition of Bolsheviks. This possibility was pointed up in the estimate as a major challenge, which Soviet counter-action must meet headlong. It was emphasized that the U.S.S.R. must meet the challenge before long if it does not want to see the present weak defensive conglomeration transformed into an effective and aggressive alliance.

However, the estimate listed the North Atlantic Union as a liability for the time being. Comprised as it is of "weak allies who require daily transfusions of blood from America," it was compared to previous coalitions whose weak links caused the eventual breaking of the whole chain. In this connection Hitler's example was cited and his failure attributed, at least in part, to his commitments to weak allies, like Italy against Greece, Hungary against Yugoslavia, and Finland and Rumania against the U.S.S.R.

A further comparison was made between the allies of the United States and those of the U.S.S.R. Thus the military might and prowess of Communist China was contrasted with those of the Nationalists. Poland and Czechoslovakia, Hungary and Bulgaria were favorably compared with France and Italy, Belgium and the Netherlands.

(3) The estimate noted that the Soviet possession of the atomic bomb had restored military equilibrium and deprived the United States of whatever advantage it might have enjoyed in this particular field.

(4) It listed certain apparent inadequacies in the American theory of war. It maintained that the Joint Chiefs of Staff had no co-ordinated or effective plan of grand strategy. Whatever they had, it was judged unacceptable to the military experts of their allies.

(5) Much was made of interservice feuds, which were said to have revealed serious deficiencies in what the estimate called tactical planning on an operational scale and in our policy of "balanced weapon development." It was added that preoccupation with spectacular new weapons retarded the businesslike development of conventional armaments the United States would need for a campaign of attrition, which it would inevita-

bly face on a European or Asiatic battlefield when confronted with the land masses of its Bolshevik enemies.

(6) The estimate cited reports of Soviet intelligence that highly acclaimed secret weapons proved dismal disappointments in actual test, necessitating costly and time-consuming redesigning, retooling and retesting, and seriously delaying adaptation of tactics to new equipment.

(7) The estimate reported in detail an analysis prepared by General Sarayev, a former military attaché at the Soviet Embassy in Washington, in which rampant confusion in the theories of war and a low intellectual approach to new forms of warfare on all levels of the American officers' corps were described.

(8) The effectiveness of atomic weapons and of strategic bombing was discounted.

(9) Another report, signed by Colonel Anatoli Y. Galkovsky, called attention to an absence of ideological orientation in the American armed services and a failure on their highest echelons to anticipate the political problems an American expeditionary force would have to face in any European country with large pacific, pro-Communist, Communist, and pro-Russian factions.

(10) A tendency to underestimate the military potential of the U.S.S.R. was emphasized together with an alleged inability of our general staff to comprehend the potentials of a global guerilla warfare waged by Bolshevik partisans, presumably compelling us to wage a small-scale war in the face of our preparations for a gigantic aerial atomic conflict.

(11) A committee headed by Commodore Mikhail N. Dorokov and Colonel Konstantin S. Kulkin submitted a report in which the failure or tardiness of civilian mobilization and allegedly lagging industrial preparedness were emphasized.

(12) They estimated that at least two years would be needed, despite the expensive peacetime maintenance of certain war-essential industries, to remobilize America for any new global war to come.

This part of the estimate concluded that the United States appeared incapable of either defending itself against a strategic assault or of delivering one with the prospect of decisive victory at the outset. This situation was expected to deteriorate rather than improve between 1949 and 1956, due largely to a mounting economic crisis which, it was forecast, would necessitate reduction in taxes and result in the reorientation of the American people's interest "from international adventures to pressing domestic problems."

The estimate further concluded that the United States would experience insurmountable political difficulties in its European theater of operations and would prove incapable of coping with the political unrest, civil war, revolution which would inevitably flare up in Western Europe either prior to or shortly after the arrival of our expeditionary forces.

Finally the estimate concluded that sooner or later the United States would be compelled to fight a land war of attrition in front of a restive hinterland, at the end of a long supply line, with an industrial base in Europe that could never meet even a small portion of the needs of our expeditionary forces.

Thus, the experts said, "the defeat of the United States in such a war would be inevitable with all the resultant consequences of such an eventuality in the political and economic field."

THE ECONOMIC ESTIMATE OF THE SITUATION

The glaring optimism of the Military Estimate was surpassed in the Economic Estimate of the Situation. An intriguing feature of the latter was the signature of Professor Eugene S. Varga, acquiescing fully with his colleagues in the official party theory of cumulative economic crisis in the United States.

Highly technical and intensely dialectical, the estimate tried to prove the rapid and progressing decline of American capitalism by citing the testimony of American economists.

Innumerable tables, charts, and diagrams accompanied the presentation to confirm Stalin's contention that "the present economic crisis is the most serious and profound world economic crisis that has ever occurred." [1] In a special report an economist named Cheprakov described the "progressive impoverishment of the workers in the capitalist countries." Another report listed "the true state of unemployment throughout the capitalist world," and averred that there were six million unemployed in the United States.

The Economic Estimate concluded with a statement by Molotov: "There are capitalist countries that have accumulated considerable wealth and substantial experience; they have natural resources and all kinds of other wealth. But capitalism as such has outlived its day and now dooms these countries to economic instability and catastrophic depressions, to periodic revolutionary shocks."

Specifically the report mentioned that a prerequisite of crisis is the "wiping out of the accumulated savings of certain classes, similar to such an event in the Stock Market collapse in 1929." It acknowledged the retreat of American small investors and speculators from the stock market, but it predicted a wholesale wiping out of savings as a result of the collapse of inflated real-estate prices, leading to foreclosures or, on the other hand, to catastrophic losses by mortgage holders. The report estimated that real-estate prices would drop by 60 to 80 per cent within four to six years, fatally reducing the investments or savings and increasing the commitments of the "mass of the American people."[2]

Drawing up the chronology of the developing crisis, the Politburo's economic advisers reported that American capitalism had reached its peak in 1943, that the recession that followed reached its first climax in 1946; it was then restimulated with spending on the cold war; it reached another climax in 1949. Despite future efforts to restimulate it, the crisis would henceforth move toward deepening recession, which was to reach depression proportions in 1954.

By 1956, the United States is expected to be in the throes of economic disaster, radiating its catastrophic effects to the countries economically tied or militarily allied to it.

The years 1954 and 1956 keep recurring throughout the two estimates as years of specific significance. On the one side, 1954–56 was described in the Military Estimate as the period in which the military consolidation of the Atlantic Union could be expected. On the other side, 1954–56 was described in the Economic Estimate as the period in which American depression would attain catastrophic proportions.

STALIN DECIDES FOR WAR

Stalin, we are told by several informants, was not particularly impressed with the estimate of his military advisers. Their view was that the Atlantic Union could never be forged into a truly effective military alliance. The Generalissimo rejected that conclusion and insisted on an estimate that conceded the possibility of success.

The military experts also presented a remarkably low opinion of the military potential of the United States. Stalin qualified that conclusion as well. He does not underestimate the United States, and he has never succumbed to the Soviet fad of excluding the United States from among the victors over the Axis. He values the contribution of the United States and appreciates the immense power that contribution so convincingly revealed between 1941 and 1945.

On the other hand, Stalin was deeply impressed by the reasoning and documentation of his economists. It may be that psychological reasons were dominant in this attitude, that he appreciated such an apparently foolproof endorsement of his own theories.[3] But Stalin is too practical to flatter himself, especially in a matter involving the future of Russian bolshevism. The fact remains that Stalin accepted the conclusions of the economists and now bases his plans on the inevitability of an American depression in 1954 and a world depression in 1956.

However, the conclusion he reached from this prognosis was different from that of his experts. The latter urged a preventive war to forestall the consolidation of the Atlantic Union and to exploit the concurrent economic crisis, a contradictory plan that was repugnant to Stalin's orderly mind.

He believes that a preventive war against the United States would promptly halt development of the American economic crisis, forge the American people into a united national front of immense strength, lend tremendous impetus to the anti-Russian sentiments of all Americans, and add a dynamism to American aggression that would make it invincible in the offensive and impregnable in defense.

Thus a conventional, old-fashioned war, even with newfangled weapons, was ruled out by Stalin.

But war was not.

Patterning his concept of war after Lenin's theoretical ideas and his own experience gained in the service of revolution and insurrection, Stalin developed his plan for a new kind of war. He will unleash it at the most propitious moment at the most propitious place, to invigorate the economic crisis, to smash the Atlantic Union, to undermine American dynamism at home and abroad. Through planned chaos and disintegration, Stalin expects not merely to reisolate the United States but to eliminate it altogether from the race and thus to terminate victoriously the "epoch of world revolution."

The decision reflects clearly Stalin's fundamental attitude on the issue of war. On the surface this attitude seems to reflect a basic cleavage if not an insoluble dilemma in Stalin's mind. He firmly believes that capitalism is the chief culprit in bringing on wars. "Capitalism in its imperialist phase," he wrote, "is a system which considers wars to be a legitimate instrument for settling international disputes, a legal method in fact if not in law." [4]

While he does not expect the complete collapse of capitalism in his own generation, he is convinced that one or two additional wars could accelerate its decline and fall. Thus Stalin both favors and abhors wars. He favors it to accelerate the downfall of capitalism; he abhors it because it imperils socialist consolidation.

It is no exaggeration to say that the question of war or peace virtually haunts Stalin's mind. Unlike Lenin who, in Stalin's own words, "did not consider himself a military expert," Stalin has a high regard for his own generalship. Consequently, war holds out to him a tempting fascination—if only as an opportunity to test his military art in action. He solves his great dilemma in the sophisticated manner of Oscar Wilde: he gets rid of the temptation by yielding to it. [5]

Stalin's opinion of war had been bluntly expressed in a letter to Alexei Maximovich (Maxim) Gorky, first published in the twelfth volume of Stalin's *Collected Works*, issued in Moscow in the spring of 1950.

Gorky had proposed the founding of a special magazine to be called *On War*. Stalin rejected the idea.

"After having seriously discussed the problem," Stalin wrote, "we came to the conclusion that there are no reasons today [1930] for publishing such a magazine. We think that it would be much more reasonable to treat the problems of war (I speak of *imperialist* war) in the existing *political* magazines. Especially because of the fact that problems of *war* cannot be separated from problems of *politics*, of which war is an expression. . . . We are not against *any* war. We are *against* the imperialist war, as being counter-revolutionary war. But we are *for* the liberational, anti-imperialist, revolutionary war, despite the fact that such a war, as is well known, is not free from the horrors of blood shedding, but rather is full of them." [6]

This Stalinist dictum is the Bolshevik grand theory of war, an expedient theory born in the travail of their history. It was first propounded by Lenin in 1915 when bolshevism, once and for all, turned from its vague and opportunistic pacifism to its firm and noncompromising militarism. "The Socialists have always condemned wars between peoples as barbarous and bestial," Lenin wrote in the wake of this historic *volte face*. "Our attitude toward war, however, differs in principle from that of the bourgeois pacifists and anarchists. We differ from the first in that we understand the inseparable connection between wars on the one hand and class struggles inside of a country on the other, we understand the impossibility of eliminating wars without eliminating classes and creating Socialism, and in that we fully recognize the justice, the progressivism and the necessity of civil wars, i.e., wars of an oppressed class against the oppressor, of slaves against the slave holders, of serfs against the landowners, of wage-workers against the bourgeois." [7]

This is the theory of the Bolshevik total war. It was most succinctly expressed in Lenin's dictum: "Boycott war . . . is a stupid phrase. Communists must take part even in the most reactionary war." And again: "The means of combatting war are not a strike against war, but the formation of revolutionary nuclei in the combatant armies, their training for the purpose of bringing about revolution." [8]

What does this mean in practical, topical terms, in the light of Stalin's decision to wage war against the West?

It means that according to Communist dogma any war the West might wage against the U.S.S.R. is an "unjust war" that must be *sabotaged* by all means fair and foul. But any war the U.S.S.R. might wage against the West is a "just war" that must be *supported* by all means fair and foul.

This means that the machineries of sabotage and support are in existence even today within the countries of Russia's potential opponents. Concealed Bolsheviks and clandestine sympathizers are entrenched within the armed forces of all democratic countries, with instructions to subvert their units in moments of great emergency, to undermine morale, to interfere with military efficiency, to smash combat effectiveness, to defeat the unit even without interference by the Russians. This means that agitators stand behind these saboteurs, ready to exploit setbacks and difficulties, all the psychological and economic strains of the war, to drive the people to civil war, to class struggle, to rebellion, to revolution.

This means that Bolshevik Russia wants war because the revolution is not possible without war and Russia's survival is not possible without world revolution. But this also means that Bolshevik Russia wants war on its own terms and will unleash it only when those terms are secured and the preconditions of the "just war" are fully assured. On this grand theory of war is based Stalin's own operational master plan. From it developed his world revolutionary theory, the Stalin Doctrine.

Part Two

YEARS OF INDECISION

4.

THE
BOLSHEVIK
MASTER PLAN

PLANS FOR FUTURE operations are among the most carefully guarded secrets of all countries, and properly so. They are, in fact, so secret that American linguistic imagination had run out of words when we were called upon to find a security classification above Top Secret for Operations Plan Overlord, the invasion of Europe in World War II. When a search of the dictionaries yielded no solution, the nonsense word Bigot was used to indicate a secret that was more secret than Britain's Most Secret. The handful who became privy to this enormous confidence were called Bigoted in the hush-hush language of an awestruck army of Unbigoted.[1]

In an operations plan a belligerent (or one who aspires for the role) bares his aims and intentions, the elements of his strength, the courses of action, his logistics, the exact timing of his moves, the forces to be used, his reserves, the direction of his attack, all his alternative plans for evasions, retreats, and defeats. Should such an operations plan ever fall into the hands of the enemy, he could win the battle simply by adapting his own plans to the secrets of his opponent.

It is, therefore, small wonder that the most elaborate precautions are taken to guard this precious document. Even so, it is possible once in a great while for an operations plan to fall into the enemy's hands. During World War I, for example, the British Admiralty intercepted a message the German Admiralty radioed to Admiral Hipper and thus learned the German operations plan for the Battle of the Dogger Bank.[2] During World

War II, the Nazi operations plan for the invasion of the Low
Countries went astray when a German courier plane carrying
those plans lost its way and made an emergency landing in
Belgium.[3]

There were other instances when operations plans were sold
in the black market of espionage, some of them for fabulous
sums. But lost or found, bought or sold, we knew of no operations plan ever given away free of charge, and even advertised
like a good buy in the bargain basement of history—until we
came across a lecture Stalin had delivered to students of Sverdlov
University in Moscow.

It was April in 1924, but late snow still covered the streets
when Stalin drove to Dolgoruki, an industrial suburb, where
the highest educational institution of bolshevism was situated.
His visit to the Tverskaya brought back memories of the struggle
for power. Just around the corner from the university stood
the Communist party's illegal printing house. Stalin remembered well the old Caucasian fruit stand which the Bolsheviks
kept in the basement of the house to fool the Tsar's secret police.
He recalled how he himself had visited the stand, ostensibly to
buy apples from his native Georgia, but really to disappear
through a trap door into the long shaft that led to a large underground room where *Robotchy,* Moscow's forbidden revolutionary journal, was printed.

"We have come a long way since 1905," Stalin mused as he
looked across the tracks of the nearby Byelorussian-Baltic railroad station, to the Zhukovsky Military Academy of Aviation
and to the Khodinka airfield where young aviators of the Red
Army practiced in brand-new Junkers planes. The district was
full of memories and reassurances. Like the backdrop of an
impressive stage setting, Petrovska Palace stood inert in the
background. There in Kasovski's eighteenth-century masterpiece Napoleon lived in 1812, and the Tsars before and after
him. They were all gone, shadows of the past! They shall never
return! The park surrounding the nobleman's palace had been
renamed the Park of the Comintern. "Well, we shall see!" [4]

On this late April afternoon, Stalin was on the errand of his
life. Lenin had died three months before, not unexpectedly but
still at an awkward time, before the question of succession had

been satisfactorily settled. Stalin was determined to settle the question in his own way. His plan had been worked out in minute detail. This visit to Sverdlova was one of those details. He went there to deliver a series of lectures, probably the most important lectures ever delivered before the impassive, scholastic audience of a university. In those lectures Stalin laid before the Communists of Russia his interpretation of Lenin's teachings. And he served notice on the world that henceforth Russia would be guided by those rules.[5]

This particular lecture was to be his seventh talk. It was entitled "Strategy and Tactics." It gave away what is in fact the Soviet Union's greatest politicomilitary secret—the pattern of its *basic operations plan.*

Stalin's introductory sentence left no doubt about the purpose of the plan: "Strategy," he said, "is the determination of the direction of the main proletarian onslaught in this or that phase of the revolution, the elaboration of the best plan for the distribution of the revolutionary forces (the main reserves and the secondary reserves), and the endeavor to carry out this plan during the whole period of this or that phase of the revolution." [6]

The *basic operations plan* presented the three phases of the Russian revolution. The first two phases may be disregarded. since they cover specific Russian conditions. But the crucial third phase, *"after the October Revolution,"* concerns us all today. This then is the verbatim transcript of the third phase, the secret which Stalin revealed to the world almost as a contemptuous gesture, like a master chess player granting advantages to an inferior opponent.

Aim: The consolidation of the dictatorship of the proletariat in one country where it could be used as a fulcrum for the overthrow of imperialism in all countries. This revolution transcends the limits of one country, and begins the epoch of world revolution.

Essential forces of the revolution: The dictatorship of the proletariat in one country, and the revolutionary movement of the proletariat in all countries.

Chief reserves: The peasantry and the intermediate strata of the population of one's own country; the proletariat of neighboring countries: the revolutionary movement in colonial and dependent countries; and the conquest and achievements of the dictatorship of the proletariat.

Indirect reserves: Antagonisms and conflicts between non-proletarian classes of one's own country, which the proletariat can turn to account in order to weaken an adversary or strengthen its own reserves. Also antagonisms, conflicts, and wars between capitalist states hostile to the proletarian state, disputes which the proletariat can turn to account for its own purposes—maybe an offensive, maybe maneuvers to cover an enforced retreat.

Chief line of attack: Isolation of the petty-bourgeois democracy; isolation of the parties affiliated to the Second International whose policy it is to come to terms with imperialism.

Plan for the distribution of the revolutionary forces: An alliance between the proletarian revolution and the nationalist (liberationist) movements in colonial and dependent lands.[7]

If we read the plan with the care it fully deserves, we can discover a passage in every one of its items and paragraphs that specifically concerns us today! Stalin himself assured us that this plan is no temporary or expedient design. It is a permanent scheme, impervious to basic changes as time goes by: "Strategy is concerned with the essential forces of the revolution and with its reserves," he said. "It changes as the revolution moves on from one phase to the next, but remains unchanged in its principles." [8]

Stalin became a world revolutionary, not by temperament or disposition, but by design. The record is clear that during the early days of the Bolshevik conspiracy, during the first two decades of this century, he fought for the Russian and not for the world revolution. He was, indeed, the Bolshevik prototype of the patriots whom Lenin ridiculed as "chauvinists" and whom he abused for their devotion to "the defense of the fatherland" [9]—the very slogan which Stalin picked twenty-seven years later for the banners of his Great Patriotic War.[10]

If Stalin's great conflict with the ghosts of Marx and Lenin on the question of nationalism versus internationalism was not particularly remarkable for an ingenuity of intellectual argument, neither was it devoid of practical skill, determination, and purpose. His intense nationalism had no selfish overtones. He had nothing in common with Alexander Pope's "foolish patriot" or with Dr. Johnson's "patriotic scoundrel." Stalin achieved in fact what William Cowper Brann thought was impossible: he developed his patriotism on an empty stomach. It was born of the spirit in which Patrick Henry told the First Continental Congress: "I am not a Virginian, but an American," and which inspired Stephen Decatur's famous toast in Norfolk: "Our country, right or wrong."

It is important to remember this great driving force of Stalin's political life if only because, for some time, Stalin's intense nationalism developed in him a defensive philosophy. It was a feeling of protective guardianship that denied, and even feared, aggression for aggression's sake. Always ready to move boldly to protect *his* Russia, Stalin nevertheless refused to indulge in the daydreams of the permanent revolutionists.

It is in this basically defensive attitude that Stalin has now undergone the great change of life. Under the mounting onslaught of the cold war, awed by the realization of America's primeval power when aroused, he decided to abandon his defensive philosophy. He made up his mind to go over to the attack "in the defense of the fatherland."

He is now frankly out to conquer the world, at the mounting rate of his conquests of recent years, at the break-neck schedule of the timetable the Politburo drafted in January, 1949. This concept of "World War for Socialism" is no belated endorsement of the Marxist principle, the prodigal theorist's return to the bosom of his spiritual father. It is not motivated by any sentimental solicitude for the welfare of foreign proletarians or oppressed nationalities.[11]

Stalin favors world revolution because it furthers Russian aims and assures Russian victories. So today he appears in the role of the world's foremost advocate of world revolution and of its recognized supreme commander in chief. However chauvinistic his motivation may be, and how much it may be influenced by Pan-Russian considerations, Stalin is no mean master of the world revolution, no mean strategist and tactician of the proletarian upheaval. In another master plan he drafted in 1927, he described the exact preconditions for proletarian revolutions in the capitalist countries and even "the line" the Bolsheviks of Russia intended to follow.

What is that *line*, Tovarish Stalin? [12]

"Our Party calling upon the proletarians of the separate countries to get ready for the coming revolution," Stalin answers, "to follow carefully the course of events, and to be ready under favorable conditions to break the capitalist front independently, to seize power and to shake the foundations of world capitalism."

How will the victory of the Bolshevik Revolution in Russia influence world revolution?

"The victory of socialism in Russia is not a self-sufficient fact but a support, a means for hastening the victory of the proletariat in all countries," Stalin answers. "The victory of the revolution in Russia constitutes the beginning and premise of the world revolution."

What, then, is the specific role of the U.S.S.R. in the world revolution?

"The world revolution will develop the more rapidly and thoroughly," Stalin answers, "the more effective the assistance rendered by Russia to the workers and toiling masses of all other countries will be."

Yes, but how? By what will this assistance be expressed?

"It will be expressed by the victorious country, Russia, stirring up and supporting the revolution in all countries," Stalin answers, "by rising against the rest of the capitalist world, attracting to itself the oppressed classes of other countries, raising insurrections in them against the capitalists, acting in case of need even with military force against the exploiting classes and their states." [13]

If the lecture to the students of Sverdlov University was the strategic exposition of the master plan, here is its tactical implementation. A clearer exposition of Bolshevik intentions is hardly needed. And a more authoritative can hardly be obtained. It comes from Stalin, quoting with approval the words of Lenin.

It is indeed the "Plan of Destruction"—as Stalin himself eagerly stated it to the Third Congress of the Communist party of Russia. "The dictatorship of the proletariat and peasantry," he said, "that is to say the outcome of our revolution, is not the organization of order but the organization of war."

This is the historical foundation on which the Stalin Doctrine is built.

5.

THE BIRTH
OF THE
STALIN DOCTRINE

FOR MANY years the Stalin Doctrine remained a vague theory of world domination. It was not as vulgar and senseless as the Nazi New Order, suggested by the line in the Horst Wessel song: "Today Germany, tomorrow the world!" But it was still a boisterous, brash, and boastful design, compounded of the adolescent enthusiasm of a successful revolution and of the megalomaniac dreams of Ivan the Terrible.

Then one late autumn night in 1940 it became a concrete, detailed, and systematic program that laid down on paper, in black and white, the fate and future of 2½ billion human beings throughout the world.

The Stalin Doctrine thus predated the Truman Doctrine by more than a half decade. It was born on October 21, 1940, in the notorious nocturnal toil and trouble that lends a fantasmal air to many a Kremlin scheme.

That night young Vladimir Mikhailovich Zhelezhnyakov accompanied his wife, Olga, to an extraordinary theater of ad-lib poetry in which actors and audience perform on equal footing. The young woman fancied herself as an accomplished poet. Vladimir Mikhailovich was rather bored by poetry. He looked at the world with more prosaic eyes, as a graduate of Moscow University's Institute of International Affairs, and as a young attaché of the Narkomindel, the commissariat of foreign affairs.

Shortly after midnight they returned home and were fast asleep when there was "the Knock" on their apartment door. Olga heard it first. She crept out of bed without awakening her

44

husband. She went to the door and opened it. There in the hall stood two men, a short one and a tall one, in the uniform of the NKVD. The short one had the one star and two stripes of a major on his shoulder mark. The slender red braiding of NKVD-on-Kremlin-duty was hardly visible. He spoke softly and in a low voice:

"Permit me, Olga Yakovleva," he said. "We want to talk to Vladimir Mikhailovich." They knew their names. Of course; they were from the NKVD.

Olga Yakovleva called across the hall to her husband in the bedroom: "Vova," she said, trying to sound casual, *"they* have come to talk with you."

They conducted him to a waiting car downstairs. It was the familiar big dark green limousine of the NKVD standing away from the street lamp, in the discreet shadow of the autumn night. A few minutes later he was being driven at break-neck speed down the long Bolshoy Lubyanka at the end of which the examining magistrates of the Narkomvnudel (the commissariat of the interior) waited for the arrival of customers every night, coming in cars just like the one in which Zhelezhnyakov was riding.

But the big green limousine did not turn into the Ilyinka. They were leaving the Kitay Gorod. They passed the Metropol Hotel and the Bolshoy Theatre. Zhelezhnyakov suddenly realized that he was *not* under arrest. A feeling of importance seeped into his muscles. They tightened and pulled him up on his seat. The young diplomat was a new man when the green car rounded the corner and turned into the Kremlin, its silent passage accompanied from then on by the shrill ringing of alarm bells.

He no longer had any doubts; this was official business. So narrow is the margin in Russia between arrest and assignment.

The car stopped in front of the big office building that houses the Soviet Union's highest authorities. Vladimir Mikhailovich was rushed to an elevator and taken to the third floor, then along a long and dark corridor at the end of which were tall double doors with numbers on them. They passed No. 10, then 9 and 8, then 7 and 6, then 5 and 4 and 3. At No. 2 they stopped. The NKVD major knocked on it—but a knock mellow with reverence.

A colonel opened the door and stuck his head out. The major saluted stiffly. He pointed at Zhelezhnyakov. The colonel beckoned him in. A minute later Vladimir Mikhailovich was standing in front of Stalin and Molotov.

He looked around in the paneled conference room, which he saw for the first time but about which he had heard so much from colleagues. The inner sanctum! Sitting around the table in apparent discomfort were Vladimir Potemkin, a deputy foreign commissar; Vladimir G. Dekanosov, another deputy foreign commissar then acting as Soviet ambassador to Berlin; Arkady A. Sobolev, secretary general of the foreign commissariat; Division Chief Alexei Merekalov; Counselor Astakhov, from the embassy in Berlin; Division Chief Kuznetsov; and a number of his lesser colleagues from the Narkomindel.

The conversation, carried on in a steady murmur without modulations, continued, with Stalin doing most of the talking. He stopped only to take a drag on his cigarette or to listen to the answers to questions he posed.

Vladimir Mikhailovich tried to fit himself into the environment. At first he failed to make out the meaning of Stalin's soliloquy. But then, like eyes which become accustomed gradually to darkness and can actually see through it, he began to understand it all.

Stalin was talking about the future of the world, about the new situation created by Germany's emergence as a world power, and about the status quo represented by England.

England never ceased to fascinate and puzzle him. "It has a weak army," he said. "The British navy no longer deserves its previous reputation. Its air arm is being increased, to be sure, but there is a lack of pilots. If England dominates the world in spite of this, it is due to the stupidity of the other countries that always let themselves be bluffed. It is ridiculous, for example, that a few hundred Britons should dominate India."

Stalin liked to look far—far beyond Britain's decline and fall. But he was confronted with new realities: Germany, for example, and the enigmatic United States. As always, he had maximum and minimum objectives—that shrewd scheme which allows for mutations in tactics but not for sudden reversals or changes in strategy. The maximum objective was stated in his *basic operations plan:* "The overthrow of imperialism in all countries."

Now, in 1940, it was high time to fix the minimum objectives, especially since Hitler, too, thought of a "delimitation of interests on a world-wide scale." It was high time, indeed, to think of those "delimitations"!

Even seven years later, in 1947, when Zhelezhnyakov [1] dictated the experience to one of our interrogators in Austria, the memory of that night was fresh in his mind. He was called in, as one of Dekanosov's confidential secretaries, to take down the blueprint of the Stalin Doctrine for the archives of the foreign commissariat, to prepare the secret record of the nocturnal conference for future generations of Soviet diplomats. Later he became useful to us as a kind of notary public to certify the authenticity of the Bolshevik master plan.

The plan was by no means foolproof. It had its share of blunders. Zhelezhnyakov himself became the victim of one of them. When Stalin made the first draft of his Doctrine, he regarded the victory of nazism over Britain and France as an accomplished fact. So he looked to Germany for partnership. Even on April 13, 1941, at a railway station in Moscow, Stalin sought out the German ambassador, threw his arm around his shoulder, and said: "We must remain friends and you must now do everything to that end." Then he told the German military attaché: "We will remain friends with you—*auf jeden Fall!*" [2]

Exactly eighty-one days later, Russia and Germany were at war. And on the third day of that war, Olga Zhelezhnyakova and her little son Sasha were killed by a German bomb in her native town of Fastov. On that same day Zhelezhnyakov volunteered for front duty. He was assigned to an infantry regiment commanded by Colonel Rogozhin. He was captured by the Germans in the Battle of Kiev and spent the war in a prison camp in the Reich. By then he was thoroughly disillusioned by the sordid spectacle in which he himself had played the minuscule role of a skittish extra. He looked toward his liberation with doubt. And so, when the Americans reached his camp, he decided to start a new life. The last link with his past was the affidavit he gave one of our interrogators, describing the events

of October 21, 1940, the night on which the Stalin Doctrine
was born.

According to Stalin, his affidavit told us, the world is divided
in three parts and, therefore, its conquest must proceed in three
stages, simultaneous if possible, progressive if it need be. One
is the Socialist World led by the U.S.S.R. The other is the
Imperialist World led by the "Anglo-Americans." The third is
the Colonial World led by its own national revolutionaries.

There were other divisions: Asia, which holds the chief attraction to the Kremlin from the point of view of continental
totality; the Euro-Asian borderland that extends from Greece
to Iran; Northern Europe with Sweden as its fulcrum; the
Middle European area with Germany as its fulcrum; the African
area; and the Western Hemisphere. We have listed them in the
order of their appearance in the plan.

Within these large territories there are *priority areas* of immense magnetic attraction to the U.S.S.R.[3]

(1) Highest in priority is the area south of Batum and Baku
in the general direction of the Persian Gulf, which is described
as *"the center of the aspirations of the Soviet Union."* [4]

(2) The second priority area of *equal* importance is Turkey
where the U.S.S.R. is bent upon, in the plan's own language,
*"the establishment of a base for land and naval forces of the
U.S.S.R. within range of the Bosporus and the Dardanelles."* [5]

(3) The third priority area is Yugoslavia, which has recently
slipped out of Soviet hands but whose reconquest is regarded
as an essential precondition for the execution of the plan.

(4) The priority area next in importance is Sweden whose
"perennial neutrality" is a matter of permanent puzzlement to
the U.S.S.R.

(5) The priority area fifth in line comprises the Baltic Sea
and the passages from the Baltic into the North Sea (Store Belt,
Little Belt, Oeresund, Kattegat, and Skagerrak) over which the
U.S.S.R. is determined to establish control similar to its projected control over the Dardanelles.

(6) The sixth priority area is Afghanistan, as well as the highlands of Asia with Tibet as its fulcrum, a direction in which the
U.S.S.R. is actually moving at the time of this writing.

(7) In seventh place among these priorities are Hongkong and

French Indo-China with Burma and the Malay Peninsula forming subpriority areas within the same complex.

(8) Next in priority are France and Italy—but from here on
the plan moves up into the rarefied air of the world revolution
where territorial priorities lose their importance and ideological
priorities come to the fore.[6]

These priorities represent most that is left of the plan still
awaiting implementation. When it was originally drafted, it
included references to Bulgaria (then a top priority on the list);
Finland (whose status is not yet definitely settled); Hungary
and Rumania; the Danube River, which was regarded as a territorial problem by itself; Austria (whose status today is similar
to that of Finland); Poland; the Baltic states.

In Asia it included China, India, Indonesia, the Philippines,
and the British possessions throughout the continent which the
Comintern once described as "links in one and the same international revolutionary chain, constituent parts of the profound
general crisis of capitalism."

Since then, to use words of the Communist International,
"an enormous mass of humanity was swept into the revolutionary torrent." Many of the areas listed in the plan as future objectives could be checked off as "received."

As if by a miracle the Stalin Doctrine survived a war that
Hitler planned as a war of extermination and that Stalin himself
feared would see the end of the Socialist experiment even in
Russia. But if such fears were truly expressed, as averred by
certain Western diplomats who enjoyed Stalin's confidence during the war, they did not persist long. Stalin believes in the
inexorable triumph of his Doctrine with fatalistic superstition.
Even in 1927, he laid down two premises for his thesis of world
revolution and drew two conclusions. According to him, the
distribution of spheres of interest among the continental powers
ended early in the twentieth century. It was followed by the
appearance of have-not powers which claimed a share in the
spoils of imperialism. This led to World War I, which, in turn,
led to revolution in Russia.

This was Stalin's first premise based on available historical
evidence. His second premise was that a first move to repartition
an already divided world would be followed inevitably by a

second attempt. He concluded that this "second attempt will cost world imperialism much more than the first." In 1945 he saw his prediction confirmed. World War II was over. Out of it emerged the Soviet Union as the colossus of a new imperialism.

The time was ripe and the stage was set for that continuing war whose strategy and tactics were laid down in Stalin's master plans and whose aims were outlined in the triumphant Stalin Doctrine.

This is how the cold war started.

6.

THE "PEARL HARBOR"
OF THE
COLD WAR

IN THE mind of the student of history there can be little doubt that the year 1945 was a landmark in that strange contest we have come to call the "cold war." Unlike Dexter Perkins, the learned historian of American foreign policy, we believe that dates *can be* decisive and that it *is* possible "to cut the seamless web of history in two according to the calendar."

There is, indeed, a strange and mysterious affinity between events and dates. In the Soviet orbit, especially where meticulous planning has replaced that kind of haphazard history that Tolstoy described as "but a tissue of disconnected accidents," dates have the overwhelming impact of reminders—not unlike the dunning letters of banks reminding one of the maturity of promissory notes.

In Stalin's orderly mind, years—both past and future—acquire the almost tangible characteristics of landmarks. The various Five-Year Plans are such landmarks. His cold war, too, is planned in stages.

From the Russian viewpoint, the cold war started in the winter of early 1945, when it became evident to Stalin that the wartime co-operation of the Allies would not continue after the war. Perhaps he had read by then, with sneers and anger, Walter Lippmann's little book on *U.S. War Aims,* in which the plea for an "association of the Great Communities" was first expressed.

Lippmann voiced apprehensions which, from abundant evidence on hand, must have been foremost in Stalin's own mind as well. Thus Lippmann wrote: "We can advance toward a universal society," but virtually in the next line he qualified this further by saying:

"But should we fail to arrive, we can stand with great advantage upon the order which the United States, Britain, the Soviet Union, and China can establish by maintaining the coalition they have formed in this war. If, however, we cannot hold this achievement, we can still find a large measure of security within the Atlantic Community." [1]

This alternative was both distasteful and menacing to Generalissimo Stalin, especially when it was spelled out in Lippmann's concluding chapter, entitled "The American Destiny." In that chapter Lippmann wrote:

"Fate has brought it about that America is at the center, no longer on the edges, of Western civilization. In this fact resides the American destiny. We can deny the fact and refuse our destiny. If we do, Western civilization, which is the glory of our world, will become a disorganized and decaying fringe around the Soviet Union and the emergent peoples of Asia. But if we comprehend our destiny we shall become equal to it. The vision is there, and our people need not perish." [2]

From such prophecy Stalin shrank with all the violent suspicion of his Asiatic mind. To him those "great associations" meant but alliances against the Kremlin, carefully forged links in a massive chain against the U.S.S.R. To his mind the "universal society" of which Lippmann spoke so eloquently—or the "One World" concept which Wendell Willkie gave to a bewildered world—must mean only a society or a world under Russian domination.

Pitting his own concept of a "Russian destiny" against Lippmann's idea of an "American destiny," Stalin could not believe that the latter could ever triumph over the former, or even that the two could coexist as the enthusiasts of Russo-American collaboration predicted. Had he really believed in such a possibility—as he sometimes gave the cunning impression he did [3]—he would have denied and destroyed the whole philosophical foundation of his faith. And that would have gone, in a radical and rude manner, against the basic tenets of bolshevism.

That he was determined never to yield, and especially to the United States, became fully evident during the closing months of the war and especially during the secretive weeks which preceded that kangaroo court of history—the Yalta Conference of Stalin, Roosevelt, and Churchill.

Although then the impression was created that everything had gone smoothly between the Allies, the fact is that Roosevelt's departure for Yalta was preceded by an exchange of those "extremely stern messages" which Mrs. Roosevelt has recently cited as symbols of the rapid deterioration of Russo-American relations.[4]

Roosevelt was advised at that time of certain Soviet negotiations with a group of Polish Bolsheviks who functioned in liberated Lublin as a quasigovernment. Apprehensive that Stalin might prejudge an otherwise delicate political situation, he wrote to the Generalissimo on December 16, 1944, requesting him to refrain from any definitive action before their forthcoming meeting at Yalta.

Stalin replied on December 27. He told Roosevelt, virtually in so many words, to mind his own business.

Two days later Roosevelt answered Stalin and told him that the brusque message "disturbed and deeply disappointed him."

No formal answer was received to this note. Stalin's answer was a bold and unilateral action. On January 5, 1945, ignoring Roosevelt's earnest plea and scorning his expression of disappointment, the Soviet Government announced that it had recognized the Lublin Committee as the Government of Poland.[5]

If anyone with a keen sense of history desires to fix the exact date of the outbreak of the cold war, he may regard January 5, 1945, as that day.

From then on Stalin was waging two wars simultaneously. One was the hot war against a tottering Germany and, in time, Japan. The other was a calculated cold war against his wartime allies in the West.

The Yalta Conference was, in fact, the first major battlefield of this new cold war. It was a clandestine battlefield on which vision was badly befogged by the preoccupations of our leaders with their own problems and by the prevalence of preconceived ideas, one of which seemed to be that the U.S.S.R. was a fair and trustworthy ally.

WHAT HAPPENED AT YALTA

A great deal has been written about Yalta, often aiming to prove that Stalin is a knave and Roosevelt was a fool.[6] It should be pointed out that Mr. Churchill, the third negotiator at Yalta during the crucial days of February 4–11, 1945, is not one of those who have written thus of his confreres.[7]

It is also of interest that Mr. Churchill, though his role at Yalta was a somewhat ambiguous one, is not placed in the pillory by the lesser men now writing, despite the fact that it was his attitude toward recognition of the Curzon Line in Poland that forced Roosevelt reluctantly to accept Stalin's Polish terms. Again, it was Churchill's indifference to China that, in the final analysis, led to United States acquiescence in Russia's Far Eastern designs.[8]

Mr. Churchill, with his customary chivalry, will undoubtedly clear up his part in the Yalta Conference when, in the course of his memoirs, he reaches that point. But there was one Yalta decision that he did not influence. It was a single item on the Conference's agenda, yet an item of overwhelming significance in any objective appraisal of the moods, achievements, and consequences of the Crimea Conference.[9]

It was the question of Soviet participation in the Pacific war.

The rather low place this item was given on the Yalta agenda did not reflect the exceptionally high priority it had in the minds of those Americans who sat around the conference table in the refurbished ballroom of Livadia Palace.

Anyone reading the verbatim transcript of the Conference must be struck by the small amount of discussion devoted to this subject. Poland's case was thrashed out in prolonged argument. Even the vote of the Ukraine and Byelo-Russia in the as yet unborn international organization received thousands of words of tepid debate.

But no one seemed eager to discuss *one* item of the agenda. When mentioned at all, it was treated gingerly, in circumspect words, in haphazard subsidiary sentences, in oblique references, as if no one really cared to bring up the matter. In reality, Americans—and possibly Russians—were thinking of little else than Japan.

This beating about the bush caused an unscheduled extension of the Conference. It was planned to conclude the conversations on February 10, draft a declaration on that day, and then adjourn. But the last day was drawing to its close and the subject was still being avoided.

A last meeting was hastily called. It was the closest and most secretive meeting of them all. It was devoid of drama or fireworks. In but a few words which nevertheless reveal hard, shrewd, and unrelenting bargaining, the decision was reached. Judging by his words, Stalin was more solemn than usual. Roosevelt, through his growing exhaustion, showed signs of elation. Churchill hardly opened his mouth.

A ten-paragraph top-secret "agreement regarding Japan" was drawn up. Stalin was the first to sign it, then Roosevelt, finally Churchill. The Conference adjourned. A copy of this precious IOU—the written agreement of the U.S.S.R. to join the war against Japan—was taken to Washington by Lieutenant William M. Rigdon, keeper of the secret papers. There it was separated from the rest of the documents and placed in Mr. Roosevelt's personal safe, in the War Room at the White House. Very few of the President's confidants knew about its existence.

Today's divergent critics of Yalta deal with the subject of Byelorussia's and the Ukraine's extra vote in the United Nations and Soviet participation in the Pacific war in the same short breath—as if these two matters were identical in significance and consequence. Such a treatment is, of course, nonsense. Reading between the lines of the Yalta protocols, one is often inclined to recognize this distinction in Roosevelt's and Stalin's attitude to all questions discussed. Their very verbosity on such questions as Poland, reparations, UN procedure, the Dardanelles, Bulgaria was merely a smoke screen to conceal their preoccupation with victory at all cost.

To say, as journalists and others have, that Roosevelt blundered, that he was taken in by Stalin, is to ignore much that is already known and to presume that what is still unknown will support faulty prejudgment.

At Yalta, diplomacy was fused with the military necessities of the Japanese campaign and Roosevelt proved a masterful coordinator of the two. When Stalin underwrote the Pacific war,

the President gained for his military advisers on the Joint Chiefs
of Staff the one and only concession they expected at Yalta. Eventual Russian participation in the war against Japan was a
promissory note the Joint Chiefs had been holding since
Teheran, in 1943. Since September, 1944, they had been urging
Roosevelt to collect on it. They stood behind him at Yalta,
reminding him every day, and urging him in no uncertain terms
to present the note—now.

When Stalin at last agreed to honor the note, Roosevelt was
relieved. The Joint Chiefs, in their own detached way, were
jubilant.

If anybody "blundered" in Yalta at all, it was the Joint Chiefs
—but even their "blunder" was most proper under the circumstances. Their decision to bring the U.S.S.R. into the Pacific war
was based on a crucial document drafted in the fall of 1944 by
the intelligence section of the War Department General Staff. It
provided what the Joint Chiefs regarded as the best estimate of
the complex Far Eastern situation. Its pessimism, its exaggeration of Japanese potentialities made Russian participation in
the Pacific war seem to them virtually imperative. The Joint
Chiefs either had to reject the estimate of their intelligence
experts or call for Russian aid. They decided on the latter course
and thus unwittingly stampeded Roosevelt into supporting
them.

It was an unfortunate and altogether wrong estimate, its
authors being deceived by a purely military and quantitative
evaluation of the enemy, a treacherous trap into which even the
greatest military leaders are likely to fall occasionally.

Later, we found that the War Department had prepared two
estimates rather than one; but somehow, the more accurate and
from our point of view optimistic evaluation of Japanese potentialities was pigeonholed by a special intelligence outfit in the
assistant secretary's office, which allowed only the pessimistic
report to go up to the Joint Chiefs and through them to
Roosevelt.[10]

An estimate—prepared for Secretary Forrestal in the Navy
Department and explicitly advising *against* Soviet participation
in the Pacific war on the grounds that it was not required by our
own military necessities—reached conclusions almost literally

identical with the optimistic evaluation of the War Department. It, too, ended up in the same Pentagon pigeonhole.

In the spring of 1945, the two optimistic estimates were still vainly competing against that impressive report of doom favored by the top level in the Pentagon and the sole guide of the Joint Chiefs. Even in June, 1945, on the eve of Los Alamos and after the defeat of Germany, it was still the basis of a highest-echelon prediction that the war against Japan would last till the fall of 1946, then approximately fifteen months away. Five weeks later the Japanese surrendered unconditionally.

At Yalta, too, Soviet duplicity and the strange morality which underlies all Soviet agreements with foreigners was shown up in an incident which we believe is revealed here for the first time. The incident is to our minds the absolute proof of the Kremlin's basic insincerity in all its dealings with the U. S. It also places the Yalta document in a new and different light, virtually justifying us if we should scrap that contract and disregard it in its entirety, in all its implications for the postwar world.

At the time of Yalta, a group of Bolshevik agents under the leadership of Edward Osubska-Morawski, Boleslaw Bierut, and Rola Zymierski functioned in Lublin as a committee for national liberation and, since January 5, as the quasigovernment recognized by Russia. On our part, we stated unequivocally that the United States Government, in the words of Secretary of State Edward R. Stettinius, continued "to maintain formal diplomatic relations with the Polish Government-in-Exile in London." [11]

At Yalta Stalin agreed to demolish his own clay structure of "Polish governmental authority," to dismember his government of stooges, and to create a new and more representative democratic authority. He affixed his signature to the binding agreement of Yalta which stipulated that "the provisional government which is now functioning in Poland should . . . be reorganized on a broader democratic basis with the inclusion of democratic leaders from Poland itself and from Poles abroad. . . . This Polish Provisional Government of National Unity shall be pledged to the holding of free and unfettered elections as soon as possible on the basis of universal suffrage and secret ballot.

In these elections all democratic and anti-Nazi parties shall have the right to take part and to put forward candidates." [12]

The publication of the Yalta agreement created panic in Lublin. A cabinet meeting was held and Nikolai A. Bulganin, Stalin's personal representative in Lublin, was summoned to explain the strange contradiction between Stalin's assurance given to his stooges that they would be the sole government of Poland, and his new commitments to Roosevelt and Churchill.

At that time Bulganin was not yet the powerful Politburo member he is today. But his star was rising rapidly, especially since the days he had spent in Marshal Zhukov's camp as the Red Army's political commissar and Stalin's personal "observer" with the marshal.

A professorial man of great persuasive power, Bulganin was nevertheless stumped for an answer when confronted with the facts of the Yalta meeting. He confessed that he had no explanation to offer but promised to fly to Stalin at once and to gain the necessary clarification.

Stalin was more than willing. He authorized Bulganin to tell the Communists of Lublin that the Yalta agreement was but a temporary compromise—what Lenin called a zigzag in history. Eventually, he assured him, his promise to the Lublin Poles would cancel out his promise to Roosevelt and Churchill.

Bulganin flew back to Lublin with the message. He said, in effect (and we heard his words repeated by one of the men who had been actually present at this momentous Bolshevik palaver):

"The Yalta declaration is a scrap of paper. It was necessary to satisfy Roosevelt and Churchill—but we will not abide by it. We will go ahead with our plans as stated to you by the Great Stalin. I give you my word that you have nothing to fear. You will be *the* Government of Poland, no matter how those elections might turn out and whatever might happen in the meantime. Be steadfast and have faith in Stalin!"

This meeting between Bulganin and the Lublin Poles took place on February 17, 1945. It was then exactly five days after Jonathan Daniels, one of President Roosevelt's administrative assistants, released the Crimea Declaration of Yalta to the American people from Washington. So within five days Stalin had overthrown the very foundation on which the postwar collaboration between West and East was supposed to be based.

The studied hypocrisy inherent in all Bolshevik assurances given to the West can be further documented on the basis of two additional reports. We received them separately—one in 1946, from Prague; the other in 1945, from Budapest.

In December, 1946, the well-known foreign correspondent Leo Lania was visiting Prague on a special mission from a New York organization then ministering to millions of displaced persons. Prague was at the time of his visit still a citadel of democracy. Its Communist premier, jovial Klement Gottwald, was then regarded, even inside some of our own intelligence organizations, as a "moderate Bolshevik who would never destroy the democracy of the Czech Republic." [13]

When Lania visited him, he found Gottwald in a robustly democratic mood. He was encouraged to ask the Premier the sixty-four-dollar question:

"Does the Communist Party eventually plan to rebuild Czechoslovakia on a Soviet basis?"

But Gottwald answered without hesitation: "The system of the Soviets and the dictatorship of the proletariat is not the only way to Socialism. The struggle against Nazism and the victory over it—these events of great revolutionary importance—have created in a number of countries and in our country, too, conditions for peaceful development of the already attained revolutionary gains toward Socialism."

This was sensational enough, but Gottwald was just gaining momentum: "I even think," he said, "that such a path to Socialism, different from the Soviet example, is not only possible in our country but that we have already started on this road, and have, indeed, come part of the way.

"Our program states clearly," Gottwald concluded, "that the Czechoslovak government considers the nationalization of production as finished. In our country private enterprise has the same possibilities and right as the nationalized industries. In Czechoslovakia the coalition of the Communists with the other parties should be preserved and remain the main force for our further successful development." [14]

There were no ifs and buts and whens in Klement Gottwald's statement. However, it was in sharp and peculiar contrast with a confidential dispatch an informant sent us from Hungary in 1945, in the immediate wake of the country's "liberation" by the Red Army. This man, a Hungarian by birth, served with the Allies throughout the war. He later succeeded in infiltrating a Communist cell in Debreczen, where the first postwar cabinet of liberated Hungary was formed.

One night his cell was alerted to listen to a lecture by "Matyi" —described as a recent arrival from Moscow. Matyi turned out to be Mátyás Rákosi, one of the few surviving colleagues of Béla Kun, whose Communist regime in 1919 gave a bitter foretaste to all Hungarians of the Bolshevik millennium. On his arrival in Debreczen, Mr. Rákosi was still wearing the uniform of a Red Army general. But by the time he was ready to address his comrades, he shed this symbol of his allegiance and donned the simple dark suit that he is still fond of wearing today.

The group to which our informant belonged was not an élite cell. It was made up mostly of recent converts, including some who had not long before been Nazis. But Rákosi addressed them as if they were a small and intimate band of conspirators to whom the greatest state secrets could be entrusted. At the very moment when Communist protestations of loyalty to their non-Communist partners in the new coalition government were loudest, Mr. Rákosi revealed the true intentions of his party and the actual nature of his instructions from Moscow.

"I want you, comrades, to hold fast," he said. "Never despair. It won't be long. I assure you, comrades, that within two or three years, or even sooner, we shall be in sole control of Hungary. I am looking forward to the day when at the head of a truly democratic Hungary I can report to Comrade Stalin that Hungary has been cleansed of all reactionaries and is now worthy of his confidence and love."

Similar speeches were made to Party stalwarts in Bucharest by Gheorghe Gheorghiu-Dej upon his return from a trip to Moscow in 1945; and by Gottwald to his Politburo in May 1946, just a few months before he assured Leo Lania of the contrary. The intelligence that reached us here, more than 3,000 miles away, surely was available to other members of the coalition governments on the spot. One can but marvel at the simple faith those men had in the assurances of their Communist partners. At that time, of course, there were British and American, as well as Russian military missions in Budapest, Bucharest, and

Prague, so the confidence of the democratic members of the coalition was somewhat bolstered by the faint hope that the West would aid them in their resistance to Bolshevik expansion. How badly we disappointed them!

We have no right indeed to censure those men for their failure to prevent Mr. Rákosi from making good his pledge to Stalin ahead of time. Those countries were sold down the river even prior to their liberation. They were received in the Kremlin on a prearranged delivery schedule.

These incidents should bring into the sharpest focus the manner in which the Kremlin deals with us. From the viewpoint of Bolshevik ethics, Stalin and Rákosi, Gottwald and Bulganin had acted correctly. They received their absolution for the duplicity in their dealings with us in advance, from Lenin himself. On pages 84 and 85 of the twenty-seventh volume of Lenin's collected works, they read and reread passages that became ingrained in their minds and are reflected in all their actions:

"That history usually moves in zigzags, and that Marxists must make allowances for the most complex and whimsical zigzags of history, is indisputable.... The attitude of Marxists toward the zigzag course of history is, as a matter of fact, similar to their attitude toward compromise. Every zigzag of history is a compromise, a compromise between the old, which is no longer strong enough completely to reject the new, and the new, which is not yet strong enough completely to overthrow the old. Marxism does not abjure compromises; Marxism deems it necessary to resort to compromises." [15]

Thus Lenin's ghost stands behind every one of the treaties and agreements the U.S.S.R. signs with the outside world, from Hitler's Germany to Roosevelt's America to Mao's China. It may give its solemn pledge today and may affirm it with the great seal of the Soviet state, but this, too, may be just a zigzag of history, a mere compromise. We should realize this before we complain, as President Truman did to the Shah of Iran, that Russia never keeps its promises.[16] We must realize that Marx and Lenin and Stalin created a new ethical code for the proletarian revolution. Most of our defeats and disappointments in the cold war are due to our failure to recognize these new ethics when we see them in action.

7.

THE BYRNES ERA OF *QUID* FOR NO *QUO*

THE OUTBREAK of the cold war was marked by skirmishes both before and after the Yalta Conference. They were not yet on the heroic scale of later conflicts. Most of them were concealed from public scrutiny by the secrecy of the war days. Even so, they should have been sufficient to provide for us the warning signals we needed so badly in our naïveté to put us on guard in our relations with the U.S.S.R.

In *Speaking Frankly,* James F. Byrnes remarked that "those of us who were familiar with Soviet activities following the Yalta Conference found our high hopes mingled with great concern." [1] If Mr. Byrnes was familiar with those "Soviet activities," he showed but slight concern when, as Secretary of State, he had a great opportunity to deal with them and to counteract them with appropriate American activities.

The opening Russian moves in the cold war, following its "Pearl Harbor" on January 5, 1945, were made prior to Mr. Byrnes's appointment to the State Department. But by the time he moved into the Secretary's musty office in the Old State Building, there were enough Soviet moves in evidence to suggest to him greater caution in his dealings with the U.S.S.R., and advise against the policy of one-sided conciliation which marked the greater part of his term in office.

These moves included, in the order of their occurrence:

(1) February 24. Soviet nonco-operation with U.S. and U.K. members of the Allied Control Councils in Rumania, Hungary, and Bulgaria.

(2) February 27. Unilateral Soviet interference in the internal affairs of Rumania, in the form of the brutal *démarche* Andrei Y. Vishinsky delivered in person to King Michael of Rumania in his familiar manner of the prosecutor.

(3) March 2. First Soviet refusal to implement the Yalta declaration concerning Poland and its refusal to broaden the democratic base of the Polish Government.

(4) March 17. Soviet violation of the simple terms contained in the 1943 Declaration on Liberated Europe, and Mr. Molotov's mendacious answer to allied protests over these repeated and flagrant breaches.

(5) March 24. Soviet decision not to send Molotov to the founding conference of the UN scheduled to open in June in San Francisco.

(6) April 6. Molotov's attitude in his conference with Truman at the White House, telling the new and then inexperienced President of the United States that the U.S.S.R. would tolerate no interference with its "interpretation" of the various agreements.

(7) April 18. Soviet refusal to abide by an agreement to allow representatives of the Western allies to proceed to Vienna, a refusal that was countermanded on May 19, and again enforced on June 10.

(8) June 25. Soviet refusal to transmit to the United States Government frantic Japanese requests for mediation with a view toward peace.

Here, then, was the pattern of the cold war as Russia was waging it even before we became aware of it. The Russians themselves were most careful to conceal the skirmishes under a thin veneer of friendliness. The Soviet comic magazine *Krokodil* of those days, with various cartoons, depicted in the most amicable fashion Russo-Anglo-American co-operation.[2] *Pravda* and *Izvestia* were printing fulsome praises of our war effort. Stalin himself told our ambassador, Mr. Averill Harriman, when the latter advised him of Mr. Roosevelt's death: "President Roosevelt has died but his cause must live on. We shall support President Truman with all our forces and with all our will." [3]

Even later, during Mr. Hopkins's visit to Moscow, he continued to acknowledge our contribution to victory, when he said that "without our intervention in the last two wars, Germany could not have been defeated." [4]

How sincere these expressions of friendship were no one outside the high walls of the Kremlin is qualified to judge. If they were intended to mislead—as is apparent now—they succeeded remarkably well. We were deceived into trusting in continued Russian good will and co-operation, even after Mr. Molotov behind closed doors at San Francisco had laid down in unmistakable terms the rules of Soviet foreign policy and the terms of co-operation. They were strict and one-sided rules, and harsh and selfish terms. [5]

Even then, our government failed to recognize the pattern. Our own diplomatic skill and machinery were at their lowest ebb. President Roosevelt had been monopolizing so long and so completely the conduct of our foreign relations that the State Department had become hardly more than a diplomatic messenger service. His death left a vacuum in our diplomatic machinery that was felt tremendously in the face of the increasing aggressiveness of Soviet diplomacy.

The then Secretary of State Mr. Edward R. Stettinius was an ebullient, cheerful, and well-meaning man, but he brought to his high office but slight knowledge and little understanding of the basic issues of the day. Moreover he was too preoccupied with the establishment of the United Nations and with the preparations for the San Francisco Conference to devote adequate time to the diplomatic war developing rapidly between the West and the East. [6]

The Acting Secretary left in sole charge in Washington the career diplomat, Joseph C. Grew, lacked the political acumen to cope with the mounting crisis. He was hopelessly out of touch with events and events were hopelessly out of touch with him. He was further handicapped by infirmity. Those of us who had an opportunity to watch from close quarters the State Department of those days were dismayed by the realization that at that crucial moment of history, the United States had a diplomatic agency in name only, and virtually none in fact. [7]

The situation changed considerably—but not for the better—with the resignation of Mr. Stettinius and the appointment of James F. Byrnes to this key office of the American Government. [8]

There is a shrewd distinction in the old definition, "The politician looks only to the next election, while the statesman looks to the next generation." Until his sixtieth year, James Francis Byrnes looked only to the next election. Then suddenly, his eyes became focused on the coming generation.

Only seven years previously Byrnes's name could be included in a book called *Dixie Demagogues,* by Allan A. Michie and Frank Rhylick. The authors described him as a powerful ally and a dangerous enemy.[9]

Even then Michie and Rhylick had to concede that the title of their book was a misnomer in so far as Byrnes was concerned. The evolution of a politician into a statesman started more than a decade ago, and by January, 1937, Mr. Byrnes was generally regarded "as a representative of the New South, a talented leader who might become one of the most powerful forces of liberalism."

In 1945, this prediction assumed a far broader meaning. "Jimmy" Byrnes no longer fought President Roosevelt's Congressional battles or aided him in the mobilization of the country as "assistant president." The metamorphosis from the artful politician was almost complete. The dexterous lawmaker had turned into ardent peacemaker, using but few of the methods of the floor of Congress in his diplomatic negotiations, indeed, to the eventual detriment of his diplomacy. His speeches were no longer made for the Congressional Record but for the record of history. "The objective is peace," he said on May 20, 1946, "not peace founded upon vengeance and greed, but a just peace, the only peace that can endure." [10]

It is a matter of some regret for us who fully appreciate the noble principles of Mr. Byrnes to censure him now for his very devotion to them. In his eagerness to bring peace to the world, Mr. Byrnes overlooked many factors, including his own diplomatic inexperience as contrasted with the ruthless skill of his Russian partners. He was recalled from sulking retirement by a new president who subconsciously feared a Byrnes in sulking retirement. There was little his country could offer to a man who had once been a U.S. senator, Associate Justice of the Supreme Court, "assistant president," and whose eyes were clearly set on the presidency itself. He served notice on Mr.

Truman that the only position he would consider was that of Secretary of State, and Mr. Truman seized upon the suggestion, since he sought eagerly a witness to Roosevelt's personal diplomacy and a privy to its secrets in the midst of his own inexperience and lack of information.[11]

But once Byrnes appeared in the Old State Building, after the sentimental pomp of an unusually festive swearing-in ceremony, he felt suddenly the weight of his new office. There were documents on his desk waiting for him, political papers, economic estimates, position reports, background briefings, all the classified missiles of modern diplomacy written in the highbrow lingo of the modern diplomat. They dealt with problems both divergent and complex, requiring not merely a sweep of a particular brand of imagination, but a factual knowledge that cannot be gained in a lifelong preoccupation with the domestic scene. It is a technical knowledge that comes from long and painstaking study of the world at large, and Mr. Byrnes was never much interested in that particular subject.

But Jimmy Byrnes was a man of immense drive and passionate industry. He was determined to "learn the stuff." He asked friends to recommend books on international affairs so that he could "catch up and brush up" on diplomacy. He did do an incredible amount of reading during those early days but there was but little time left to him, in the midst of the hectic chaos, to read up on diplomatic history and revolutionary techniques, a fusion of which Soviet diplomacy represented. As we watched his perambulations, they appeared sometimes pathetic, sometimes painful. Upon one occasion, in a press conference, he touched upon the Russian claim to the Dardenelles and announced that we would oppose Soviet insistence upon a settlement "confined to the Black Sea powers."[12] A correspondent innocently asked the Secretary to enumerate those Black Sea powers only to find Mr. Byrnes, flushed with anger, turning abruptly to another questioner. Then in the privacy of his office the Secretary sent out his messenger for a map of the Black Sea to familiarize himself with the topography of the area.[13]

Despite an immense amount of briefing to which he was subjected, nevertheless he failed to learn all that was to be known about the political and geographic disputes of the day with which he had to deal. Thus during his first big meeting in London he found Molotov raising impatiently the question of Eastern Europe—a question for which Mr. Byrnes found himself unprepared. He tried to gain a postponement but Molotov insisted and the question of Eastern Europe had to be placed on the agenda at once. The meeting had to be adjourned to allow the Secretary of State to familiarize himself with the unexpected subject. But then it developed that there was no expert in his entourage in London who could brief him completely on Eastern Europe. A frantic call was sent to Washington, instructing the State Department to fly an expert to London at once. Just then the Department did not seem to have one either. Its top man on Eastern Europe, Cavendish Welles Cannon, one of this country's hardest working and most brilliant foreign-service officers, had just been transferred out of the Department to a diplomatic post in Lisbon, Portugal, and in *Western* Europe. So the Department called Cannon in Lisbon, ordered him to London to brief Byrnes on Eastern Europe, and to stand by while the problem stayed on the agenda of the Council of Foreign Ministers.[14]

As time went on Byrnes's knowledge of diplomacy and political issues of the international scene broadened to a remarkable degree. But he himself developed into a lone wolf, depending upon himself and a very small coterie of journalistic and diplomatic friends for advice, a recluse in the maze of the State Department. The rarefied air of diplomacy seemed to have turned his head, and members of the working press, who used to find in Jimmy Byrnes a jovial and co-operative target, now discovered a creeping haughtiness in his attitude to both men and issues. They knew that Byrnes had by then attracted to himself the usual satraps of Washington's diplomatic correspondence, that he had been confining his contacts to a small circle of pundits, perhaps to silence their barbed criticism that used to pain him during the early stages of his term. He called to his hotel apartment the opinionated writers of Washington columns, chiefs of the Washington bureaus of the big newspapers, surrounding himself with the cream, to be sure, but skimming the rest in his contacts with the press.[15]

Gradually Byrnes was found echoing the lofty but impractical ideas of his new friends, their unrealistic internationalism, their vague theories born in the travail of writing a daily column from Washington. By then Byrnes himself appeared impervious to and, indeed, resentful of criticism. He imagined that there was little that he had to add to his newly found but comprehensive knowledge of world affairs, and that he needed no advisers to implement that perfect knowledge. In reality Byrnes never became fully equipped for the tasks confronting him. His refusal to learn continuously the tricks of his new trade, the characteristics of his opponents, and especially the historical background of diplomacy, eventually prevented him from becoming what he so ardently hoped to become—a truly great Secretary of State.

The result for the United States and the world was nothing short of disastrous. No matter how one hesitates to pass definitive judgment at this short perspective of history, one cannot escape the conclusion that the Byrnes era of American diplomacy—from June, 1945, to January, 1947—caused inestimable damage to our position in the postwar world, a damage which our diplomacy failed to repair in subsequent years of trials and errors.

Mr. Byrnes approached his task with an amiable joviality and the desire to please all in a game in which you can please but few to succeed. In the old game of give and take he preferred to give and give and give, and to take but little in return, until he discovered that he had little more to give away to strike what the Russians call a bargain. Edouard Benés of Czechoslovakia once said that you can always make a deal with the Kremlin, all you have to do is to meet them a little more than halfway. What was but a sardonic quip with Benés became something of a cornerstone of the Byrnes diplomacy. By the time he discovered the fallacy of the system and the dire consequences of his initial generosity, it was too late to repair the damage.

It was thus during the Byrnes regime that the U.S.S.R. scored its first and decisive victories in the new cold war. They were victories that now enable her to resist our frantic counteroffensive without losing a single inch of the ground gained during the *laissez-faire* era of Mr. Byrnes.

These crucial Soviet victories became inescapably evident during the Paris Peace Conference, in the summer of 1946. That conference represented the crowning achievement of Mr. Byrnes's year in the State Department. He worked hard and with unselfish devotion to the cause, without realizing that what was produced by his enlightened and humanitarian effort was not peace but the prelude to war.[16]

PAX AMERICANA VERSUS PAX SOVIETICA

In Mr. Byrnes's peace program traditional American ideals clashed with European realities. The basic principle of his peace program revolved around an attempt to combine international law with international justice in providing a lasting peace for Europe.

Most of the American ideas for a European peace were crystallized several years before when President Roosevelt and Secretary Hull decided during the war to draft a peace plan to avoid the chaos and uncertainties that characterized the years of transition after World War I.[17] Some of these ideas were carried into practice in the proposals of Mr. Byrnes, but he was not bound by them. His envisaged Pax Americana was different from both that of 1919 and the draft of the more recent planners. He preserved much of President Wilson's moral idealism, but combined it with a diplomatic realism that seemed to augur well for the future of Europe.[18]

The moralism in the American peace program was expressed in the Atlantic Charter, especially in Articles 1 and 2.[19] From the American viewpoint, both articles are still valid today, but their execution is found difficult if not impossible in view of innumerable departures from the principle of self-determination.

The position and influence of Mr. Byrnes were enhanced by the fact that the United States had no territorial claims in Europe, but wanted to see certain territorial changes on ethnic and economic rather than on purely political or strategic grounds.

American plans for a future Germany were embodied in Secretary Byrnes's proposal envisaging a twenty-five- (or forty-) year control of the Reich—a plan which he regarded as his major diplomatic opus and his chief contribution to European peace.[20] The issue of Austria was separated from the German complex.

On the Continent, the United States was interested in an

equitable peace for both victors and vanquished. Thus, for example, qualified support was given to the claims of defeated adversaries, including Hungary and Bulgaria, despite the fact that the government of the latter was not yet recognized. It was remembered, however, that in 1919, too, the United States with Italy championed Bulgaria's cause in Paris in opposition to Britain and France.[21]

On the whole, the Pax Americana was planned as a product of compromise, reducing to a considerable degree American influence in Europe as well as the prospects of a lasting peace.

By contrast, the Soviet Union's elaborate peace program was firm and authoritarian. It tolerated no contradiction. It was visible to all (but Mr. Byrnes) in the *faits accomplis* with which Russia confronted her fellow peacemakers.

Without waiting for a formal peace conference, in a series of arbitrary, almost unilateral agreements concluded with the provisional governments of defeated adversaries in the immediate wake of the war, the Soviet Union had annexed Estonia, Latvia, and Lithuania; it took Karelia from Finland, Bukovina and Bessarabia from Rumania, its wartime enemies. It received the Polish Ukraine and Carpatho-Ruthenia from its wartime allies. It compelled Rumania to cede Southern Dobruja to Bulgaria, and Hungary to transfer considerable territories to Rumania, Yugoslavia, and Czechoslovakia.[22]

The future of these territories was final and their fate excluded even from review by the peace conference. This part of the Pax Sovietica had already then added thousands of square miles to Soviet territory. The regions are inhabited by people whose transfer to Soviet sovereignty was accomplished without consideration for wartime promises and assurances, and Article 2 of the Atlantic Charter.

The Russian peace policy was dominated by only one consideration—the future security of the Soviet Union in the military sense of the term. It was this same consideration which motivated the signing of the Russo-German pact of 1939, enabling the Soviet Union to expand its frontiers without the threat of German opposition or interference. The frontiers which Russia established with Hitler's consent in 1939–40 closely approximated her present boundaries. They may be regarded as the main security line behind which the Soviet Union feels militarily safe.

Victor in a costly and difficult war, Russia was bent on extending her security line even farther to the west through the creation of a second security belt composed of nominally independent countries under Russian domination. This determination was not influenced by the introduction into modern warfare of atomic energy, which diminishes the defensive value of land masses as buffers. On the contrary, the Soviet design received further impetus from it, inducing the Soviet Union to push her basic security boundary as far west as possible, to remove Russian targets beyond the range of foreign airfields.

Mr. Byrnes should have noticed and should have protested that from the Russian point of view only minor issues were left to settlement by the Peace Conference. The Soviet Union itself appeared with no territorial claims before the twenty-one nations. But it supported the claims of the countries designated to form her new greater security belt.

Poland and Bulgaria were the chief beneficiaries of Soviet support. The outlines of a Russo-Yugoslav rift were already visible.

Poland had full Russian support in establishing her western frontiers on the Oder and the Neisse and in retaining control over the German Baltic ports of Stettin and Kuestrin. The Soviet Union, moreover, insisted on leaving the control of the Danube in the hands of the riparian states, all of which are within the Russian security belt.

The primary long-range factor in the Russian peace program concerned the future of Germany. During calls of various European diplomats on Premier Stalin, they were told of the Russian leader's belief that the possible comeback of Germany was the sole threat to a lasting peace in Europe. Stalin expressed his determination to keep Germany disarmed permanently.

"The revival of the Reich as a balance of power still animates reactionary circles not merely within Germany," he was quoted as saying. He explicitly referred to Miss Jenny Lee, who remarked about Germany's potential role in the House of Commons on May 10, 1946: "Let me say in public what we are all saying in private. Germany and Austria at this moment are diplomatic battlegrounds, they are battlegrounds—sadly we must admit it—in which the former Allies, this country, America, Russia, France and the rest, are maneuvering with one another for present position and future support."

The Paris Peace Conference did open, somewhat, Mr. Byrnes's eyes to Russian realities and methods. "I should be less than frank," he said upon his return to the United States on October 18, 1946, "if I did not confess my bewilderment at the motives which the Soviet Delegation attributed to the United States at Paris. Not once, but many times, they charged that the United States had enriched itself during the war, and, under the guise of freedom for commerce and equality of opportunity for the trade of all nations, was now seeking to enslave Europe economically. Coming from any state these charges would be regrettable to us. They are particularly regrettable when they are made by the Soviet Government to whom we advanced more than 10 billion dollars of lend-lease during the war and with whom we want to be friendly in time of peace." [23]

But irritation with the U.S.S.R. provoked in him petty responses. He turned bitterly against Henry Wallace, who advocated a still milder foreign policy in the face of the developing cold water, even while Mr. Byrnes was waging it, as yet meekly himself, on one of its active fronts. He turned bitterly against the Czechoslovak delegation, a hapless group in Paris under the pathetic leadership of Jan Masaryk, when its members felt obliged to applaud politely a Russian attack against Mr. Byrnes. He turned to Ernest Bevin for solace in a strange about-face, coming as it did after a period of feuds and bickerings. In London and in Moscow in 1945, and during the London session of the UN General Assembly in 1946, Bevin assumed an attitude toward Russia that caused Lippmann to write: "The line followed by Mr. Bevin in his first ten months was not consistent with the promises and the doctrines of the British Labor Party. Mr. Bevin's policy has been to carry on the policies he found when he took office and to adhere to the line laid down by Mr. Churchill and the old hands at the Foreign Office." [24]

During those months Bevin kept up a running feud with Byrnes, whom he accused of being "an appeaser of the Russians." In Paris, too, Bevin preferred to work with Senators Vandenberg and Connally, whose "firmness of policy" he trusted as much as he distrusted Byrnes's "weakness and appeasement." [25] But Byrnes made his *rapprochement* with Bevin even to the degree of agreeing to support a morbid Palestine policy in the face of the opposition of President Truman and the people of America.

The haphazard Byrnes diplomacy reached its low point during the Secretary's impromptu visit to Stuttgart to enlist, quite openly, German aid for the cold war against Russia, much in the manner that seemed to bear out the Stalinist prediction. It was a strange spectacle, this fraternization with a vanquished enemy against a wartime ally, holding out hope to a dazed and incredulous German audience, still unstripped of Nazi taint and war guilt, of substantial concessions at the expense of Russia. Byrnes assured them that "the United States will not support any encroachment on territory which is indisputably German or any division of Germany which is not genuinely desired by the people concerned." [26] This statement was as unrealistic as it was premature. It revealed still another metamorphosis in Mr. Byrnes and highlighted the inconsistencies which were the characteristic marks of his regime.

In the meantime, back in the United States, a restive public was treated to another set of inconsistencies. Mr. Churchill went to Fulton, Missouri, and, in the presence of the President of the United States, accepted the Soviet challenge to meet headlong in a cold war. Here was a peculiar combination of a statesman freed of all official responsibilities since 1945 and the President of the United States burdened with the responsibilities of international co-operation, joining in an act of realistic hostility, if only in response to the sustained provocations of a prodigal ally. It was difficult to make out the meaning of history at this peculiar junction. Mr. Truman endorsed Churchill's clarion call but he also seemed to approve Wallace's violent censure that followed in its wake.[27] He appeared to approve both Byrnes's conciliatory policies and Senator Vandenberg's misgivings. But just when Truman himself decided on a firm course and Byrnes, too, resolved to get tough with the Russians, the two men found themselves farther apart than at any time during their hapless collaboration.

It was growing personal animosity rather than disagreement

on policies that separated them. The President was gaining a firmer hold on foreign affairs, but without the help he properly expected from his Secretary of State. The White House, he found, was but seldom considered when Byrnes was at large making policies. As a matter of fact, Mr. Truman was but rarely taken into the confidence of Mr. Byrnes on the issues of American relations with Russia.

During those days Washington was treated to a spectacle of feuding between the President and his Secretary of State. Inevitably their feud was carried into the open. On one day in Washington an important friend went to see Mr. Truman in the morning and mentioned that he had an appointment with Byrnes for the afternoon. The President appeared singularly unimpressed by our friend's decision to consult the Secretary of State. Oh, he exclaimed in effect, what's the use of talking to that busybody?

The same condescending hostility confronted this important American when he met Mr. Byrnes in the afternoon. He was, in fact, appalled to hear the Secretary of State refer to his President by a name, not only vulgar but contemptuous. It was evident to all on Washington's inside track that the honeymoon was over and that the divorce was but a matter of time.

The circumstances of Mr. Byrnes's departure from the State Department are either obscure or unpleasant to contemplate in so far as they are known. Pressure was brought upon the President to "get rid of Byrnes" from a strange assortment of friends and Mr. Truman appeared by no means disinclined to yield to their pressure. He was, indeed, impatient to vacate the place for his favorite candidate, the man he liked to describe as "the greatest American of this generation," General of the Armies George Catlett Marshall, then in China on a delicate fact-finding mission as the President's personal emissary.

With General Marshall's entry into the State Department, American diplomacy gained that firmness and consistency of purpose it so sadly lacked under Stettinius and Byrnes. The towering genius of George Marshall, his unique humanitarian appeal to all, the orderly discipline of his mind, and his devotion to routine gained in a long military career attracted at once the imagination of the American people who were becoming increasingly impatient with the improvisations of U.S. diplomacy. During those days, a Washington columnist looked to the Old State Building with moist eyes and had the vision of George Washington himself entering it as Truman's new Secretary of State. There were many of Washington's unique qualities in Marshall and his tenure in the State Department brought out most of them.

General Marshall is undoubtedly one of the greatest men of this generation or of any generation of Americans. We respected him from our vantage point of the intelligence services as the man who usually made the right decision in spite of repeatedly wrong intelligence reports. The Russians respected him for his long and selfless advocacy of a second front across the English Channel. But if the Kremlin expected a drifting or improvisation under Marshall, it was in for a set of unpleasant surprises. Under Marshall the United States seized the initiative from the Russians and managed to hold it to the regrettable day on which illness forced the General to give up his strenuous diplomatic assignment.

Some of the achievements of the Marshall era should be, to be sure, properly credited to his Under Secretary of State, Dean G. Acheson. The remarkable approach to the problems of atomic energy, the introduction of the foreign-aid program known as the Truman Doctrine, and especially the concept of the Marshall Plan were all born in the State Department under the happy constellation of Marshall and Acheson. Looking back on those purposeful months of American diplomacy and upon the sudden and unexpected victories our side was to gain in the cold war, one is inclined to say that Mr. Acheson was destined to be the ideal Under Secretary rather than Secretary of State. Whatever it was, those months of the Marshall-Acheson era will live in the history of American diplomacy as its most positive period since the days of Jefferson and Monroe.

Marshall's attitude to the U.S.S.R. had no sentimental undertones or the conservative ideology one would associate with the philosophy of a professional soldier. It had the forthrightness that characterized his actions throughout his life, without even a trace of bellicose provocation. The motivation of Marshall's diplomatic moves was simple enough: he realized that the cold war was on, inexorably on, and that we had to do something about it unless we accepted defeat in advance. But he insisted, far more than Byrnes before and Acheson after him, on the democratic process in the conduct of our cold war. Thus it came to pass that the Marshall era of American diplomacy was among its most liberal periods as well.

Outstanding achievements of that era were, of course, the Truman Doctrine and the Marshall Plan. What could have become a third achievement equal to the two in importance and consequence was muffed completely in the face of an unprecedented campaign of vilification on behalf of a discredited foreign regime. It was thus that Marshall was prevented from carrying out his own recommendations presented to the American people in a document of singular wisdom upon his return from his presidential mission to China. The Russians, in turn, were quick to detect both the strengths and the weaknesses of the Marshall era. They shifted their attention from Europe, chosen as our own major cold-war front to Asia, which the Kremlin selected as the major front of Stalin's cold war. Thus the struggle was waged on fronts thousands of miles apart, but waged with unceasing vigor on both sides, even as we accepted the challenge in our belated recognition of the Soviet scheme.

STALIN'S CASE AGAINST THE WEST

Despite the creeping insidiousness with which Stalin managed to sneak the cold war upon us, the record of Soviet diplomacy is not entirely black. Above all, Stalin did not begin his cold war in the Japanese manner, i.e., without an open and frank declaration of hostilities. There are at least four documents extant which may be regarded as Stalin's declarations of the cold war.

One is his note to Roosevelt, the one dated December 27, 1944, in which he reaffirmed his determination to proceed in the solution of all outstanding problems without regard for the sensitivities and the interests of his wartime partners.

The second document is preserved in a series of shorthand notes Mr. Byrnes took at the conference table at Livadia Palace in Yalta. Most of them concern Stalin's views on Poland, Germany, and the question of postwar collaboration with the allies. They reflect, in retrospect, his grave doubts and also his deter-

mination to make the Soviet views prevail by all means at his
disposal, fair or foul.

The third document is the full transcript of Stalin's conferences with Henry L. Hopkins in Moscow in the summer of
1945. This document is reprinted in Mr. Sherwood's historic
Roosevelt and Hopkins, on pages 887-912. They should be read
again and again, with close attention, both by our policymakers
and by our people at large.

There is, however, a fourth document, not in the public
domain, which we regard as equally, if not more, important. It
is the confidential report of a prominent Polish diplomat from
Moscow to his Foreign Office in Warsaw. It described Stalin's
frame of mind upon his return from the Potsdam Conference.[28]

The Generalissimo was ill and in a bad mood. The conference
displeased him, not so much by the issues discussed, but by the
inferiority of the peoples with whom he had to deal. "There was
no flexibility in them," he said. In the seats long occupied by
Roosevelt and Churchill, he now found Truman and Attlee,
Byrnes and Bevin. He was particularly suspicious of Attlee and
Bevin, long known for their opposition to Communists and
communism, representatives of the kind of obsolescent socialism
which Stalin despises more than capitalism and even imperialism.

Then, too, the news of the A-bomb was received and spread.
Although he refrained from discussing the subject then, feign-
ing studied indifference and disbelief, today we know that he
resented deeply allied secrecy maintained around all that concerned the Manhattan Project. In his opinion this project should
have been developed by all allies, and not merely their Western
branch. "Millions of Russian soldiers could have been saved
from horrible death," he was quoted as having said to our informant, "had our American allies told us about the A-
bomb. They pushed us into one offensive after another. Senseless
offensives, now they appear to be. We could have waited behind
our strong lines, without marching against the heavily fortified
inner lines of Germany, waiting for the atomic bomb to do to
Germany what it did to Japan. But no! We were never told of
that weapon! Don't you think," he asked, "that there was a
calculated design behind all this? Was it not calculated to kill

off as many of our soldiers and political workers as possible, preys of the Hitlerite beast? I think it was." [29]

These thoughts deepened the developing anti-American sentiments in Stalin's mind. By the summer of 1945, that mind was soaked in suspicion and distrust.

Then Stalin's faith in the United States received a final shock by the sudden termination of Lend-Lease. According to the record of an informant, "... the abrogation of Lend-Lease hit Russia more than it was ever suspected abroad. It virtually undermined her post-war economy and threw out of kilter carefully laid plans for industrial rehabilitation. Gromyko frankly told me that Stalin at first refused to believe the news when Molotov informed him of the brusque American note. He instructed the Soviet Ambassador in Washington to ask for an extension to enable the U.S.S.R. to initiate at least the first phase of its post-war recovery and was further shocked when Novikov told him that, in view of Washington's peculiar mood, no such extension could be obtained." [30]

Stalin's suspicion froze into weary distrust when Soviet application for a U.S. loan, designed to offset the loss of Lend-Lease, "got lost in the State Department" and when the Department of Commerce, "upon explicit instructions from the State Department," began to embargo exports to Russia, especially of machine tools and heavy industrial equipment.

Stalin on his part persisted in refusing to accept blame for the deterioration of relations or to attribute the verbal belligerency of certain Americans to their own weariness over repeated Russian provocations. He insisted that Russian moves and actions were all justified by a strict adherence to the Yalta and Potsdam compacts, and regarded our actions as flagrant violations of the letter and the spirit of those agreements.[31]

Stalin was quite sincere in this belief and actually believed his own monstrous rationalizations. This blind spot in his attitude toward America made him increasingly intolerant of American expressions of disillusionment. He became inclined to exaggerate the significance of vitriolic editorials in privately owned American newspapers. He tended to attribute far too great significance to and expected far too serious consequences from the threats of individual Congressmen speaking but for themselves or airing *only* their private opinions.

He underrated the intelligence and equanimity of the American people and expected them to rise and march against the U.S.S.R. or scatter A-bombs over her, at the bugle call of head-line-hunting after-dinner speakers. He failed to appreciate the true position of our military and naval officials in our political order but believed that they have an actual influence on the political leaders of the country when it comes to deciding the crucial issues of war or peace.

It cannot be said that Stalin didn't expect such a turn of events. "It is not so difficult to keep unity in time of war," he remarked at Yalta, "since there is a joint aim to defeat the common enemy, which is clear to everyone. The difficult task will come after the war when diverse interests tend to divide the allies. It is our duty to see that our relations in peacetime are as strong as they have been in war." [32]

And again: "I think that the task is to secure our unity in the future, and for this purpose, we must agree upon such a covenant as would best serve that purpose." [33]

Stalin recognized the United Nations Charter as such a covenant, especially its Article 27. But he foresaw difficulties. "My colleagues in Moscow," he warned, "cannot forget the case which occurred in 1939 during the Russian-Finnish war, when Britain and France used the League of Nations against us and eventually expelled us and isolated us." [34]

The old fears returned, the hoary apprehensions reappeared, and inevitably the security of the Soviet world from Berlin to Vladivostok, from Petsamo to Baku became uppermost in Stalin's mind. "For the Russian people," Stalin said in February, 1945, when discussing postwar boundaries, "the question of Poland is not only a question of honor but also a question of security. Throughout history, Poland has been the corridor through which the enemy has passed into Russia. . . . It is in Russia's interest that Poland should be strong and powerful, in a position to shut the door of this corridor by her own force." During those days Stalin frequently used the phrase: "I owe it to the Russian people to secure their frontiers against all comers." His idea of a *cordon sanitaire* consisting of not one but two security belts developed in the late '30's. It was revived in 1945-46, stronger than ever.

He said: "History shows that when any state intends to make war against another state, even not adjacent, it begins by seeking frontiers across which it can reach the frontiers of the state it wants to attack. Usually an aggressive state finds such frontiers. She always finds countries willing to 'lend' her a frontier." [35]

In the face of "the new Western hostility" and repeated demonstrations of anti-Russian sentiments, Stalin decided to prevent anyone in the Soviet orbit from "lending" such frontiers to anyone in the West. The Yalta agreement established an "area of paramount Soviet interest" in Poland and Czechoslovakia, in Hungary and Rumania and Bulgaria, but Stalin now felt that Soviet interests were not too paramount after all. His fears were not completely groundless. Democratic opportunities, encouraged by us and Britain, were pitted against the prospects of the new totalitarianism of Russian rule. The clash was inevitable and violent, even though in 1946 it was confined to the minds and hearts of a gallant band of would-be conspirators against the illegal Sovietization of their hapless countries. [36]

There were other straws in the wind, all of them indicating to the restive Soviet mind a deliberate Western encroachment on vested Russian interests or calculated insults against the U.S.S.R. December 6, 1945, particularly, was a bitter day in the Kremlin. On that day America wrote off $25,000,000,000 Lend-Lease aid to the British Commonwealth and agreed to grant Britain $4,400,000,000 in credits. A few months later France received a loan of $1,400,000,000—but a Soviet note, asking for a similar loan, was still adrift among the desks and drawers of the State Department.

The United States was preparing the Bikini tests of its fourth and fifth A-bombs; Congress approved a continuation of the Selective Service Act; American planes appeared over Yugoslavia; and Britain and the U.S. signed an agreement for the economic merger of their occupation zones in Germany. To Stalin's mind, postwar history turned a full cycle. So in Moscow, he sat down behind a microphone to denounce "international reaction" and the "plotters of a new war" in the strong and bitter words of a disillusioned ally. [37] The man who was waging his cold war surreptitiously resented even the slightest Western move that appeared as a counterstroke to his own clandestine campaign. By the time 1946 was drawing to a close, Stalin became determined to step up his quiet campaign and to move boldly, without consideration for treaties or sensitivities. He called in Vishinsky and Zorin, two of his deputy foreign ministers. He ordered them to work out a system of satellite co-ordination—a kind of Bolshevik *Gleichschaltung* patterned after the notorious Nazi prototype. With such an example, Vishinsky was quick to create the design. He selected Poland as the proving ground for a new type of Bolshevik *coup d'état*—the seizure of power from a coalition in which Communists already play a dominant role. It was, as historical precedents went, a grotesque version of the conventional *coup d'état* in that it was staged against a government of which the rebels were part and not against the régime of an opponent.

Workers were trained for "mass action" and learned the "art of demonstration." "Those of you living in a free and orderly country," Mr. Ferenc Nagy of Hungary once told us, "cannot conceive the effect of some tens of thousands of workers marching the streets in disorder and threatening some cabinet minister, judge, or public official with removal if he denies their demand. The legally constituted government (in which the Communists still represent a minority) is helpless against such mass demonstrators because force cannot be used against them. . . . If there should chance to be a man in the government who resists their demands, they respond with an outbreak of strikes and with production stoppages leading to economic disintegration." [38]

Agents provocateurs were assigned to sensitive areas to create disorders; to incite anti-Semitic riots in rural areas; to prepare apparent sabotage in industrial plants. The activities of these operatives were used to justify raids and the expansion of the scope of police activities. This was the last step but one. All that was left was to "discover" members of the non-Communist parties involved in "conspiracies and espionage activities" against the "new democracies." Accusations were made, witnesses were procured, and faked incriminating evidence was provided. The terrain was well prepared for the last stage of the *coup*—and the

Bolsheviks moved fast, with the precision of the Moscow-trained apparatus executing the Moscow-made plan.

When the shouting subsided (there was little shooting in these *coups*) the government that took over power looked remarkably like the one just ousted from office. But there had been a decisive change. By a process of selective sterilization, only its Communist members retained their political virility. Their non-Communist colleagues returned with a new voice—that of the eunuch.

The Polish *coup,* in the spring of 1947, was the first. It was over even before it could be recognized as such. The forces under Vice-Premier Stanislaw Mikolayczyk obliged the Bolsheviks by departing from the country overnight at their own volition.

The Hungarian *coup* of May 31, 1947, was somewhat similar to the Polish. It ended with the expulsion of Premier Ferenc Nagy and the seizure of dominant control by Communists, under Vice-Premier Mátyás Rákosi.[39] It was followed, in September, 1947, by the Bulgarian *coup,* when the Communists hanged Nikola Petkov, heroic leader of the Agrarian opposition, who refused to go abroad just one jump ahead of his executioners.[40]

Next in line was Rumania. It fell to the Bolsheviks on December 30, 1947.[41] In less than one year the Kremlin subdued four "liberated" countries, and turned them into helpless satellites, without moving a single Red Army soldier, without firing a single shot, or crossing a single border.

There was then only one country left behind the iron curtain in a somnambulist state of quasi-independence. It was Czechoslovakia. Although its government had co-operated with the Communists and supported Soviet foreign policy in an unequivocal manner, it had not been left unbruised by the affection of its Russian friends. In 1945, a Czechoslovak delegation negotiating a friendship pact in Moscow was held up virtually at gunpoint and told to hand over Subcarpathian Ruthenia—or else. Needless to say the Kremlin had its way. Czechoslovakia surrendered its easternmost province, and its population of 800,000 lost souls.

By 1948, the sand of Czechoslovakia's borrowed time was also running out. Its conquest needed just a little over a week. The campaign which had begun on the eve of February 20, with the arrival of Valeri Zorin, one of the Minindel's deputy ministers, ended on February 28, with his departure. On February 27, a new cabinet of Communists and reliable stooges was sworn in by a dazed and partially paralyzed Edouard Benés.[42]

When Czechoslovakia succumbed at last to the unbearable Soviet pressure, the demise of Central Europe's democratic paragon was accepted with glee and satisfaction in the satellite countries that had preceded her into the oblivion of the "people's democracies." During those days a significant little story made the rounds in Hungary. It described an incident during an inspection trip of Vice-Premier Rákosi in a region close to the Hungarian-Czechoslovak border.

Driving through a wheatfield heavy with promise in the sunny May of Hungary, Rákosi stopped his car to talk to an old peasant who tipped his battered hat to the new nobility.

"Well, Uncle János," Rákosi began, "how do you like this world of ours?"

"I like it fine, Comrade Excellency," the old man said.

"What do you like most about it?"

"Oh—I like everything, Comrade Excellency."

"Don't you like the fact that your son, only a railway porter a year or so ago, now is stationmaster in Küküllö?"

"I like it fine, Comrade Excellency."

"And how about your daughter? I hear she is studying in a teacher's college in Budapest. Don't you like that?"

"I like that especially fine, Comrade Excellency."

"Now come, János, tell me. What do you like most?" There was a pause. Then the old man said:

"I like most, sire, that those damned Czechs are now also in the Soviet orbit."

8. THE KASENKINA INCIDENT AND THE BERLIN BLOCKADE

IN 1947 and early in 1948 the Russians worked furiously and fast on the execution of the Vishinsky plan to co-ordinate Eastern Europe. As Stalin looked contentedly at Poland and Hungary, at Czechoslovakia and Bulgaria, even at corrupt and turbulent Rumania stripped of its young Hohenzollern, he thought of resting a bit on the laurels of these cheap victories.

But then two incidents, unrelated, snatched him from this holiday from conquest. And more than just that—they changed his attitude toward the whole issue of war or peace, deepened his suspicion of the United States, and turned him into as coldly aggressive a foe of the United States as anyone in the Kremlin school of America-baiters. One of these incidents was the Berlin Blockade and the handling of its diplomatic end by Ambassador Walter Bedell Smith in Moscow. The other had no connection whatever with the Berlin imbroglio. It developed in the heart of New York quite suddenly over the personal adventures of a pathetic little Russian schoolteacher named Oksana Stepanova Kasenkina.

It may be recalled that Mme Kasenkina deserted her Soviet employers on the eve of her projected departure for Moscow from New York, where she worked in one of those strange and secretive schools the Soviet authorities maintain for the children of their officials.[1] She accepted the hospitality of a group of well-meaning White Russians whose conduct in the incident was both proper and prudent and who cannot be blamed for its consequences.[2] It was, rather, Mme Kasenkina whose fears and indecisions precipitated the crisis. Just when she seemed safely out of the reach of her revengeful Soviet bosses, she changed her mind and sought quite voluntarily the protection of Yakov Mikhailovich Lomakin, the Soviet consul general in New York. Back in the Consulate, she changed her mind again. She jumped out of the window of her room where she was confined, so she said, in captivity, by Mr. Lomakin and his aides.

The incident was seized upon promptly in the United States as a welcome opportunity for effective anti-Soviet propaganda. With headlines blazing and loudspeakers blaring, the personal tragedy of the little woman gradually developed into an international incident. There was no question of the skill and discretion of our own officials who handled the case in a sober and dignified, and, therefore, very effective manner. But the judgment of some of the men who rushed headlong to Mme Kasenkina's bedside to take charge of her relations with press and radio were not to be trusted. Their anti-Soviet record had been remarkable for its senseless and vindictive venom rather than for its effectiveness.

Bigoted individuals should not be allowed dominant influence on the delicate conduct of our foreign relations—but soon it became evident that such persons had gained complete control of the case. By inspiring headlines and stimulating the news stories below them, they drove the State Department to a diplomatic action whose severity was out of all proportion to the incident. Its hand forced by the clamor of drummed-up public opinion, the Department demanded the recall of Consul Lomakin for abuse of his diplomatic privileges.

It must be understood that Lomakin was no ordinary consul. He occupied a very high position among the Soviet diplomats in the United States. In fact, we had reason to regard him as one of the highest-ranking diplomats of them all. Moreover, certain information led us to believe that Lomakin, a former chief of the Tass News Agency, was the head of the Russian political intelligence service in the entire Western Hemisphere. In that capacity he was closely tied into all Soviet agencies in charge of international relations: the Minindel, the Ministry of Foreign Trade, the foreign branch of the MVD, and, above all, the For-

eign Affairs Administration of the Communist party's Central
Executive Committee. He was, it seems, an important official in
the legendary mold of Chekhov's inspector general.

Moreover, Lomakin was more reasonable in his personal attitude toward America and Americans than any other Soviet
diplomat in our midst. Perhaps this was due to the fact that he
loved baseball in general and the Yankees in particular. An
ardent Bolshevik and a blind disciple of Stalin, he nevertheless
showed enough independence and honesty to confess admiration
for at least some of our political institutions as well.

Lomakin kept aloof from American Communists and their
fellow travelers. Gregarious and hospitable as he was, he preferred the company of Wall Street financiers, industrialists from
Pittsburgh, Detroit, and Cleveland, and other representatives of
our big business who, on their part, flocked to his cocktail parties and dinners in the Consulate.

He was, in a quiet but effective way, a positive factor in
Russo-American relations, one in a rapidly diminishing group
of pro-American Soviet officials left behind from the short term
of Maxim M. Litvinov in Washington. It was, therefore, both
ill timed and ill advised to pick on Lomakin and to hand him
his passport in a nebulous diplomatic fracas whose propaganda
value had already been skillfully exploited.[3]

Up to the point at which the State Department withdrew
Lomakin's consular exequatur, the U.S. made the most of the
case, managing to maintain the initiative despite frantic Russian efforts to wrest it from us. But in the moment of Lomakin's
expulsion we lost the initiative to the Russians.

The U.S.S.R. is traditionally sensitive on this particular score.
It tolerates no infringement upon the prestige of its diplomats.
Slight affronts against quite insignificant Soviet diplomatic offi-
cials bring prompt retaliation with disproportionate resentment.

The news of Lomakin's expulsion stunned the Minindel, already upset by the American furor over the Kasenkina case and
by the great success of the "Voice of America" in advertising the
event in its short-wave transmissions to the U.S.S.R.[4] Unused
to such triumphs, our diplomatic wallflowers in Moscow appeared jubilant at the obvious effectiveness of this propaganda
among the little people in the Moscow streets. Their jubilation

was reported to the Minindel, where it caused Mr. Molotov to fling particularly virulent bouquets of his famous profanities at his hapless aides, from Comrade Efreev, his personal secretary, down to his MVD driver.

Even while the question of blockaded Berlin was occupying the center of all diplomatic attention, Molotov's report on the Kasenkina case moved Stalin to give the Lomakin affair priority over all outstanding issues. He instructed Molotov to retaliate for Lomakin's expulsion with the immediate closing of the U.S. Consulate General in Vladivostok and with the withdrawal of a permission for the establishment of a U.S. Consulate in Leningrad.[5]

We thereby suffered a serious diplomatic defeat. To the U.S.S.R. the closing of her consulates in New York and San Francisco represented nothing of any consequence. First of all, the whole of the United States is wide open to the scrutiny of Soviet officials on overt and covert missions. Second, the U.S.S.R. maintains a network of resident spies throughout this country with bases of their own, independent of the closed Consulates.[6] Third, the designation "Consulate" was at best a meaningless concession to Western diplomatic usage. No sooner was the "Consulate General of the U.S.S.R." closed in New York, than it reopened virtually unchanged as the "Consular Branch of the Embassy of the U.S.S.R." to perform to this day all the functions of its "abolished" predecessor.

We, on the other hand, became deprived of a major diplomatic listening post at the far end of the gigantic Soviet Empire —in fact, of our sole official foothold in the Bolshevik Far East. We cannot share the indifference of some Americans to the loss of an American Consulate in Vladivostok. Hemmed in, over-guarded, under constant surveillance, their telephone tapped, their conversations recorded, their mail rifled, their lives spied upon, our diplomats could nevertheless make at least some observations. And their long Trans-Siberian journey to and from their post provided opportunities now lost to the U.S.[7]

However, the closing of our Vladivostok and Leningrad Consulates was not our sole loss in the skirmish. The nebulous case had far greater consequences, including a change—a crucial and probably fatal change—in the Kremlin's political and military timetable.

Although General Smith surprisingly fails to correlate the two incidents in his memoirs, it is a fact that the Kasenkina affair, a minor tactical episode, seriously interfered with his own major strategic maneuvers to settle the serious Berlin crisis that had been bothering the world since April 1. On that date, the Soviets in Berlin ordered a land blockade of the Allied sectors of the former German capital by refusing to allow United States and British supply trains to pass through the Russian zone.[8]

The news of Lomakin's expulsion reached Moscow during the night of August 20–21. Less than forty-eight hours later Stalin invited the Western envoys, who had been negotiating with him about the means of lifting the Berlin blockade, for a second conference. Apparently he was in a jovial mood. But his attitude on Berlin was stiffer. He was demanding and uncompromising. Molotov, who lacks Stalin's tact and charm in his dealings with foreigners, did not even bother to conceal his abrupt attitude with a mask of joviality. "Before he had been restrained and courteous," General Smith wrote, "but now he became truculent. His pleasant manner disappeared, and we wrangled over each word and every sentence in our proposed directive to the military commanders in Berlin." [9]

General Smith is inclined to attribute this change to Stalin's disappointment over our refusal to agree to some of their conditions on the rest of the German question. In any event, immediately following the meeting of August 23, Stalin turned his back on the West. He returned to his interrupted vacation in the villa that once belonged to the merchant prince Zensinov. A few days later, the Politburo instructed Molotov "to let the Berlin negotiations end in disagreement." What happened there, during those few days, causing the failure of a major diplomatic move—a failure that was to cost us millions of dollars spent on the air lift?

The Russians' conduct during the negotiations over the Berlin blockade remains one of the major mysteries of the cold war. The fact is that it mystified us as much as it puzzled at least a few of Russia's own diplomats who could themselves offer no explanation for the sudden rupture in the conversations, and that, apparently, in the moment of signing an agreement.

A still-active official of the Soviet Foreign Ministry with whom we had several private conversations of great frankness and elaborate secrecy suggested to us a theory that seems plausible enough to recommend itself as at least a clue to the solution of the mystery. "I examined everything I could find in our own archives and in your published reports on that particular conference," he said, "but I could find nothing to justify the breakdown of the negotiations, the well-known consequences of the breakdown, and the Generalissimo's stiff attitude since August 1948. In the absence of tangible evidence I had to search for intangible proof. Now, upon reading General Smith's memoirs, I think I have discovered it."

He then pointed out the following passages in our ambassador's memoirs as helping him in the development of his "clue":

We met Stalin for the second time on August 23. He was still jovial, and after greeting us in a friendly fashion, said quickly, "Gentlemen, I have a new plan." I remarked that Stalin's reputation as a strategist certainly had been justified, because he had anticipated us, but that we too had a new plan. "Good," Stalin rejoined, "we can compare them."

We proceeded to a paragraph-by-paragraph comparison, and I was pleased to see that the two drafts were close to each other in many respects. . . . But before we had time to become too elated, Stalin gave us a dash of cold water by insisting that something be said in the agreement about the plan to establish a Western German government. I reminded him that he had not made suspension of these plans a condition of the agreement. He persisted, however, that some mention of this question be made and suggested the following paragraph be included in a four-power communique:

"The question of the London decision was also discussed, including the formation of a Western German government. The discussion took place in an atmosphere of mutual understanding."

Taken by themselves, these words would seem harmless enough to the average Western reader—indeed, they might seem desirable, as indicating a friendly understanding. But in this context they were dynamite. The people of Germany and all Western Europeans knew very well that it would have been impossible for us to have discussed this question in an "atmosphere of mutual understanding" unless we had secretly accepted the Soviet condition and had agreed to abandon the Western German government idea in exchange for some blockade concessions. . . . I said that I would inform my government of Stalin's desire, but that I did not anticipate that the United States could accede to any such wording unless the proposed paragraph also contained the definite statement that "no agreement was reached on this subject."

For all practical purposes, I believe the conference really ended at this moment. . . . At our last meeting with Stalin, we had agreed to meet again on the date fixed for the military government to conclude their discussions. But before this day came I heard that Stalin had left Moscow on vacation, and I knew beyond question that the Politburo intended the session in Berlin to end in disagreement.[10]

The clue which our informant deduced from these paragraphs may be difficult for a Westerner to comprehend. "Stalin's decision was due," he said, "not to any basic disagreement on the fundamental issue, but rather to his anger at the stubborn and uncompromising attitude of Ambassador Smith during these closing minutes of the negotiations."

According to him, it was the common practice of Soviet diplomacy to smuggle extraneous passages into communiqués announcing the conclusions of negotiations. Sometimes the trick was not discovered at all until the damage was done and the U.S.S.R. gained its end. Sometimes Stalin's or Molotov's opposite number exclaimed: "But we haven't even discussed the matter!" And Molotov answered with a poker face: "Very well, let us discuss it now."

On one specific occasion, Molotov declared that the contested passage was sneaked into the communiqué "by mistake" and agreed quite readily to remove it. This, in fact, was what happened during the 1945 London conference of the Council of Foreign Ministers, at exactly two thirty in the morning, when its protocols came up for signature. Suddenly Molotov invited James Byrnes to his table and said that his staff "had, 'by mistake,' included the Soviet document on Bulgaria in the Russian text of the protocol." He asked quite sheepishly if, after all, it could not be accepted. Byrnes promptly answered that it could not. Molotov made the alternate suggestion that the first part of a Byrnes proposal on Bulgaria be combined with the second half of his own draft. Byrnes asked him: "How about accepting the American proposal in full?" And, to the amazement of all, Molotov agreed. The incident lasted for a whole hour. It was three thirty in the morning when the conference came to an end.[11]

But this is how the Russians do business. And this is what our own diplomats, used to the methods of puritan diplomacy, cannot comprehend or emulate. "Generalissimo Stalin was quite prepared to listen to a counterproposal on the part of Ambassador Smith," our Soviet informant advised us. "He never has rigid terms or inflexible conditions in mind." Indeed, Stalin is wide open to horse trading, ready to exchange a set of compromises on our part against some concessions on his. This, in a measure, was the secret of his success with Roosevelt. After Teheran and Yalta, too, after those citadels of the diplomatic *quid pro quo*, he was prepared to settle down to a long and quiet era of horse trading, unprecedented in the history of diplomacy. It would have slowed down, to be sure, the machinery of peacemaking, but it would have been effective nevertheless to prevent the machinery of war from coming into motion.

The brusquely negative attitude of the Western envoys toward his terms and bargaining gestures over the Berlin blockade suddenly convinced him that, for what to him seemed distinctly ulterior reasons, we refused to play his game of slow-motion diplomacy. His explanation was that we had no interest in peace. The truth was that we had no experience in old-fashioned Oriental horse trading applied to modern diplomacy.

While this explanation is admittedly far fetched and seems to do injustice to the fine diplomatic achievement of General Smith, it is reprinted here because it came to us, in all seriousness, from a responsible Soviet diplomat. It may be frivolous to accept a view that the fate of the world depends on such whimsical details on human relations. And yet there is substantial evidence to confirm the Russian's theory and to blame, at least in part, Stalin's caprice for the intensification of the cold war.

For it is an undeniable fact that it was only after the Kasen-kina incident and the breakdown of the Berlin talks that Stalin called his experts together to answer for him the three crucial questions of war or peace; it was only in the wake of those two disappointments that he ordered an acceleration of the tempo and a change of the rhythm of his preparations for war; it was only in the wake of those blows to his personal vanity and Russian prestige that he carried the cold war to all the fronts of Europe and Asia, invigorating, promoting, and spreading it in three continents.

At the end of 1948, the cold war was waged on innumerable fronts. Indeed it became a global cold war. It extended from France and Italy to China and Viet Nam; from Spitsbergen to the Dardanelles; from Greece to Chile, Bolivia, and Colombia. It was waged in a variety of manners, according to a set of divergent rules, on a puzzling mutation of past patterns, revamped, changed, and modernized, as the forces of Bolshevik Russia applied them to new victories and defeats.

Part Three

HOT FRONTS OF THE COLD WAR

9.

PATTERNS
OF
DESTRUCTION

WHEN THE grandfathers of the socialist revolution drafted their program, they outlined but one single schematic pattern, in the famous second chapter of the *Communist Manifesto*.[1] International bolshevism has traveled a long way since 1847. Today it is so far advanced on the road to "the final result of the revolutionary process" that it can draw on innumerable past patterns for any future conquest.

Outstanding among them is the *Russian pattern,* or revolution by armed insurrection. This is the pattern of a minuscule minority seizing power in the disorder of a "bourgeois-democratic" revolution. The steps are, first, to create and then to exploit chaos, and, finally, to move with speed and martial precision behind the smoke screen of disorder, to capture the most sensitive points of the state authority and organization.

In its progress political aims are completely subordinated to technical means. It was one of the Bolsheviks' basic tenets that no political minority, such as they were in 1917, can ever carry a revolution to success unless it resorts to the methods of armed insurrection.[2] To this end they created the original Red Guards, a small professional army of revolutionary activists that survives today within every Communist party of the world, including the Communist party of the U.S.A.

The Bolsheviks invented superbly efficient tactics for their Red Guards. One of them was called "invisible maneuvers." As it is still practiced today, squads of men prepare for their assignments at the revolutionary H-hour by "visiting" the localities of their allocated mission. Thus one squad may establish the exact position of the master switch they will have to throw in the power station. Another may survey the terrain of the reservoir where they will turn off the big town's water supply. Still others may observe the railway switch they are to throw to derail trains bringing loyalist reinforcements.[3]

One of the secret textbooks used in every school where bolshevism still trains its Red Guards is called *The Road to Victory*. It has the subtitle, *A Theoretical Discussion of Marxism and Revolution*. Its author, "Alfred Lange," [4] compressed the basic theories of the Bolshevik struggle for power into six chapters. Their titles speak for themselves.

Chapter One is devoted to "The Particular Art of the Uprisings." Chapter Two discusses "The Choice of the Right Moment." Chapter Three deals with "The Concentration of Forces." Chapter Four advises "Attack at Any Price." Chapter Five surveys how the concentration of the enemy can be prevented. The sixth chapter contains Lange's conclusions.

"An effective fight for the destruction of the armed forces of the enemy demands that it be waged not just from the outside but also from the inside," he wrote. "At the moment of the final conflict . . . an armed fight against the police and the military [is needed] and a physical battle for the military, that is to say, an active, desperate fight with the counterrevolutionary elements for the winning over of the mass of soldiers." [5]

Another secret textbook is called *The Organization of Revolutionary Strikes*.[6] Its author is Ernö Gerö, today the second-ranking Communist in Hungary, troubleshooter of the Communist-dominated Hungarian Government. He devoted special attention to the organization of strikes in the United States. They include all kinds of strikes, from slowdowns in factories to the strike of schoolchildren against their teachers. Farmers' strikes in Iowa and Nebraska, in the early '30's, are described in great detail as the prototype for Bolshevik agitators, and the aim toward which they are to strive in their propaganda and agitational work in the rural areas of America.[7]

These books are current texts, not only in the old Lenin School of Moscow, which is the acknowledged university of the seven lively arts of revolution,[8] but also in the new Cominform

School in Budapest, whose rank is but slightly below that of the Lenin School.[9]

A confidential informant, who succeeded in working his way into the school and spent one full term studying the rudiments of revolution, reported to us that the Cominform School had among its students several Americans who had gone to Europe on the GI Bill of Rights. In their application they asserted their intention to study in such universities as the Sorbonne or the London School of Economics. They did matriculate in those schools but then they continued clandestinely to Budapest and spent the year studying the techniques of insurrection. They are now back in the U.S., submerged in the community, trained operatives of the Communist underground.

An important branch of the Budapest school is the school of activists. It turns out "professional revolutionaries" in a two-year course. The curriculum of that school includes military as well as ideological training and a complete course in subversive activities from psychological warfare to sabotage.

A graduate of the school is supposed to know:

1. How to handle light arms (up to and including heavy machine guns) of his own country, as well as a great number of foreign armies.

2. How to use all weapons at the disposal of police and how to defend oneself against them.

3. How to break the codes of governments.

4. How to wage what is called the conspiratorial type of warfare, street fighting, action behind and in front of the barricades, fighting adapted to various topographical conditions; partisan warfare behind enemy lines during conventional hostilities, civil war.

5. How to conduct civil-war intelligence to establish the location of food supplies, warehouses, utilities, communication centers, railway stations and yards, telephone exchanges, and similar institutions essential for the proper functioning of an organized state.

6. How to wreck trains, slow down or stop production, destroy machinery in key factories, demolish centers of re-

sistance such as hostile newspaper plants, police stations, etc.,
destroy assembled cargo in warehouses.

7. How to propagandize and agitate among soldiers, workers, the intelligentsia; how "to raise the mob spirit" in order
to start masses "on the go."

8. How to infiltrate into the state apparatus, into key
civilian institutions like utilities, industrial plants, banks;
how to bore from within preparatory to the uprising to sap
the strength of the opposing forces.

9. How to conduct counterintelligence against "traitors
and imperialist spies," and how to secure the "conspiratorial
character" of "the Organization." [10]

This is but a partial list. No aspect of subversive tactics and
conspiratorial civil war is ignored in this curriculum.[11] An
American graduate of the Lenin School described the "con-
spiratory type of warfare" in the following words:

"It is related to the boring-in process, street fighting, and how
to *'mobile'* [move around] in blocks, the blocks in a city, the
workers in a plant; how to develop a general strike out of a local
strike; how to develop a general strike into a city uprising, a city
uprising into a national uprising, coordinating all these different uprisings. Then how to lead this thing, once it is raised, once
these men are on the warpath, how to direct them.

"Then we come to something like open warfare. We break
these people down into groups; we make armies on the basis of
the immediate emergency of the moment, or whatever the situation may be." [12]

Here, too, the pattern follows the early Bolshevik example.

The Bolshevik Red Guard had a few thousands of officers and
men, but their shock troops, called the "advanced workers" and
commanded by a fanatic named Antonov, had only about one
thousand. They were divided into squads of ten each. The
squads were further subdivided for specific operations: one man
going alone to kill the railwayman in charge of a switch; three
men going to a bridge to disarm its drowsy guards; ten men assigned to the "capture" of the central telephone exchange; one
man to pull a switch and blackout street lights in a certain part
of the city.[13]

There are many other patterns, too. Thus we can designate a new type of the Bolshevik *coup d'état* as the "Czechoslovak pattern"; the large-scale civil war the "China pattern"; the guerilla-type civil war the "Burma pattern." Infiltration on an international scale may be called the "Iran pattern." Among the patterns in store for future use in countries as yet unconquered are the "Indonesian pattern" and the "Swedish pattern," to be applied to India as well.

Today the Russian pattern is most evident in the tactics of the Communist parties of Italy and France, a pattern of harassment by activists, training for the day of their armed insurrection.

10.

THE RUSSIAN PATTERN
IN ITALY
AND FRANCE

A time comes when there is demoralization above, a growing revolt below; the morale of the army is undermined. The old structure of society is tottering. There are actual insurrections; the army wavers. Panic seizes the rulers. A general uprising begins.
M. J. OLGIN: *Why Communism*

COMMANDED BY Luigi Longo, a battle-hardened Communist soldier of fortune from the North, the Red Guard of Italy is said to have 200,000 men. In our judgment 80,000 is closer to the truth.[1] Most of them are concentrated in the densely populated and highly industrialized northern regions of Liguria, Piedmont, Lombardy, and Emilia. They provide the personnel for still another pattern—the Franco-Italian pattern of slow insurrection and harassment.

The Red Guard is the Grand Army of the Italian revolution. The shock troops, the action squads, total no more than 5,000 men. They are organized in cells of five men each, with specific tasks assigned to them for which they are, at this very minute, executing reconnaissance missions and invisible maneuvers on the Antonov pattern.

Some of these men are not even known as Communists. They live in rural areas, away from the big cities. Their orders are to refrain from all contact with the movement, some even masquerade as opponents of communism. They are thus required to stay underground until H-hour—then they will rush to their battle stations to execute with trained skill the assignments given to them long in advance, perhaps even years ago.

One man from Liguria may go to Lombardy to wreck a particular train, passing at a certain time over a specific bridge, thus blocking passage across that strategic bridge of reinforcements or supplies, isolating an entire region by this one stroke. Another man may go to a hydroelectric station in Bolzano, make his way into the control room, club the man sitting in front of the board, turn the switch, and throw a whole region into darkness.

The Red Guards are superbly trained and well commanded by men who went through all the schools of Communist activism during their long exile from Mussolini's Fascist regime. "Commander" Longo himself, who heads the military administration of the Italian Communist party's Executive Committee, received his *military* training in the Soviet Union's top-ranking service schools as well as in the civil-war schools of the Comintern and Cominform.

An accomplished practical soldier, as well as a trained professional, Longo has held the highest positions in the Communist international military hierarchy. He was one of the chief political commissars in the Spanish Civil War. During the fight for Italy's liberation in 1943–44, he commanded several partisan brigades with gallantry and skill.[2]

But it is the career of the legendary "Dario" that is really typical of the Red activist. His real name is Ilio Barontini. Born into a middle-class family in Cecina sixty years ago, he became an engineer. As a student, at the age of fifteen, too young to practice his chosen profession, he joined the Young Socialist movement. In 1921, he joined the Communists.[3]

When the Fascists sought to arrest him, Dario—with Togliatti and other Communist leaders—escaped to Moscow where he spent long years in day-and-night training for his future duties as a Communist military commander. He graduated with honors from the Frunze Military Academy in 1936, and was promptly sent to the Spanish Civil War to act as political commissar of the Garibaldi Brigade. He went on to Ethiopia in 1938 to organize guerilla bands; then to France to aid in the organization of the First Maquis; and eventually to Northern Italy to lay the groundwork for the partisan's "war of liberation" in Italy. Dario, at long last fighting on native soil, rose to general command in Italy's own Garibaldi Brigade.

There is supposed to be in Italy a Soviet liaison staff clandestinely co-operating with the staff of the Red Guards, aiding in the preparation of tactical plans, but also supervising the Stalinist loyalty and dependability of the Red militia. Some of these Russian agents were originally attached to the Soviet Repatriation Commission at Salsamaggiore but failed to return to the U.S.S.R. when the commission was abolished. Instead they went underground to serve as weapon teachers or technical inspectors with regional commands. Their number has recently been enlarged with the steady arrival of newcomers directly from Moscow.[4]

The pattern drawn up for the Italian Communist party is one of harassment, hit-and-run fighting on a really large scale. The Party's instructions do not include seizure of power *at this time*. On the Communist timetable Italy is marked to fall into the orbit only during or after a World War III in which it will, inevitably, play its part as one of the chief bases of the West.

In the meantime, the Communists are required to undermine the stability of the government and thus prevent Italy from ever becoming too strong a bastion of the West. Their tactics include strikes in public utilities, provocatory and guerilla action against the police, in which, incidentally, they are sufficiently infiltrated; raids against "Fascists," which term includes everybody not in their own camp; and, above all, large-scale "propaganda demonstrations," abrupt and furious, to show their strength and ruthless determination much in the manner of a fleet showing its flag.[5]

Occasionally small bands of activists are allowed to come out into the open to stage such demonstrations. Thus in November, 1947, just as the Friendship Train was crossing the United States with food for France and Italy, the Communists of Italy were ordered to stage a series of violent outbreaks. The experience of Naples during those days was a clinical example of their tactics. The activists of the neighboring villages received orders to assemble for "direct action." They were then driven in trucks into Naples to "spread confusion and terror far and wide." [6]

Such tactics of harassment include clamorous fist fights in Parliament to undermine the status and respectability of that democratic body. On February 14, 1950, the Communists decided to create disturbances on the floor during an important policy speech of Premier Alcide de Gasperi. Their purpose was to make bigger headlines than those announcing the Premier's policies and thus to monopolize a parliamentary session that would have otherwise belonged to Gasperi. In fact, the Communists tried to assault de Gasperi himself. The task was assigned to Luigi di Mauro, one of the youngest deputies, and one of the leaders if not the commandant of the activists within the Italian Parliament. Next day the Communist press of Italy hailed di Mauro's misplaced alacrity with unrestrained enthusiasm.[7]

The signal for such demonstrations is flashed secretly to Party organizations or is given openly by inflammatory speeches of Party leaders. When *Unita,* official organ of the CPI, reprinted a Togliatti speech in which the chief of the Italian Communists called for an "intensification of agitation against the government," his specialists staged raids throughout the country; they cut down telephone poles, took policemen as hostages, opened the jails. The nation was terrified—for just one day. Then the goon squads disbanded and disappeared, each man to his own neighborhood and his daily job, as they had gathered to despoil.[8]

Aside from keeping the country in a permanent state of high nervous tension, these tactics have several operational aims:

(1) They are designed to "habituate" authorities to Communist disturbances and, thereby, to relax their vigilance and reduce gradually the intensity of their defensive measures.

(2) They are intended as maneuvers for the activists, to test certain important tactical problems such as, for example, the time needed for a column of trucks to reach a certain destination from a secret assembly point; the strength of police forces thrown against individual assailants or for the protection of certain key points; possible interference, pro or con, by the populace; the efficiency and effectiveness of illicit interference with the operations of public utilities; and similar tactical problems of civil guerilla war. All the experience thus gained goes

into the war books of Italy's Communist activists, enabling them to plan and plot with painstaking exactitude for H-day.

The outstanding feature of the Italian Communist underground is that it is based on the organization of partisans trained in guerilla warfare and eager to return into action.[9]

From a strictly military point of view, Italy has the most effective Communist organization in Western Europe. The potential danger this fact represents to our plans can hardly be overstated.

In France, the military organization of the Italian Party is duplicated but it lacks the efficiency and discipline of the Italian apparatus despite wartime training and experience in the *Francs-Tireurs et Partisans*. The military zeal and qualifications of a Barontini are equaled if not surpassed in men like André Marty, the fabulous "General Joinville," whose real name is Alfred Mallert, and Laurent Casanova—some of Luigi Longo's counterparts at the head of French activists.[10]

But men more typical of the *French* pattern of harassment are Benoit Frachon and Gaston Monmousseau, labor leaders on the strategic echelon, or Ambroise Croizat and Antoine Demusois, their colleagues on the tactical level.

The center of gravity of the French Communist offensive is in the labor movement, and the chief weapon of the Communists in France is the strike. It is not necessarily the *general* strike which is regarded as a weapon of last resort in extreme emergencies, likely to fail when called indiscriminately. They prefer the *pinpoint* strike at key points within key industries and utilities, with what is called their radiation effect, capable of paralyzing even those functions of the state and nation that are otherwise unaffected by stoppage.

In this connection, relatively obscure French Communist leaders like Lucient Midol and Raymond Tournemaine, who control the activists among the French railway workers, and Marcel Paul, who, as secretary general of the departmental union of public utilities in the Paris region, has his specialists at the key electric power switches of the republic, gain greater significance for the plan than even Maurice Thorez himself.

Periodic failures of strikes called by the Communist party's central committee mislead us into believing that the Bolsheviks are losing their influence with the French workers. Thus, in the early winter of 1950, it was reported from Paris:

"The West European Communist campaign to delay or halt shipment of U.S. Atlantic Pact arms shipments suffered a stinging setback.

"In France, which will receive the bulk of the war material, the government's declaration of war against Red strikes and sabotage appeared to be paying off. A two-hour rail strike called by Red Leader Maurice Thorez and his aids to test Communist strength among railway workers never got started. There were only a few stoppages, in Marseille and suburban Paris.

"At Cherbourg, where the bulk of U.S. arms are likely to arrive only 80 of 1200 rail workers struck. In the mines, usually responsive to Red demonstration orders, the Communist 'warmup campaign' was a little more successful, but even there only some 30 per cent observed a demanded 24-hour walkout." [11]

The chief clue to the Communist's strength is not the failure of the 1,120 Cherbourg rail workers to strike, but the ready response of 80 to Thorez' appeal. The French pattern emphasizes quality above quantity—the revolutionary efficiency of the lone-wolf operator (the single activist) over the inefficiency of the mass. Even during the recent war, the French underground was organized in two branches. One was the huge Maquis which fought brilliantly *after* the Normandy landing but spasmodically and hesitantly before it, filling even President Roosevelt with misgivings as to the real effectiveness and value of the French resistance. The other was a much smaller army of activists assigned to specific and carefully chosen tasks. They did such a magnificently thorough job of sabotage that occasionally it even interfered with the progress of our own advances over the railroads and bridges and roads they demolished to slow down German mobility. The Monsieur Dupont who left his bakery shop in Finistère for an hour or two, blew up the munition dump of a German regiment on the outskirts of the town, and returned to his *brioches* and *croissants* with the world's most innocent expression on his face; or the young curé from Auxerre who, called to a dying parishioner, actually went out into the woods of Yonne to operate a clandestine radio station in touch with the

Allies—such specialists are numerous within the labor movement.[12]

In France, which has bled so profusely in a succession of wars since the days of Napoleon, and where the discrepancy between birthrate and deathrate is the greatest in Europe, the idea of peace has a particular fascination for all. The Communists make the most of it, embellishing the French pattern of destruction with still another tactical element.

Paris was the center of the Communist-inspired peace movement of the middle 1930's, even as Hitler was preparing his war against France. Then Georges Cagniot, a quiet professor from Montigny-les-Cherlieu, was the spark plug of the Communists' "pragmatic pacifism," as secretary general of the World Committee against War and Fascism.

His seemingly abstract and pacific preoccupation pays ample dividends in today's "direct actions." The French section of Moscow's Permanent Peace Committee finds a way to intervene in any of the nation's daily problems if it provides an opening for the Bolshevik wedge. Thus in Algiers more than sixty "peace committees" were formed to prevent an anti-Communist campaign of the authorities that the Cominform on its part described as "a campaign of repression by the colonial authorities against democratic organizations." [13]

These are illuminating items of a report, dated January 20, 1950, which the French "section" of the Permanent Peace Committee sent to Cominform headquarters at 56 Valeriu Braniste in Bucharest. The report was entitled: "Response of the working people of France to the transportation of war materials under the North Atlantic Defense Pact."

Item: "Throughout France, workers at many enterprises actively collect funds for the heroic Saint-Nazaire dockers who voluntarily gave up their jobs, having refused to unload American arms."

Item: "Peace committees are being formed in many factories, as for example, in the Luvalette factory in Saint-Ouen."

Item: "Workers in the Duval plant in Isay-les-Moulinaux stopped production of tanks parts."

Item: "In Toulon, arsenal workers refused to load arms on a ship. Sixteen shops in the arsenal simultaneously stopped work.

Six hundred dockers and crane drivers in Nantes also refused to unload war materials."

Crane operators are high among the key workers organized as activists by the Communists to achieve effectiveness in the pinpoint strikes of their trial areas. The Cominform's great interest in work stoppages in arsenals and war-essential factories reveals the Soviet Union's chief preoccupation with the central question of war.

In the French pattern, pacifism is shrewdly conjoined with anticolonialism. Today they are both used to sap France's strength, not merely by keeping her disarmed, but also by stripping her of all overseas possessions. The great colonial struggle of the day Moscow conducts against the West is concentrated on the most vulnerable link in the chain—on France. The Soviet recognition of Ho Chi Minh of Viet Nam was accompanied by a national campaign of French Communists, who demonstrated against their own government's policy in Indo-China upon orders from Moscow. Their action was in line with Lenin's famous principle known as "working for the defeat of one's own country." [14]

The permanent Bolshevik campaign against the French Government's stand in Indo-China has been masterminded in Moscow and forced upon the French Communist party whether they liked it or not. It all reached a high point of intensity in January, 1950. The so-called peace movement had all the ingredients of the French pattern: temporary stoppages of work in selected key industries, demonstrations, meetings, the adoption of resolutions, and parades by "mothers with sons in Indo-China."

The workers of the Renault factory, which manufactures some of the equipment needed in Viet Nam, held a big demonstrative meeting just to show what they could do in the event of a serious emergency.

Temporary work stoppages were organized in Toulon, the arsenal city; in the strategic Lens coal mines; in Rouen; and, again in the words of the Cominform, "in the arsenals of Lorient, Tarbes and Saint-Nazaire."

The S.S. *Pasteur*, a troopship about to sail for Indo-China, was held up for forty-eight hours by her crew demonstrating against the Viet Nam war. The workers of Marseille staged a temporary work stoppage to manifest their solidarity with the crew.

Then Marseille railwaymen left their places of work for twenty-four hours in another solidarity strike. Two other ships plying between France and Indo-China, the *Lyon* and *Belfort*, delayed their departure when the Communists interfered with their sailings.

The demonstrations continued unabated. On February 14, the Associated Press reported from Nice that "about 1,000 workers, answering a call from the Communist-led General Labor Confederation (CGT), dumped a truck containing war material in the bay.... Official sources later confirmed that the material was part of a pylon for a V-2 rocket ramp. It was to be loaded aboard a freighter scheduled to sail Thursday for Oran." [15]

These ingredients of the Franco-Italian pattern of harassment should be viewed in the light of Lenin's definition of armed uprising. He described it as "the highest place of the revolutionary crisis," [16] and Stalin declared:

"No impassable line should be drawn between a 'revolutionary upsurge' and an 'acute revolutionary situation.' ... Usually the former passes unnoticed on to the latter. Our task consists in preparing the proletariat even now for the decisive revolutionary battles without waiting for the moment when the so-called acute revolutionary situation will arrive." [17]

11. ACTION IN ASIA

WHILE THE Franco-Italian pattern represents the "revolutionary upsurge," the pattern of China and Viet Nam demonstrates the "acute revolutionary situation." But it demonstrates far more. First, it shows the development of an imperialist war into civil war along the exact lines of Lenin's theories and predictions.

Second, it demonstrates the use of armed force as an aid to the Bolshevik Revolution.

Third, from our own point of view and most important, it demonstrates how the Americo-European coalition of democratic powers can be weakened by striking at them indirectly.

The China pattern was described in remarkable words by Secretary of State Dean Acheson, in a speech to the National Press Club, on January 12, 1950:

Nobody, I think, says that the Nationalist Government fell because it was confronted by overwhelming military force which it could not resist. Certainly no one in his right mind suggests that. . . .

After the war, Chiang Kai-shek emerged as the undisputed leader of the Chinese people. Only one faction, the Communists, up in the hills, ill-equipped, ragged, a very small military force, was determinedly opposed to his position. He had overwhelming military power, greater military power than any ruler had ever had in the entire history of China. He had tremendous economic and military support and backing from the United States. He had the acceptance of all other foreign countries, whether sincerely or insincerely in the case of the Soviet Union is not really material to this matter. Here he was in this position and four years later what do we find? We find that his armies have melted away. His support in the country has melted away. His support largely outside the country has melted away and he is a refugee on a small island off the coast of China with the remnants of his forces.

As I said, no one says that vast armies moved out of the hills and defeated him. To attribute this to the inadequacy of American aid is only to point out the depth and power of the forces which were miscalculated or ignored. What has happened in my judgment is that the almost inexhaustible patience of the Chinese people in their misery ended. They did not bother to overthrow this government. There was really nothing to overthrow. They simply ignored it throughout the country. They took the solution of their immediate village problems into their own hands. If there was any trouble or interference with the representatives of the government, they simply brushed them aside. They completely withdrew their support from this government and when that support was withdrawn, the whole military establishment disintegrated. Added to the grossest incompetence ever experienced by any military command was this total lack of support both in the armies and in the country, and so the whole matter just simply disintegrated.

This magnificent analysis ended with this conclusion:

The Communists did not create this. The Communists did not create this condition. They did not create this revolutionary spirit. They did not create a great force which moved out from under Chiang Kai-shek. But they were shrewd and cunning to mount it, to ride this thing into victory and into power.

Our troubles in China are not of recent origin and we have had ample warning to prepare ourselves for them. Lenin regarded imperialism as a corroded chain bound to break at its weakest links, and looked to China as one of the weakest links of the chain.[1] Although Stalin expected the chain to break "next" in India and Germany, he identified himself with Lenin's basic remark that "the East ... has definitely been drawn into the common whirlpool of the revolutionary movement." He said:

> To put it briefly, the chain of the imperialistic front should break, as a rule, where the links are most fragile and, in any event, not necessarily where capitalism is most developed, or where there is a certain percentage of proletarians and a certain percentage of peasants, and so on.
>
> This is why statistical calculations concerning the proportion of the proletariat to the population of a given country lose, in the solution of the question of the proletarian revolution, the exceptional importance so eagerly attached to them by the bookworms of the Second International who do not understand imperialism and who fear revolution like the plague.[2]

Chinese nationalist leadership under Sun Yat-sen, hard pressed by the war lords, seized upon the pattern thus prescribed by the Russians and allied itself with the Marxist pattern and the Moscow front. This alliance was not broken until 1927, when the Russian design became evident to all.

At that time the "Old Marshal," Chang Tso-lin, was in control of Peking. Himself one of the implacable foes as well as the target of Sun Yat-sen and Chiang Kai-shek, he decided to strike at them by striking at their Soviet allies, whom he held mainly responsible for his own troubles.

In April, 1927, the "Old Marshal" decided to move—and his action that followed dealt a mortal blow to the Sino-Russian alliance. It did more than that. It opened for all time certain Chinese eyes to Russian designs as it should have opened other eyes abroad, especially in the United States where the fate of China has always been followed with close interest and never ending apprehension.

Carefully planned and efficiently executed, the Soviet Embassy was raided in Peking, in what was an expedient and timely violation of diplomatic immunity.

Immense quantities of documents were seized. Among the papers was the master plan for the complete bolshevization of China.[3] The "Old Marshal" saw to it that copies of the master plan reached Chiang Kai-shek at once. That was the end of the Comintern-Kuomintang alliance. All Communists were eliminated from Chiang's entourage. Some of them were liquidated in the traditional Chinese manner. Others just disappeared without a trace in a purge that shook China from Mukden to Shanghai.

Communism became discredited in China.

In March, 1927, in Shanghai, a small international force including American sailors and marines watched apprehensively the Communist Eighth Route Army from behind barbed wire and sandbags. The Chinese were trying to make up their mind whether or not they should overrun the foreign settlements and eliminate all foreign influence from China. Commanding the Eighth Route Army was a young man, then virtually unknown to the outside world. His name was Mao Tse-tung.[4]

He had 100,000 men under his command. The West had only 3,500. But nothing came of this uneven showdown. A month later, in the wake of the "Old Marshal's" sensational discovery in Peking, Mao and his Eighth Route Army were fleeing from the gates of Shanghai to South China where they remained until 1935.

The Communists of Mao Tse-tung never wavered in their loyalty—never for three decades. Their party was founded in May, 1921, by a group of university students in Peking. Mao himself was too poor to be a student. But as a youth of seventeen he had obtained a position with the university library where he spent his days and nights, educating himself. Early in its history, the Party enrolled him as one of its first members. His shrewd intellect and great popularity, coupled with other positive traits of a remarkable character, brought him rapid advancement and eventual leadership in the Party.[5]

It is the chronology of developments rather than their ideological meaning which reveals to us the China pattern in all its bizarre aspects. Up to the early winter of 1947, a Kuomintang-

Communist pact seemed probable although Chiang properly recognized that it would not prove feasible for long. No pact with the Communists does. Their eagerness to join Chiang's government was motivated by their weaknesses. They lacked material strength but were confident that they would be able to bore from within once they were inside the government.

Generalissimo Chiang anticipated the Bolshevik design. On February 11, 1947, he notified the Communist delegation, waiting in Nanking to get the terms of collaboration, that "its presence was no longer desired." [6] The breach was followed promptly by an uprising in Formosa and then by a violent upsurge of Kuomintang military activity. A large-scale offensive was started against the Communists. It yielded Yenan, the Communist stronghold, to national government forces. [7] The civil war was on.

The Communists needed a full year to gather their strength, to organize their forces, and to arm themselves with weapons the Japanese Kwantung Army surrendered in Manchuria and which the Russians "abandoned" to them. On March 12, 1948, their steamroller started to move—without Russian assistance.

Ssupingchieh was the first to fall to Chinese Communist forces. Tsinan fell in September; Chinchow and Changchun in October. By November 1, the Communists were in Mukden. On January 31, 1949, they entered Peiping. On April 20, 1949, the Chinese Communists crossed the Yangtze. The civil war was won. [8]

From this point on the great decision we shall have to make is whether or not we shall allow, by inaction, nationalism in China to be perverted and brought under the complete domination of Moscow. We must do as much as possible, and do it now, to prevent it. It is idle to talk of Titoism in China, just as idle as expecting any other forms of "foreign" influence taking root and shaping the destiny of China. Appreciating the basic national psychology of the people, we expect no Titoism to develop in China after the Yugoslav pattern. Neither do we expect the Chinese to fall blind victims to communism as it is directed from Moscow. [9]

But we can expect dissidence to develop and spread and even activate itself in the form of the kind of resistance to the Kremlin that Mao and his men showed to the Kuomintang. Whether we call it Maoism or Chinese national communism or just plain Chinese nationalism, it is a reality with which we have to deal and upon which we must count in making our plans.

Careful investigations [10] failed to turn up any Russian equipment in the hands of Mao soldiers. Even the prime minister of Chiang's refugee regime in Formosa had to concede that there were no Soviet troops, concealed or otherwise, fighting on Chinese soil at the side of Mao's battalions.[11] The great number of technicians one can now find in Peking are, in reality, MVD emissaries. They are watching Mao and his regime with the suspicious eyes of the police, rather than aiding him in a solution of his innumerable technical, social, political, and, above all, economic problems.

The strict quantitative limitation of Russian aid suggests a theory that, if tested and proven correct, could go far in a proper evaluation of relations between Mao and the Kremlin. It appears that in China the Polish pattern was applied and failed.[12] This is a pattern of giving rope to *both sides* in a struggle, but just enough to hang themselves separately, as long as they can find no common ground on which to hang together. It appears that Mao won in China—despite Russia.

Not all the arms the Japanese left behind in Manchuria were given to Mao. He was given just enough to equip *no more than 20,000 combatants* for a limited campaign against the demoralized forces of Chiang Kai-shek. Moscow expected that this would lead to a stalemate and eventually to a defeat of *both* adversaries —Chiang's by the Communists, and the Communist's at the hand of the nationalists. There is some reason to believe that the Kremlin even expected the nationalists to make a comeback and stay in power. In that case the Communists of Mao would have been relegated to their old cave-dwelling existence in the remoter regions of China.[13]

Aside from the quantity of arms Mao was allowed from the depleted Japanese arsenals, other evidence seems to support these speculations. One such indication is the Kremlin's decision to maintain its chief diplomatic agencies in China at the court of Chiang Kai-shek until Mao's victory was an accomplished fact. Another is the Oriental intrigue the Soviet Ambassador was known to have been conducting, both in Nanking and in Canton, against Mao.[14] Still another was the maintenance—just in case—of Li Li-san, Mao's bitter enemy and Moscow's willing stooge, in Mukden, even while Mao was scoring his victories over Chiang.[15]

Another indication is that after long Soviet delay in recognizing Mao, there followed still another delay in demanding for him a seat in the United Nations. In the subsequent clamor for that seat—accompanied by Soviet walkouts from UN bodies—it was easily forgotten that not until early in 1950 did the U.S.S.R. decide to champion China's cause in the United Nations, although it recognized Mao in September, 1949.

We regard Mao's long sojourn in Moscow, in the winter of 1949–50, as still another indication of flaws in this important pattern in Asia. Contrary to general opinion in the West, we maintain that Mao gained far more than he was compelled to yield in the Russo-Chinese treaty of February 14, 1950.[16]

Such Asiatic treaties have to be read between the lines. This particular one, too, is full of loopholes. Mao succeeded in adding to it a series of shrewd paragraphs which enable him, at a moment's notice, to turn away from Moscow even while remaining faithful to the letter, though not to the spirit, of that strange alliance.[17]

There is already, we believe, a *new* Chinese pattern in the making in Moscow. It is a "pattern of the two Chinas"—one inside and the other outside the Great Wall. From now on Russia will work hard, with its best agents on the spot, to confine Mao's rule to the ancient area inside the Great Wall, while retaining control of the vast subcontinent outside the Wall.[18]

The United States must take this new pattern into full consideration and try to discover, through intelligence and analysis, how Mao plans to react to it. On the accuracy of our prognostications and on our countermeasures depend our future in China, and China's future in a free world.

Bordering on China, as well as on the Chinese pattern, is the complex problem of Viet Nam.

In French Indo-China the blunders of a bewildered French administration have aided and abetted the Bolsheviks in creating still another pattern—revolution by guerilla warfare. The his-

tory of French administration in Indo-China since the termination of World War II is a nightmare of old-fashioned colonialism with the whip removed, but with the whip-hand attitude
remaining. Senseless oppression alternated with unwarranted
leniency; extreme friendliness followed by extreme hostility;
reckless promises unnecessarily made—then wantonly broken.
Administration has been inexcusably incompetent. Administrators like Admiral d'Argenlieu and Governor Bollaert, and visiting observers like General Revers, generated intrigue and
counterintrigue, and promoted Japanese collaborators to positions of political supremacy.

Thus, on March 6, 1946, the French signed an accord with Ho
Chi Minh, perennial mystery man of southeast Asia and agent
of the Comintern, recognizing *de facto* control of the northern
part of the country by the government he headed. Ex-Emperor
Bao Dai was then one of Ho's advisers.

Months of negotiations followed at Fontainebleau with Ho
himself leading the Viet Nam delegation. But they failed to
result in agreement on anything except a temporary *modus
vivendi*. Then on December 19, 1946, at Hanoi, French soldiers
began to move against Ho's followers around the city. It has
since been civil war to the death in Indo-China.[19]

In 1946, in Fontainebleau, Ho was strong and France was
weak. In 1950 the situation appeared to the French to be re-
versed. In the meantime France built up a garrison of 130,000
imported soldiers in Indo-China, men and supplies that are a
serious drain on her weak economy and an even greater strain on
her political unity. In its determination to pack more and more
divisions into Indo-China, France unfortunately ignores the new
truth that the strength of a colonial power is measured by the
weakness of the army it needs to police a colony or maintain
control over a dominion.

Whether proper French policy and adequate French administration could have tied Ho's regime to the West, no one can say
with certainty. Certainly Ho is a Marxist. Just as certainly the
bulk of his support in Viet Nam is nationalist, not Marxist. The
proper French policy would have been to satisfy nationalist am-
bitions and other needs of the Viet Namese, giving Ho the
choice of sacrificing his support at home or in faraway Moscow.

It has been years since Ho Chi Minh has been in Russia. In the meantime, and particularly during the war years, he had apparently renounced die-hard communism of the Stalinist pattern. At least, he went to extreme lengths in denying his Communist affiliation when interviewed by Harold Isaacs some time ago.[20]

Indo-China is an important strategic plum to gain or hold. In Ho's Northern provinces exportable tin, tungsten, zinc, manganese, coal, and lumber are mined and produced in abundance. The country forms an 800-mile-long land bridge between Communist China and British Malaya. It also borders on Burma and Thailand. Its harbors of Haiphong and Saigon provided the bases for the Japanese from which to launch their attacks on Indonesia and Singapore, and from which they supplied their forces in the Philippines.

But it is not the mineral wealth or strategic importance that makes the Viet Nam pattern so important in the overall plan of destruction. Nor is it Ho's Moscow-given task to conquer Viet Nam against impossible odds.[21]

Ho's task is to keep General Mercier's 130,000 troops—the bulk of the French Army—occupied in a distasteful colonial campaign away from home. His task is to force the French into making deals with Japanese collaborationists and former Nazi soldiers who fight for them in a revitalized foreign legion. His task is to compel the French to fill their prisons with Viet Namese nationalists.

Ho's task is to place an unbearable burden on the French budget, to give ammunition both to French Communists at home and to the nationalists throughout Asia—in other words, Ho's task is to keep the unrest going, sustain chaos and disorder, until the time arrives for the "acute revolutionary situation."

The economic and military repercussions of the Viet Namese campaign are widespread. Prior to the conflict, Indo-China was the rice bowl of southeast Asia, exporting over a million tons a year. Today her rice paddies lie fallow. Her annual export has fallen below 100,000 tons. The result is that southeast Asia starves—and hunger raises new Asian resentment against colonialism.

How much support Ho's guerillas can or will get from their new neighbor, Communist China, is a matter of slight importance. Even without a single rifle or a single bullet, by his sheer presence in the mountains, Ho fulfills the task allocated to him. How well he fulfills this task was shown on February 18, 1950, when the French General Staff, in a secret memo to Washington, asked permission to divert their share of Atlantic Pact weapons to Indo-China. The sound of the Viet Namese guerilla's rifle carries far. Its shot can be heard in the Elysée Palace in Paris as well as in the Pentagon in Washington.

The Viet Nam pattern is applied with appropriate alterations to Burma, to the Malay Peninsula, and the Philippines—to most of the southeast Asiatic area which has recently been moved high up on the Soviet list of territorial priorities.

"This entire region," G. D. H. Cole wrote, "up to the very frontiers of India, fell an easy victim to Japanese aggression in the period after the Pearl Harbor attack; and in most of them there was no serious resistance on the part of the native inhabitants. There was, indeed, hardly anywhere any readiness to collaborate with the European rulers in opposing the Japanese. . . . They had not been partners in any [Western-model] democracy and had no ground for disliking Hitler or the Japanese militarists any more than they disliked the British, or the French, or the Dutch." [22]

The feverish uprisings of 1947 and 1948, in Burma, Malaya, and the Philippines, seem to have subsided—but unrest continues to boil under cover.

In Burma, civil war on the Viet Nam pattern has seriously retarded the country's economic recovery and knocked it also off the list of the great rice exporters of southeast Asia.

In Malaya, conditions of apparent tranquillity, created by rather brutal police reaction to violent nationalist-Communist provocations, are unlikely to endure. Once the division between native Malays and the large population of Chinese settlers is alleviated and other inner weaknesses of Malay nationalism eliminated, the uprisings are likely to start anew to the detriment of the European planters whose continued safety is a chief concern of the present administration.

The Republic of the Philippines, an independent sovereign state since 1946, is an American problem and an American responsibility in the eyes of the world. During World War II, the peasant masses of the Philippines supported the resistance movement, while the landowner and the trading classes for the most part collaborated with the Japanese. Yet we put some of the collaborators into power and turned the Hukbalahap, the national resistance movement, over to the Communists, only too willing to receive them into exclusive custody.[23]

This, and some postwar economic measures forced down Philippine throats, created an anti-American opposition that should not be ignored. It includes considerable peasant forces, as well as some powerful groups in the Congress of Labor Organizations—printers, tobacco workers, cooks, waiters, and bartenders.

The peasants are led by Mateo del Castillo, who shares with labor leader Guillermo Capadocio, and Mariano Balgos, active leadership of the guerillas as well. Capadocio and del Castillo went through the Comintern schools of Moscow.

In the Philippines, as China and Viet Nam, in Burma and Malaya, *the U.S.S.R. is waging war against us by proxy.*

From time to time, however, direct aid arrives from "somewhere in Russia," usually from Petropavlovsk on Kamchatka, main base of Soviet aid to its allies in southeast Asia. Now and then a camouflaged Soviet submarine sneaks into one or another Philippine bay secretly held by a company of Huks. It unloads some arms, some ammunition, food and medicine which the guerillas need badly.

But it also brings Bolshevik tracts, the writings of Lenin and Stalin, and an occasional traveler from Moscow to explain their meaning.

One such visitor said not long ago: "You have as much right to gain your complete independence as the Americans had in 1776." To show them how it is done, he gave the Huks a slim little volume, printed in their own language in large type for all who could read.

It was Stalin's major opus, his treatise on the nationalities question which Lenin had praised so highly in his letter to Maxim Gorky almost forty years before. The book that took forty years to reach southeast Asia might take no more than another five or ten years to start a conflagration throughout a region ripe for revolution and—alas—bolshevism.

12.

THE DARDANELLES PLOT

We do not want to fight, but, by jingo, if we do . . .
The Russians shall not have Constantinople.
Popular song by GEORGE WARD HUNT, 1878

IN THIS gigantic cold war whose grand strategic plan we here seek to reconstruct, the U.S.S.R. has still another immense advantage. It is occupying what the German general staff called *"die innere Linie"*—the inner line. This is a strategic advantage that enables an aggressor to strike in any direction of his own choosing while pinning down the defenders at innumerable points along the boundaries of the central position.

Thus, for example, the Soviet Union succeeded in focusing military and diplomatic attention on Berlin by the simple and inexpensive device of blocking the passage of trains and trucks and barges across their zone to the Western-held zones of the German capital. But while we were pouring manpower, high-octane gasoline, and millions of dollars into what appeared to be a major engagement of the cold war, the Russians utilized their inner position to strike at another spot [1]—at China, whence we had gradually retired as tension apparently subsided.

In another instance, in 1947–48, our attention was focused on China. General Wedemeyer was there conducting a hectic tour of inspection; high-pressure propaganda placed the country in the center of our diplomacy and gained economic aid for the lost cause of the Kuomintang.[2] Just then the Russians decided to strike at another spot whose jeopardy was concealed from our attention. This is how they conquered Czechoslovakia.[3]

When the U.S.S.R. from its vantage point appears to strike out against Italy or France, the time will come to decide whether we want Finland to fall helplessly under the Communist ax. And when Russia raises the issue of Sweden we will do well to watch developments in Iran or Trieste or Turkey—especially Turkey.[4]

In each case the pattern will be slightly altered and adapted to specific conditions of time and space. Against Turkey, for example, emphasis will be most likely on strong military pressures. The din of war will be skillfully concealed by the din of propaganda. Though Russia will carefully refrain from apparent direct involvement in whatever extemporaneous shooting should occur, the possibility of a world war in the wake of those pressures cannot be ruled out. The West, we are convinced, will fight to save Turkey from the Russians.

With the U.S.S.R. haughtily aloof as usual, the dirty work will be allotted to some handy national liberation forces. In this instance they will fight their own guerilla war to gain "the lost lands" of Kars and Ardahan.[5]

In the shadowy parade of international relations, the affairs of Russia and Turkey stand out in sharp relief with their morbid ambivalence of love and hate. For many years between 1920 and 1936, the Soviet Union and Kemal Ataturk's new republic were on the best of terms.[6] When Marshal Voroshilov once visited him on the exercise grounds of his army, the Turkish dictator exclaimed to his officers somewhat in the grand manner of Mussolini: "Look hard at these Russians! They may one day be your leaders in war!" [7]

But since 1936, Russo-Turkish relations have gradually frozen into the cold war's coldest front.

At Montreux in July, 1936, with Russian consent, Turkey won the right to remilitarize the Dardanelles and to close them if it were at war or even threatened by aggression. The Red Fleet alone was given complete freedom to pass through the Straits in peacetime and during a defensive war.[8]

The treaty never satisfied the Kremlin. How could it? Stalin sees in a refortified Dardanelles a *place des armes* for a march against the U.S.S.R. and not a passage for his own fleet to the wide-open spaces of the Mediterranean. This is Stalinist reality. The Montreux convention was a figment of Litvinov's diplomacy—a scrap of paper. Ever since Montreux, Soviet preoccupation with the Dardanelles has reappeared with monotonous regularity in all the Kremlin's international talks.

It was one of the chief bones of contention during the secret talks Neville Chamberlain's emissaries conducted in Moscow in 1939 under the leadership of William Strang, today one of Britain's foremost career diplomats but then a mere subaltern in His Majesty's foreign service. It is a pity that the records of those talks are left to gather dust on Britain's and France's secret shelves. Their publication would add some significant touches to the complex Soviet pattern of destruction. They would reveal, among much else, that it was chiefly the Kremlin's insistence on booty from unvanquished opponents that caused a breakdown of the negotiations. Diplomat Strang was frankly exasperated at the Soviet demands at the expense of peaceful and weak neighbors, and reported to Whitehall that one can hardly do business with Russia.[9]

What the Soviet Union failed to gain from Britain and France, it sought from Nazi Germany. On November 13, 1940, during his long talk with Hitler and Ribbentrop, Molotov talked about Turkey the longest. The transcript of his soliloquy was found in the secret archives of the German Foreign Office.

"I want to discuss first the problem of Turkey," Herr Molotov told Hitler. "Both during the Crimean War and in 1918–19, the Turkish Straits proved England's historic gateway for attack on Russia. The Soviet Government has only one aim in this respect. We want to be secure from an attack by way of the Straits. We would like to settle this question with Turkey—not only on paper but in reality."[10]

A few hours later, during his final conversation with Ribbentrop, Molotov returned to the Dardanelles: "Paper agreements would not be sufficient," he said. "We will insist on effective guarantees."[11]

Twelve days later the Germans were told what the Kremlin meant by those "effective guarantees." When Molotov returned to Moscow he took along the draft of a pact between Germany, Italy, Japan, and the U.S.S.R., with two secret protocols attached. One of them was the outline of a new convention to settle the question of the Dardanelles.[12]

Stalin rejected it as still another "scrap of paper." In his own handwriting, he gave Molotov his ideas of a solution. Molotov then spent hours redrafting the German draft and translating Stalin's blunt directive into some form of a diplomatic note. On November 25, the new draft was set and approved by Stalin. At eight P.M. Molotov's secretary called the German Embassy and asked Ambassador von der Schulenburg to rush to the Kremlin at once, to the familiar room on whose tall double doors the nameplates are changed so often. Then, in the late fall of 1940, the plate read: "Molotov, Chairman, Council of People's Commissars." *

Molotov was unusually solemn as he told the German Ambassador: "The Soviet Government has studied the statements of Gospodin Ribbentrop and is prepared to accept the draft of the proposed Four Power Pact—provided . . ." With this, he handed to Schulenburg a copy of the *note verbal* from which he read in his halting monotone: ". . . provided that within the next few months the security of the Soviet Union in the Straits is assured by the establishment of a base for land and naval forces of the U.S.S.R. within range of the Bosporus and the Dardanelles by means of a long-term lease." [13]

Molotov's draft was leaving nothing to the imagination: "In

* Molotov retains the same Kremlin quarters though his title changes. A few weeks after this date the sign read: "Molotov. Deputy Chairman, Council of People's Commissars." Such changes are often meaningless. A visitor after Molotov's "demotion" in 1941 reported to the German Foreign Office: "Molotov received me in the same study that he had formerly, surrounded by his usual staff in the Kremlin. . . . The only difference was the nameplate at the entrance. . . . There was nothing to indicate that his position with Stalin was shaken or that his influence . . . had suffered any diminution." This same observer, among the most astute of them all, reported only seventeen days before that Molotov's new assignment "actually means a considerable abridgment of his former authority. The reason for it," he added, "may be sought in the recent mistakes in foreign policy which led to a cooling off of the cordiality of German-Soviet relations, for the creation and preservation of which Stalin had consciously striven, while Molotov's own initiative often expended itself in an obstinate defense of individual issues." Almost identical speculation accompanied Molotov's departure from the foreign ministry in 1949 when his "demotion" was attributed to his failure to improve Russo-American relations. The fact is that only the nameplates change, but Molotov's role in the hierarchy, and his influence in the Politburo and as Stalin's shadow, remain constant and paramount.

case Turkey declares herself willing to join the Four Power Pact, a guarantee of the independence and of the territory of Turkey should be included. Should Turkey refuse to join the Four Powers they agree to work out and carry through the required military [sic] and diplomatic measures."

Turkey's statesmen had fitful sleep during those uncertain days of World War II. Even the slightest whisper in Moscow or Berlin or London awakened them. It did not take too long for this roar of Molotov to reach Ankara. It came by way of Japan, from the brilliant and well-informed Turkish Ambassador in Tokyo, who reported on Foreign Minister Matsuoka's visit to Germany in the spring of 1941. According to the Ambassador's report, Ribbentrop had told Matsuoka:

"Confidentially, Excellency, our present relations with Russia are correct—but no more. After Herr Molotov's visit, during which we invited Russia to accede to the Three Powers Pact, the Soviet Union made conditions which are unacceptable. They involved the granting of bases on the Dardanelles. The Fuehrer had not concurred. We are not inclined to let the Balkan Peninsula fall under Russian domination." [14]

What Russia could not win from Britain and Germany, it hoped to get by default from the United States. On August 10, 1946, the Kremlin sent a new note to Turkey demanding those military bases on the Dardanelles. The note was a warning to all to let the U.S.S.R. settle the perennial problem with Turkey alone.[15]

Fortunately by then the United States was slowly awakening to Russian diplomatic realities. We tapped the hand of Russia with the hesitant gesture of a discreet man in a crowded subway train who thus quietly warns a pickpocket that his fingers have been felt in the wrong pocket. The fingers withdraw but the thief remains at large.

These Russian moves to gain and hold the Turkish Straits have been widely discussed. But it is revealed here for the first time that still another move was planned on a far more ambitious scale for the summer of 1949. For this we have abundant evidence, the kind of glamorous evidence only the Balkans can supply.[16]

Involved in the plot were a Russian major; his mysterious companion who emerged for but a fleeting moment from the dark underworld of postwar espionage; another young officer of the U.S.S.R.; and an officer courier of the Turkish general staff, on a journey to Ankara carrying some vital documents from the Turkish military attaché in Moscow. They all died within a month—in the late spring of 1949.

The plot seemed to have no survivors at all. But then a man left Red Army Military Intelligence Directorate in Moscow. This man succeeded where all before him had failed. He brought documents with him which had wandered from corpse to corpse across half of Europe. He revealed the strange story behind the deaths of these men—one of them in search of freedom; another in search of money; a third in search of nothing in particular, just caught in the crossfire of the cold war.

The deserter's story was backed by those documents—a dictionary, some leaflets, and a folder of maps, all printed in Germany.

According to that man, the plot started where it eventually ended: at 19 Znamensky, seat of the Red Army general staff. From there it zigzagged to Leipzig. In this famous German graphic center, its thread can be picked up best.

In the fall of 1948, a special courier of the Red Army general staff arrived in Leipzig with a sealed pouch. It was addressed to Major General Dudorov, chief of staff of Lieutenant General Dubrowski, commander-in-chief of the Soviet occupation forces in Saxony.

The Soviet generals found a set of manuscripts and the drafts of certain general-staff maps in the pouch. One of them was the manuscript of a simplified Russo-Turkish dictionary with such ready-made sentences as an invading army must know. Also included were the maps of certain Turkish regions, exceptionally large-scale maps, similar to those printed during World War II, for the guerilla bands fighting behind German lines.

Without the specific instructions that accompanied the pouch there would have been nothing particularly unusual in this shipment. For several years Leipzig's graphic-art industry had been used by the Red Army general staff to print some of its most secret documents and maps. In one instance a 50-thousand-mark contract was given to a group of printers to produce over one hundred different general-staff maps, including maps of Magdeburg and Schleswig-Holstein in Germany, and those of various Chinese regions. Russo-Spanish and Russo-Chinese military dictionaries were also printed in quantity, as well as various manuals indicating the lively interest of the Red Army in distant countries.[17]

In addition, the pouch contained manuscripts for certain *tactical* leaflets. They were all in Turkish. Their nature indicated the true purpose of the dictionaries and maps as well. The whole shipment had the highest security classification known to the Red Army general staff.

This shipment from Moscow had nothing of the leisurely nature of previous print orders. It had a deadline of April, 1949. It was most specific on this goal.

General Dudorov assigned his aide, Guard Major Byelusov, to supervise the project. Major Chernyaev, a printer by profession, was placed in technical command.

Work progressed satisfactorily until March, 1949. Then one morning Major Chernyaev failed to report for work. A search of his apartment produced certain clues. It was assumed that he had fled across the border, probably to the West. A checkup of the printed stores revealed that several sets of secret maps, certain leaflet samples, and key manuals were missing.

A general alarm was flashed to the border detachments of the MVD. The frontier was closed promptly and tightly. Nothing happened. Then two days later in the dense woods near Altenburg, bloodhounds of an MVD special squad came upon the body of a man already badly mauled by beasts. Even so it was quickly identified as the body of Nikolai Ivanovich Chernyaev.

Nearby the hounds found still another corpse. All efforts to identify it failed, and it was assumed that it had probably no connection with the Chernyaev case at all. But autopsies revealed that both men had been killed at about the same time and both with bullets fired from the same automatic rifle, the type of submachine gun carried by MVD guards on frontier duty.

None of the documents missing from Leipzig were found on either of the bodies. A most painstaking search of the area disclosed no additional clues. Even so, Major Byelusov feared that a crucial operations plan of the Soviet Government had been betrayed. State secrets as vital as any in modern times were on the point of disclosure, if they had not already been disclosed by the man or men in possession of the missing documents.

Byelusov remained in Altenburg to supervise the investigation which now extended to the MVD guards in charge of the frontier section where the shooting occurred. He had a quiet check made of all frontier guards. He found that a junior lieutenant of an MVD detachment named Olishev had disappeared without a trace.

Byelusov by then was convinced that Chernyaev was a spy. He had probably been approached by a foreign agent who learned the nature of what he was printing and persuaded him to smuggle some of them out of Leipzig. The two no doubt were to meet in the woods near Altenburg and escape together to the West. Instead they had been shot by a third man. This third man, Byelusov felt certain, was Olishev. No trace could be found of the young lieutenant.

In the meantime the diplomatic branch of the MVD in Moscow received reports of several attempts of an unidentified Russian to contact the Turkish military attaché. The Turks never responded to these calls, but the MVD did. One of their operatives, masquerading as a representative of the Turkish military attaché, arranged a rendezvous with the man in Gorki Park.

The man who appeared was, indeed, Olishev. When he realized his mistake, he ran out into the street, into the traffic, and threw himself under a passing car.

None of the missing documents were found on his body. The story did not end with Olishev's suicide. There was yet another man marked for sudden death—an innocent bystander, but destined to pay with his life for a secret that was never entrusted to him. He was an officer of the Turkish general staff, named F. Guzaltan, serving as the courier of the Turkish military attaché on the Moscow-Ankara route.

On June 1, 1949, Captain Guzaltan was handed a pouch by his chief, the military attaché, in the mailroom of the Turkish Embassy in Moscow. He was admonished to take special care of his precious diplomatic cargo. It was hardly more than a routine warning. Yet the conversation was reported promptly to the MVD by spies from inside the Embassy. Immediate connection was effected in the imagination of Soviet counterespionage agents between the missing documents, which they could not find on Olishev's body, and Captain Guzaltan's diplomatic bag in which they were believed to be.

No one knows exactly what happened to Captain Guzaltan during the early part of his trip to Ankara. But on June 2, he was found unconscious in his compartment, wounded by an unknown assailant. There was no gun on or near the body.

The Turkish Embassy was *not* notified of the tragedy. The mortally wounded young officer was removed to a hospital in Sochi where he died a few days later, without, so the official Soviet account of the tragedy later averred, ever regaining consciousness.

Only then was Guzaltan's chief, the Turkish military attaché in Moscow, advised of the case. He was told that his young aide had committed suicide in a moment of deep depression.

No trace could be found of the diplomatic pouch he carried. Energetic representations were made to Moscow and then, sure enough, the pouch turned up just as mysteriously as it had disappeared from the train. It bore unmistakable signs of tampering. Its seal had been broken. Someone had read its contents. There were fingerprints of strangers on the documents, obviously of the men who photostated them in the MVD.

But the Olishev papers were not in the bag. Captain Guzaltan was the innocent victim of an MVD zealot who fired the fatal shot when the young Turkish diplomat tried to resist an attempt to steal the pouch from under his nose.

What bearing has this melodrama on our contention that the U.S.S.R. had, in the summer of 1949, definite military designs on Turkey?

The answer is contained in the documents themselves which the MVD never recovered despite this manhunt. They had been concealed by one of Olishev's old friends, a schoolmate, then serving at Red Army military-intelligence headquarters. Later they were smuggled out of Russia.

The papers outlined in detail a plan to revive the old claims to the Dardanelles. They also revealed the decision to accompany diplomatic and propaganda offensives by overt military moves, Soviet-trained Turkish partisans carrying a Russian-incited civil war to the soil of Turkey. The papers include a full description of a proposed military and diplomatic move and the forces to be employed. They reveal the entire Dardanelles pattern in the matter-of-fact language of the Red Army general staff.

Captain Guzaltan's body was taken to Ankara where it was buried in an impressive military funeral. He did not die in vain. In sacrificing his life, he alerted Turkey to the threat it was facing; and the Turks responded to the danger signal with promptness and efficiency. Colonel General Gurman, chief of the general staff, ordered his forces to battle stations and thus foiled whatever was left of the plans after its disclosure.

The danger to Turkey is by no means over. The Dardanelles pattern continues to occupy a most important place among the Soviet Union's highest priority expansionist designs.[18]

It may be that it will be applied to Norway even before the time of its reapplication to Turkey will be considered propitious. For Norway, like Turkey, controls an important strategic spot that the U.S.S.R. covets almost as much, and in much the same manner, as it desires the Dardanelles.

That spot is Spitsbergen, or, in Norwegian, Svålbard.

Spitsbergen is a group of mountainous islands in the Arctic Ocean, about 370 miles due north of Norway, halfway to the pole. Discovered by Norsemen in 1194 and rediscovered by Barents in 1596, the islands were for centuries the resort of whalers of several nations. Norway periodically asserted her claims to the islands. Following action by the 1919 Peace Conference, a treaty was signed in Paris by the United States, Great Britain, Denmark, France, Italy, Japan, the Netherlands, Sweden, and Norway, which neutralized Spitsbergen under the flag of Norway, and granted international concessions to, among others, the U.S.S.R.[19]

There are immense quantities of coal on the islands; an estimated 9 billion tons. There are large deposits of low-grade iron ore and some gypsum. Signs of oil also have been reported.[20] However, it is not her mineral wealth but her strategic position that causes the U.S.S.R. to eye Spitsbergen with covetous eyes.

"There are eight great industrial areas in the world today of sufficient productivity to be significant factors in a full-scale war," General Carl Spaatz of the U.S. Air Force wrote in his final report as chief of staff. "All of these key areas lie above 30 degrees north latitude, and the two great land masses on which they are located—the Eurasian and North American continents—have one region of common tangency: the Arctic Ocean with its impassable ice cap. Although the polar ice cap is impassable to ships or surface forces, it offers no barrier to aircraft flying above it. The shortest air route between the central United States and the Urals, between Alaska and Germany, or between Greenland and Japan, lies directly over the polar region." [21]

Similar views have been held by many other famous airmen, from General William E. Mitchell to Colonel Bernt Balchen. In a speech in Norway, in the winter of 1947, Balchen bluntly declared that the Arctic would be a focal point in any future war.

In the fall of 1948, Colonel Balchen was dramatically recalled to active duty with the U.S. Air Force. His reactivation on a secret mission was one of several moves on both sides of the cold-war front in which the Arctic region figured most prominently. Sir John Cuningham, first sea lord of the British Admiralty, visited the Arctic Ocean with important elements of the Royal Navy's home fleet, followed by units of the U.S. Navy, including submarines. The U.S. Navy held several large-scale cold-weather maneuvers in the North Atlantic, one of them alone involving 31,000 officers and men, 65 ships, and 31 aircraft squadrons. Prolonged Arctic experiments were conducted in the Hudson Bay area by the U.S. and Canadian armies. The U.S. Air Force sent B-50 bombers to Alaska on rotating training missions.

The U.S.S.R has developed and now maintains important military and naval installations on Rudolph Island, northernmost of the Franz Joseph group, about 82° N. Soviet submarines make frequent appearances as far north as 86°, and undergo severe tests in extreme cold. The Russian Air Force is conducting "ice reconnaissance" patrols from bases on Dixon Island and Tixie Bay, so that "scores of polar flyers" may "acquire the special training and skill needed for their work in the Arctic.[22]

Military preoccupation with the Arctic is matched by diplomatic activities. The three great powers, the U.S., the U.K., and the U.S.S.R., are jockeying for positions on Greenland as well as Spitsbergen. In the Arctic one can find confirmed what Director Harold Sverdrup of the Norwegian Polar Institute told us in Oslo: "The friendly Arctic has been stripped of its former mysteries. The airplane has turned it into an open book for all to read without much eye strain." But there is a certain peril in this new familiarity—one of which the Norwegian Foreign Office, uneasy custodian of strategic Spitsbergen, is fully cognizant. And it has an overwhelming reason.

While the United States is still casting but a distant shadow over the area, the Soviet Union is actually and physically present in this nominally neutral region. On Spitsbergen the Russians maintain a vital outpost based on three mine concessions, at Barentsburg, Grumant City, and the Pyramids. The Soviet holdings determine the whole strategic value of the entire archipelago. Of the vast region, only the area around Isfjord is available for the establishment of air and, probably, submarine bases. From Cape Linné, at the westernmost entrance to Isfjord, to the Pyramids, at the easternmost end of the fjord, the Russians command the vital passages to the whole area.

Norway insists on painstaking neutrality on the islands, which are, in fact, completely disarmed and demilitarized. The Russians, who maintain about 2,000 husky miners in their concessions, know this and have no complaints. What they want is, in fact, the remilitarization of the islands along the lines of their Dardanelles plan.

In 1944, and again on January 10, 1947, the U.S.S.R "raised the question of revising the international treaty of 1920 which assigned the islands to Norway." On February 15, 1947, in secret session, the Norwegian Parliament voted against bilateral discussions with the Soviet Union and recommended that the U.S.S.R. submit their request to the other signatories of the 1920 treaty.

Since then in quiet and informal diplomatic conversations behind the closed doors of the Norwegian foreign ministry, the Kremlin renewed its "suggestion" that "joint Russo-Norwegian military bases be established on Spitsbergen." The meaning of such "joint control" is only too well known to the Norwegians as well as the Turks. They are determined to deny Russian demands and look hopefully to the United States to support their stand.

The Dardanelles pattern as applied to the Far North and the Far South of Europe seems remote and strange to the observer from America. And yet it is potentially the most dangerous of all patterns. The Russians seem to be as determined to gain recognition for their claims in Turkey and the Arctic Ocean as we are to reject those claims. This is why, in the light of past documentation and recent intelligence, we are inclined to regard the Dardanelles pattern as, indeed, the pattern of the *casus belli*.

13. THE SOURCES OF SOVIET CONDUCT IN THE MIDDLE EAST

THE U.S.S.R. has definite designs on the Middle East, but, contrary to the estimate of the Pentagon,[1] they are of a *revolutionary* and not of a *military* nature.

The Soviet Union's current appraisal of revolutionary potentialities in the Middle East is not far different from the conclusion reached at the Baku Congress of 1920. At that time, delegates concluded that, with the probable exception of Turkey and Persia, the Middle East was not yet ripe for a revolution along Marxist-Leninist lines.

Even while the U.S.S.R. thus adopts a wait-and-see attitude as the cornerstone of her short-range policy, she believes that time is on her side. She expects that, in the long run, despite temporary setbacks, diplomatic defeats and effective military exclusion, she *will* gain paramount influence in an area in which the new Anglo-American coalition now rules supreme—and gain it with revolutionary rather than military forces.

The Russians believe this is not sheer wishful anticipation. The Soviet Union has done much to gain the respect of various strata of the Middle Eastern populations, and not merely the discontented. It has no record of oil imperialism. Despite perfunctory alliances with governments and revolutionary groups both right and left, the U.S.S.R. has refrained from making any really binding commitments to anyone—even the regional Communists.

Soviet long-range planning depends on a Communist network functioning clandestinely in the Middle East. The network consists of an astonishing large number of organizations, associations, brotherhoods, federations, splinter parties, and unions. Most of them work at cross purposes, often without visible means of support, and joined together only by their orientation toward the U.S.S.R. in a nondogmatic but unconditional allegiance.

According to a claim issued at the 1947 London Conference of Communist Parties, there are a total of 24,400 "registered" Communists in the Middle East, out of a population of 71 millions. An estimate, prepared by the United Press in May, 1947, counted only 13,700 in the area.

Our estimate exceeds both claims. On the basis of Communist admissions, election returns, the circulation figures of regional Communist publications, and other data of primary index value, we believe that Communists and *active* supporters number 126,300 in the Middle East.[2]

Even this estimate does not include the workers and employees organized in trade unions known to be wholly or partly under Communist control. In Egypt alone there are 465 such unions with an estimated membership exceeding 150,000. The Iranian oil workers' union embraces about 95 per cent of the 60,000 workers employed by the Anglo-Iranian Oil Company. The total trade-union membership in Communist-dominated labor organizations is now past the quarter-million mark.

This potential political grouping is in its period of *Sturm und Drang*. At present, Communist or quasi-Communist parties may function openly only in Israel. In Iran strong Communist influence persists in the Tudeh party. In all other Middle Eastern countries, Communist parties are outlawed and underground.

Outward compliance with the law reduces the strength of communism in the area. The Stalin portraits travelers once found in many a modest Arab cottage are disappearing. The great wartime popularity of the Soviet Union has waned. And yet, Communist influence remains considerable.

This is largely due to the fact that in the Arab world, the Communists identify themselves with the aims, hopes, and aspirations of widespread, intransigent, intolerant, impatient nationalism and irredenta in the region. This well-nigh complete Communist identification with its political environment produces a set of odd contradictions.

Thus, for example, Iraqi Communists participated in the violent anti-British riots of 1948 at the side of the remnants of Ali Rashid's pro-Nazi mob, while in Egypt, Communists ally themselves with the pro-British Nahas Pasha against the anti-British King Farouk.

In Lebanon, Communists set themselves up to defend Christians against the "intolerance of Islam," while in Syria they follow a line of extreme Islamism. Ruad Qaran of Lebanon fought against the French in 1936 and for them in 1943. Dr. Khalil Budayri, a prominent Jerusalem physician, was a member of the Arab Higher Committee and supported the Mufti, while another Palestine Communist, Labib Fuleyhan, defied the Mufti and co-operated with the Jews.

Similar contradictions are reflected in the leading personalities. The head of the Syrian Communists is Khalid Bakdash, a Kurd; Egypt's Communists are led by Henri Curiel, a Jew; Arab Communists of Palestine by Emil Touma, a Christian.

Most of the Communist leaders of the Middle East, like Touma, Salim Khayyas, Nicola Shawi, Dr. Sami 'Alam-al-Din, are wealthy members of influential upper-middle-class families. Also, they are, like Shawi of Lebanon, products of the Jesuit University of Beirut, or graduates of Oxford, like Touma.[3]

The Soviet Union's dependence on such a heteroclite group of zealots is motivated by its realization that in the Middle East situation quality far outweighs quantity. In fact, the astonishing effectiveness of communism in the Middle East, and its continued growth despite suppression, are due to the integrity, devotion, and competence of its leaders. It is commonly conceded that only the Communists as a whole are immune from the financial corruption and political gluttony which are characteristic of so many political leaders in the Middle East.

If communism is to engulf the Middle East in the lifetime of Mustafa Al-Aris,[4] it will be because it has allies vastly more powerful than his. As specified by a survey prepared by Sidney Glaser for the Bolton Subcommittee of the House Committee on Foreign Affairs, there are "destitution, unemployment, illiteracy, oppressive taxation, undernourishment, and starvation,

wretched conditions of public and private health, neglect and
corruption." [5] All these factors figure in Moscow's plans.

Recent Soviet documents, to which we have had access, recognize the new military significance of the Middle East. One of
them, a directive of the Central Committee of the Communist
party, set down this appraisal of Palestine:

"It is situated at the approaches to the Suez Canal, the central
link of world communications which connects the capitalist
centers of Europe with their colonial possessions in Asia and
Africa.... Palestine, located in the very heart of the Near East
could well serve as a base for the imperialist domination of all
Arab countries. The aggressive strategy of Anglo-Saxon militarists is closely bound up with the designs of the British and American oil trusts which want to preserve their monopoly over the
oil resources of the Arab world." [6]

The existence of a firm British policy made the absence of
clear-cut, plausible, workable, long- and short-range Soviet
policy keenly felt in the Kremlin. In the early fall of 1943 the
Politburo sent Ivan Maisky, then vice commissar of foreign
affairs, on a long fact-finding tour to Egypt, Iraq, Iran, and
Palestine. Maisky's report was to be the basis for a definitive
Middle Eastern policy.

Shortly after Maisky presented his report to the Politburo,
the Middle East became the scene of widespread Russian activities. They included the cultivation of minority groups having
racial or religious affinity with Soviet ethnic groups (Armenians,
Kurds, Druses, Assyro-Chaldeans, Turkomans, etc.), using the
clergy, including Patriarch Alexei, Archbishop Kostania, and
Imam Rassulov as propagandists; expression of guarded sympathy with regional political organizations, right or left, in any
struggle for independence from the West; dissemination of
direct and indirect, overt and covert Soviet propaganda; direct
revolutionary interference in Iran.

The Maisky recommendations resulted in a long series of
specific events in which the U.S.S.R.:

(1) Established diplomatic relations with Egypt.

(2) Recognized the republics of Syria and Lebanon; established diplomatic missions in Damascus and Bagdad.

(3) Sponsored a visit to Moscow by the Greek Orthodox patri-

arch, Alexandros III, and arranged for a return visit to Lebanon and Syria by Patriarch Alexei of All-Russia.

(4) Sponsored a trip by Professor Ashot Der Karekini Abrahamian, dean of Armenian studies at Erivan University and secretary of the Armenian Holy Synod, to establish close ties with the 200,000 Armenians in Syria and Lebanon.

(5) Established clandestine contact with the fanatic, pro-Mufti faction of the Arab High Committee lead by Jamal Al-Husseini, and instructed the Communist organization of Palestinian Arabs (the League for National Liberation) to support the Mufti, temporarily at least.

(6) Instructed all Communist organizations to promote the concept of national liberation as the militant revolutionary principle best suited to the Middle East.

(7) Supported Communist infiltration into trade unions, especially in Iran, Lebanon, and Egypt; promoted or exploited a series of quasipolitical strikes.

(8) Promoted the establishment of a series of front organizations, such as the Lebanese Friends of Soviet Russia, the Iraqi Anti-Zionist League, etc.

(9) Arranged for the repatriation of thousands of Levantine Armenians, assigning a first secretary of the Soviet Legation at Beirut to the task.

(10) Assured non-Communist revolutionists in Iraq, Iran, and Palestine of asylum in neighboring Soviet territories.

In so far as Palestine was concerned, the Soviet Government appeared to maintain a strict and unrelenting anti-Zionist attitude even as late as April, 1947. A directive of the All-Union Lecture Bureau of the Ministry of Higher Education, issued for its itinerant propagandists and providing the official line on all aspects of the Palestine question, contained nothing but vituperations against the Zionists, while embracing the cause of the Arabs.

The directive described a Zionist state in Palestine as a "reactionary Utopia," and cited Stalin as a chief witness to prove that Jews, "who lived in different countries, had no national ties and represented no national community." [7]

Basic in this anti-Zionist attitude of the Soviet was the belief that world Jewry was opposed to Bolshevist aspirations, that

Jews were largely nonproletarian, and, therefore, difficult to regiment and bolshevize.

The reversal of this established policy and the introduction of a pro-Israeli, but not pro-Zionist policy, were long in coming. The drift had started even during World War II. At the Teheran conference, Marshal Stalin indicated that the U.S.S.R. was not completely opposed to establishment of a Jewish state. But the first open indications of a more conciliatory attitude had come during 1945. At the World Labor Conference in London, the Soviet delegate announced that his government favored and proposed to support a projected Jewish state; on November 26, 1945, the U.S.S.R. made a formal proposal that the Big Five lay the groundwork for such a state.

By late 1946, the new Palestine policy was fixed in Stalin's mind and discussed in the Politburo. This was the decision which, when made, changed the course of Jewish, Russian—and possibly Anglo-American—history in the Middle East. Evidence that the new policy involved the whole area, and not merely Palestine, came from Stalin himself during an unpublicized conference with Ernest Bevin on May 15, 1947.

Bevin sought the interview on the eve of Egypt's submission of its case against Britain to the United Nations. When the Foreign Secretary arrived in Stalin's study in the Kremlin, he found the Soviet Premier eager to discuss the whole Middle East in general and Egypt specifically. In the course of the conversation the Generalissimo told Bevin that in his view Soviet interests in the Middle East did not conflict with those of Britain—as long as British moves were not directed against the U.S.S.R. He gave Bevin definite assurance that the U.S.S.R. would stay aloof from the Egyptian affair. While it may be doubtful that Secretary Bevin accepted Stalin's assurances at face value, the fact remains that the Russian leader did go on record with these sweeping assurances.

What then are, Generalissimo Stalin's assurances notwithstanding, the salient features of Soviet policy in the Middle East? They are two:

(1) The elimination of Britain from the whole area whereby the Kremlin hopes to pull the last remaining prop from under the tottering structure of the British Empire.

(2)   The generation of violent anti-American sentiment in the region to prevent the U.S. from replacing Britain in her eastern Mediterranean Monroe Zone.

The basic Soviet policy on the control of the Middle East is as follows: "The U.S.S.R. has no territorial claims in the region, but will never tolerate the transfer of Palestine or any independent Middle Eastern country to exclusive sovereignty of any single power."

That sentence is the crux of Soviet policy in the Middle East. It was translated directly, without abridgment or ellipsis, from an issue of *Voyennaya Mysl* (*Military Thinking*), the publication of the Soviet General Staff for the senior officers of the Soviet General Staff.

The views of the American General Staff were expressed on April 10, 1950, by General J. Lawton Collins, Chief of Staff of the U.S. Army. "The Middle East," he said, "is one of the great strategic areas of the world. There isn't any question in the world about that. It is the link between Asia and Europe and Africa." [8]

Though the Soviet Union is unlikely to undertake an old-fashioned war to control this important tricontinental bridgehead, neither is she likely to abandon hope of inheriting it from the United Kingdom and the United States. The problems, both fundamental and imposed, both social and economic, both political and military, which the vast region presents will for long continue to challenge the ingenuity and patience of East and West. For both will continue to strive for the same goal: control of that immensely valuable parcel of power-political real estate— the Middle East.

14. THE HYPOTHETICAL SWEDISH BLUEPRINT

BEYOND THE immense tapestry of accomplished conquests which now hang in the trophy hall of the Kremlin, diligent hands are at work on the embroidery of the new conquests of tomorrow. In the center, half completed, is the Swedish pattern that may be applied to others unfortunate enough to be bordering on the U.S.S.R.'s expanding frontiers.

The Kremlin distrusts Sweden despite the frantic protestations of neutrality by the Swedes, their record of international pacifism unbroken for more than a century, and a demonstration of their incomparable skill in fence sitting in the midst of history's greatest conflicts.[1]

For the Kremlin has no illusions about Swedish neutrality in the cold war. Neither is it particularly reassured by the fact that Sweden refused to join the North Atlantic Union. Sweden is somewhat like Olive of the cartoons, her affections torn between Popeye, this lovable Sinbad of the West, and Bluto, the Eastern brute wielding the club of a caveman.

Soviet preoccupation with Sweden has a long and remarkable history, tied closely to the *grande dame* of Leninist diplomacy, Madame Alexandra Kollontay, who lived in Stockholm for decades, first as a politicking exile from Tsarist Russia, then as the Soviet Union's friendly and popular envoy extraordinary and minister plenipotentiary.[2]

Sweden has never ceased to interest the Russians. It attracts them with unexpected revolutionary possibilities, hinted in occasional Communist strength at some municipal election in the Far North.[3] But most of all, it fascinates them with its military advantages, available to all comers who reach out for them.[4]

Virtually no month in the year passes without one or two alien planes crossing mysteriously the borderline of Sweden's skies. They are presumed to be Soviet planes on reconnaissance missions mapping the Swedish countryside and remapping it. The archives of the Red Army's aviation department must be overcrowded with Swedish obliques. Nothing remains concealed from them, neither a new rail line running into Boden, the mysterious fortress city of Sweden, nor a new pylon built around Lulea to hold the wires that carry additional electric power into the harbor, nor a new engine brought for the Kiruna-Narvik run of the Arctic railroad over which plenty of the world's best iron ore travels.[5]

The Swedish Communist party is small and quiet. The contacts of their leaders with Russia are spasmodic and even superficial. True, Nils Holmberg did teach at the Lenin school in Moscow; Hugo Sillen and Knut Senander did occupy high positions during the halcyon days of the Comintern. But the Swedish Communists are not very different from the Swedes in general. They are peaceful, calm, egocentric, and conceited, and they dislike others to tell them what to do. If there is a Swedish Communist who answers to the prototype of the Bolshevik leader, he is Hilding Hagberg, the man who turned the north into a Communist stronghold in his own and the Bolshevik party's early years. But Hagberg, too, is growing in years and inclines to take his politics and aquavit in his stride.[6]

In many ways the Swedish and the U.S. Communist parties represent a common problem to the U.S.S.R. They are both important instruments of Soviet foreign policy: the first as an ancillary movement because of Sweden's territorial proximity and the dangers inherent in such a capitalist neighbor; the latter because of its role in breaking down the resistance of the United States to Soviet expansion and world revolution.

And again, both are infirm and impotent, lacking that Bolshevik *savoir vivre* which make the Italians under Togliatti and the French under the Thorez-Duclos-Cachin "troyka" such redoubtable allies.

The Russians do not dream that they can ever depend on

Sweden to fall by itself into the morass of communism. Neither
do they count upon their Swedish "section" to bring about such
a collapse. A special pattern must be used to bring Sweden into
the orbit. The pattern was tried in the United States when
Henry A. Wallace was induced to form a third party, the failure
of which is ascribed to the unreliability of its non-Communist
promoters and, to a large extent, to Wallace himself. No one in
Moscow questions the basic efficiency of the idea and its eventual
effectiveness under more favorable circumstances in a more
intelligent alliance.

In fact, had we discussed the strategic aims of bolshevism as
far back as 1935, we would have called this particular part of
the plan of destruction the American pattern. It was then eluci-
dated in no unmistakable terms by the Comintern, in one of its
resolutions on the report of Ercoli.[7] The pattern survives without change in the official textbooks of the Cominform, but it no
longer applies to the United States in its new role as a gigantic
world power.

Today it applies chiefly to Sweden. The Kremlin recognizes
that the Swedish proletariat cannot be content "with the organization of only its class-conscious vanguard that is prepared
to follow the revolutionary words." In plain English this means
that Swedish communism is not nearly strong enough to direct
revolutionary action.

Thus alliances have to be made, a third party must be created,
"neither Socialist nor Communist...but it *must be* an anti-
fascist party and *must not be* an anti-Communist party." [8]

And even if the formation of such a party meets with great
difficulties, individuals who fit the pattern must be gathered,
cultivated, and used against the enemy.

At one point on the march of bolshevism (between now and
1956), the Bolshevik master plan calls for Sweden to be torn from
her Western Popeye and pinned irresistibly in the arms of her
hairy Eastern suitor. How will this be done?

The Soviet Government will view with increasing alarm certain constellations in the Swedish sky that will be visible only
from Moscow's political observatory—a familiar trick of the
Kremlin's diplomatic astronomers. Such a constellation might
include "secret airdromes leased to the United States in regions

adjacent to the Soviet border," or "a confidential treaty that the chiefs of the Swedish General Staff concluded with the American Joint Chiefs," or "the stockpiling of American arms for an overland invasion of Soviet territory"—anything along these lines.

A diplomatic offensive will be mounted with positions on the front pages of *Pravda* and the *Ny Dag,* Sweden's own official Communist daily. There will be mass meetings and *démarches,* and plants in the foreign press, and an influx of correspondents to Stockholm to watch the spectacle.

The Swedish Government will turn to the West for guarantees, but all it will get will be words of enormous determination unbacked by a genuine show of force. The Swedes are far too sophisticated and realistic to depend on anything less than assurances that the United States would go to war should the U.S.S.R. menace its territorial or even political independence. Such an assurance will not be forthcoming.

The pressure from Russia will increase. A united front of Scandinavian communism, from Denmark to Norway and Finland, will resound with resolutions, opinions of small minorities which will be presented to the people of Russia as *the* voices of Finland and Norway and Denmark.

The first report of Soviet troop movements will be "leaked" through "neutral sources" to the Western press. A news magazine in New York will print a red-and-black map showing the ring of V-2 platforms the Russians will be building on the Baltic coast opposing Sweden, ready to reduce Malmoe within two hours. A ring of platforms for guided missiles will suddenly grow up all around Sweden. The transfer of the Fourth Tank Army from Leningrad to Petsamo will be officially announced in Moscow.

Tension will mount and with it the native nervousness of a nation which has not tasted war for 138 years. There will be pressure on the government to yield. But Moscow will never explicitly say just what the Swedes are supposed to yield.

Just then Stalin will submit to an interview, by mail, preferably with an American correspondent. He will state that the U.S.S.R. is menaced by Sweden's belligerent intentions. He will assure the world that all the Soviet Union wants from Sweden is peace and international collaboration in the face of threats on the part of Anglo-American warmongers.

In the ensuing controversy over divergent interpretations of Stalin's words the government of Sweden will dissolve Parliament and call for new elections. A caretaker Cabinet of specialists will be formed.

A third party called the Peace party (or rather Progressive Peace party) will make its appearance. It will represent itself as the only political party which could guarantee peace to Sweden for another 138 years.

It will join a coalition formed in despair to maintain political continuity and place two members in the Cabinet. One of them will be a clandestine member of the Communist International and an agent of the Kremlin. The hectic and restive meetings of the Cabinet will be recorded by a Bolshevik and transmitted to the Soviet intelligence service.

The first round will be won.

The pressure will continue. The Western press will report the movement of additional Soviet contingents, and soon Sweden will feel like a man ensconced in armor but with no spear to defend himself. It will be a distinctly uncomfortable feeling. The Cabinet will fall. Another Cabinet will be established.

The new Cabinet will be formed by some obscure professor described as the "grand old man" of the Progressive Peace party, the man who promised peace for another 138 years. He will announce that he has accepted an invitation to go to Moscow to discuss the possibility of a friendship and neutrality pact with "the great Soviet Union."

The nation will sigh with relief. The Kremlin will check off Sweden. That is exactly how far it wanted to go.

But Sweden's perennial neutrality will be over. Sweden, too, will become a satellite. But before this hypothetical Swedish blueprint can be tested in action, the Kremlin will have to take care of Finland, the last remaining country in "the orbit" to which the pattern could be applied. And the Kremlin is moving steadily and irresistibly to demolish the precarious independence of Finland.[9]

The Russians have a "troyka" boring eagerly but, just now,

not too successfully from within Finland. It is the strange trium-
virate of Kuusinen, Lehen, and Leino.

These three people—a woman and two men—form a bond
which is as strange in its romantic implications as it is powerful
in its political determination. Hertta Kuusinen, today the first
lady of foreign communism, is a born Bolshevik, daughter of
Otto V. Kuusinen, companion and friend of Lenin and Stalin
during their exiles in Finland. Next to Dimitrov and Gottwald,
Kuusinen was the most important member of the Comintern
executives. Today he is president of the Karelo-Finnish Soviet
Republic.

His daughter was once wife of Tuure Valdemar Lehen who,
under the alias "Alfred Lange," wrote the major theoretical
textbook for the Comintern's action schools from which we
quoted a few passages on page 96.[10] Lehen himself is a graduate
of several Comintern schools, and of the highest military
academies of the U.S.S.R.

In World War II he fought in the Red Army against his own
country and rose to the rank of a Red Army lieutenant general.

His rival for Hertta's affection, but his companion in Bolshevik conspiracy, is Yrjö Kaarle Leino, an agronomist who is
Miss Kuusinen's present husband. He too is a graduate of the
two major educational institutions of modern bolshevism: the
prisons of his own country and the Comintern schools of Russia.

The Finnish Communist party is remarkable for its abject
subservience to Moscow. Its leaders, almost without exception,
were trained in the conspiratorial schools of the U.S.S.R. The
great majority of them served in the Red Army. In them, the
U.S.S.R itself has a general staff inside Finland, a fact which may
facilitate the application of the satellite pattern to the country.

But the Finns are not easily intimidated. The Communists
have never had influence in the army. They lost control of the
police when Leino was deprived of the interior portfolio in the
Cabinet shake-up of 1948.

The Party, too, has fallen from its halcyon days. A skilled and
courageous Social Democrat, Fagerholm, managed to checkmate
the Communists just as they had deployed for the kill.

Until the early winter of 1950 the situation seemed to be
developing against the Communists and for the democratic

coalition. Then in the elections for the presidency the tide suddenly turned.

Our press hailed the re-election, in March, 1950, of President Paasekivii, himself a pro-Russian liberal, as a great triumph for democracy. But the Communists piled up 22 per cent of the popular vote, an unprecedented demonstration of Communist strength and an alarming straw in the wind. Signals like this the Kremlin never fails to heed.

How and when the pattern will be applied.to Finland no one can tell. Operations against the little country are on the agenda of Soviet empire builders. They may be started with lightning speed, on the pretext of an artificial issue such as the alleged harboring of "anti-Russian war criminals," of which much was made during the turbulent 1950 election campaign.

The Soviet Union is never embarrassed by the low quality of such charges. Neither was she impressed by energetic Finnish denials of their validity. If she nevertheless allowed the charges to die down, it was but a temporary concession, motivated by the U.S.S.R.'s preoccupation elsewhere, and not by any consideration for truth or justice in her relations with her former enemy and most reluctant satellite.

In the meantime Finland remains on the danger list. She will find it hard if not impossible to avoid a fate now common to all the other fallen countries in the satellite commonwealth.

15.

PATTERNS
WHICH
FAILED

In the wide arena of the world, failure and success are not accidents as we so frequently suppose, but the strictest justice.

ALEXANDER SMITH in Dreamthorp

IF THIS roll call of the victories of Soviet imperialism conveys an idea of invincibility we must correct the impression. Stalin and his aides are not impervious to failure. Like Alexander Smith's fragile literary gentleman, they are most sensitive to the bites of the critical mosquito. And since they live in the tropical swamp of intrigue and conspiracy where mosquitoes swarm, they are exposed to bites to an extraordinary degree. They can be foiled without elaborate stabs to their hearts. They can be killed by pinpricks.[1]

Such a pinprick resulted in the demise of an ignoble Soviet scheme in the spring of 1946. It was administered by a nameless Allied mosquito, a young intelligence officer then serving with one of the Western missions in Prague, Czechoslovakia.

The incident in which he figured prominently ended in one of our tangible victories of the cold war. It deserves to be studied in meticulous detail in our war colleges and diplomatic schools. It also shows that there *is* a defense against the revolutionary plots of the U.S.S.R., provided that the plot is recognized in advance and counteracted with boldness.

In that late spring of 1946, Czechoslovakia was on the eve of its first postwar general elections. The country, still remembering the betrayal at Munich, maintained the friendliest relations with the U.S.S.R.

"Expressing the deep gratitude of the Czechoslovak nation to the U.S.S.R.," the declaration of the new national front stated, "the government will unwaveringly maintain, as the leading line of Czechoslovakian foreign policy, the closest alliance with the victorious great Slav power in the east." [2]

But Moscow was not satisfied with such lyric protestations of loyalty. It wanted more tangible evidences and appeared to be determined to get them, too, in the elections scheduled for May 26, 1946. The old Comintern war horse, Klement Gottwald, for many years Dimitrov's deputy in the Comintern Secretariat, was then vice-premier—as well as the Kremlin's chief representative —inside Zdenek Fierlinger's coalition Cabinet. [3] In the Soviet Legation was Valeri K. Zorin as minister with plenipotentiary power to act upon a directive a special courier had brought from Moscow.

The directive stated in the simplest terms that (1) the Communist party *must* emerge as the largest party in the May 26 elections; (2) Klement Gottwald *must* become prime minister forthwith; (3) Vaclav Nosek *must* be given the interior portfolio, and Vaclav Kopecky was to be made propaganda minister; (4) the Communists *must receive absolute majority* within the Cabinet irrespective of their majority in Parliament. Then it added an impossible; (5) "All visible interference with the elections must be avoided."

Now this was no easy directive to implement. Zorin and Gottwald asked themselves: How could they "deliver" if they were not allowed to "interfere"? The dilemma appeared insoluble. Zorin flew to Moscow in great haste to ask for a "clarification." When he came back, and told Gottwald the answer, the election seemed to be in the bag.

Gottwald carried the news to a hastily called meeting of his own Politburo. Marshal Konev's Third Mechanized Army, he told them, was still in Austria, preparing for a leisurely withdrawal to the Soviet motherland. It was *not* supposed to pass through Czechoslovakia. But now its long voyage home was to be rerouted. It would enter Czechoslovakia after all on May 25, just twenty-four hours before election time. It would bivouac, stretching out from one end of the country to another. Then rumors would be spread that Konev was there to stay unless a parliament was returned the U.S.S.R. could *really* trust. Such a parliament would have to have a Communist majority!

A few hours after the Politburo meeting in which Gottwald revealed the plan to use the Red Army as an ancillary revolutionary force, Captain "X," an officer of the United States, received a report on the proceedings. He recognized the significance of the intelligence and left at once for Austria to check on the authenticity of the report. He observed that Konev's tanks were being prepared for imminent departure. A bit of fraternization with Red Army personnel brought additional confirmation: the Third Tank Army was to start on May 23, with a new marching route that included Czechoslovakia, all the way from south to north.

The young American captain had no time to lose. Reluctant to use communication facilities in Prague or Vienna, where Soviet agents were tapping and monitoring every wire, he flew to General Eisenhower's headquarters in Frankfort, Germany.

There he persuaded his superiors to carry out a plan he figured would stop Konev's tanks in their tracks. All they had to do was to publish the news of the ruse to show the Soviets that their secret had leaked to us and that we were sharing the information with the Czechoslovak people whose elections *they* tried to influence.

The cold war was in an early stage. There was still considerable pro-Russian sentiment at Frankfort. The captain was nevertheless granted permission to publish the news. He gave it to a few selected correspondents and urged them to give top priority to it on the wires. It was the eleventh hour.[4]

Then, on May 23, no more than two or three hours prior to his H-hour, Marshal Konev received orders from Moscow to keep his Third Armored Force in Austria "until further notice." The whole armed demonstration of rumbling tanks was canceled. Czechoslovakia gained two years of grace before it was forced to succumb. There are today, in every one of the combat areas of the cold war, men like Captain "X." We know some of them. In ingenuity, determination, and skill they seem not inferior to him. Yet they seem to be far less effective.

It is not their fault. They must operate in the ambiguous, vague twilight of a diplomacy which cannot recognize its dominant role in the war between West and East. From their point of view our so-called "total diplomacy" is either totally nonexistent or a total failure.

Captain "X" told this in no uncertain terms when we asked him why his success was restricted to that one incident of 1946 and whether this did not indicate that the Russians are, after all, impervious to effective counterattack.

"Oh," he answered, "Prague was not my only scoop, but the others were on a far smaller scale. I could never again obtain permission to execute my ideas that, believe me, were on a scale comparable with the *coup* which I aborted.

"Do not blame my superiors on the spot! They are helpless victims of our Washington bureaucracy. They have orders to lie low and observe their diplomatic responsibilities. Don't be beastly with the Bolshies! There was a time when we could operate with a somewhat freer hand. It was nothing illegal or something a civilized nation should be ashamed of! It was the legitimate work of intelligence officers who recognized an opportunity when they saw one. During those days, remember, the Bolshies had a lot of trouble in Hungary, Rumania, and Bulgaria. Well—it was us, the small fry, who caused the trouble.

"But what happened? The Russians complained to Washington and we were clubbed on our heads. Withdrawn, scattered, admonished, demobilized. Some of us disobeyed. We continued to work singlehanded, without official support. But the Russians were emboldened by the prompt Washington reaction to their complaints, so they launched more complaints.[5]

"We had a personal stake in the cold war. We made friends in those friendly countries. They were the best. Intellectuals. Artists. Politicians. Most of them came up through the underground movement where we first met them when we parachuted into their countries. Suddenly we heard they were Nazis or Fascists—those men who fought against the Nazis on the spot while their new Bolshi partners in government did paper work for the Comintern in Kyuibishev.

"It didn't make sense. Then they started to disappear. The night before we had a drink with Béla or Jan or Valeriu. Next morning they could not be found. They were in jail, beaten to pulp or stood up against a blank wall under the glaring light of the examining magistrate's lamp. Gogol has come to Eastern Europe! [6]

"Next we heard that they had 'confessed.' Then word came that they had been taken to Russia. The Siberian labor camps of the MVD are crowded with our friends—and we were not allowed to do anything about it.

"Let me tell you one story about Washington. I was no longer with the 'organization' but I was working as a free lance in —— because some of my friends, who were still at large, needed help. One day a man came to me and asked me to get him out of the country. Now there are many stories about the help our agents are giving to those desperate people, but the actual aid they give is really very little. This particular man did contact our people in official places but was turned down, despite his credentials. This was a *bona fide* case, no *agent provocateur* stuff.

"We needed something like fifty dollars to prepare the man's escape. I did not have the money. So I went to another small fry who was spending his interneship as an intelligence man in one of our offices. He listened to my story sympathetically, then asked me to write out a 'project' memo so that he could send it on to Washington. There it was supposed to be passed by a project review board that authorizes such expenditure—or rejects it.

" 'Hell,' I said, 'I have no time to lose. I need the dough now. The guy is in danger!'

" 'I'm sorry,' the poor little man answered. 'These are regulations. But to tell the truth,' he added, 'I don't think you have a chance getting this project approved. Washington frowns upon such protection cases.'

" 'Okay,' I said, 'how about *lending* me the money?' He coughed up the fifty bucks. I got the guy out of the country. And I still owe our man those fifty smackers.

"We Americans, Britons, and French had a right to operate in those countries. Some of them we liberated. Others we helped to conquer. But the Russians, strangers themselves, kept on complaining, and Washington refused to let us work or stay. What fools we are, brother, what fools! [7]

"One day in Budapest someone got away with my jeep. In the garage where I kept it I was told that it was a Red Army captain who drove it away. And sure enough, later during the day I found my jeep parked in front of the Russian control commission's office. I went in and found my man, and asked him to give me back my jeep. He just laughed and pretended not to understand English, German, Hungarian, Czech, the languages I tried on him. Then a Hungarian clerk in his office who spoke Russian told him all about it in Russian. He still laughed and said 'Nyet.'

"I was boiling mad. I went downstairs to General Sviridov's office and told his aide that I had to see the general on business, secret, urgent, official. I was taken in to him at once. He laughed, too, when I told him my story, but said there was nothing he could do about it. He was not allowed, he said.

"I boiled over. 'Look, General,' I said, 'what kind of an army is this where a captain is allowed to steal my jeep and a general is not allowed to give it back?'

"I got back that jeep at once.

"This is an example of how one has to work with them. You don't take anything lying down. They can't take it. Now it is too late. They are holding too many of our men and we are holding none of theirs. They have the jump on us and we will never overtake them—or hardly ever."

The success of some of our men shows clearly how vulnerable our foe really is to this kind of attack. But for reasons that are too many to enumerate and too delicate to discuss, we are holding back and abandoning the whole field to the Russians.

The British have a different idea. While we do not concede that British Intelligence is doing all that the Russians claim, it is at least more intelligent and compassionate in handling those "protection cases" than we are. It is also far more discriminating in its selection of "cases." While it does burn its fingers upon occasion, on the whole it is doing a bang-up job in probing for the Achilles heel of the Soviet body politic in Eastern Europe.[8]

However, it was not on the smallest but on the largest scale of positive political action that Great Britain showed the world the way and demonstrated in practice the best method of foiling those excellent designs Stalin enumerated in his operations plans.

It happened in India.

. The vast subcontinent was marked by the Kremlin for early revolutionary action. In 1924, when elaborating upon the basic operations plan, Stalin posed the rhetorical question: "Where will the revolution begin? Where, in what country, can the front of capital be pierced first?" As usual, he answered it himself.

"It is not impossible that this may be in India for example. Why? Because there we find a young and militant revolutionary proletariat which has an ally in the shape of the national liberation movement, unquestionably a very powerful and important ally; because in that country the revolution faces a notorious enemy, a foreign imperialism, devoid of all moral authority and deservedly hated by the oppressed and exploited masses in India." [9]

Even a few years ago it seemed that Stalin would be proved as infallible in this prediction as in some others. But then, by sudden and effective action, the Labor Government of Great Britain removed India from Stalin's timetable by the simple process of granting her the independence she was clamoring for in the impressive voices of Gandhi and Nehru.

Even Konni Zilliacus, whose laudatory remarks are usually reserved for the Soviet Union, found nothing but praise when he discussed the Labor Government's actions in Asia: "When Japan collapsed," he wrote, "the Labor Government, with the help of Lord Louis Mountbatten, the leading man of the spot, adopted a relatively enlightened policy towards Burma that eventually conferred Dominion status and the right of secession (promptly exercised) on that country. This progressive policy, also followed in India, [was] due to in part to the advice of the Colonial and India Offices." [10]

From a strictly revolutionary point of view, India is no longer in the danger zone. The British Government has shown itself second to none in fighting the Bolsheviks with their own weapons and arguments. Britain's enlightened action was not confined to the foiling of Stalin's India pattern. Similar British patterns were applied to Burma, to Egypt, and to Palestine. If disquiet continues in some of the "liberated" places it is due to our followup rather than to the original action.

Look to Indonesia to see how a pattern can succeed from the Russian point of view and then fail as a result of proper and energetic action on our part.

Our stock hit a low and Communist sympathies were strong when, after VJ-day, the Netherlands troops, which came to reoccupy Indonesia, fought the "natives" in the uniform and with the equipment of our own Marines who, back in the States, were actually trained for this kind of close combat against the Japanese. Their tanks did not even have their U.S. markings removed. The bullets which killed Indonesians were manufactured in the United States and Great Britain.[11]

No wonder that Communist agents were popular as they moved up and down the islands, reminding the inhabitants of the "Program of the Communist International" which mentioned "uprisings in Indonesia" among its prognostications and plans, as one of the "links in one and the same international revolutionary chain, constituent parts of the profound general crisis of capitalism." [12]

Our setback was temporary. We did in Indonesia what we later failed to do in Indo-China. We put pressure on the Netherlands to come to terms with their subjects. Because today the United States of Indonesia is a reality, another Soviet pattern has been foiled. It was no accidental tribute to the United States that the first stamp printed by the new sovereign republic had the picture of George Washington on it.

Despite the evident successes of these enlightened policies, we abandoned our successful diplomacy and replaced it with an old-fashioned colonial policy.

"We are like a chess player who, failing to develop all of his pieces, advances two or three pawns and one knight, hoping to capture the king," Walter Lippmann wrote on April 4, 1950.

"The French colonial army, Bao-Dai, a little American money and some arms, a little bit of Point 4, a few visiting warships, and a lot of ringing declarations are not enough to make a policy that has any prospect of success. The problem is too big for measures of that kind. We shall have to rise above the notion that it can be dealt with by giving some help to the French, and we shall have to put the problem in a different and larger frame of negotiations where, through the medium of the United Nations, the leading powers of Asia and the influence of the whole world can be brought to bear upon it.

"That, one might say, would be total diplomacy in action." [13]

As the West succeeded in defeating the Soviet pattern in India, but helped it to success in China; as we foiled it in Indonesia, then helped it to triumph in Indo-China; so we thwarted it in Greece and Iran, only to allow it to succeed elsewhere on the Bolshevik perimeter.

The failure of the Greek pattern is too well known to require detailed description. For a long time it looked as though the U.S. would stand idly by as Greece, too, like Newton's apple, pulled by the gravity of the times, fell into the orbit. We did feel somewhat uneasy about the policies of Mr. Churchill in Greece. There was a little story—certainly apocryphal—making the rounds in Athens, which still describes best the general direction of those policies. On his trip to Athens at Christmastime in 1944, Mr. Churchill was introduced to Archbishop Damaskinos, slated to become the regent of Greece. The Prime Minister pulled General Scobie, the British commander, aside to inquire:

"Who is this Archbishop Damaskinos? Is he a selfless prince of the clergy interested only in matters spiritual, or is he a scheming prelate devoted to more temporal things?"

"I am afraid, sir," General Scobie allegedly answered, "he is the latter."

"Good," Mr. Churchill was quoted as saying. "He is our man!"

When the whole and unbiased story of British intervention in Greece is told—and the sooner someone tells it the better, if only for our own democratic education—we shall be appalled by the Whitehall's conduct in the liberation of an ally. During those days a British diplomat in Athens told a member of Parliament: "The last thing we want is Liberal democracy in Greece. It would turn into Communism!" [14]

In reality there was no such danger at that time. The danger developed as a result of British aid to collaborationists, including the quislings of an organization called "X," even against the liberal, non-Communist elements of the resistance and liberation movements. This was frankly admitted by Mr. Churchill in his memoirs, in which he wrote:

"Late one night at this time [December 6, 1944], I drafted a telegram to our General Scobie, who had come to Athens with 3,000 men to fight the Germans, that he must no longer consider himself neutral between the Greek parties, but on the contrary, should sustain Premier Papanderou and not hesitate to fire on Communist assailants." [15]

This kind of British "diplomacy" was running amuck in the closing days of the war. In Greece it had but one aim: to prevent the establishment of a republican government. Churchill was determined to play the role of the kingmaker.

Had it not been for Mr. Churchill's misguided efforts the Greek pattern might never have been applied by the Kremlin. It cost the West billions of dollars and an effort that staggers the imagination to remedy a situation created by a blind and uncompromising policy.[16] And yet, the Greek aid program, so magnanimously underwritten and financed by the American taxpayer, was by no means wasted. It showed that we do have the ability to defeat a Soviet pattern at the very spot where it threatened to become most dangerous. This is perhaps particularly important because the elaborate military action we financed failed to break the strength of the guerillas of Markos Vafiades.[17] Again in Greece, it was not the grandiloquently planned stab at the heart, but the pinpricks of stray mosquitoes that defeated an ambitious Soviet pattern. These pinpricks reveal the inner weakness of the pattern itself. Today we know that:

(1) There was dissension in Greek Communist ranks, even on the highest echelons of the guerilla movement. The establishment of a government by Markos in the mountains was an arbitrary act. It was executed without Moscow's prior approval, and maintained in the face of its grudging acquiescence. The U.S.S.R., these days quite ready to recognize dissident governments, failed to grant recognition to the Markos regime throughout its existence. When Moscow did intervene in the internal affairs of the Greek "section," it did so only to insist upon a purge, and upon the liquidation of the Vafiades section, for

"Titoist" deviation.[18] It was the Moscow-inspired purge rather than the Washington-inspired offensive that defeated the guerillas and brought their campaign to a standstill.

(2) There was dissension within the Cominform leading, as we all know, to Tito's deviation. The military "successes" of the guerillas were not victories. They were due to their mobility, enabling them to apply Stalin's own evasive tactics, and retreat rapidly in the face of imminent defeat. Such retreats were made possible by the collaboration of Bulgaria, Albania, and especially Yugoslavia, opening their borders for such withdrawals.[19]

Tito's departure from the orbit closed this important avenue of escape to those Greek guerillas who remained faithful to Moscow and continued their hit-and-run campaign under new commanders. The proximity of Titoism itself went far to strengthen the hand and the faith of men who continued to regard Markos Vafiades as their leader.

The fate of Markos himself is obscure. We had various reports but none could be verified. Most interesting was the one which described his escape to Yugoslavia where he is now supposed to be training a Greek division, recruited from among his own partisans for the showdown battle between Moscow and Belgrade.

Another intelligence report which we received in the late summer of 1949, and for which corroboration was obtained from several sources in the early winter of 1950, indicated that the Kremlin itself wrote off its Greek pattern as a failure. In a special Politburo session held on August 21–23, 1949, it was decided to liquidate the Greek guerilla movement, and more than that, to assure Greece of future tranquillity from those quarters. A plan was worked out to partition Albania, the only remaining territory to which Greek guerillas could retreat, and to attach its southern section to Northern Greece, while annexing the North as a Yugoslavia purge of Tito.

This plan, we were told, was communicated semiofficially to the American Government as one of the baits to catch this country's approval for a projected liquidation of Tito. We had no means of tracing this communication to the State Department. But we did trace it to the Soviet Embassy in Washington where, we were advised by a reliable informant, the document had been duly received through diplomatic channels with instructions to Ambassador Panyushkin to bring it to the attention of the Secretary of State.[20]

TROUBLES IN YUGOSLAVIA

The failure of the Greek pattern, caused by the inner weaknesses of the Soviet conspiracy, is dwarfed by the deviation of Yugoslavia, the greatest blow Soviet expansionism has suffered in the postwar world. It is now generally recognized, some such experts as Freda Utley and Rebecca West notwithstanding, that the clash between Stalin and Tito represents the gravest rift in Communist unity ever to occur, not excluding the Stalin-Trotsky and Stalin-Bukharin rifts. The latter were domestic clashes, threatening to undermine the Communist rule only inside Russia. The former is international, threatening the success of Communist domination of the world. It is the kind of rueful conflict which Stalin, way back in 1928, described as "a deviation which cannot be regarded as a trifling matter." [21]

In 1929, in another significant address to his party's central committee, Stalin provided the actual keynote for what, in 1936–37, and in 1948–49, became the leitmotivs of the campaigns against Trotsky-Bukharin and Tito-Piyade respectively.

"If we," Stalin said, "in our own ranks, in our own party, in the political General Staff of the Proletariat, which is directing the movement and is leading the proletariat forward, if we tolerated all this, what would it mean? Would it not mean that we want to send the revolution down hill, demoralize our socialist construction, flee from difficulties, surrender our positions to the capitalist elements?" And then he added the menacing alternative: "Either you carry out this demand of the party, in which case the party will welcome you. Or you do not, in which case you will have only yourselves to blame." [22]

We are inclined to agree with Stalin's conclusion that unless the Bolsheviks "overcome the Right deviation and the conciliationist tendency, it will be impossible to overcome the difficulties" which confront them.

In the summer of 1948, Europe was a great deal more excited than the United States by the news of the Cominform break with the Yugoslavs. The reports and editorials in the continental press were entirely different from those in the United States. In the U.S. the news was received with tempered excitement, distrust of Tito, unwillingness to forget past policies of the Yugoslav regime, and with some acceptance of the theory that it was a fake fight designed to get Marshall Plan aid for Yugoslavia.[23]

Europeans are better trained in Marxist dialectics than Americans. They discovered immediately the real unbridgeable break for they knew the U.S.S.R. never forgives two crimes of Communists: (1) attacks and unfavorable reflections on the Soviet Union; and (2) separation of Marxism-Leninism from Stalinism. Europeans were thus quick to detect these two elements in the Cominform's criticism of Tito's policies and to recognize that they made reconciliation impossible so long as Tito remained in power.

For some time in 1947 and 1948, the rift was the best-kept secret of the postwar period. The first confidential report of an impending Tito-Stalin break reached us in December, 1947, in the wake of the first Cominform conference in Poland, over the signing of a secret military protocol whose story we shall tell later in this chapter. Documentation was not at that time complete. But in March, 1948, a rapid alienation of the Kremlin's affections from Marshal Tito became the keynote of all reports reaching us from behind the iron curtain. Here, then, in authentic detail is the whole inside story of the Stalin-Tito rift.

The rift began, not in 1948 or in 1947, but in fact already in 1946. In the early spring of that year, a program was drafted by the Yugoslav Economic Planning Commission, under the chairmanship of elder-statesman Moshe Piyade. It provoked great consternation in the Kremlin, if only because it displayed a concept of economic independence. Belgrade proposed to rely upon trade with the West, an orientation that was severely frowned upon by Moscow.[24]

The plan was the practical implementation of an older scheme, called "Bihatch Program" after the secret meetingplace of Tito's partisans where, in 1942, in the midst of war, an economic blueprint had first been drafted.[25]

The success of the Bihatch Program was dependent on (1) substantial reparations from the Axis, and (2) good economic

relations with the West, including financial assistance from the
U.S. The Yugoslavs expected the U.S.S.R. to aid forcefully in
the gaining of reparations. At the same time, Belgrade told
Moscow that it would "not look favorably" on Soviet efforts to
subordinate Yugoslavia's Western trade to "larger political and
strategic considerations."

The Kremlin was appalled by such intransigence and Stalin
summoned Tito to Moscow for a conference. "What you are
doing is merely to revive the old NEP," he fumed. [The NEP
was the New Economic Policy of Lenin under which, during the
1920's, individual entrepreneurs were permitted to function.]
When Tito appeared unshaken by these words, the Russian
leader told him: "You are repeating Lenin's old mistakes." [26]

This sounded like sacrilege to Tito's chief brain truster, old
Moshe Piyade. A contemporary of Stalin, he had employed his
sixteen years in Serbian prisons to translate the works of Marx
and Lenin—but no writings of Stalin—into Serbian. Tito and
Piyade never forgave Stalin's "heresy." They are both Marxist-
Leninists who refuse to accept the so-called Stalinist adaptation
of the theoretical and ideological structure of communism.

At that time in 1946, Moscow still had two important representatives in Tito's innermost circle. One was Andriya Hebrang;
the other was Sreten Zujovich. The eventual expulsion of these
two from the Tito Cabinet, and their arrest by General Alek-
sander Rankovich's secret police actually precipitated the
U.S.S.R.–Yugoslav crisis. After Stalin's 1946 interview with Tito,
Hebrang and Zujovich were secretly expelled from the central
committee of the Yugoslav Communist Party. But strangely
enough they were allowed to retain their high ministerial positions.[27]

However, from then on, Hebrang and Zujovich were regarded
as "Moscow stooges," invulnerable only so long as the façade
of Communist unity was to be maintained. But when, early in
1948, Moscow decided to move in for the kill, Hebrang and
Zujovich were transferred directly from their offices in the
Ministries of Planning and Finance to cells in the Central Prison
of Belgrade.[28]

Shortly after his Moscow conference in 1946, Tito laid down
the line for Yugoslav Communists. "We fought the war on the

Bihatch Program," he said to confidants in November, 1946. "We did not intend to change it." Soviet reaction to this statement was immediate. Russian observers on the spot went so far as to voice their disapproval even to British diplomats.

It soon became clear to Tito and his aides that the Bihatch Program was being sabotaged by the U.S.S.R. Without vigorous Soviet support, Yugoslavia failed to gain the *substantial* reparations which she had sought. Then, in September, 1947, the newly established Cominform declared war on the Marshall Plan, and sought openly to prevent Tito's doing business with the West.

Tito's reaction was renewed determination to see his program through. The challenge was accepted by Stalin. The showdown followed.[29]

The temporary establishment of Cominform headquarters in Belgrade was no evidence of Tito's solidity with Moscow. It was the opposite. It was, in fact, infiltration. One of Russia's foremost international revolutionary experts, Pavel Yudin, was selected to lead this work.[30] It was indeed within the Cominform that the smoldering feud between Moscow and Belgrade developed into an open break. For Tito's insistence on *economic independence* was but one of two major reasons for the split. The other was his even more determined insistence on *military sovereignty*. This was revealed to us in startling detail in a secret document to which we gained access in August, 1948. It came to us unsolicited and without warning, in the form of a photostat of the original. The circumstances of this acquisition, the source from which it reached us, and the motivations of our informants left no doubt in our minds as to the authenticity of the document. It also convinced us, at a time when such belief was by no means widespread, that Tito's break with Moscow was final and irrevocable.

The document turned out to be a secret annex to the resolution adopted by delegates of nine European Communist parties, meeting in Poland at the end of September, 1947, which announced to a startled world the establishment of a Communist Information Bureau, in fact, the revival of the Comintern.

It was a protocol entitled "Military Measures." Under the pact, the countries in the Soviet orbit agreed in effect to place all their military resources at the disposal of the U.S.S.R. for eventual integration into the armed forces of the Soviet Union. Thus they were supposed to sign away a vital aspect of their sovereignty: their control over their own military apparatus. They were to agree to the establishment of a new Greater Red Army, to be co-ordinated by a single General Staff, under the control of a single command authority, completely dominated by the Soviet Union from Moscow.

The document itself was drafted in Moscow, by the military administration of the Communist party's Central Executive Committee, under its then chief, Lieutenant General Joseph Shikin, one of the late Andrei Zhdanov's lieutenants and confidants.[31] It was approved by the Politburo and taken to Warsaw to be forced down the throats of the satellites. The conference was almost over when Zhdanov, in a feigned afterthought, called on Shikin, who flew in from Moscow that day, to present the draft to the delegates.

There was evident consternation and bewilderment in the silence which greeted the reading of the document. Then Zhdanov spoke, in violent terms, using the strongest and most colorful language of which a Bolshevik is capable, urging acceptance of the protocol "without debate." It seemed there would be no debate. Then one of the Yugoslav delegates, Edvard Kardelj, turned to his colleague Milovan Djilas. A few sentences passed between the two. Finally Kardelj rose to make a speech.

All eyes turned on him. Jacques Duclos of France called out in subservient haste: "There will be no debate." Joseph Révai of Hungary echoed the slogan: "There will be no debate." Zhdanov sat still, with a pained expression, perhaps caused by the physical pain of his long and progressing illness, pouncing upon him in moments of tension. Malenkov, his fellow delegate from the U.S.S.R., stayed silent, his arms folded on his tunic, the faintest of all smiles playing on his lips.

Duclos repeated the call: "There will be no debate!" Now Kardelj echoed it himself. "No," he said, "there will be no debate! But on behalf of the Yugoslav delegation I would like to state that we have no authority to sign the protocol."

Was this mutiny? But then again, it may have been just exaggerated prudence on the part of Kardelj and Djilas, quite plausible in a Communist party as disciplined as the Yugoslav section of Comrade Josip Broz. Kardelj waited for an answer, for a question, or for any reaction at all to his statement, but none seemed to be forthcoming. So he rose again and, in the fluent Russian he learned in Dolgoruki, a Moscow suburb where he taught the history of the Comintern at the Communist university named after Sverdlov, he said:

"I suggest that the organs of our section be consulted on the issue and that we adjourn until my delegation obtains the proper authorization." He paused for a moment as he added: "One way or another." The possibility of an alternative left the delegates in restive mood, but they agreed to adjourn when Malenkov, without consulting Zhdanov, raised his hand placidly to signal his approval.

While the delegates waited in Warsaw, General Milovan Djilas flew to Belgrade in a military plane with the draft of the military protocol. The next afternoon he was back in Warsaw. An extraordinary meeting of the conference was promptly called. The tension was unbearable in the hall, where the air was poisoned by the heavy smoke of Russian cigarettes. Nerves were on edge when Wladyslaw Gomulka, one of the Polish delegates, opened the meeting and called on Kardelj to announce Belgrade's decision. But before Kardelj could rise, Zhdanov jumped to his feet and delivered a thinly veiled warning to the two Yugoslavs, as if calling on them to make up their minds, in this last minute, should the news from Tito run contrary "to the will of the majority." He sat down in great pain, his left arm pressed against his body, his fingers aimlessly grasping the empty air. Then Kardelj rose:

"I regret to say," he announced, "that the Executive Committee of our Section cannot approve of the proposed protocol and has therefore instructed us to refrain from affixing our signatures to the document." [32]

TITO'S DEVIATION

When the whole story was in, chiefly through Malenkov's private report to Stalin and Molotov, the Kremlin was quick to recognize Yugoslavia's refusal as a serious breach in the Cominform front. Although it was assumed that Tito alone would not have challenged the authority of Moscow and that he had the backing of his Politburo, or even its instructions, the Kremlin hoped to settle the controversy in a man-to-man talk between Stalin and the Yugoslav dictator. So orders were sent to Belgrade, summoning Tito to Moscow, not in his capacity as Marshal of Yugoslavia and head of its Cabinet, but as a disciplined Bolshevik functionary subject to higher commands.

The meeting between Stalin and Tito started out quietly enough, but then, in a crescendo of vituperations, it developed into a verbal brawl, probably the first Stalin experienced since his debates with Trotsky. It was Stalin who lost his temper. Tito answered him in measured words, something like this:

"Of all the popular democracies," he said, "Yugoslavia is the only one which has no common frontiers with the U.S.S.R. We are, in fact, 150 kilometers from the Soviet border, but only about 40 kilometers from the frontiers of the West, across the Adriatic Sea in Italy. It is evident that our soil would be the first to be attacked by the Anglo-Americans should they ever decide to unleash an imperialist war against the U.S.S.R.

"The protocol requires us to join in any war in which the U.S.S.R. might be involved, and to integrate our armed forces with those of the Soviet Union for better or for worse. There is a contradiction there, in so far as Yugoslavia is concerned, in those two separate commitments. We are too isolated and in a too precariously advanced position to be able to afford the luxury of a war with the West unless our survival is assured. And how are we going to defend ourselves if our forces form part of an army with which we have no territorial or logistic contact?"

Tito was allowed to return to Belgrade—a decision the Russians must regret to this day, since attempts were made shortly after to get him out of the way. When assassination proved too difficult in Belgrade, or probably when it threatened to expose the conspiracy to the efficient, Moscow-trained Yugoslav secret police, attempts were made to lure Tito out of the country and to liquidate him on foreign soil. An invitation to Moscow met with polite refusal. So the Cominform was instructed to call still another meeting, this time on the level of the chiefs of states, to discuss loose ends left by its conference in Warsaw. Tito laughed out loud when the invitation arrived with an R.S.V.P., and the proviso that "the premiers of Cominform countries, or their highest-ranking Communist functionaries, are expected to attend."

Tito asked for the agenda of the meeting and was given one, hastily compiled, featuring another report by Zhdanov "on the international situation." Here was the loophole Tito awaited. "Foreign affairs are the *ressort* of the Ministry of External Affairs," he advised the Cominform. "Yugoslavia will be represented by *Gospodin* Stanoje Simič, our minister of foreign affairs."

This was a calculated insult the barb of which was not likely to miss. *Gospodin* Simič was not even a member of the Communist party. Not only did Tito refuse to go himself, but he did not allow any of his party comrades to make the trip either. All he was willing to send was a remnant of the *bourgeoisie*— the most expendable among his Cabinet ministers.[33]

The struggle was on, Tito still holding the initiative, but with the clandestine forces of Pavel Yudin's Cominform apparatus in Belgrade moving in for the kill. Then one night, in his White Palace, Tito received a phone call from General Rankovic, his interior minister and chief of Security Police. The one-time tailor sounded jubilant as he announced: "Their game is up. They are all in jail."

"They" included the biggest catch next to Yudin himself, General Yevgeni Zhukov, one of the Red Army's chief representatives in Belgrade. Here was the end of a career that was as shady as it was romantic, and perhaps the end of a man who had played with fire already far too long without ever burning himself. But now he was in jail, a prisoner of Tito who was thus openly challenging and boldly defying Zhukov's mentor, the Foreign Department of the mighty MVD.

Yevgeni Zhukov was one of the perennial "foreign" residents of Belgrade, sitting out all the regimes that came and went in the cavalcade of Serbian politics. Back in the Tsar's Russia he was an officer of the guards, devoted to Nicholas II with the fervor of a religious fanatic. He escaped from the revolution and made his way to Belgrade, where a group of Russian monarchists found welcome refuge under the wings of the pro-Romanov family of the reigning dynasty. For years afterward, a

Tsarist Embassy was still functioning in Belgrade, the only one of all the capitals of the world. And gathered around the Tsarist ambassador was a motley crowd of exiles, dreaming of return to Holy Russia.

Yevgeni Zhukov was one of the most fanatical among them. He stood fast in his loyalty even after the Embassy finally pulled down its colors. He continued to edit a small monarchist paper in Belgrade and to be one of the centers of Tsarist activities, the strings of which all centered in his hands.

Old King Peter I was followed by his son Alexander on the throne; then Alexander was killed in Marseille, and his place taken by Prince Regent Paul; then Paul was overthrown and young King Peter II installed; and then the Germans came. Throughout the years, Zhukov stood his ground. He was a confidant of all comers and on the best of terms with the Germans, whose intelligence service found in him a willing operative.

In 1944, the Red Army was standing outside the gates of Belgrade, with Tito's partisan divisions marching up from the south. On October 20, Belgrade was liberated. The first man to greet Marshal Tolbukhin, commander-in-chief of the Red Army forces, was Yevgeni Zhukov, the renegade monarchist.

But he was no renegade. He now appeared in the gray field uniform of the Red Army itself, with the khaki-braided shoulder marks of a major general. The two men embraced. Zhukov's long exile was over.

Throughout his years of exile, throughout his leadership in monarchist movement, Yevgeni Zhukov was a Soviet spy, the best paid and most respected secret agent of the MVD's foreign department, with links to the highest in the Party, army, and government. This man was chosen to keep Tito in check. Later he was picked to bring about his liquidation.

But in Tito and his partisans, Yevgeni Zhukov met his nemesis. While there were but few undetected Cominform spies inside Tito's entourage, the Cominform clique in Belgrade was honeycombed with Tito's spies. They reported on everything, including a secret visit Malenkov made to Belgrade, on forged papers, in elaborate disguise, to discuss the problem with Yudin and Zhukov on the spot. But Tito's agents discovered his presence, shadowed him throughout his stay, listened to his phone conversations, and treated him as if he were a capitalist spy. This is, at least, how Malenkov himself described his treatment to Zhukov. Their conference ended on a sweet note. Zhukov received the orders to get rid of Tito. Next morning Tito received word of Zhukov's latest instructions.

It may be difficult for one who is unfamiliar with the techniques of Bolshevik conspiracy to follow the course of the intrigue. For one familiar with it, the Tito-Zhukov bout was the fight of the ages, fought with the consummate skill of two admirable blackguards. Tito enjoyed the fight. Zhukov had some doubts.

Then the word came from Moscow to strike. The message was intercepted, the code read by Rankovic's cipher clerks. That night his OZNA agents raided Zhukov's house. When the perplexed Russian arrived in the secret police's jail, he found all his conspirators assembled under guard. Among them was the young partisan lieutenant, a member of Tito's personal bodyguard, who was supposed to fire the lethal shot. He was not one of the prisoners. He was there as a witness—the man who broke the case and saved Tito's life.

Tito was still amused. "They forget," he said the morning after Zhukov's arrest, "that I was trained in the Cheka school in the Lubyanka." That was more than Zhukov could say of his training.

Zhukov's arrest ended the Kremlin's hope that Belgrade would return to the fold. But what of the future? The greatest speculation revolves around the probability of immediate strategic changes which may upset the whole Soviet pattern and timetable in the Balkans and disrupt an uninterrupted land front from Stettin to the Dardanelles. With Yugoslavia's departure from the Soviet bloc, the Adriatic Sea is even now effectively closed to the Soviet Union, despite Albania's precarious loyalty to the Kremlin.

But the Tito-Stalin schism must be considered chiefly as a failure of the Cominform pattern, for its effect on the Communist ranks in Europe and Asia. The immediate effect of the Tito affair became visible in the investigations and purges of all Communist parties everywhere in Europe. Not only various high-ranking officials in Politburos and Orgburos, but small regional officials down to secretaries of cells, were tested as to their loyalty. Thousands of them, big fish and small fry, were weighed and found wanting. Communist stalwarts like Rajk of Hungary, Clementis of Czechoslovakia, and Gomulka of Poland were liquidated, some of them by hanging, others by imprisonment, still others by fatal ostracism. For Tito's defiant break with Stalin brought to light everywhere a new line of anti-Russian thought among the Communists of the world.

Up to the Tito break, a sincere Communist under criticism as an anti-Stalinist had nowhere to go, provided he wanted to remain a Marxist. He could not join to the Trotskyites, for they represented in his eyes a small and uninfluential sect. He could not go to the Socialists, for he counted them too mild, reformist, and opportunistic. He could not, above all, become an anti-Marxist. If he broke with Stalinism, he was a lost sheep.

The Tito formula of independent Marxism-Leninism is the solution thousands of Communists have yearned to apply since the Moscow purge trials of 1936–37. Now the road was open. The Communist who joined the independents could keep his faith, he could continue to believe in the necessity of some co-operation with Russia and in its social and economic reforms, but he needed no longer remain subject to the dictates of a foreign power.

Tito's supporters stress constantly that Belgrade is no new Moscow, that Tito is no Stalin. But the leaders of the Yugoslav regime are and intend to remain Marxists. They think that, with Yugoslavia's mixture of industrial and agricultural economy and the progress they have made in the campaign to win support of youth, they are in a good position to attempt a full-fledged Marxist experiment that does not follow strictly the Soviet pattern specifically created for the satellites.[34]

In this is epitomized the failure of still another pattern of destruction. However, we may do well to remember that these failures were due largely to certain weaknesses within the basic pattern rather than to any effective outside interference with it. The failure of the Greek pattern, especially, seems to indicate that dollars and cents, planes and tanks, guns and bullets are capable by themselves of containing the Russians along the peripheries of their expansion. This is a fallacious belief. It is costing not inconsiderable sums to the American taxpayer, and anguish to the democratic world.

That containment can be accomplished cheaper and with more resounding results through direct assault, if carefully planned, shrewdly timed, and boldly executed, was demonstrated by Mr. Byrnes when he, at last, decided to abandon his futile policy of conciliation and to fight the cold war on Russia's own terms.

In the case of Iran the Kremlin blundered into an impossible situation. But it was left to two brilliant aides at Mr. Byrnes's elbow in the State Department to discover the opportunity for our greatest victory in the cold war. One of them was George V. Allen, at that time chief of the State Department's Office of Near Eastern Affairs; the other was Charles Bohlen, the Department's chief tactician in all our skirmishes with the Russians. They urged Mr. Byrnes to take up the case of Iran; they advised him on the course to follow; and they aided him brilliantly in the development and execution of his campaign. The result was our only major victory in the cold war—aside from the dearly bought successes of the Marshall Plan and North Atlantic Pacts.[35]

It will be remembered that during World War II, Russia, the U.S., and the U.K. were granted permission to send troops into Iran, partly to counteract German intrigue, but chiefly to secure the steady flow of American Lend-Lease shipments to Russia.

On November 24, 1945, the government of the United States sent a note to the U.S.S.R., as well as to the United Kingdom, raising the question of withdrawal of foreign troops from Iran. It reminded the Soviet Government that "the United States has already reduced its forces in Iran during the present year [1945] from a maximum strength of approximately 28,000 to less than 6,000." Simultaneously it advised the two allies that American military authorities in Iran would complete withdrawal of all American forces by January 1, 1946, inviting the others to follow suit.

The decision of the U.S. was partly motivated by intelligence that under the protection of the Red Army a puppet government had been established in Iranian Azerbaijan. The rest of the story may best be told in the succinct words of Mr. Byrnes himself, whose contribution to this Western victory deserves respect and emulation. He wrote:

> We repeatedly warned the Soviet Union that the United States, as well as the Soviet Government, was pledged by the Teheran Declaration signed by Roosevelt, Stalin and Churchill to protect the sovereignty of Iran. I personally stressed to Stalin that, if Iran protested to the United Nations, we would support Iran. But all our efforts failed to convince the Soviet Government that we would fulfill our Teheran pledge. Therefore, when Iran appealed to the Security Council, we acted.
>
> As so often happens in public affairs, the main battle was fought over a subsidiary issue; the right of Iran to present its case to the Security Council. I felt that if a precedent was established that denied any country the right of speedy access to the Security Council, the United Nations would be crippled from birth. I felt so strongly, in fact, about both the issue of Iran's sovereignty and the issue of ready access to the Security Council, that I personally argued the American case before the Security Council. Soviet resistance extended even to the point where Mr. Gromyko "walked out" on the Security Council. But firmness and the United Nations won.
>
> Generalissimo Stalin announced the withdrawal of his troops in a telegram to the president of a news agency rather than to the Security Council. And then, last December, [1946] the puppet regime collapsed. The people of Iran were not fooled by Soviet propaganda. When Allied observers went into Azerbaijan with the Iranian authorities they were greeted with cries of "Long Live the United Nations." [36]

One is inclined to agree most wholeheartedly with Mr. Byrnes's concluding remark: "It is a cheer we should not forget in the months and years ahead."

The Bolsheviks can "take it" as well as they can "dish it out." The failure of their Iranian pattern was regarded in the Kremlin as just one of those zigzags of history of which Lenin said: "When one enjoys an overwhelming superiority of forces one can succeed by a direct frontal attack. When forces are inadequate, detours, waiting periods, zigzags, and retreats may be necessary. That history usually moves in zigzags, and that Marxists must make allowances for even the most complex and whimsical zigzags of history, is undisputable."

Translated into the more lucid language of the West, this means that Soviet withdrawal from Azerbaijan was but a temporary expediency and that in the failure of the Iranian pattern the West gained merely a temporary respite, an uneasy armed truce, on one of the cold war's hottest fronts.

This, then, ought to be the lasting lesson we learn from the patterns which failed.

Part Four

AT BATTLE STATIONS

16.

STALIN DEPLOYS HIS FORCES

BETWEEN November 6 and 9, 1949, the heavy iron curtain of Russia was lifted four times in rapid succession. It remained raised barely long enough to allow just a few quick glimpses. But it was enough for some of us to see behind it feverish work on the deployment of the Soviet world for the Great Stalin Plan in the coming showdown with the West.

Glimpse number one showed Politburo chieftain Georgi Maximilianovich Malenkov standing in the glittering center of the big parade that annually marks the anniversary of the October Revolution. He warned that World War III "will be the grave not only of individual capitalist states, but of the whole world capitalism." [1]

Glimpse number two showed Marshal Konstantin Konstantinovich Rokossovsky of the Red Army going to Warsaw as minister of defense and commander-in-chief of the *Polish* Army, in the strangest appointment since Gaius Caligula bestowed the priesthood and a consulship on his horse Incitatus.

Glimpse number three, somewhat vague and perplexing, showed Premier Antonin Zapotocky of Czechoslovakia at the uranium mines of Yachimov, watching the loading of pitchblende by forced slave labor and the sealed trains starting on their long journey to the two Atomgrads in the U.S.S.R.

Glimpse number four, the most blurred of them all, showed the shadowy figures of two German generals, Vinzent Mueller and Otto Korfes in Potsdam, recruiting ex-Nazis and ex-Wehrmacht men for still another satellite army. [2]

Meanwhile, in front of the iron curtain, Foreign Minister Vishinsky was performing his familiar act in the best tradition of the diplomatic music hall. At Lake Success he proposed to the Big Five the signing of a nonaggression pact "to strengthen peace." In vaudeville such acts are known as "fillers"—to keep the audience amused while the scenery is changed behind the curtain. Neither audience nor management pays particular attention to "fillers." But Vishinsky, excellent actor that he is, put his heart and soul into the slight interlude and managed to divert our attention from the main act for which Russia was preparing the stage behind his broad back.

Apparently there was no intelligent reaction to the intelligence from Czechoslovakia and Germany. It failed completely to impress itself upon the public mind. Editorial reaction was nil. No one made an attempt to put it in its proper place in the developing drama of the world.

To most it seemed that these four episodes revealed behind the iron curtain were individual incidents, haphazard and unrelated. But these four items in the news of the day told a coherent, correlated story. Above all, they indicated the route of Soviet deployment: Poland, Czechoslovakia, and Germany. Then they showed unmistakable signs of a return of the Soviets to Europe from their detour to Asia. Third, they revealed, in Malenkov's words, the direction of their ideological deployment—world revolution and the collapse of world capitalism.

There was, to be sure, a quantitative and qualitative inner distinction between the four episodes in the varying degrees of their importance. The Malenkov speech was a reiteration; Zapotocky's trip to Yachimov was a confirmation. But the recruiting of ex-Nazis into a new German Red Army and the Rokossovsky mission to Warsaw were straws in the wind, an ill wind to the West.

Here again we failed to recognize a major engagement in the cold war, for the Rokossovsky appointment was the first step in a premeditated move to deploy the Soviet forces for the showdown. The strange assignment of a Russian marshal to command a nominally alien army was, indeed, by far the most important show of Stalin's hand. But the announcement of Rokossovsky's mission to Warsaw was only one in a series of significant events which occurred with gunfire rapidity during that pregnant summer of 1949.

(1) In that summer, the U.S.S.R. detonated an atomic weapon that was powerful enough to shake the world far beyond her own closely guarded borders.

(2) At about the same time, during a top-secret conference in Stalin's private quarters in the Kremlin, the campaign against Tito was mapped in full detail.

(3) Members of the Politburo, including key men like Molotov, Mikoyan, Beria, and Bulganin, were relieved of their administrative duties and assigned to new secret tasks on the highest strategic level.

(4) The whole war machine of the U.S.S.R. was revamped. Major changes were made in the Red Army and the Red Fleet, in personnel as well as in organization. The Soviet General Staff was given a new chief, General Sergei M. Shtemenko. Even more important, Colonel General Joseph Shikin was quietly removed as head of the Political Administration of the Red Army.

(5) The war against the Church was brought into the open. Cardinal Mindszenty of Hungary was imprisoned; Archbishop Beran of Czechoslovakia was detained; Archbishop Vyszinsky of Poland was intimidated. Wholesale imprisonment of clerical loyalists occurred throughout Eastern Europe.

(6) A mad and bloody purge swept across the steppes of satellite communism with some of the greatest names of international bolshevism ending on the gallows. Everywhere, from the Baltic to the Adriatic, from the Oder to the Black Sea, the most loyal henchmen of the Kremlin and Stalin's personal bailiffs assumed complete control and absolute power in a stringent move to stop the spread of Titoism.

(7) The peace campaign of the Kremlin, designed to keep us disarmed and disunited while Russia prepared for war, went into high gear, the highest since the middle '30's. Huge, co-ordinated demonstrations were held in Wroclav, Paris, Colombo, Moscow, and New York, patterned after that basic directive of all peace campaigns, the 1935 resolution proposed by Italy's Communist leader Palmiro Togliatti, alias Ercole Ercoli.[3]

(8) A rash of loyalism broke out within the "sections of the Comintern," the regional Communist parties, from down under

in Australia to 35 East Twelfth Street in Manhattan, the national office of the Communist party of the U.S.A. Evidently obeying instructions from "that house" in Moscow, on the corner of Vozdvizhenka and Mokhovaya, whence international bolshevism gets all its directives, they declared one after another, that "if the outbreak of a counter-revolutionary war compels the Soviet Union to set the Red Army in motion for the defense of Socialism," they will call upon the toilers within their own countries "to work, with all the means at their disposal and at any price, for the victory of the Red Army over the armies of the imperialists." [4]

These, then, were some of the stones that went into the making of the mosaic of Stalin's strategic plan. The most important single item, the clue to the entire enigmatic design, was Marshal Rokossovsky's assignment to Poland.

Although this particular move came upon us with dramatic suddenness, apparently surprising even our statesmen, there were more than indications—there was actual information four months in advance—that the appointment was impending.

We had such information. We assume that our Department of State had the information, too. Our informants advised us that Rokossovsky had been recalled from his headquarters in Liegnitz, Germany, on August 14, 1949—and was for several weeks in Moscow, in secret conferences with Marshal Vasilevsky and Sokolovsky and, above all, Marshal Bulganin. The latter attended these conferences in a threefold capacity, as the Politburo's representative in all military matters, as the Politburo's expert on Poland, and as Rokossovsky's mentor and personal friend.

It was upon Bulganin's recommendation that Rokossovsky was picked for the unique assignment of commanding what is, for all practical purposes, a foreign army. In the U.S.S.R., such a recommendation means far more than a mere gesture of confidence and friendship. On the part of Bulganin, it means a guarantee to his colleagues that Rokossovsky will not betray their trust. On the part of Rokossovsky it means personal and ideological subservience to Bulganin.

In Rokossovsky's life Bulganin means the difference between glory and obscurity, even life and death. A hustling and ambitious officer, a typical product of the opportunistic senior officers' corps of the Red Army that came into prominence in the wake of the Tukchachevsky scandal, Rokossovsky lost his bearing in the difficult and stormy year of the purge of 1937. Although commanding a cavalry corps of the Leningrad military district, he was arrested, dumped into the big yellow jail of the GPU. He lost some of his teeth and four of his ribs were broken while he enjoyed the hospitality of the late Yezhov's secret police.

Then, suddenly, Rokossovsky was released from jail. His ribs were healed, his teeth replaced. He was given command of an army, then of an army corps. How can such ups and downs in a man's life be explained? Simply enough. Rokossovsky had an influential friend. He was Nikolai Alexandrovich Bulganin, one of the men rising fast to supreme prominence in the U.S.S.R.

Rokossovsky picked his mentor well. By 1946, Bulganin was an alternate of the Politburo; a full member in 1948; a member of the Supreme Soviet and chairman of its powerful Committee on Foreign Affairs; member of the Orgburo; deputy chairman of the Council of Ministers; minister of the Armed Forces; marshal of the Soviet Union.

In view of Rokossovsky's experience in the Leningrad jail, it would be foolish to assign to him personally too much importance and influence. Not Rokossovsky but Bulganin is the master of Poland's new destiny—continuing a job which he began in 1944 as Stalin's personal representative with the Communist Committee of National Liberation, for a time the shadow government of Poland. He then played a major role in the outbreak of the cold war, one that made the Yalta agreement a scrap of paper.

Even before the arrival of Rokossovsky in Poland, the Polish Army was singled out as the testing ground for experiments in military infiltration. After the seizure of power by the Polish Communists, the secret of Russian control over the Polish Army was maintained outwardly. But behind the façade of a national army apparently composed of Polish nationals was the reality of an international force honeycombed with Russian officers, most of them in staff or key command positions. A trusted politico-military officer of the Red Army General Staff, Lieutenant General Korchich, was sent from Moscow to act as chief of staff of the Polish Army. He had absolute control over the 150,000 officers and men of the Polish Army in which the Red Army of the U.S.S.R. had no fewer than 10,000 of its own officers.

With the progress of Communist indoctrination of a young proletarian officers' corps, the number of Russian officers was reduced to 3,000, but all now serving in Poland are in key positions or serve within the general staff which is hardly more than a branch of the Red Army's own general staff.

Few Poles are allowed to serve in the air force, which is completely controlled by the Russians. The Polish Navy, an effective fighting force superior in all respects to the clumsy naval force of the U.S.S.R., has been reorganized by Russian officers and was, in fact, the first branch of the Polish armed forces which lost its separate identity.[5]

THE DEPLOYMENT OF THE MARSHALS

Since Rokossovsky's arrival in Warsaw, the progress of integration has been stepped up. Today, one can no longer speak of an independent or national army in Poland. It became part and parcel of the Red Army of the U.S.S.R., or, as the Russians prefer to call it, of the advanced armed force of the proletarian world revolution.

Rokossovsky's assignment was not an isolated case.

In December, 1949, word reached us from Sofia that another satellite army had been placed under the supervision of still another Soviet marshal. This time it was the bullet-headed Ukrainian Feodor I. Tolbukhin, wartime commander of the Third Ukrainian Army group, who was made commander in chief of the revamped, enlarged, reoriented Bulgarian army. In his new position he continues to share authority with General Damyanov; but there are indications that Damyanov, too, will soon be branded a chauvinist for his determination to keep the Bulgarian Army Bulgarian.[6]

Tolbukhin's wartime colleague, Rodion Y. Malinovsky, is busy in the Far East, building a new Chinese Army, a new Northern Korean Army, and redeploying his own Red Army in the great *Aufmarsch-plan* (deployment plan) for the integration of Asia. Another one of Tolbukhin's colleagues, Ivan Fedorovich Petrov, advises the Hungarian Army—with the customary Soviet passion for anonymity of such advisers.

In Czechoslovakia, Marshal A. I. Yeremenko made his appearance, together with another senior officer of the Red Army General Staff, who is also a functionary of the Central Committee's Military Administration. His name is A. S. Gundorov. He was Ambassador Zorin's military aide during the *coup d'état* of 1948.[7]

At the turn of the half century, more and more information reached us about progressive expansion of Soviet military control throughout the Soviet world and of the deployment of topranking Soviet officers to key command positions beyond the Russian borders. It is impossible to discount these moves as routine developments. On the military map a pattern is gradually forming, a pattern that suggests to us the contours of the Great Stalin Plan in its important military sphere.

In this connection two intelligence items of supreme significance reached us in Washington. One came from Russianoccupied Germany, the other from Budapest in Hungary. From Germany came the news that Marshal Gregory K. Zhukov had arrived there to take supreme command of all Russian armed forces in the west. From Budapest came the news that Marshal Ivan Konev had arrived there to take command of all Russian armed forces in the south. Their assignments indicate the line of advance of the Soviet forces. Of the two, Zhukov's reappearance on the scene is of greater significance.

On October 1, 1946, General Eisenhower remarked that he had not heard from Zhukov for a year.[8] The inference was that Zhukov had fallen from grace and was no longer in favor. Soon afterward contradictions were received concerning Zhukov's fate. One of them related that he had been removed from his high post as the ranking marshal of the U.S.S.R. and replaced as commander in chief of all ground forces by Konev, in the wake of a bitter political controversy with Bulganin.

The other version related that he had been assigned to command the Soviet Union's southern armies with headquarters in Odessa, in preparation for an imminent march against Iran and the Middle East, including Greece. The latter version seemed then plausible in view of Soviet preoccupation. It appeared confirmed by agents and road and train watchers, reporting troop movements in the direction of Iran and Turkey, and the arrival of Russian officers in the mountain strongholds of the Greek guerillas.

The contradiction was never resolved. We had corroboration of the intelligence that Zhukov was in Odessa. It seemed that he was ill. He lived in a hospital of the trade unions, spending his days, so our informant reported, in quiet pursuits, occasionally going to church on Sundays. The report was explicit to the smallest detail, even listing Zhukov's telephone number where he could be reached. We never made an attempt, but we tried to gain additional information without much success.

The Zhukov mystery was long unsolved, and even in 1949, General Bedell Smith seemed to accept the version of disfavor when he wrote: "Great military leaders like Zhukov, whose ideas about co-operation with the West presumably conflicted with the Molotov policy, disappeared from the Moscow scene to posts of relative obscurity so quietly that it was hardly noticed." [9]

In recent months the Zhukov mystery took a new turn. The first hint of a change in his status was the appearance of Zhukov's name—virtually the only one thus mentioned—in Professor Pankratova's history textbook for secondary schools, prepared with infinite care and under the special supervision of Glavlit censors. He was given sole credit for the conquest of Berlin. [10]

Then, in a little-publicized lecture to an officers' club within the Kremlin walls, in which he surveyed informally the lessons of World War II, Stalin himself included Zhukov's name among "the splendid generals of a new type." And more than that, he mentioned him in first place, ahead of Konev, Vasilevsky, Tolbukhin, Govorov, and the late Vatutin.

Last, Zhukov was seen entering at regular intervals the fine eighteenth-century "palace on the Znamenka," which houses the Ministry of the Armed Forces and the Red Army General Staff. On its walls are inscribed the names of history's great fighters for freedom. Over its portal stands the quaint inscription: "If any will not work, neither let him eat."

Zhukov is working again. He occupies the center position in a new focal area of Soviet military activity in eastern Germany. His reappearance on the scene of his greatest triumphs marks the end of a situation which plagued Western intelligence for another reason as well. Until quite recently, the Western command of the Red Army was subdivided in three major headquarters: one at Liegnitz under Marshal Rokossovsky, who was the senior officer of the "troyka"; another in Karlshorst under Marshal Sokolovsky, who was second in the top command; and a third in Baden, under Colonel General Kuznetsov, the junior member of this distinguished group.

Then in 1949, Sokolovsky was recalled to Moscow. His place in Germany was assigned to a comparative newcomer, a young lieutenant general named Vassily Chuikov. His appointment to the important post at Karlshorst was astonishing, if only because of Chuikov's second-layer position and relative obscurity. No successor to Rokossovsky in Liegnitz was announced. A few months later it was inferred but not so stated that Chuikov would take care of that command as well.

The Karlshorst post is largely political, strictly conditioned by directives from home and not particularly difficult to run; all one has to say is *"nyet, nyet, nyet"* to all the suggestions of the other allies in Berlin. But the Liegnitz post is one of the major commands—if not the major command—of the Red Army. It was most unlikely that it would be assigned to a senior officer of Chuikov's junior rank. Soon it turned out that it was not. Chuikov's name was used merely as a smoke screen to conceal the fact that Rokossovsky's command had been given to Zhukov. There never was much publicity about this Liegnitz outpost of Soviet militarism. So it need not astonish us that Zhukov's assignment to Liegnitz was not accompanied by fanfares of propaganda. But the unusual secrecy in which his transfer is still being shrouded is indicative of considerations other than the mere habit of secrecy. The Soviet leaders refuse to announce Zhukov's return to the Red Army's most important active field command to conceal the new mission assigned to the growing Red Army in the West, and to its specific assignment within the new Soviet plans.

With Zhukov back in Germany, General Chuikov can devote undivided attention to his real duties in Berlin. There, in the Soviet zone, wearing a uniform grimly reminiscent of Hitler's Waffen SS, a new Soviet army is being created in what the Germans wryly call *Uternehmung Kanonenfutter*—"Operation Cannon Fodder." This is the designation all Germans on both sides of the great divide give to the thinly concealed effort of the Western allies and the Russians to let the Germans be the Hessians again in the military phase of the coming showdown between East and West.

In this scheme General Chuikov has an important and familiar role. A colonel at the time of Stalingrad, he rose rapidly in rank and influence, due chiefly to his association with Field Marshal Friedrich Paulus, General Walther von Seydlitz-Kreuznach, and the group of German senior officers who surrendered with them at Stalingrad. The morning after their surrender, the dream of resurrection was already in the minds of these German professionals, and that dream eventually aligned them with the Bolsheviks for World War III.[11]

The man who first recognized the gleam of hope in the eyes of those German generals, and who knew best how to exploit it, was Colonel Chuikov. One of the ablest German-language officers of the Red Army General Staff, he was assigned to conduct the interrogation of the most glittering group of prisoners any army ever took up to those 1943 days of Stalingrad. He reported his discovery and his idea to Nikolai A. Bulganin, future member of the Politburo, then chief political officer at the Red Army's Stalingrad headquarters. Chuikov asked permission to utilize this German group in a slick game of political warfare. Ever ready to recognize a chance, the Kremlin was quick to grant the necessary permission.

The surrendered generals were established in a schoolhouse at Dimitrov, a town not far from Moscow. They were encouraged to form their own organization, later called the Union of German Officers—in reality a skeleton general staff of a phantom army, then planning the rebirth of a new German army from the defeat of the old. Chuikov remained with them in Dimitrov, nominally as a liaison officer, in reality as their boss.

The Paulus-Seydlitz group, under the new leadership of others, has since moved out of the seclusion of Dimitrov, first to Kaliningrad (formerly Koenigsberg in East Prussia), then into the very heart of Russian-occupied Germany and to the historic center of Prussian militarism, to Potsdam. New men, like Vinzent Mueller and Otto Korfes, assumed active command while the fatally ill Seydlitz and the still-bewildered Paulus watch the play from the wings, in their role as military elder statesmen.[12]

Chuikov is in Germany chiefly to be close to his group of German somnambulists. The dream of Seydlitz, first dreamed in the tiny wooden shack on the outskirts of Stalingrad after his capture, is closer to realization today than at any time since 1945.

When Zhukov went to Odessa, his place at the head of the Soviet Union's mighty ground forces was taken by Ivan Konev, the Red Army marshal with a head like a billiard ball. For years he occupied third place, behind Vasilyevsky and Sokolovsky, in the new Red Army hierarchy. And even today, after Zhukov's return, he is firmly entrenched in fourth place.

But he, too, moved out of the Znamenka, into the field. His new command post is at Székesfehervar in Hungary. His forces are composed of the Soviet troops stationed in that country, but chiefly of the new joint Red Army forming out of the integrated satellite forces. The two posts, Zhukov's in Liegnitz and Konev's in Székesfehervar, are equals in rank and importance. Together they represent the most potent military force anywhere in Europe—as a matter of fact, anywhere in the world.

This, then, is the order of battle of Russia's marshals as they return mysteriously to the posts they occupied during World War II. Their journeys, concealed completely or carefully camouflaged, reveal a pattern of military revitalization—indeed, of mobilization.

Their reappearance on the scene of their recent glories is but one subordinate phase of the greater Soviet deployment for the day and for the precise execution of the plan. The return of the marshals is an event of immense significance, even though they might have come merely to watch rather than actually to cross the Rubicon.

17.

THE MOBILIZATION OF THE COMINFORM

THE DEPLOYMENT of the marshals is a most significant move. It shows that the U.S.S.R. is now determined to back up its dynamic diplomacy with military force, if need be.

Under "ideal revolutionary" circumstances the Red Army is not allowed to intervene in what the Bolsheviks call direct struggle. It is not allowed to wage an old-fashioned war. Wars are to be kept pure in their imperialist character so that they may develop, according to plan and schedule, into civil wars. With the Red Army involved in one or another, this plan may go astray. An army, both within or without Russia, may even become the source and the force of civil war *against* the Bolsheviks of the U.S.S.R. Thus the Red Army is kept intact and deployed only as an auxiliary force of the world revolution.[1] It is the sword of Damocles that hangs by a thin thread over the heads of those the Kremlin has singled out for conquest or destruction. It stood *behind* Mr. Vishinsky when he went to Rumania to overthrow King Mihai's government; it stood *behind* Mr. Pushkin, the NKVD diplomat, when he organized the *coup d'état* in Hungary; and it sends token forces—sometimes only a single Soviet marshal—into Poland when collaboration is found lagging. This is why in China, in Greece, in Viet Nam, the leaders of the national liberation movements wonder at the strange aloofness of the Red Army general staff.

The major militant force of the world revolution is the Cominform. We have seen in the description of the various patterns how sections of the Communist International, namely the regional Communist parties of individual countries, and the apparatus of the Cominform, namely the full-time professional revolutionary organization, work throughout the world on the basis of central directives received from Moscow.

For a long time, international bolshevism was, so to say, a civilian force. It fought its battles in the streets and in the factories. Its weapons were mass terror, political murder, the general strike, and the armed insurrection. Its wars were called rebellions, uprisings, revolutions. It frowned upon organized armies and navies, unless it could infiltrate them, to bore from within, and to shatter them as bulwarks of the bourgeois state. Even in 1928, the Communist International proclaimed the injunction that "armies, which form a constituent part of the bourgeois state apparatus, must not be democratized but broken up." [2] And Lange, in his Lenin School textbook for bolshevism's fledgling agitators and activists, wrote: "An effective fight for the destruction of the armed forces of the enemy demands that it be waged not just from the outside but also from the inside." [3]

But then suddenly international bolshevism found itself with a number of organized armies on its hands. There was, above all, the Red Army of the U.S.S.R.; [4] then all the armies of the satellites; the active partisans of Asia; the immense reserve forces of the Communist underground of World War II that fought its full-scale battles with tactical perfection. The Russian bosses of the Comintern faced the waxing dilemma of what to do with this unexpected growth of organized military strength within their own ranks, what to do to prevent it from becoming a Frankenstein's monster.

If it is allowed to sprawl and spawn, it might gain uncontrollable strength and turn against its master. If it is dispersed and abolished, bolshevism might deprive itself of a gigantic new force that may gain for it the victories on regular battlefields that could never be gained, or only in decades, in street fights and general strikes.

The dilemma was solved, as all such dilemmas of international bolshevism are, in the immense privacy of the Politburo of Russia's own Communist party.

When in September, 1947, the Comintern was revived under a new name, a secret protocol provided for the complete military co-ordination of all Cominform countries including France and Italy which are in the Western and not in the Soviet orbit.

For delegates from the Bolshevik countries of Eastern Europe, adherence to such a pact was a matter of no particular consequence. But for Jacques Duclos and Etienne Fajon, delegates from France, for Luigi Longo and Eugenio Reale, representatives of Italy, it was an act of high treason, if only because the secret pact outlined in detail plans for a co-ordinated military action against the West, including infiltration into the armed forces, sedition throughout the military apparatus, subversive activities and sabotage against the war economy of "the enemy" —including Duclos' own France and Longo's own Italy.

. Interior Minister Jules Moch of France is in possession of a copy of the secret protocol which thus indicts Duclos and Fajon, as well as, indeed, the Communist party of France, of high treason and conspiracy, not only against their own country but against the North Atlantic Alliance on which, to a large measure, France's own survival depends. Mario Scelba, Italy's minister of the interior, could also easily obtain access to the pact if he is not already in possession of a copy. It may be useful for them to review the situation created by the adherence of the French and Italian Communist parties to a military protocol under Russian domination, while their own governments adhere to a defense alliance binding them to the West. However, this is a matter for the countries directly involved to decide, even though their decision may affect the security of their allies as well.

The adherence of Hungary, Rumania, and Bulgaria to the pact raises a different kind of question. These are former Axis satellites whose defeat by the Russians was vastly aided by us. They are bound by the peace treaties which they signed freely in Paris, and which we ratified by solemn Congressional action. Their adherence to the military clauses of the Cominform *Resolution* represents a violation of those peace treaties. The U.S.S.R., which under those treaties is supposed to be our chief guardian over them, is an accomplice to their violation.[5]

The need for co-ordination and integration of the military establishments behind the iron curtain was described in the preamble of the protocol as "developing from the aggressive designs of the Anglo-American imperialists and their social-democratic stooges." The new alliance itself was described as defensive in character.

An addendum to the protocol provided for its implementation in explicit terms. It created a military administration within the Cominform with headquarters in Budapest, at 5 Akadémia Utca, to be specific. A Hungarian Communist whose Party alias is Mihály Farkas, a former printer's devil from Kosice who had spent half his life in the service of the Comintern and rose to clandestine military prominence during the Spanish Civil War, was appointed head of the committee, in fact, chief of a full-time, full-fledged Cominform Military General Staff. Today Farkas is Hungary's minister of defense.

The protocol, now fully implemented, created a new military force—the greatest single coalition army ever assembled in peacetime under a single command authority, with a single operational aim, under unified tactical training, with standardized equipment, and with a single logistic support.

According to the best available information, the Greater Red Army now comprises the following standing forces:

U.S.S.R.	1,360,000 (effective combatants, excluding reserves)
Poland	350,000
Czechoslovakia	200,000
Hungary	180,000
Rumania	300,000
Bulgaria	130,000
Albania	18,000

or a total of 2,538,000 officers and men of first-line troops in a state of readiness, many of their units at battle stations, with about 5,000,000 men in their organized reserves under continuous training.[6]

The military compact of the Cominform confronts us with a situation which is as dangerous for the continued tranquillity of the world as it is without precedent in political and military history.

But from the viewpoint of the satellites as well, the Greater Red Army created a situation that is entirely different from previous conditions within their military organizations. Originally, in 1945–47, the Kremlin showed no interest in the armed forces of its young satellites and did not require the Communist parties to claim the defense portfolios in the coalition cabinets in which they participated. With the exception of Bulgaria where an ex-instructor of the Frunze Military Academy, Russia's West Point, and one of the chief organizers of the International Brigade during the Spanish Civil War, a Bolshevik soldier of fortune named Georgi Parvanov Damyanov was named minister of war; and in Yugoslavia where Tito naturally retained the defense portfolio, the Communists allowed their partners in the coalition to catch and keep the ministries of war or defense.

In Hungary, the job was assigned to a toothless old democratic soldier, a general named Bartha, a member of the Small Landholder party. In Czechoslovakia it was, until recently, in the hands of Ludvik Svoboda, the Bohemian farmer's son who rose to his high post in hard fighting on both military and political battlefields, and gained the Kremlin's confidence as well as its Order of Lenin without ever joining the Communist party of Czechoslovakia. In Finland, the portfolio went to a social democrat. In Rumania, it was given to two professional soldiers, Generals Lascar and Damaceanu, both technicians (specialists) with no political affiliations.

But as the Kremlin was drifting toward a possible eventual military alternative in its long-range plans, the defense portfolio in satellite cabinets became as important a Communist plum as the interior portfolio, with its control over the police, was until then.

After Tito's deviation, in the summer of 1948, the drift became a mad rush. Mihály Farkas, chief of the Cominform's Military General Staff and prime mover of all military intrigues in the satellite world, became Hungary's minister of defense. In Rumania, the two specialists were replaced by Emil Bodnaras, son of a Ukrainian sharecropper who joined the Communists at the Fainious Artillery School of the Royal Rumanian Army, and then rose to second place behind Ana Pauker in the Rumanian Communist party. Bodnaras' appointment to his new post was symbolic of the trend: he became minister of national defense without relinquishing his control over the secret police.

In Czechoslovakia, General Svoboda continued in his post but was hemmed in by an influx of high-ranking Communists in the military and civilian posts of the army and air force.

Throughout the satellite world, native graduates of the various Soviet military schools and senior veterans of the Spanish Civil War were moved into key positions. Satellite armies were ruthlessly purged of all elements the Kremlin would not trust, including fanatical Communists with some Titoist coloration. Among the top-ranking officers who ended their lives either on the gallows or by bullets fired at the base of their brains, was Colonel General George Pálffy–Oesterreicher, chief of the Hungarian General Staff.[7] In Czechoslovakia, for example, Svoboda is virtually the only surviving member of the old officers' corps of the Masaryk-Benés republic.

With the assumption of control over their armed forces by the satellite countries' most trusted Communist leaders and with the elimination of all untrustworthy elements from staff and command positions in the satellite armies, the integration process was successfully concluded. The Greater Red Army was a reality.

It may be that the pact, as we said before, was directed against the signatories as much as it was aimed at the West. The secret protocol was designed, on the one side, to create a gigantic new Communist armed force of unprecedented strength, with bases and garrisons throughout the satellite world, and with clandestine outposts deep within the military body of the West. On the other side it demolished the independence of six national armies within the Soviet orbit and thus assured, or at least hoped to assure, that they would never turn on the U.S.S.R.

Whatever it did, it brought militarism to its crossroads. Previously, armies were bulwarks of reactionary forces and statism. Now they became major instruments of world revolution. Marx was often confronted with the reactionary aspects of militarism and despised it in all its manifestations. He regarded the proletarian masses of the world as the revolutionary army, but he suspected even the motley military forces of the American and French, the Prussian and Hungarian revolutions, an attitude justified by Napoleon's "Eighteenth Brumaire" in 1799, and his nephew's coup d'état in 1851, when the military forces of the revolution were expropriated for purposes of imperialism.[8]

Marx and Engels never dreamed that one day generals and admirals, bedecked with medals and gold braid and insignia, would become standard bearers of their revolutions. But Lenin did. In September, 1917, when the October Revolution was but one month away and yet seemed still remote, he wrote: "The Soviets are a new state apparatus, which, in the first place, provides an armed force of workers and peasants; and this force is not divorced from the people, as was the old standing army, but is most closely bound up with the people. From the military standpoint this force is incomparably more powerful than previous forces; from the revolutionary standpoint, it cannot be replaced by anything else." [9]

The Bolsheviks had more than thirty years to breed a new type of military men: the professional revolutionary who is also a professional soldier, who knows as much about dialectics as about ballistics, who can apply his revolutionary tactics to war just as he can adapt his military tactics to revolution. Hundreds if not thousands of Bolsheviks from all walks of life and from all countries of the world sat for many years on the benches of the Soviet Union's highest military schools, from the Voroshilov Superior War Academy in Moscow to the Kalinin Military Academy of Logistics at Kiev. They graduated from those schools with high honors and with high ranks in Russia's own Red Army.

Mehmed Shehu of Albania graduated from the American Vocational School of Tirana in 1932 and from the Frunze Military Academy of Moscow in 1946, a true cosmopolitan. Franz Honner of Austria graduated with the 1935 class, six years after Georgi Parvanov Damyanov of Bulgaria, who not only studied but later also taught at Frunze.

Ruggero Grieco of Italy, Rudolf Slansky of Czechoslovakia, Edwin Hoernle of Germany, André Marty of France, Nieh Jung-chen of China, Jorge Frianeza of the Philippines, Tuure Valdemar Lehen of Finland are but a few men whose names we picked at random from the long roster of foreign Bolsheviks who studied military science and tactics in the Russian West Point.

These men and their fellow graduates, scattered throughout the world, are now joined together in one great military fraternity. They form the practical link between the proletarian masses and the professional military forces of the new world revolution.

18.

HOW STRONG IS RUSSIA

IN THE operations plan he drafted in 1924, Stalin enumerated "the essential forces and chief reserves" of the world revolution. He spoke of the revolutionary movements in all countries, of the semiproletarian and petty-bourgeois masses in the highly developed countries, and of nationalist movements in colonial lands and dependent areas. In 1924, most of these forces were potentialities rather than realities, hopes rather than actual masses bent on rebellion. But today, only a little over twenty-five years after the drafting of the operations plan, Stalin has at his disposal a Grand Army of the Total Revolution that includes:

(1) The armed forces of the U.S.S.R. and of the satellites.

(2) The propaganda of world communism.

(3) The diplomatic arm of the U.S.S.R. and its satellites.

(4) The sections and the apparatus of the Communist Information Bureau.

(5) The permanent peace organization.

(6) The militant organization of science in the satellite world.

1. THE RED ARMY AND AIR FORCE

The Red Army of the U.S.S.R. is the product of Stalin's "Great Patriotic War" of 1941–45. It is an entirely new army which has no technological or ideological connection or association with the defunct military force that died with Marshal Tukchachevsky in the grand military purge of 1937, or with the enigmatic military forms which melted away, as if by magic,

193

under the heat of Hitler's offensive in 1941. Stalin created his new army in the image of the Tsarist generals who defeated Napoleon: "Let the heroic examples of our great forebears—Alexander Nevsky, Dimitri Donskoi, Kuzma Minin, Dimitri Pozharsky, Alexander Suvorov, and Mikhail Kutuzov—inspire you in this war," Stalin called out to the new recruits of the Red Army on November 7, 1941.[1]

In the course of World War II, this new Red Army, according to historian Pankratova, became "a fully seasoned army which had mastered the tactics of maneuvering, encircling, and annihilating the enemy."[2] Even in the development of his new strategy Stalin was guided by the example of the Tsarist's generals. Looking back on the war in February, 1946, he described how he had devised the strategic counteroffensive against the Germans, which in fact caused the Nazi defeat, on the basis of historical patterns. "This was also very well known," he said, "to our great Commander-in-Chief Kutuzov who destroyed Napoleon by a well-prepared counteroffensive."[3]

Stalin was prepared to go to extreme length in his apotheosis of the Tsar's generals and to defend them against all comers, not only bourgeois authorities on warfare but even the classics of Marxism. "Engels once said that of the Russian Commanders of the 1812 campaign the only one deserving attention was General Barclay de Tolly," Stalin said. "Engels, of course, was mistaken for Kutuzov as a commander stood head and shoulders above Barclay de Tolly. And yet, one still may find people who will defend this mistaken pronouncement of Engels."[4]

Stalin's adherence to and admiration for the armies of 1812 is reflected in the spirit which he inculcates in his new Red Army. All, or virtually all, the elements and symbols of morale promotion are remnants of the Tsarist armies, producing incongruities one would scarcely expect to find in a revolutionary force.[5] But the recent war showed that this emulation of an imperialist force represents part of the strength of the new army.

The physical strength of this army is epitomized in its numerical superiority over its potential opponents. While the army of the United States has an authorized strength of only 670,000 men, and the British army has only 345,000 officers and men, a reliable estimate puts the Red Army's peacetime effective strength at 2,150,000 officers and men. This figure excludes all para- and semimilitary formations, the militia (organized police), and the troops of the MVD and MGB.[6] The Red Army is organized into six armies, and has approximately 160 divisions, with about 10,180 per division. By contrast the North Atlantic Pact envisages a total of 36 divisions to be put into the field by its eleven member nations by 1955. Right now there are only 22 divisions on the Continent and only twelve of them are in any shape to move. Italy's six divisions are ill equipped. The Netherlands have no army to speak of.[7] Even the armies of Belgium and France are far from representing an effectively organized striking force, as opposed to the fully mobilized Greater Red Army of the Cominform countries which we described in a previous chapter.

The organization of the Red Army consists of new type very mobile rifle divisions (with 11,000 men in each) which are moved entirely by motor; of old-type rifle divisions which still depend on animal transportation; of mechanized divisions (of 12,500 to 13,000 men in each) with forty or more self-propelled heavy-armored guns, twenty or more heavy tanks, sixty to seventy T-34 tanks, mortars, howitzers, at least twelve 132-mm rocket launchers, 37-mm AA guns in each division. Tank divisions of 10,500 men in each have 182 to 210 T-34 tanks, forty to fifty heavy tanks, twenty to twenty-five heavy-armored self-propelled guns, in addition to the familiar mortars and howitzers, and the not-so-familiar rocket launchers, in each division.

Artillery divisions of 10,000 men each have medium and heavy guns, including 76-mm and 122-mm guns, 122-mm and 152-mm howitzers. Immense emphasis is being placed on new weapons, such as rocket launchers and guided missiles. New tactical plans are being designed which take into consideration the absolute weapons that made their appearance after the war.

The Russian Air Force, under the Ministry of the Armed Forces, is organized in two major groupings in the West and Far East. There exists an independent long-range striking force directly under the High Command. The establishment of this force indicates that the U.S.S.R. has now embraced the idea of strategic bombing while previously it frowned upon all aerial

assaults not in tactical support of ground operations. The existence of this force under General Gumarov is a distinct indication of Soviet designs and intentions in an intercontinental war.

The militarized formations of the Ministry of the Interior
(MVD) and other secret-police units have their own air forces.
A civilian air organization is maintained as a paramilitary force
and as the reservoir of the Air Force's personnel needs. As to its
strength, the U.S.S.R. Army Air Force is said to have from 8,000
to 16,000 first-line operational planes, with a personnel of 600,-
000 to 700,000 officers and men. The best available information
places the material strength of the Red Air Force at 7,500 first-
line planes, including such recent developments as the Ilyushin
12 supertransport and the Tupolov bombers, said to be copies of
the B-29's.

According to Soviet figures, U.S.S.R. aircraft production
amounted to 120,000 planes over a period of three years between
1944 and 1946; present-day production is estimated at 60–10,000
planes per year. However, deficiencies of precision-instrument
production and delays in completing blueprint designs retard
full development of the Red Air Force, despite the fact that at
the present moment 70,000 scientists and scientific workers aid
in meeting material needs of the Red Air Force. Stalin's personal
interest in the Air Force is regarded as a major boost. The
U.S.S.R. also has bomb sights, radar, and other wartime developments, but constant autocriticisms indicate technical deficiencies.
A recent trend in Soviet aircraft development is the building of
superior jet planes, patterned after German designs, and long-
range bombers, under the overall supervision of General
Tupolov.[3]

2. THE RED FLEET

Despite the growth of the Red Fleet during the last five years,
concentrated mainly in an oversized submarine force, the Soviet
Union will not become a major seapower capable of commanding the seas beyond her immediate maritime interests until 1966.
This is the unanimous opinion of qualified observers in the
United States and Great Britain, who base their estimate on
meager published data but voluminous intelligence reports. But
they concede that with a gigantic industrial base now being

prepared and a construction program planned for the next twenty years, the Soviet Union eventually will join the naval constellation now dominated by the United States and the British Empire.[9]

Since Generalissimo Stalin's pronouncement on July 21, 1945, that the Russian people want "a still stronger and mightier Navy" and "will create new fighting ships and new bases" for it, Soviet seapower has played a major role in all diplomatic considerations. Very little is known of this navy and even less of the strategic purposes it may one day serve. The role it may play in present Russian plans has been sensationalized and overstated.

As to its strength, the Red Fleet of today is far stronger and much better equipped than at any time during the past twenty-five years. As seapowers go, however, it is still a minor force, occupying third or fourth place among naval powers. It owes much of its present strength to the aid it received from the United States and Great Britain during World War II.

A total of 545 combatant vessels of varying size were supplied the Soviet Union by the United States between 1941 and the end of the war. The largest single unit was the 7050-ton *Milwaukee*, a light cruiser built in 1918. (This ship was later returned to and scrapped by the U.S. Navy.) Among other vessels lend-leased to Russia were torpedo boats, submarine chasers, patrol frigates, minesweepers, landing craft, and icebreakers. In addition, four floating workshops were delivered to the U.S.S.R., providing the nucleus of a Russian fleet train.

A relative contribution was made by Great Britain, which released the old battleship, *Royal Sovereign* (29,150 tons), and built scores of smaller craft for the Red Fleet. The total combatant tonnage which Russia obtained from her allies amounted to almost 200,000 tons, or approximately one fourth of the total tonnage she had in 1941, prior to losses suffered during the war.

Russia's battleships are either antiquated (some of them were built as long as thirty-five years ago) or badly scarred by war. On the other hand, the much-advertised German claim that the *Marat* had been sunk and the *Oktiabrskaya Revolutia* disabled was effectively refuted in February, 1944, when a Russian naval force built around these battleships shelled German defenses along the Estonian coast. The present building program calls for the completion of three to five 35,000-ton battleships, the largest vessels ever built in the Soviet Union. Some of the intact Italian ships were transferred to the Soviet Union.

On the basis of recent developments in the war at sea, Russia's weakness in cruisers is her greatest naval deficiency. The small number of cruisers available to her fleet automatically excludes her as a major seapower, at least for the time being. An ambitious construction program provides for several new cruisers of approximately 8,000 tons each, to be added to the Red Fleet's six modern *Kirov*-class cruisers, which now form the core of Russian seapower.

WORLD'S GREATEST UNDERSEA POWER

The present-day strength of Russian seapower is concentrated in what appears to be the world's largest submarine fleet and it is in this category that the Red Fleet represents a formidable offensive force and a major factor in the Soviet's armed strength. The Red submarine fleet is now estimated at not less than 200 units, but it is possible that Russia has up to 400 submarines, counting the German U-boats she captured intact or slightly damaged in Baltic ports.

Naval experts consider a fleet of 300 submarines sufficient to decide a *guerre de course* (commerce war at sea), even against fleets which may be superior in surface strength, provided the submarines are handled with skill and economy. They attribute the failure of the Nazi Fleet largely to its initial weakness in U-boats. Germany started the war with hardly more than forty U-boats of which only ten to twelve were operational. But with this inadequate force, German U-boats sank the British battleship *Royal Oak* and the aircraft carrier *Courageous* during the opening months of the war, and inflicted heavy damage on Britain's mercantile marine.

The wartime record of Soviet submarines gained the respect of international observers. Breaking out of an ingenious mine blockade with which the Germans succeeded in bottling up the Soviet Baltic Fleet, the Russian subs sank about 1.2 million tons of German shipping between June, 1941, and October, 1943, in the Baltic Sea alone. The total destruction of German tonnage which Soviet propaganda credited to Russian submarines is obviously exaggerated, but there is reason to believe that Soviet undersea craft destroyed or damaged 960 German vessels, totaling over 1.8 million tons.

Russia's ability to build and repair submarines is quite considerable. The 200-ton *Malodki*-type subs are fabricated in inland factories, particularly at Gorki, and shipped by rail to assembly ports. The range of the *Malodkis* limits their use to short operational cruises. But they are effective as defenders of a coast against invasion.

The Russians themselves indicated their confidence in their subsurface strength when they agreed to the destruction of German U-boats captured by the Royal Navy instead of claiming their share. A total of 114 U-boats were sunk subsequently in what became known as Operation Deadlight, in the presence of Russian naval observers.[10]

The Red Fleet's greatest improvement over its prewar strength was made in the category of small and smallest combatant craft. In torpedo boats alone Russia received 185 vessels, or six times the number of boats she had prior to the war. Her own thirty torpedo boats, most of them inherited from the Tsarist Fleet, are now ready for the scrap heap.

This fleet of small craft has particular significance for Russia, as her defense system is based on a network of canals which connect her major naval outlets. Some of these canals are known to both geographers and strategists everywhere in the world, but the existence of others is clouded by secrecy which also attends Russia's future canal-building plans. German forces which captured some of the canals were surprised to find that, contrary to common belief, some canals permitted the passage of light cruisers.

Russia's network of canals is designed to remedy a deficiency caused by the length of the Soviet coastline and the wide separation of first-class bases. This compels the Russians to maintain four independent and self-contained fleets in the Far North, in the Baltic, in the Black Sea, and in the Far East, in addition to three flotillas on the Amur and Dnieper Rivers and the Caspian Sea. The system of canals when completed will permit the transfer of entire flotillas, even from the Arctic Ocean to the

Black Sea, by direct overland route. Only major units will need
to be tied down with individual fleets. Their screens, escorts, and
trains can be assembled rapidly whenever and wherever they are
needed.

The Red Fleet receives an immense appropriation from the
Soviet budget. In 1941 alone, over 12 billion rubles ($2½ bil-
lion) was allocated to the Soviet Navy. The rate of new construction of which Soviet industry is capable was revealed in
1939–40, when 280 new surface ships were built. Although no
accurate data are available as to ships now being built or projected, it may be assumed that the rate of postwar construction
has reached prewar level in 1947 or 1948. At the rate of 150–200
ships and craft per year, and with the same emphasis on seapower which Russia has put on her ground forces, the Red Fleet
might reach the major league of maritime powers by 1956.

During this period she can expand the industrial base on
which modern seapower is founded, replace or modernize her
obsolete units, and construct new vessels along unprecedented
lines, revolutionizing naval architecture. How far atom strategy
will interfere with or modify her present plans is, of course, a
matter of conjecture. Articles in the official journal of the Red
Fleet indicate that Russian naval experts expect no immediate
changes and intend to proceed with plans stemming from the
preatomic age of seapower.

Russia will need in the meantime the freedom of the seas for
her mercantile marine, which grew to immense proportions
during the war. It is this overall maritime field rather than the
purely naval field that determines Russian foreign policy in its
pressing need for warm-water ports. The possession of a merchant marine now exceeding one million tons is dominant in
shaping Russian intentions and immediate plans for ports in
the Mediterranean, the North Sea, and the Persian Gulf.

3. THE REVOLUTIONARY USE OF THE ARMED FORCES

The war theory of the Russian General and Naval Staffs is
unique in so far as it forms only one part of the Soviet grand
strategic concept. In this concept military considerations are
fused with revolutionary requirements. The armed forces are
used as auxiliaries of the revolution.

Stalin revealed his military ideas in startling frankness in the March, 1947 issue of *Bolshevik,* the chief theoretical journal of the Communist party. It was in answer to a letter from Colonel E. Razin who asked Stalin to clarify for him the official Kremlin attitude on the German military philosopher Clausewitz. Stalin's answer was organized in three sections: (1) an affirmation of the thesis that Lenin's appraisal of Clausewitz has grown obsolete; (2) an excellent critique of Clausewitz's military theories; and (3) a brief exposition of Stalin's own theses of war. Stalin strongly criticized Colonel Razin for his failure to take the strategic counteroffensive in consideration.

"I speak of a counteroffensive after a successful offensive by the enemy in which, however, decisive results have not been achieved, and during which the defender gathers his forces, goes over to the counteroffensive, and inflicts upon the enemy a decisive defeat.... Even the ancient Parthians understood such a counteroffensive when they lured the Roman commander Crassus with his armies into the interior of their country, then went over to the counteroffensive and destroyed him." [11] As we have seen, he attributed Kutuzov's success against Napoleon to this same grand strategic concept.

American military experts regard Stalin's letter as the fullest and frankest expression of his basic strategic and tactical ideas. In this connection Paul M. Kober wrote in *Military Affairs,* journal of the American Military Institute: "It should be clearly understood that Stalin's letter, despite its informality, is an authoritative policy document, and that no military theories are now being taught in Russia that in any way conflict with the ideas here expressed." [12]

Though the significance of these passages from Stalin's historic letter cannot be overemphasized, they refer only to Stalin's theories in the purely military field. This is but one role, the conventional role, the Red Army is supposed to play in the Bolshevik order of things. Stalin's concept of the Red Army *per se* was outlined in no uncertain terms in a speech on the tenth anniversary of the Army. It was reprinted in June, 1941, as a morale builder, during the opening days of the war against Germany.

"What are the peculiarities which constitute the source of

strength and power of our Red Army?" Stalin asked. "In distinction from other armies, our Red Army has the peculiarity that it is a weapon for liberation of workers and peasants from the yoke of landowners and capitalists. Our army is an army for the liberation of the toilers. . . .

"Our people and army constitute one entity, one family. . . . We love, respect and care for our army. . . .

"What does love by a people for their army mean? This means that such an army will have the strongest rear, and that such an army is invincible. What is an army without a strong rear? Nothing. . . .

"A second peculiarity of our Red Army is that it is an army of brotherhood among the peoples of our country. . . .

"This is a pledge that at the most critical moment our army will find the greatest support from the millions of masses of each and every nationality inhabiting our immense country. . . .

"*The third peculiarity of the Red Army consists of the spirit and feelings of internationalism which imbue our entire Red Army. . . . Our army is an army of world revolution, and an army for workers of all countries. . . . This circumstance is a source of strength and power for our army, because our Red Army has an innumerable number of friends and allies in all parts of the world, from Shanghai to New York, and from London to Calcutta.*" (Our italics.) [13]

The strategic concept based on this catalogue of Bolshevik virtues was outlined in detail in the classic manual of the Red Army, in Marshal Boris Shaposhnikov's *The Brain of the Army,* a two-volume work on the role and functions of the General Staff in war.

A young Tsarist officer at the time of the Revolution, Shaposhnikov joined the Red Army and soon became one of its intellectual leaders. He attracted the attention of Stalin, who encouraged him to incorporate his ideas in a book. This book, although published in 1927, has never lost its hold on Stalin's imagination. Stalin is said to know its basic tenets by heart. Visitors to his office or private quarters discovered Shaposhnikov's book on his desk and night table. Stalin himself said that during World War II, passages from it provided his daily reading. The Marshal's death a few years ago did not diminish his influence, and now he joins M. V. Frunze, one of the two original builders of the Red Army (the other, of course, was Trotsky), as one of the philosophers of the Soviet Union's reoriented armed forces.

Shaposhnikov accepted Clausewitz's basic tenet that war is a continuation of policy by other means, but he proposed to go far beyond it. According to him "war is both the highest form and the most important weapon of politics."

"Wars are conducted by states," Shaposhnikov wrote, and "not by the armed forces alone. Wars cannot be locked within the confines of strategy which is the specialty of professional military men, because war is a definite form of social relations and not merely an armed struggle for the annihilation of others. In the final analysis, victory is gained or defeat is suffered, not by armies, but by peoples as a whole. With them is defeated or helped to victory the entire machinery of the state in whose hands the direction of the war must be concentrated." [14]

The practical strategic consequence of this doctrine is the alternate use of politics and of war, either singly or jointly, as circumstances demand. This type of war is not directed by any one military organization, but by the supreme political organization of the state, in Russia's case the Politburo.

Thus war assumes a total and permanent character. Every act of the state and of its individual parts represents a tactical move to implement the strategic concept. From this point of view, a speech delivered by Foreign Minister Vishinsky at Lake Success, the general strike of French workers, the building of a new power plant in the Kazakh Republic, the term papers prepared by children in Russian schools must be regarded as tactical moves.

In this concept the whole proletarian world is engaged in fighting Russia's war for world supremacy. Meanwhile the U.S.S.R. proper maintains its military might as a deterrent or as an implement of persuasion to be used only as a last resort.

OPERATIONAL THINKING

Ellsworth L. Raymond tried to gauge the operational thinking of the Red Army's generals. He studied the writings of its outstanding specialists and found unbroken preoccupation with land warfare in which they recognize the Soviet Union's best military chance. "A belief that any future war may be decided by a massed attack from the air," Raymond found, "with the lavish use of atomic and other absolute weapons seems to be discounted and even frowned upon."

As a matter of fact, Colonel V. Chalikov went on record to dispute General Carl Spaatz of the U.S. Air Force in his views on the overwhelming contemporary importance of strategic aviation. According to Chalikov, Spaatz exaggerated the role and importance of his particular service. "Joint operations by all types of troops," he wrote, "are far more important than aviation alone," emphasizing an idea that appears to be the major theme of current Russian military thinking.[15]

How, then, do Russian military thinkers envisage the shape of a future war? According to them it will undoubtedly start with a mass attack from the air, in which the attacker will utilize all kinds of absolute weapons, leading to a temporary economic paralysis of the attacked. On this score, Soviet military specialists state bluntly that they do not expect decision in this first phase of the future war. They are emphatic in their belief that the war will continue long after this first all-out assault. Since decision cannot be gained immediately, they expect the war to settle down to a protracted period of attrition, not unlike the period which followed the initial German attack on Russia in World War II, but on a far more gigantic scale.

This indecisive strategic assault is expected to be followed by the second phase in which conventional armaments are again expected to come into their own. Among such conventional are now listed jet planes, rocket guns, and guided missiles.

The decisive phase of this imaginary war is its third, in which the nation attacked mounts what Colonel Pavlenko, too, calls the "strategic counteroffensive." It is in this third phase that all new weapons are put to effective tactical use with an appropriate regard for vastly increased mobility and firepower.

The scope of this strategic counteroffensive knows no limitations. It aims at "the total annihilation of the exhausted and defeated army." This phase ends with what General Bronewski calls "operational pursuit on a strategic scale" in which jet planes and self-propelled rocket artillery will play a predominant role.[16]

From this description of the future war, based on original Soviet sources, it is evident that the Russians expect to be attacked in the first phase, and to mount the strategic counteroffensive in the third. Despite the departure from Clausewitz's theories, they still agree with the German military philosopher that geography is the invincible ally of the Russians. It is their geographical advantage which permits them almost endless retreats in depth which, they believe, will enable them to withstand the second phase and prepare for the third during its protracted period of attrition.

4. THE PROPAGANDA MACHINE

The farmers of Nebraska may be supporting a number of strange causes, but they can hardly be accused of supporting the causes of Moscow.

And yet, during the 1935 Congress of the Communist International, they were honorably mentioned by the Comintern's keynote speaker whose task was to review the "victories of the past ten years" (1925–35, remarkable, in fact, for Bolshevik defeats from China to Germany).

In his global report to the first plenary session of the Comintern, German delegate Wilhelm Pieck (today president of the Soviet-controlled East German regime) praised the Iowa and Nebraska farmers for what he called "their organized strike against capitalist exploitation." He gave them full credit for "a major contribution to world revolution." [17]

Bolshevism knows well how to gain the utmost benefit from such innumerable inadvertent aids—from statements made in a convention of the National Association of Manufacturers; from the way of life of Washington dowagers; from an article Mr. Truman wrote for a New York weekly some years ago; from the low quality of Hollywood pictures; from the amount of whisky consumed annually in Henderson, Kentucky—all the way to the suffocating heat of a New York summer day among the tenements of Hell's Kitchen.

As a matter of fact, these are actual items all used by the Bolsheviks in an undeclared war: the war of propaganda.

While in the United States propaganda is derided and
frowned upon, in the U.S.S.R. it is raised to an exalted position,
is utilized without qualifications and used as an instrument of
power, first, to serve the Soviet Union's foreign political aims,
and, second, to advance world-revolutionary designs under
dominant Russian leadership.

Propaganda is, in fact, tool number one in the vast arsenal of
international bolshevism.[18]

The propaganda departments of the U.S.S.R. employ 1,-
401,000 full-time, paid, professional workers. This number
exceeds by about 400,000 the personnel employed in the political police organization of the MVD. It does not include the
millions of Party and State officials who, in their capacity as
"political workers," must act as part-time propaganda functionaries, and who in special emergencies swell the numbers
engaged in propaganda up to about 5 per cent of the total
population.

This standby rank and file, the skeleton of the complex Agitprop organism, include graduates of the Sverdlov School of
Propaganda or of the Highest Party School; agitators of the
Political Administration of the Armed Forces; propagandists of
the innumerable regional organizations (there are 25,000 of
them in the Leningrad party committees alone) ; thousands of
workers, teachers, librarians, motion-picture operators, lecturers, and other minor functionaries in the Agitpunkts (propaganda centers), down to an official called "conversationalist." He
is the amoeba among Soviet propagandists, a one-man cell, his
efforts aimed at the individual. He disseminates prepared propaganda in seemingly casual conversations with fellow citizens in
the Russian town and country. The Agitprop regards him as its
most valuable prop.

Soviet propagandists are rarely allowed a quiet period of
routine activities. Like an automobile engine that is purposely
kept racing, the Soviet political machinery is deliberately maintained in a perpetual state of stringent haste, permitting no
mental relaxation, even for occasional short breathing spells.

From time to time, the urgent propaganda drive is forced into
higher gear. Special campaigns demand partial or full mobilization of propaganda manpower. During a nationwide election

campaign "more than 3,500,000 agitators conduct propaganda in the election districts." Propaganda personnel aiding in one recent bond drive numbered 5,000,000. Campaigns to increase agricultural production are conducted by "an army of 1,000,000 rural agitators." An ordinary production drive in the factories involves "the mobilization of 1,500,000 industrial propagandists."

The greatest mobilization involves 10,000,000 propagandists, agitators, and political workers. It has occurred but twice in history. The first was in 1938, coincident with the publication of *The History of the Communist Party of the Soviet Union* (Bolsheviks), edited by a special commission of the Central Committee under Stalin's personal supervision. This is the official version of events, presented to fit the Stalinist party line and to aid in the prevention of unwitting deviations from it.

The second total propaganda mobilization started after World War II and continues today on behalf of the first postwar Five Year Plan. Based on the old Five Year Plan formula and pinned to Stalin after whom it is named, the campaign is designed to promote reconstruction and rehabilitation. The drive renews itself from year to year, claiming the full energy and time of 10,000,000 Soviet citizens. This means that more than 5 per cent of the 180,000,000 population are working day after day calling the rest of their work benches, the scaffoldings, the mines, the fields.

Both the major and the minor campaigns are kindled at the apex of the propaganda hierarchy and then carried like an Olympic torch across the whole land, gaining momentum as they spread. However abstruse some of the themes, slogans, or subjects may be, they soon become the major topics of Soviet conversation everywhere—often, as planned, excluding other topics.

HOW IT WORKS

The execution of the gigantic Soviet propaganda program is entrusted to an immense and intricate network of agencies. In them, as in most Soviet agencies, there exists an organizational dualism, Party and State separately administering policies. Party and State (theoretically) also establishing them. Actually, propaganda policy is ordinarily shaped by the Communist party, either in the Central Committee, or in the Politburo. Only very seldom does the State's executive organ, the Council of Ministers, make a policy decision involving propaganda and agitation. The major policy decisions are made by the Central Committee. The few that originate with the State usually emanate from the Ministry of Education.

Not only policy but most of the propaganda efforts and agitational work are the responsibility of the Party. The agency which performs these duties—a sort of Propaganda Ministry—is the Central Committee's second bureau, the Administration of Propaganda and Agitation. It is this which is known as Agitprop. Two other subsections of the Central Committee also are devoted to propaganda: the Political Administration of the Section of Military Affairs, and the Propaganda Department of the Section of Foreign Affairs. The latter has charge of the Soviet Union's international propaganda effort, including such activities as those conducted by the Cominform.

In the government, as distinguished from the Party, propaganda is centered in the Ministry of Education. All teachers are, in the final analysis, propaganda functionaries. The Ministry has a number of subsidiary propaganda agencies for administrative or control purposes.

The Agitprop itself is organized in five divisions: (1) Division for Party Propaganda and Agitation, (2) Division for the Press and Publishers, (3) Division for Schools, (4) Division for Cultural Enlightenment, (5) Division for Science and Scientific Inventions and Discoveries.

Each of these five divisions has several subdivisions, departments, branches, and sections. Most important of all is the Division of Current Events, which is also in charge of foreign affairs and co-operates with the Agitprop of the Department of Foreign Affairs within the Central Committee.

This organization is duplicated throughout the hierarchical and geographical organizations of Russian communism; *okrug, oblast, krai, city, and raion* committees of the Party. From the bottom to the top of the huge pyramid, each Agitprop resembles in structure all the others, except that only the Central Committee in the apex has a foreign department.

Although he is not himself a member of the Politburo, the

chief of Agitprop ranks among the top twenty-five Russian leaders. At present this post is occupied by D. T. Shepilov, a relatively young man, former editor of *Pravda*. The overwhelming importance of the post of chief propagandist is signified by the fact that at one time or another it was occupied by Stalin himself, and by Zhdanov, when he was second only to Stalin in his party eminence. Shepilov's immediate predecessor was Mikhail Suslov, who is now reputed to be a candidate member (alternate) of the Politburo in charge of propaganda mobilization and the international peace campaign. Suslov rather than Shepilov is the man behind the immense propaganda war the U.S.S.R. is conducting against the West.[19]

No single instrument better exemplifies the gigantic scope of this cold war than a mysterious radio station called the Stalin Transmitter. It was built at the Generalissimo's personal order somewhere in the Ural Mountains, far beyond the reach of the German invaders. Up to 1943, the station was in charge of Comintern broadcasts, together with a 500-kw station called Moskva Imeni Kominterna, administered by the *Minsviazi* (Ministry of Communications), but disseminating the propaganda of the Third International. Its call letters, RW-1, were familiar to all listeners of Soviet broadcasts.

The mystery station was built with Lend-Lease material shipped by RCA to *Narkomsviazi* in Kuybyshev. It soon became the Big Bertha of World War II's all-out propaganda campaign. Starting out with 750 kws, its power was gradually increased until it reached the unusual strength of 2,500 kws. It is, by about five times the most powerful station in the world, capable of transmitting medium- and long-wave broadcasts over unprecedented distances, guaranteeing almost certain clear reception.

Big Bertha was used for a variety of purposes: it jammed German broadcasts beamed to the U.S.S.R.; and then in turn it beamed effective propaganda to the Germans, and later to the Japanese, penetrating deep into the hinterlands on both fronts; it guided Red pilots all along the combat zones; it served as an overall electronic aid in many a secret operation.

Its most spectacular feat is revealed here for the first time: Big Bertha was the phantom station which heckled Adolf Hitler and **Dr. Paul Joseph Goebbels** during their most important speeches, shouting, "Lies!" and similar invectives on synchronized wave lengths from 1,500 miles away. It was apparently the heckling of this unknown station which more than anything else succeeded in driving Hitler off the air for protracted periods of time.

Today, despite the mounting intensity of the cold war, Big Bertha is relatively quiet. It operates with only 500 kws—but it has 2,000 in reserve to be used when and if Generalissimo Stalin declares a supreme propaganda emergency. It bears watching by all who are interested in the outcome of the cold war. It may yet become an audible seismograph, roaring a warning in a voice that talks with the unprecedented stentorian strength of 2,500 watts.

The Stalin Transmitter is also attached to the propaganda section of the Agitprop's Department of Foreign Affairs. The tools employed by the 400 men in this department are, like Big Bertha, all capable of being heard afar. A propaganda line laid down in Moscow goes out, via the Foreign Affairs Department, to Communist Party magazines, newspapers, bulletins, lecturers, even conversationalists, in every nation where a Party cell exists. The department is particularly effective through the Cominform and in those countries which belong to that propaganda organization.

5. THE MACHINERY OF TOTAL DIPLOMACY

Blocking the visitor's view as he sets out on a sight-seeing tour from the heart of Moscow is a huge red Victorian building. It is called in hushed tones "the Lubyanka" by Muscovites with a keen respect for authority. It is the headquarters of the MVD, used to accommodate thousands of political prisoners since the days of its first head, Leo Dzershinsky.

Looking out of a window of the Lubyanka, one's eye follows the broad boulevard as it turns northwest into busy Kusnetsky Most, to another huge building of equal fame throughout the world: the edifice of the Soviet Foreign Office, or Minindel.

Drawing the sight-seer's attention is a statue of Vaslov Vorovsky in front of the Foreign Office. A martyr of the Soviet Foreign Service, Vorovsky was one of the two Soviet diplomats killed at their posts by assassins. He was murdered in Lausanne in 1923, four years before his colleague Pavel Voykov met a similarly sudden death in Warsaw.

To the hundreds of Minindel officials streaming to their desks in the morning, Vorovsky's statue is more than a mere memento of the hazards of diplomacy. To them it is a reminder that Soviet diplomacy is still in its *Sturm und Drang* period; that many accounts, opened in 1917–18, are still not satisfactorily settled today.

Since 1917, the U.S.S.R. has had only four foreign ministers (they were called commissars till January 1, 1946) : Chicherin, Litvinov, Molotov, and Vishinsky, while the U.S. has had nine Secretaries of State, and Britain has had nine foreign secretaries since 1917.

A similar constancy has not been evident in the ranks of Soviet diplomats stationed abroad. Especially in recent years, the entire diplomatic corps of the U.S.S.R. has undergone a grandiose transfusion to siphon new blood into the old Soviet foreign office.

Today there are hardly any old-timers in the Soviet diplomatic corps. But while the replacements may be newcomers to foreign lands, they are by no means novices in diplomacy. Tailormade for their posts, they are fully indoctrinated in what Vladimir Potemkin once aptly called "the duties peculiar to a Soviet envoy." [20]

It would be erroneous to assume that these young diplomats were haphazardly chosen for important posts, that their nomination was a form of patronage, or that they are mere fronts for secret agents surreptitiously working behind the diplomatic façade. Very often they are the agents themselves. The appointment of Foma Trebin to Venezuela reveals the consideration which today determines the selection of a Soviet envoy. Venezuela is recognized by the Soviet Union as one of the world's foremost oil-producing countries. Accordingly, an oil expert in the person of Trebin was chosen as the first Soviet minister.

To the Syrian-Lebanese post the Minindel named Daniel Solod, a graduate of the Tiflis School, which specializes in the problems of the Middle East. Alexei D. Chiborin, envoy to Egypt, is an alumnus of the same school, as was Abdurrahman

F. Sultanov, perennial secretary in the Cairo Legation. Much of the experience accumulated in Iran and Afghanistan is taught theoretically at Tiflis and applied practically in Beirut, Damascus, Cairo, Teheran, and Kabul.

The size of Soviet diplomatic missions has often been represented in exaggerated terms. One hears of scores, if not hundreds of diplomats allegedly attached to Russian embassies and legations. The fact is that even if the Soviet Union wanted to overstaff its foreign missions, it could not do so for lack of qualified personnel. There are an average of thirty to forty persons attached to major Soviet diplomatic missions, but only a fraction of the staffs are *bona fide* diplomats. The rest is composed of chauffeurs, doorkeepers, domestics, clerks, who enjoy no diplomatic privileges or immunities. The secret agents, MVD operatives, saboteurs, are among these men of nondiplomatic status. [21]

A relatively large diplomatic staff is maintained in Turkey, with fifteen accredited diplomats, and in Norway, with fourteen diplomatic representatives. By contrast, Britain has twenty-three and the United States forty-eight officials of diplomatic status in Turkey. The U.S. has twenty-eight diplomats attached to its Oslo Embassy. The largest Soviet diplomatic mission outside London, Paris, and Washington is maintained in Stockholm where the Soviet Union has twenty-four diplomats as compared with forty-three Americans and twenty Britons.

The ways of Soviet diplomacy puzzle onlookers and intrigue those who come into professional contact with them. And as mysterious as the protagonists of today's Soviet diplomacy are the aims of the foreign policy entrusted to their seemingly untried hands. The present informational vacuum sharply differs from the days of Georgi Chicherin and Maxim Litvinov, when Russian envoys were popular figures in the drawing rooms of the countries with which the Soviet Union maintained diplomatic relations. Emerging from the revolutionary underground, from Tsarist prisons, or from shabby basement dwellings to which the poverty of exile confined them, Soviet diplomats shone brightly on the international firmament of the late '20's and early '30's.

In London, for example, men like Leonid B. Krassin, Gregory

Sokolnikov, and even Ivan I. Maisky are remembered as conformists who seemed to have succeeded in adjusting themselves to the manners of the old school. In Washington, the days of Alexander A. Troyanowsky are cherished by the dowagers of Massachusetts Avenue who now look to 1125 Sixteenth Street as if it were an exotic abode on some Tibetan hilltop. Teheran recalls the easygoing days of Feodor Rothstein, who ruled supreme in the munificent compound of the Soviet mission whence his successor, a young unknown named D. V. Sadchikov, now haunts the waking hours of the Premier of Iran.

The Krassins, Sokolnikovs, and Rakowskys are all gone—and gone with them is the era of the Soviet Union's *laissez-faire* diplomacy. Under Lenin and his Foreign Commissar Georgi Chicherin, the Narkomindel (Narodnyi Kommissariat Inostrannyk Del, People's Commissariat of Foreign Affairs) and its numerous diplomatic outposts were merely instruments of foreign policy. Revolutionary activities were left to the Comintern and its agents abroad.

To Lenin, the bonton of Soviet diplomats was an expedient weapon, designed for foreign consumption. Indeed, in a letter to his Commissar of Justice, on February 28, 1922, he cautioned the domestic agencies of the Soviets against patterning their own actions after the Narkomindel's example in good behavior. Advising Comrade Kursky to refrain from relying on foreign law books in drafting the new Russian civil code, Lenin wrote: "You must not ape the People's Commissariat of Foreign Affairs. You must refrain from flattering and appeasing Europe. On the contrary, you must go to the limit in codifying the intrusion of the State in legal relations between individuals, as well as in other bourgeois matters."

But while Lenin endorsed and supported the pleasant smile on the Narkomindel's face turned to the West, Josef Stalin always opposed the separation between diplomatic and revolutionary activities abroad. He blamed Chicherin's aristocratic background and bourgeois upbringing for this separation and for the condescension with which Soviet diplomats regarded Communist agitators. The long-slumbering Stalin-Chicherin clash on this score was brought into the open on March 10, 1921, at the tenth Congress of the Russian Communist party. It came in the wake of the publication of a series of articles by Chicherin in which he outlined the tasks of the Narkomindel as he envisaged them. Stalin pitted his own ideas against what he called Chicherin's reactionary concepts. He said:

"Comrade Chicherin is inclined to deny the existence of controversies between the capitalist countries, to exaggerate international unanimity among them and to underrate the inherent contradictions between these imperialist groups, controversies and contradictions which do exist and which inevitably lead to war. . . . It is on these controversies that the activities of the Narkomindel must be based. The *raison d'être* of the Narkomindel is to take stock of these controversies, to exploit and to manipulate them." [22]

It is not without significance that both Lenin's long-lost letter to Kursky and Stalin's old speech were revived in 1946, by republishing them for the benefit of the Soviet masses.

The great change over within the Narkomindel, from an instrument of foreign policy to an instrument of world revolution, was almost complete in 1944, when Stalin regarded the time as both ripe and expedient for the abolition of the Comintern. By then, most of its functions and a great majority of its functionaries were transferred to and firmly entrenched in the Narkomindel.

Far more important and revealing than the routine organizational structure of a foreign office are the men in charge of its groups, divisions, and sections. Still at the apex of the Minindel's hierarchy today is Vlacheslav Mikailovich Molotov, the link between the Politburo which formulates and the Foreign Office which executes Soviet foreign policy. Immediately under him are two distinctly separate layers of top executives. One is composed of the Foreign Minister and four Deputy Foreign Ministers, whose positions correspond to American Under-Secretaries and Assistant Secretaries of State. The other is a "brain trust" of counselors and advisers, a flexible group of specialists enlarged or reduced as necessities require.

SATELLITE DIPLOMACY

Today the immense machinery of Soviet diplomacy has an auxiliary tool in the diplomatic apparatus of the satellites. In the wake of a total purge which eliminated virtually all non-Communists from the foreign services of Poland, Czechoslovakia, Hungary, Rumania, Bulgaria, and Albania, satellite diplomatic missions are used to spearhead Soviet interests in such allied fields as propaganda, intelligence, and espionage.

The case of the Hungarian Legation in Washington, D.C., shows the prototype of diplomatic infiltration. In fact, for a time the Hungarian Legation was one of the chief outposts of the Cominform in the United States.

Left behind in the Legation by a departing non-Communist staff in the summer of 1947 was a mild little man named Endre Sik. He was widely introduced as a prominent Hungarian poet, in charge of Hungary's cultural relations in the U.S. Our first meeting with Dr. Sik, at a jovial Legation party that characterized our early relations with Hungary, supplied the external confirmation of the reputation that preceded him. In the formal party of tuxedoed guests, he alone appeared in a rumpled gray suit—apparently the only one in his whole wardrobe, since we have never seen him wearing another. He wore his gray hair in unruly locks. He had an esoteric look in his blue eyes, and huge holes in the soles of his shoes, which he displayed with negligent glee. From head to toe, Sik was the continental prototype of the poet.

Until 1945, Sik was a member of the Hungarian Communist colony of Moscow. In fact, his very existence was unknown outside a small group. He was respected for two virtues: for his unconditional devotion to Stalin and his passion for anonymity.

In 1937, Sik celebrated his twentieth year in Russia. A young Hungarian officer in World War I, he was captured by the Russians on the eastern front. This son of a Hungarian rabbi, whose other son became one of Hungary's most distinguished Catholic *monsignori,* became an ardent Bolshevik, determined to devote his life to the world revolution.

In selfless and hard effort, Sik worked himself up to an important position in the Comintern. He specialized in African affairs and in the Negro problem of the United States. Since 1935 he has been preoccupied with the question of Ethiopia, a fact that caused him to reveal himself to Farago, who had then just written a book on that country.

A prudent and ascetic man, he survived all purges in which most of his friends and some of his closest associates perished. We have good reason to believe that the decline and fall of at least some of his friends and associates were directly connected with Sik's own survival. He was the GPU's informer both within the circle of his friends and the petty bureaucracy of his office. We succeeded in establishing definitely that his closest associate, a young Hungarian intellectual and idealist, was delivered to the GPU by Sik on charges resulting from nothing more than the young man's doubts shared in artless confidence with his boss and friend.

In a total transformation of character, essential for survival in Stalinist Russia, he abandoned all affinity with his Hungarian past. He applied for Soviet citizenship, married a Soviet woman, and fathered two Soviet children who never bothered to pick up even a few Hungarian words.

Nevertheless, Endre Sik was among the first of Moscow's Hungarian expatriates to return to Budapest with the Red Army. He came as an obscure Bolshevik whose chief ambition seemed to be to gain recognition for his poetry from the Hungarian masses. But the poet was given a diplomatic post in the reorganized Foreign Ministry, then still under the control of the Small Landholders party. In 1946, Sik was sent to Washington.

Sik's Comintern past attracted our attention to the shy poet. We decided to develop a few contacts among men regularly visiting him. Upon the occasion of one such visit, Sik abandoned all pretense of being merely the cultural attaché. Without observing even the simplest precautions, in front of a stranger, he emerged as the Big Boss, sending instructions to Hungarian Communists in New York and Cleveland in explicit terms, camouflaged only by the dialectics of ordinary Bolshevik lingo. This incident revealed to us his real role in the Washington setup.

After the resignation of Minister Szegedy-Maszák and his staff, Sik was made chargé d'affaires and eventually minister. Our State Department granted him the necessary *agrement* in apparent ignorance of his real assignment.

In his camouflaged post as envoy of Hungary, Endre Sik was continuing the work he began for the Comintern—the study of

Negro conditions in the United States. On this subject he reported directly to Moscow. In view of the fact that the Negro situation is a major factor in the militant Soviet attitude to the U.S. and the chief promise of civil war (or at least a kernel of disturbance) in this country, the key character of his position should have been evident to all.

Today Sik is back in Budapest. The former poet has come into his own: he is the second-ranking diplomat of Hungary—Under-Secretary of Foreign Affairs, the real boss, as representative of the Central Committee of the Russian Communist party.

Sik's career typifies the planned infiltration of the Kremlin into the diplomatic apparatus of its satellites, as well as the totality of Soviet diplomacy as a major weapon of the U.S.S.R.

While the diplomats of the Soviet Union symbolize old forces of this grand army of the total revolution, and while even the armies and the navies represent merely "conventional forces of the last resort" whose task begins where the work of the diplomat ends, there is a new and absolute force in the U.S.S.R. which gains increasing responsibility and mounting assignments from the Kremlin general staff.

It is the militant organization of Soviet science which is working overtime on the development of absolute weapons for the offensives and defenses of the coming war.

19.

THE

BOMBS

OF ALAGOS

THE SOVIET UNION is quick to claim the birthright of most inventions. According to the Agitprop and the Academy of Sciences of the U.S.S.R., the radio was invented by A. S. Popov in 1895; the airplane by A. P. Mozhaiski "twenty years before the brothers Wright"; and the helicopter by Zhukovski in 1910. The parachute was invented by an actor named Kotelnikov; the electric arc by V. V. Petrov in 1803; the steam engine by Polzunov in 1765. The first steam turbine was built by Zalesov, and the electric lamp, called "Russian Sun," was invented by A. N. Lodygin in 1873, "long before Thomas Alva Edison." [1]

It is strange, therefore, that the A-bomb is not claimed as the invention of Soviet scientists. But even while Soviet scientists did not precede their American colleagues in the actual invention of the A-bomb, the U.S.S.R. did detonate a bomb of its own construction some time before President Truman announced to the world that such an explosion had taken place in the Soviet Union.

We had no doubt as to the Soviet possession of A-bombs in the fall of 1948, when word reached us from two independent but equally reliable sources that the U.S.S.R. did, in fact, explode at least one and possibly more atomic weapons somewhere on her vast proving grounds.

One of our informants was a high-ranking Scandinavian officer who gained his information from intelligence agents operating in the southern parts of Russia and in the north of Iran. Our second contact was an officer of the MVD detachment which guards the secrecy of the Soviet Union's atomic-energy projects. This man, a chemist by profession, was serving as a scientific courier in the MVD, and carried highly classified documents from Moscow and Leningrad, and even from Berlin, to the underground cities in the Soviet Union called Atomgrad I and Atomgrad II, which are the headquarters of the U.S.S.R.'s "Manhattan Project."

Our Scandinavian informant described to us, on the basis of numerous intelligence reports, the circumstances of the first atomic explosion in the U.S.S.R. Our Russian informant, one of the innumerable refugees who bring news from behind the iron curtain, outlined for us the immense atomic organization of the U.S.S.R. and the methods by which the Soviet Union succeeded in developing atomic energy ahead of schedule.

According to our Scandinavian source, the first Soviet atomic explosion occurred, not in "recent weeks," as announced from the White House on September 23, 1949, but early in October, 1948, exactly one year before.[2] An atomic monstrosity far different from our own A-bombs went off accidentally while being prepared for an underwater test. The accident occurred somewhere in the 110,000 square miles of the Karakum Desert, on the black sands and clay soil of which Atomgrad I was built. The desolate, uninhabited area, due east of the Caspian Sea, resembles in many respects our own New Mexican desert where Los Alamos is situated. But there the resemblance between the two A-bomb tests ended.

The clumsy handling of the first Russian A-bomb, the absence of proper security measures, and the premature explosion resulted in the killing of hundreds of bystanders, including some of the leading Soviet scientists assigned to the project. Additional thousands were killed or maimed in remoter areas. Property damage was extensive. The Soviet Government, annoyed by the embarrassing failure, decided to camouflage the first atomic explosion inside the U.S.S.R. By a unique coincidence "an earthquake of unusual intensity" occurred in the same general area at the same time. It is a matter of recorded fact that the seismographs of the world's great observatories, including that of Fordham University in New York, recorded violent tremors in the area where we now know the explosion occurred, on October

5, 1948, at 2000 (eight P.M.) Greenwich mean time.[3] The camouflage was made particularly easy as a result of this coincidence.

The unexpected explosion of this bomb gave the Russians the
key to the one remaining atomic secret they still had failed to
crack. Soviet scientists, who learned some of the atomic secrets
of the U.S. simply by reading our official reports, had known
since 1945 that "the mass of U-235 required to produce explosive fission under appropriate conditions can hardly be less than
2 kg nor greater than 100 kg." But they didn't know what scientists call the "critical mass" or the smallest amount of U-235
needed to touch off the fast chain reaction.

"They thought it would be 60 kgs of U-235, placed in two
hemispheres of 30 kgs each," our informant reported. "But they
were wrong. And they overloaded their bomb."

This overloading of the Soviet A-bomb for the underwater
test of 1948 resulted in the uncontrolled explosion, but it revealed to Soviet scientists the exact amount of U-235 needed for
the explosion. "It also demonstrated to them in practice the
principle that detonation is produced by the instantaneous assembly of subcritical masses."

With this vital knowledge on hand, the second bomb could be
assembled and detonated under proper conditions. It was ready
for the test in July, 1949. It was exploded, under perfect scientific control.

In view of the accidental nature of the first explosion, this
second test of July, 1949, must be regarded as the first truly scientific proof that the U.S.S.R. has come into the possession of the
atomic bomb. Even this proof needed checking and double
checking. It was therefore proper that President Truman did
not make the announcement until September 23, 1949.

But how about the time lag between the atomic developments
of the United States and the U.S.S.R.? And how far behind us
are the Russians with the new A-bomb?

In July, 1949, the Soviet Union's atomic development stood
exactly where our own atomic energy development stood at
five thirty A.M. on July 16, 1945, when we exploded our first test
bomb in the remote section of the Alamogordo Air Base, 120
miles southeast of Albuquerque.[4] In other words, the Russians—
even if they are in the fullest possession of all atomic secrets—are

four years behind the U.S. in the development of atomic energy for military purposes.

If one considers that in 1946 Major General Leslie R. Groves, wartime head of the Manhattan Project, told a scientific audience in Washington's Georgetown University that "the Russians won't have The Bomb in the lifetime of our children's children," these four years represent only a short interval.[5]

But this time lag of four years is likely to persist and even increase as the Russians face the gigantic task of transporting what they call their "Great Stalinist Atomic Project" from the laboratory to the assembly line.

The magnitude of this task is evident at once if one remembers that a single American plant, known as K-25 in Oak Ridge, Tennessee, built to extract fissionable U-235 from normal uranium, has a sixty-acre roof; or that a relatively small separation plant in Hanford used enough concrete for a thirty-mile highway.[6]

Even the United States, with its vast industrial might and technological skill, experienced almost insurmountable difficulties with the process of this transfer. During the years 1946 and 1947, our own A-bomb production was dangerously low—in fact, it was almost at a standstill, because of the unexpected problems of mass production.

Not until late in 1948 did we remove the bugs, improve our technique, and solve most of the problems. But even today further chemical processes, vitally needed to increase the speed and efficiency of our A-bomb production, are still in the pilot-plant stage.

The Los Alamos Scientific Laboratory, our sole A-bomb assembly plant, is now outdated and inadequate. It will take from one to three years to modernize its facilities and to systematize the assembly of the many component parts which make an atomic bomb tick. In all these years since July 16, 1945, we ourselves have detonated only eight bombs. No more than three of them were of a new, improved design.[7] The time we needed for this intermediate improvement was exactly two years and eight months. And we still have a long way to go.

Now, how about the Soviet Union? If the Russians need no more than the time we required for the change over from laboratory to assembly plant, they will not have any factory-produced bomb before April, 1952. And no matter how one calculates all the factors involved in mass production, the Russians may have no appreciable stockpile of A-bombs until about 1956.

Espionage played an exceptionally great part in the Soviet achievement as, indeed, we now know that at least two top-notch Western atomic scientists, Alan Nunn May and Julius Klaus Fuchs, were important members of the Soviet ring specializing in atomic espionage.[8]

In fact, the Soviet administrator himself who is in supreme charge of the Soviet Union's A-bomb experiments learned much about them off Bikini, in the summer of 1946, as he watched the detonation of U.S. bombs, numbers 4 and 5, from the deck of the U.S.S. *Panamint,* one of Admiral Blandy's observation ships.

He was Professor Semyon P. Alexandrov, a famed Russian metallurgist, hand picked by Stalin himself to observe the Bikini tests.

Dr. Alexandrov never even tried to conceal the true purpose of his mission. To a Russian-speaking official of the U.S. Department of Interior he confided that he had come to the U.S. to "find out all he could" about our bomb, and then to apply his new-found knowledge to Soviet atomic research.[9]

One of our informants, a prominent Russian metallurgical engineer now an exile in New York, told us all about this man Alexandrov.

"We went to college together and were close friends for many years afterward," he said. "Then Alexandrov's career skyrocketed. First, he was appointed director of the Kalinin Institute of Gold and Non-Ferrous Metals, a branch of the MVD (secret police) which is in charge of all Soviet gold-mining operations. Then he was made chief of the MVD's scientific intelligence service where all atomic espionage is co-ordinated."

But his Bikini experience was not enough for Alexandrov. He needed more time to complete his mission. So he stayed on in the U.S. as one of the Soviet delegates to the United Nations Atomic Energy Commission.

Professor Alexandrov worked overtime, under personal orders from Stalin, to produce the bomb's secrets—or else.

At that time, in the summer of 1946, Soviet scientists were more than eight months behind a deadline. The morning after Hiroshima, five of the U.S.S.R.'s leading nuclear physicists were summoned to Stalin in Potsdam for consultation. They assured the Soviet Premier that they would produce a Soviet atomic bomb by the end of 1945.

They had then just received the "Official Report on the Development of the Atomic Bomb under the Auspices of the United States Government," [10] cabled to Moscow in its entirety by the Tass News Agency. The Soviet scientists were confident that they would produce the bomb in a jiffy, by simply following the revelations of the American report.

But within a few weeks they found that key research data they desperately needed for success was missing from the Smyth Report. Especially the absence of specific information about the exact amount of uranium needed to detonate the bomb, and the critical speed at the assembly eventually frustrated all Soviet scientific efforts.

Pressed for time, Stalin's scientists decided to try another, more original approach. They now tried to construct an A-bomb of their own, with a spin or angular momentum in which the missing link of the "critical mass" could be expediently disregarded.

On December 18, 1945, a delegation of Soviet atomic scientists went to Stalin and told him that they had succeeded in making a new type of A-bomb, hardly bigger than a tennis ball. Their A-bomb was supposed to be far simpler than the American prototype and could be mass produced at once. What they described as its horizontal pulverization range was supposed to be 85 kilometers, or a little over 50 miles.[11]

This, at least, was how this sensational new Russian bomb looked on paper. But when experiments were carried out to test the theories in practice, the new atomic weapon simply refused to explode.

Angered by the dud, Premier Stalin then made a number of moves which, only three years later, resulted in the Soviet discovery of the bomb's secrets.

First, he ordered the establishment of an Atomic Energy Commission within the Soviet Academy of Sciences, supervised by a special committee of his own Politburo, with Secret Police Chief Laurenti Beria in full-time charge.

Second, he sent word to occupied Germany to round up all available German atomic scientists and ship them to the U.S.S.R.

Third, he directed the Soviet intelligence service to step up its atomic espionage, both through secret agents especially trained for the job, and through clandestine Communist party adherents throughout the world. Semyen Alexandrov was placed in charge of the network.

Under President Sergey Vavilov of the Academy of Sciences, a vast and efficient web of atomic agencies came into being. Two underground, lead-protected research cities, called Atomgrad I and Atomgrad II, were rushed to completion. A commission on physical methods of prospecting minerals, under famed, bearded Arctic explorer Otto Y. Schmidt, was established to find new deposits of uranium in the Soviet-controlled territories of Europe and Asia.

Scores of German scientists followed Stalin's invitation to the U.S.S.R. Among them were Professor Gustav Hertz, an outstanding expert on the separation of U-235; Ludwig Bevilogua, wartime aid of Dr. Heisenberg, Germany's top-ranking nuclear physicist; the great scientific administrators von Ardenne and Volmer; and many more.[12]

Still on October 29, 1946, in a long and heated conference with Stalin, President Vavilov could report no real progress. Stalin then set a deadline: the summer of 1947, and called in Alexandrov to do the job.

What Soviet scientists failed to accomplish, Russian spies achieved—within the time limit set by Stalin.

Alexandrov himself conducted this massive espionage operation from Glen Cove, L. I., where the Soviet delegation to the UN has its headquarters. He had his operatives in the U.S. He sent new spies to Canada to replace members of the defunct Zarubin network. Still others he sent to Mexico, Britain, France, Belgium, and Denmark.

At one stage of the game, two Soviet spies were brazenly flown into the U.S. from Switzerland, with clumsily forged travel documents but thinly concealing their true identity. These two Alexandrov operatives were stopped at LaGuardia Field and promptly shipped back to Europe. But others managed to penetrate to what the people of the U.S. thought were America's most closely guarded secrets.

Evidence of this fact was supplied by the late Richard C. Tolman, one of the wartime chiefs of the Manhattan Project and, in 1947, an associate of Bernard M. Baruch on the U.S. delegation to the UN Atomic Energy Commission. On the surface, Tolman was Alexandrov's opposite number at the UN, both acting as scientific advisers to their respective delegations. But in the end, the quiet New Englander became the nemesis of the young Soviet scientific spymaster.

It was in the summer of 1947 that Tolman made his alarming discovery. He was then making a special effort to read the verbatim transcripts of all speeches delivered by Soviet and Polish delegates during the UN's discussion of atomic energy. A careful study of these speeches revealed to Tolman that certain phrases used by the Soviet and Polish delegates were obviously lifted from top-secret U.S. documents. He also discovered that some of the questions they asked had been based on classified information to which only selected U.S. officials were supposed to have access.

Here was a leak of the greatest importance. But no one responsible for this breach of confidence and none of the Soviet spies whose brilliant teamwork enabled Alexandrov to score one of history's neatest espionage scoops has ever been caught, except Klaus Fuchs, by his own voluntary confession to the British authorities, and Harry Gold.

Today, some of Alexandrov's operatives are at large in the U.S., in Britain, and elsewhere in the Western world. They seem to be the charmed ones of modern espionage, for it is a matter of public record that no Soviet atomic spy of the first rank has ever been apprehended in the United States.

MOBILIZATION OF SCIENCE

We would, however, deceive ourselves should we believe that espionage alone helped Soviet scientists to the keys of atomic energy. Nuclear research has as impressive a history in the U.S.S.R. as anywhere else in the world and while Soviet propaganda is most reluctant to make rabid claims on this score, it could make them with greater justification than, for example, in biochemistry where the discovery of "Soviet penicillin" is attributed to that embarrassed lady, Professor Ermolyeva.

The earliest recorded Soviet accomplishments in this field are connected with D. V. Skobeltzin, who, in 1925, attracted attention through the use of a strong magnetic field in a cloud chamber. He thus studied the charge and energy of particles, especially those induced by cosmic rays. According to Gerald Oster, who gave us an admirable review of atomic-energy research in the U.S.S.R., Skobeltzin demonstrated that certain charged particles which are associated with cosmic rays possess tremendous energies of several million volts.

Another Soviet scientist of that period, L. V. Myssovsky, observed the tracks made by nuclear charged particles in this photographic emulsion.[13]

The discovery by the Englishman Chadwick, in 1932, of the neutron gave immense impetus to this branch of Soviet science. Prior to 1932, there were only fifteen scientists working in this field in the U.S.S.R. Between 1932 and 1941, there were several hundred. Today there are thousands working on studies associated with nuclear fission.[14]

In 1946, "three major institutes" which were carrying on extensive nuclear research in Leningrad and Kharkov "received generous financial support from the Government." Soviet scientists had even then several cyclotrons, including "a very large one" whose construction was continued even during the war. A huge 4½ million volt van de Graff electrostatic generator was completed in 1937.

On November 17, 1948, we received a complete report on atomic information concerning the U.S.S.R. from still a third source, a Soviet scientist who had worked on one of the Soviet atomic projects virtually until the day of his hurried departure in 1948.

According to Professor "X," the Soviet Union produced its first atomic bomb in the underground laboratories of Atomgrad I. It is situated in the Alagos Mountain in the Caucasus.[15] The Soviet Union has four industrial centers entirely devoted to the production of atomic energy. One is in the Sverouralsk region, due north of Swerdlowsk and Magnitogorsk. The other is in the Kuznetsk basin between Tomsk and Stalinsk. The third is in the vicinity of Irkutsk. The fourth is on the shores of Lake Siuriunda, the largest and most secret of the four.

Situated at 103–104° eastern longitude and 65–66° northern latitude, it is in the heart of the Siberian virgin-forest region called *Taiga*. It is completely isolated from the outside world, without a single road leading to it. The nearest highway passable by motor traffic is 1,500 miles away. The sole means of communication with the Siurinda Project is by air. The defenses which Atomic Energy Chief Beria established in the region are among the strongest in the whole Soviet Union. The entire area is fenced in by barbed wire charged with high-tension electricity. Control towers manned by MVD guards are at 500-yard intervals. The defense installations include the latest model rapid firing antiaircraft guns and radar.

According to the same source, the Soviet Union is now producing four atomic bombs per month. Professor "X" maintains that the U.S.S.R. is fully capable of producing a hydrogen bomb.

The atomic-energy project of the U.S.S.R. is under the immediate supervision of a special atomic committee of the Politburo, headed by Laurenti Beria, with Lazar M. Kaganovich in charge of technical supervision. The Academy of Sciences has an atomic energy commission in charge of research and development. There is a control commission on atomic security, in charge of Leo Mekhlis, member of the Orgburo, and, next to Beria, the highest-ranking secret policeman of the vast Soviet MVD–MGB system. Under this roof are seventeen scientific organizations whose work is fully or partly devoted to atomic development.

The Soviet Union's leading atomic scientists are Professors Khlopin, Joffe, Vavilov, Krizhanovsky, and of course, Academician Peter Kapitza, director of the Moscow Institute of Physical Problems of the Red Banner Order of Labor.

There are conflicting reports about Kapitza's whereabouts and standing with the Politburo. According to reports at our disposal, he is at Alma Ata, working at the S.M. Kirov State University of Kazakhstan, supervising all scientific phases of the immense atomic-energy projects of the region.[16]

In view of recent rapid developments in the field, including the discovery of the so-called hydrogen bomb, we must know whether or not Soviet scientists are capable of meeting the high professional standards of their Western colleagues. An authoritative answer to this question was given by Professor Eric Ashby of Manchester University, who had served as scientific attaché with the Australian Legation in Moscow.

According to him the quantity of scientific work in the U.S.S.R. is immense. "It is idle," he reported, "to guess at the precise number of scientific workers in the U.S.S.R, because no reliable figures are available. Thus Turin recently gave the number as 32,617 in 804 institutes, but this is certainly an underestimate. What is certain is that in all technological work (i.e., scientific work in the various Commissariats) the limiting factor is not money or laboratory space, but men." [17]

He was more specific as to the quality of scientific work in the U.S.S.R. We can summarize his tentative opinions as follows:

(1) The view held that Soviet organization and planning enables scientists to accomplish wonders is nonsense. Contrary to popular belief, there is no profound difference between the organization of science in the U.S.S.R. and its organization elsewhere.

(2) The Soviet Union may be presumed to have the same proportion of first-class scientists per head of population as any other civilized country.

(3) There is, however, a much greater "dilution" of first-class men by men of poorer quality. The result is that the *average* quality of scientific work in the U.S.S.R. is low, simply because there is an excess of low-quality workers.

(4) Certain kinds of research requiring teamwork can be done better in the U.S.S.R. than elsewhere.

(5) The U.S.S.R. seems to have built a much firmer bridge between pure science and practical application than exists in other countries.

"A great quantity of scientific work is done in the Soviet Union," Professor Ashby concluded, "because a great number of workers have been mobilized to do it. The quality of scientific work, in the Soviet Union as elsewhere, is no better than the quality of the worker."

It must be remembered that science in the Soviet Union "is

ambitiously planned, well endowed, vigorous, and healthy."

We have seen in another part of this chapter that there is, nevertheless, a discrepancy between scientific discovery and its translation into manufacturing practice when it comes to such a precision job as the separation processes involved in atomic projects and the construction of A-bombs. But in Soviet calculations, which are supercharged with the electric currents of the world revolution, the mere existence of the bomb, the mere knowledge of its secret, the mere propaganda value of the weapon are regarded as far outweighing all other practical or scientific considerations.

We must therefore ask, why did the Russians allow President Truman to score a great propaganda beat through the first announcement of the atomic explosion in the U.S.S.R.?

Why did they—who claim a historical first in all inventions from the safety pin to the radio and airplane—fail to exploit this particular invention on which Stalin himself placed a premium second to none?

There is a conclusive answer to these questions. We gained it through the prolonged interrogation of men who ought to know: high-ranking Red Army officers, now refugees from Communism, some of whom had a leading part in the recent revamping of Soviet strategy. According to them, the strange Soviet modesty about their A-bomb is due to the fact that the U.S.S.R. still has a long way to go before it will have effective atomic weapons in sufficient numbers.

In the meantime the question in the Kremlin is not how to win wars with their A-bomb, but rather how to influence people.

The instructions which the Politburo gave to the Administration of Propaganda and Agitation (Agitprop) was to play down, at least for the time being, the Soviet possession of the bomb and to play up the so-called Gromyko plan, concerning "the conclusion of an international agreement for the outlawing of the production and application of a weapon based upon the use of atomic energy for the purposes of mass destruction." [18]

Soviet propaganda was also told to insist on "the exchange of scientific information."

In other words, the Kremlin hoped that we would destroy our present stockpile and stop making more bombs, while they would continue their own experiments and improvements, without a moment's letup, until they could outstrip and overtake us.

It is a slick device which even becomes effective through the Soviet Union's world-wide propaganda drummed into the ears of peoples who naturally fear the A-bomb and distrust any diplomacy based upon it.

This is exactly what the Russians want and hope to accomplish with their propaganda, conducted with vigor and skill through the United Nations.

Possession of the secrets of atomic energy tends to bolster Russian strength, not only in the military field, but in the civilian as well. Unhampered by the divergent considerations that slow down atomic developments for nonmilitary uses in the capitalistic West, the Russians can make more rapid progress when it comes to industrial exploitation of nuclear fission. Information from Russia indicates quite convincingly that the Soviet Union places as great an emphasis on the military as on the civilian phases of atomic developments.

It is certain that the projected Soviet conquest of Asia is inexorably tied to a master plan concerning the development of atomic energy for nonmilitary purposes. Immense are, indeed, the possibilities in Asia, impossible for the human mind to visualize at this stage, with atomic energy suddenly introduced into enervated China to revitalize it with a source of power unequaled there since the legendary days of its mythological dragon. India's vast resources, Burma's mineral deposits, all the enormous untapped wealth of a neglected continent will emerge in unexpected mass and at unprecedented speed with atomic energy thus harnessed and placed at the disposal of a new band of colonizers.

HOW STRONG IS RUSSIA

Russian strength is, indeed, among the great and fascinating mysteries of history. There is a peculiar interplay of glitter and murk in this grandiose obscurantism that seems as cunningly calculated as it is, in fact, clumsily guileless. For centuries, Russia has puzzled and annoyed all, from Shakespeare to André Gide, from Napoleon to Hitler and Churchill. The enormous contrast that has always been an integral part of the Russian enigma was never better expressed than in the quizzical words with which Macaulay described a visit of an envoy from the Court of St. Petersburg to the Court of St. James's: "The ambassador and the grandees who accompanied him were so gorgeous that all London crowded to stare at them, and so filthy that nobody dared to touch them. They came to the court balls dropping pearls and vermin."

Russia's generals and admirals are as enigmatic as are her ambassadors. And she confronts us with as many puzzles as in war. Preparing for *his* war against Tsar Alexander in 1812, Napoleon spoke, in Jomini's hindsighted words, of "the grand enterprise which was to put Europe at my feet, or to wholly ruin the immense edifice which I had erected with so much care and labor." [19] His counselors warned him, "Will it be prudent to throw our army into these distant deserts, across countries made insurgent by this invasion, or by the ravages of preceding campaigns?" Others asked, "Is it wise to trace a line of operations five hundred leagues in extent through a hostile country, where the embers of ill-extinguished fires are ready to burst forth into a volcano?" Still others said, "Obstacles will multiply in our way if the enemy, led by a second Fabius, only temporizes and falls back on the center of his power and resources." [20] And yet Napoleon resolved, "among songs of victory," to embark upon his grand enterprise. "I had no desire to imitate Cambyses, or the Emperor Julian, or Crassus," he said. "All my measures were adopted with care, and every possible precaution taken to provide against disasters like theirs." [21]

One hundred twenty-eight years later, Hitler was still undaunted by the lessons of Napoleon's decision. On December 18, 1940, at his headquarters, he dictated document *OKW/WFSt/ Abt.1 (I) Nr. 33 408/40 g K Chefs,* the draft of *Fuehrerbefehl 21, Unternehmung Barbarossa,* his first operations plan against Russia. The very first sentence of the directive read: "The German Armed Forces must be prepared *to crush Soviet Russia in a quick campaign* even before the conclusion of the war against England." [22] Both plans were painstakingly prepared—and yet both failed as indeed they were bound to fail. "Great enterprises into distant countries," Montesquieu said, "perish from the very extent of the preparation required to secure their success."

On March 8, 1942, less than nine months after the outbreak of the Russo-German war, Propaganda Minister Goebbels wrote in his diary: "We are having great difficulties everywhere. For instance, in one army corps alone 18,000 horses fell during February, 795 of them from exhaustion." [23] Of the fallen men Goebbels said nothing—not until the fall of 1943, when he wrote: "Our total losses in the East, exclusive of Lapland, from June 22, 1941, to August 31, 1943 ... total 2,902,438, of whom 81,779 were officers." And yet, even then, Russia continued to puzzle him: "It is a curious thing that every individual soldier returning from the Eastern Front considers himself personally quite superior to the Bolshevik soldier, yet we are retreating and retreating." [24]

The overwhelming fact is that our leaders know as little about Russia as Napoleon and Hitler did. Napoleon complained, "At Borodino we were ignorant... We had no good maps of the country... We knew not the position of the practicable roads ... I was deceived in the military character of the Emperor Alexander, as well as in the efforts of the Russian nation to sustain him." [25]

One of Hitler's historians, an admiral named Assmann who is now obligingly serving us with the compilation of his country's defeats, revealed that the Germans had been groping in the Russian night as much as Napoleon had before them. "The General Staff estimated that Russia had available at the commencement of hostilities 213 divisions," he wrote, and then quoted from the *War Diary* of the chief of the German general staff: "We underestimated Russia, we reckoned with 200 divisions and now have already counted 360." In another place Assmann wrote: "Only meager information was available as to the number of tanks the Russians had at their disposal." Later he added, "It came as an unpleasant surprise to the High Command when the front reported the appearance of Russian tanks with 15 cm. (5.9 in.) guns." [26]

We are wont, as Napoleon and Hitler were before us, to make our plans and estimates on the basis of absentee information. Japan was wide open to us, and yet we underestimated her. Today again official Washington, unaided by its intelligence services, is in the prognostic moods of 1941. We seem to be hope-

lessly confused about Russian intentions. We are inclined to
vacillate between an underestimation and an overrating of
Soviet capabilities. When talking in terms of Russian divisions
and equipment, we sometimes speak of a formidable foe. But
when talking of Russia's industrial base, we tend to deprecate
the Soviet war potential. Both attitudes seem to us erroneous.
The Russian armed forces may not be so good as the Pentagon
represents them to be. On the other hand, Russian industrial
strength may be far greater in both absolute and relative terms
than our estimates would indicate.

A favorite but dubious Washington method of appraisal is a
comparative assessment of steel output in the U.S. and the
U.S.S.R. We are producing nearly 100 million tons of steel per
year; the Russians are believed to be producing about 25 million
tons.[27] The qualitative and quantitative elements of such a
comparison are misleading, as is the fact that the U.S.S.R. is
spending most of its steel output on the manufacture of war-
essential goods, whereas we are diverting our output, vastly
greater though it may be, to nonessential peacetime com-
modities. While peace can best be waged with fine washing
machines and refrigerators, wars are won by cannons.

Russia's strength is not in those tangible ingredients which we
are best capable of comprehending. It is in fact in one single intangible particle that Tolstoi in *War and Peace* called the Russian conceit: "A Russian is conceited precisely because he knows
nothing and cares to know nothing, since he does not believe it
possible to know anything fully."

In material terms Russian strength rests in a shrewd utilization
of space as a decisive factor; in the lavish use of manpower from
an inexhaustible reservoir; and in an uncanny ability to improve
in the art of war under the hammerblows of initial failures. In
terms of morale, the Russian people cling, as few others do, to
the sacred soil of their enormous fatherland, and are willing, as
no others do, to die cheerfully in its defense. Generalissimo
Stalin showed in the past that he knew how to mobilize the basic
elements of Russian strength, how to prepare the immense resources of the vast subcontinent, how to drive the nation ruthlessly into battle. "If we will have nothing left," he once said to
an informant, "no more men, no weapons, and no ammunition,

our women will continue the battle, pouring hot water upon the invaders."

Some of this strength may be a mirage conjured up by the Soviet Union's propaganda magicians. Soviet propaganda is indeed designed to minimize Russian weaknesses which are enormous, and magnify Soviet strength, which may not be too formidable.

But behind the large-scale propaganda smoke screen, obviously designed to weaken us while they themselves could increase their own strength, are certain visible activities which expose the Russian plot. In this report, November, 1949, was the turning point in Moscow's strategic planning. On that day Stalin began the deployment of his forces for the "inevitable atomic showdown" with the West in his long smoldering campaign in which he recognizes the United States as public enemy number one.

20.

STALIN
VERSUS
AMERICA

*Today in ... the United States, no less than else-
where, the smashing, the destruction of the "ready-
made State machinery" ... is the indispensable prerequisite of any genuine folk-revolution.*
Stalin quoting Lenin in *Foundations of Leninism*

FOR A long time, Stalin appeared both practical
and realistic in his attitude toward the United States. His attitude was influenced by two chief considerations. One was his
belief that the U.S. would not be roused to oppose him for a
long time to come. The other was his admiration for the technological skill of this country.

"We never forget that America is a capitalist country," he
said once under circumstances similar to those of today. "But
we respect American efficiency in industry, technique, literature,
and life. America was a land of free colonizers without landlords
or aristocrats. From this fact rise its strong and relatively simple
customs in industry.

"Our worker-managers who have been in America notice at
once that characteristic. They note, not without a certain pleasant surprise, that it is hard to distinguish in outer appearance the
engineer from the worker. It is quite otherwise in Europe,
where in daily life and manners still survive remnants of feudal-
ism, and its arrogant ways are carried into industry, science, and
literature." [1]

Even when he was reproaching his own American disciples for

a certain backwardness in their revolutionary zeal, he himself provided their apologia: "It cannot be denied," he said to a group of Communists from the U.S., calling on him in 1929, "that American life offers an environment which favors the Communist Party's falling into error and exaggerating the strength and stability of American capitalism." [2]

He is not so well informed of the United States as was Marx or Engels. Neither is he so ignorant as was Lenin, who wrote on August 20, 1918, an epistle "to American workers" in which he called Woodrow Wilson "the head of the American billionaires and servant of the capitalist sharks." In his letter, Lenin wrote that "the American revolutionary proletarians are destined precisely to play an especially important role as irreconcilable foes of American imperialism, which is the newest, strongest and latest to participate in the world-wide slaughter of nations for the division of capitalist profits." [3]

Stalin did not seem to share Lenin's delusion. To Roy Howard he said: "The Soviet system will not evolve into American democracy, or vice versa. We can peacefully exist side by side if we don't find fault with each other over every trifling matter." [4]

He expressed similar views in talks with Harold Stassen, Eric Johnston, Eugene Lyons, Walter Duranty, and others. When Alexander Werth of the London *Times* queried him "about the feasibility of a friendly and lasting collaboration of the Soviet Union and western democracy despite the existence of ideological discord," Stalin answered with "an unconditional yes." [5] To Elliott Roosevelt he spoke about the possibility "for a democracy, such as the United States, to live side by side in peace in this world with a Communistic form of government, such as that of the Soviet Union." [6]

Some evidence shows that Stalin was not altogether hypocritical in making these statements. He did not mean to commit himself to unconditional co-operation. "It takes two to make a bargain," he likes to say—and, as we have seen, the word "bargain" has an exalted place in his dictionary.

Another factor overlooked in the appraisal of such statements is the element of timing. This element of the *quid pro quo* and the time factor were both frankly emphasized in his famous letter of February 12, 1938, to young Comrade Ivanov, which in-

cluded the often quoted passage: "The existence of the Soviet
Republic next to a number of imperialist states *for a long time*
is unthinkable. *In the end* either the *one or the other* will have
the better of it." (Our italics.) [7]

Both these elements were thoroughly explicit in Stalin's answer to an American Labor Delegation in 1929, which quizzed
him about the practical possibilities of such coexistence. "The
matter concerns, obviously, temporary agreements with capitalist states in the field of industry, in the field of trade, and,
perhaps, in the field of diplomatic relations," he said. "I think
that the presence of two opposed systems ... does not exclude
the possibility of such agreements. I think that such agreements
are possible and expedient under conditions of peaceful development....

"The limits of these agreements? The limits are set by the opposition of the two systems, between which rivalry and struggle
go on. Within the limits permitted by these two systems, but
only within these limits, agreements are fully possible....

"Are these agreements merely an experiment or can they
have more or less lasting character? That depends not only on
us; that depends also on those who contract with us. That depends on the general situation. War can upset any agreement
whatever...." [8]

Even America as a world power is no new image in Stalin's
mind. He focused his attention on the United States as early as
1925, measuring it as an inevitable though temporarily paramount factor in world affairs. In this, as in many other instances,
Stalin showed immense prophetic power.

Looking far beyond 1925, Stalin conjured up a world that
seemed unreal a quarter of a century ago, but which closely resembles the world of today.

He noted that financial capitalism was moving its main center
across the Atlantic, from the exchanges of Zurich and Paris and
Amsterdam, and from the city of London, to Wall Street, and
that the United States was becoming the new bastion of capitalism. He foresaw an eventual "crystallization of two chief but opposed centers of attraction and ... two directions of pull toward
these centers throughout the world." He identified those two
centers as the United States and the U.S.S.R. [9]

He predicted that the United States would become not only

the *new* but the *last* stronghold of capitalism. Its collapse would mark the conclusion of what he called "the Epoch of World Revolution"—the final disappearance of the outdated capitalist world order and the victorious emergence of the new socialist world. "Not until a revolutionary crisis will develop in the United States," he said in 1929, "will we see the beginning of the end of all world capitalism." [10]

For long he expected the American revolution to ignite itself and then to burn on by the internal combustion of all revolutions. He was in no particular hurry to expedite it by external means.

"We ought to learn from the British the art of 'wait and see,' " he has said repeatedly in Politburo meetings. He used to advise his colleagues to direct their efforts toward strengthening "what we have in our hands instead of running after the bird on the roof."

He was willing to wait and to sit out the long wake, until moribund capitalism would collapse under the enormous weight of its own sins and blunders. He held with Marx and Engels that socialist revolution was inevitable, and with Lenin that imperialism was the last stage of capitalism that prepares the conditions for the proletarian revolution.

All he had to do was to look around him to see these two prognoses confirmed in the world at large, in the quickly passing show of wars and revolutions, which arrived like express trains running on close, fast schedules.

He watched calmly the United States becoming the center of world capitalism. He stood by with equal equanimity as the United States moved into the position of world power. He derived a kind of personal satisfaction from seeing his prediction come true.

"Whether the United States wants it or not," he said to Harry Hopkins, "she is a world power and will have to accept worldwide responsibility. Without your intervention in the last two wars, Germany could not have been defeated. In fact," he added these words of immense significance, "the history of the last thirty years shows that the United States has more reason to be a world power than any other state." [11]

Stalin's remark had a double meaning. It was not intended

merely to open Hopkins's eyes to the inescapable reality of
American leadership in the new postwar world, but it was also
intended to nudge the British Empire from the position of leadership it had so long held.

In his early prophecy, Stalin visualized the United States as a
partner of Britain and spoke of Anglo-America rather than of
the United States alone as the "center of attraction" confronting
the U.S.S.R. But then he expected British competition against
the U.S. to lead to the collapse of the coalition. The change in
Britain's power position from a potential rival of the U.S. to
a dependent of the U.S. deprived Stalin of an ally in his showdown with America. This circumstance, of course, has not essentially altered the balance of ultimate power. Anglo-American
rivalry may indeed still affect the current of world and Soviet
history. It already does in the Middle East, in China, and even
within the Western union, although how it will affect Stalin's
changed plans no one can now foresee.[12]

With or without rivalry, Stalin expected the U.S. to replace
Britain at the apex of the world, not by design, but by the sheer
force of its material strength. With this was coupled his realization that the U.S.S.R. could not occupy that coveted first place
in a new world until it was strong enough to remove the U.S.
from that position.

This he expected to accomplish, not by international war
which he regards as the last resort and the foolish instrument of
capitalism-imperialism, but by two parallel socioeconomic developments: first, by crises gradually sapping the strength of
America and leading to quasirevolutionary upheavals; and, second, by the Soviet Union's ability to "overtake and outstrip" a
weakened American economic system.

With hardly more than the equipment available to the oracles
of antiquity, to which he added the pragmatic researches of his
Marxist augurs working feverishly in the various Moscow institutes, Stalin first fixed the date of America's collapse and Soviet
ascendancy to undisputed power at some time in 1976—not
sooner and not later than that.

To the American mind, long-range planning with such chron-
ological exactitude may seem frivolous and absurd. We were
reluctant to accept it as an authentic report on Stalin's plan

when it was first presented by two informants: one a former scientific worker at 14 Volkonkha, the edifice which houses the Soviet Union's topmost group of geopolitical experts; the other a former aid to Professor P. A. Khromov in the Institute of Economics, an important and influential branch of the Soviet Academy of Sciences.

They assured us that the existence of such a long-range appraisal with mathematical precision applied to an intangible estimate was no figment of the imagination. It was the conclusion of a secret Kremlin document of Stalin's own making, distributed far beyond a small circle of confidants. In recent months we have gained confirmation and have no reason now to question the accuracy of the report on which this exposé is based.

Here are the salient features of that document:

In the fifty years between 1926 and 1976, Stalin expected that all intermediary powers would disappear and leave the field in a global conflict solely to the U.S. and the U.S.S.R. On his part he was ready to do everything to bring the Soviet Union to the point within fifty years where it would "overtake and outstrip" the United States.

In 1926, Stalin to this end created a fifty-year plan of socialist victory—a plan to cover the period between 1926 and 1976. He realized that such an ambitious project would be far too much for the tardy technological imagination of his Russians. So he subdivided his project into ten five-year plans, each adding its principal plus compound interest to the amortization of the final project.

As the fifty-year plan was progressing ahead of schedule—with the enthusiastic aid of the capitalist West, which was sending raw materials, machines, tools, blueprints, and its best engineering brains to Russia—the equilibrium of the world received a rude shock. A set of have-nots appeared on the scene and clamored for places in the sun with far greater haste and violence than Stalin. The deck of cards of imperialism was reshuffled. Britain and France were still trumps. But the deuces, Germany, Japan, and Italy, were wild. Before Stalin could even account for the damage, he found the U.S.S.R. relegated to seventh place in a world order, preceded by Britain, France, Germany, Japan, Italy, and a most reluctant United States.

But from the ideological defeats of the 1930's and from the military defeats of 1941–42, Stalin snatched a victory that was so decisive that it necessitated the drafting of a new timetable.

At the end of a war that seemed at one point about to ring down the curtain on bolshevism, the U.S.S.R. emerged more powerful than ever. While in 1941 she was still in seventh place, in 1945 she found herself in second place, still behind the United States of America, but far ahead of schedule.

Whereas one might suppose that the war had left little but ruins of Soviet industry, Stalin found actual improvement. Part of the $8½ billions of Lend-Lease Russia received was in the form of equipment to build new industries east of the Urals, in the place of those the Germans destroyed to the west. Enormous strides were made in the establishment of new huge industrial bases far beyond reach of the enemy.

The restoration of the devastated industries in Europe and Russia, from Petsamo on the Arctic Ocean down to the Donetz Basin on the Black Sea, and in the oil fields of Baku and Batum, have been, in effect, a tremendous postwar addition to the Soviet Union's industrial potential. And one must not ignore Russia's gains through the integration of highly industrialized satellites, such as Poland and Czechoslovakia, into the economic system of the U.S.S.R.[13]

Three of the intermediary powers, Germany, Japan, and Italy, had been eliminated. France was still in the race but running far behind the two new champions: the U.S. and the U.S.S.R. What Stalin hoped would occur in 1976 actually came to pass in 1945—more than thirty years sooner than he expected. There he was face to face at last with his great adversary, the United States of America on the eve of a premature showdown.

At first, Stalin's response to these realities was astonishingly slow. His mind was so tormented by the cruel experience of the immediate past that it seemed blunted to the challenge of the greater future. He seemed overawed by the problems of re-habilitation and reconstruction, in material and personal terms. He did not seem able to accept the new facts of world power until the opportunities of an early Soviet victory were brought unequivocally to his attention by renewed threats to Soviet security.

From a geopolitical point of view it was over Britain that the U.S.S.R. found herself in acute competition with the United States. The Soviet Union regards the present era as a supreme historical opportunity to take over all that Britain still retains by tenuous ties.

However, when after August, 1945, the Soviet Government turned to the pleasant task of picking up pieces of the British Empire, Stalin found that the conflict could not be limited to a rather one-sided bout with the British alone. Instead, in Greece and Turkey and Iran, in the Far East and in Western Europe, with money, men, and military supplies, and with votes in the United Nations, the United States supported and sustained the British Empire. The effect was to preserve Britain in that second place of the power-political alignment for which Stalin himself aspired with the tense expectations of the impatient suitor.

For many years before the adoption by the U.S. of its back-up-Britain policy, Stalin had seen in the United States merely a philanthropic power, with no selfish designs on foreign lands. It was the Politburo's conviction that while America was not available for shady deals in the black market of imperialism, like Stalin's deal with Hitler, neither would she intervene effectively in the execution of the Stalinist plan. Soviet writers never hesitated to express the view that there existed no basic controversy between an *expanding* U.S.S.R. and an *isolationist* United States. They would have been quite satisfied to emerge from World War II in number-two place, conceding first place to the United States, if only because of its vast economic potential.[14]

But now they became aware that the United States was unwilling to return to isolationism or to await with folded arms the fate the Moscow scientists predicted for her. With something like the healthy instinct of survival displayed by the rich widow in Charlie Chaplin's *Monsieur Verdoux,* and with little more than that, the United States refused to collaborate in its own assassination. It was thus, in the wake of America's hesitant decision to enter what Ilya Ehrenburg called the red-light district of imperialism, that the United States became superimposed on Soviet designs.

Today, Stalin regards "American imperialism"—our still somewhat hit-and-miss diplomacy—as the most formidable adversary of Bolshevik imperialism and the only obstacle in the path of the latter's victory.

It is remarkable, indeed, what havoc this concept of the U.S. has wrought in Stalin's mind.

One of our informants, a Polish diplomat, was frankly appalled by the vehemence with which Stalin attacked this new monster, especially since he recalled that only a few years before, the Generalissimo had discounted any threat to his plans from America. He tried to allay Stalin's suspicions and fears by reassuring him of the essentially peaceful frame of mind of the American people and of the nonimperialistic, noncolonial heritage of the U.S. Government. Stalin countered with the remark:

"You cannot suppress the natural urges of life even in the most chaste of all people. History is crowded with reluctant imperialists. The Romans, for one, never aspired for the glory of conquest beyond their narrow boundaries, if only because they despised the people they had to conquer and whom their consuls had to administer, even teaching them how to wash away the dirt from behind their ears. When their hour in history will strike, the Americans will spread their wings and leave their cozy nests, no matter what their old women might tell them about the unknown dangers of a cold strange world outside."

Today Stalin no longer views the United States with equanimity. Today he thinks that the war which he described as capable of upsetting "any agreement whatever"—the war between the United States and the U.S.S.R.—is not only possible and probable, but inevitable and even imminent. He may still be in doubt about the true intentions of the Truman administration, although he is lately inclined to include President Truman on his list of warmongers. But while he has doubts about the intentions of the Truman administration, Stalin has none about the determination of other influential circles, both in the United States and abroad. The famous and lengthening list of warmongers Mr. Vishinsky likes to reel off, with the monotony of a prayer wheel, actually originated with Stalin. He has kept a record of his candidates since the day of Mr. Churchill's speech at Fulton, Missouri, in the spring of 1946.[15]

According to Stalin, there are three categories of people who are vitally interested in bringing on another world war. Those

whom he regards as warmongers include (1) top economic leaders, the so-called capitalists, who are interested in continuous
expansion of production and markets, no matter by what means;
(2) military men, who, in Stalin's view, are not so much interested in war as in continuing tension, to keep their budgets high;
(3) a whole group of discredited and disavowed political leaders
whose only chance for a comeback lies in another war.

The "little warmongers" of Europe and Asia, he told a Czechoslovak diplomat in the fall of 1949, remind him of "the dogs of
Arabia which bark at passing caravans but fail to impede their
progress."

A man of supreme realism, he usually measures even the most
bellicose statement against the speaker's ability to act upon it.
He thinks that all the "little warmongers" can do is talk—a conviction he expressed to another Czechoslovak diplomat, now
among our informants, who called upon him in the spring of
1948, during the review of the Prague *coup d'état* by the Security Council of the United Nations. The Czech diplomat was
somewhat concerned and pointed to a Tass dispatch of that
morning, reporting a remark of Sir Alexander Cadogan, the
representative of the United Kingdom, to underscore his apprehension. Sir Alexander urged the council "to act" and, in an
unaccustomed flourish, probably influenced by misunderstood
instructions, he added "even at the risk of war."

"Do not worry," Stalin consoled his visitor, "England will not
go to war over this issue. How can she? The only contribution
that bankrupt country can make to war is the risk."

But the "warmongers of America" do not provoke from him
contemptuous parables from his arsenal of succinct Russian
proverbs. They belong to a country—the United States of
America—which, to him, is as enigmatic and unpredictable as
the U.S.S.R. is to us, but vastly more powerful and vastly less
realistic. This combination of assets and liabilities make the
United States, at least in Stalin's calculations, the great unknown
in the otherwise simple equation of international affairs.

Stalin is no longer content with simply waiting idly for the
demise of moribund capitalism in the United States by natural
causes. He realizes that he must promote and accelerate it; in
fact, he must purge America from among the contenders for
world power lest the United States prolongs its life indefinitely

and seizes from the U.S.S.R. leadership in a co-ordinated world, under the aegis of a comfortable and lucrative new ideology: pluto-democracy of the Jeffersonian-Hamiltonian brand.

For years Stalin himself and his vast propaganda machinery tried to convince the United States that isolationism was the best course for her to follow, even though she might be allowed to appear as the paramount trader on the world market, for the time being, at least. Then, when this persuasion failed to yield the desired result, Stalin suggested that a deal be made under which the world would be divided into a Soviet hemisphere and an American hemisphere, with the scantiest political intercourse between the two. When this, too, failed, Stalin tried to isolate *his* world and exclude us from it, with rude keep-out signs at first and with bloodhounds later.

This method seems to be failing, too. So Stalin finds himself compelled to resort to more radical means. He may await the 1952 presidential campaign because the election of a man like Robert A. Taft would reisolate the United States without the need of external influences. However paradoxical it may sound, Senator Taft is Stalin's candidate. But should "his man" lose the election and should an internationalist like Truman or Eisenhower win, Stalin is determined to move at what he regards as the eleventh hour.

A physical attack against the United States proper is considered, of course, even though it might never materialize. If it comes at all, it will be in the form of strategic air and submarine assaults against key targets and shipping lanes; bombardment by guided missiles launched from platforms on huge snorkel-type submarines; widespread sabotage by Bolshevik Red Guards and activists even now conducting their "invisible maneuvers" for their carefully planned "invisible insurrection."

A careful intelligence survey of the entire perimeter of the vast Soviet frontier bordering upon the friction zones of the United States revealed actual large-scale military preparations against continental America at only one strategic spot. It was in the Bering Sea region across from the American mainland on Asia's easternmost tip. An exact order of the battle of Soviet contingents and a detailed description of their military installations are available to us. Both indicate aggressive designs rather than mere defensive preparations.[16] A number of recent informants, led by Mr. Roman Goull, a Russian Arctic expert who devoted a lifetime to the vigilant observation of Soviet activities in the Far North, confirm the evidence that indicates acute Soviet designs on Alaska. They advise us that even in a remote conflict fought on distant battlefields, the U.S.S.R. intends to bring the war to American soil by actually invading and seizing our Alaskan outpost.

The operational implications of such a step are considerable. But it must never be forgotten that the United States would not be imperiled by an enemy possession of the Alaskan outpost. There must be some military design in this feverish Soviet preoccupation with the Far North but it is far too obscure for us to venture a definite opinion as to its orientation. Even so it may be stated categorically that it is the West Coast rather than the East Coast of the United States that would be in peril should the Russo-American war ever materialize.

There are, along the perimeter, two major installations which represent physical threats to our overseas commitments. One is the so-called Zhukov Line, consisting of fortifications that extend from Kaliningrad (formerly called Koenigsberg) in Eastern Germany, south-southwest to the fortified Oder Line, and north-northeast, along the strategic coast of the Baltic Sea, to Viborg, formerly Finland. The other is the so-called Malinovsky Line, the major Soviet fortifications in the Far East, centering on Vladivostok and Petropavlovsk, with important bases in the Kuriles and on Sakhalin.

Otherwise, too, the armed might of the U.S.S.R. is deployed against our new outposts throughout the world. Major points of deployment are the Black Sea area mobilized against Turkey and Iran; Hungary as a base against Yugoslavia; Bulgaria as a base against Greece; Eastern Poland and the Russian zone of Germany as bases against the West; Latvia, Lithuania, and Estonia, as well as Northern Finland and the Soviet Karelian Republics as bases against Sweden.

These are, in their broadest outline, the strong points of the physical assault planned against the U.S. More important are the means of the nonmilitary assault—the design on America's will to power, will to international participation, and will to survival.

Part Five

COLD WAR ON THE AMERICAN PLAN

21.

CONTOURS OF AN AMERICAN BLUEPRINT

THE UNITED STATES came closest to preparing its defenses against the all-out revolutionary offensive of Stalin's Bolshevik Russia on March 5, 1947, when the Truman Doctrine was born; in August 15, 1947, when the Marshall Plan was first proclaimed; and on January 20, 1949, when President Truman in his inaugural address recognized the nature of the attack and outlined not merely an operations plan to meet it, but also the logistics of the planned operations, his point-four program, and the contours of a counterattack.

Our stated aims were refreshingly ideological: to halt the spread of the "false philosophy of communism" which "maintains that social wrongs can be corrected only by violence," and to oppose to it our democracy which "has proved that social justice can be achieved through peaceful change." [1] But the operations plan which President Truman thus pitted against Stalin's basic operations plan was both too little and too late. It was propounded almost exactly twenty-five years after the revelation of the Stalinist plan. And it went less than halfway in meeting it. Our plan reflected in its essential part the view that "in a world of suspicion and distrust, peace can be maintained *only* [sic] when backed by the *military* strength to resist aggression." [2]

In its concluding paragraph, however, the statement did touch upon the broader aspects of the problem: "The Military Assistance Program is a realistic program. It is not a panacea for international ills and it alone will not put an end to the 'cold war,' but it can become an important *additional* instrument in the foreign policy of the United States, and it can play a vital role in the co-operative action directed at preventing another world war." [3] (Our italics.)

Thus was it recognized that the military assistance program is but one of the pillars on which our defense structure against bolshevism must necessarily rest. Prior to that, in August, 1947, we recognized another pillar in "the close connection between economic welfare and the preservation of free institutions." But the wisdom of our defenses should rest on the proverbial seven pillars, five of them to bolster the souls of men instead of supporting his granaries and arsenals.

President Truman's four-point operations plan contained the contours of our concept of total defense against the spread of bolshevism. Less than a decade after Franklin Roosevelt urged us to remove the dollar sign from our international relations, we allowed it to sneak back. The fact is that our defenses against the ideological and revolutionary plans of bolshevism rest almost exclusively on material means. We are not concerned with the minds of the people abroad and how they may succumb to Soviet pressure. We are chiefly concerned with just two points of their anatomy: their stomachs and, more recently, their trigger fingers.

Deficient as our defense program is on the ideological score, (and the appalling magnitude of this particular deficiency will be outlined in detail at its proper place), it is not adequate even in the military field.

The word "defense" is not even listed in the index of the Defense Secretary's second report to the President except in the designation of the secretary's office.

With the exception of fifteen to twenty words in the 357-page volume, there is nothing that would indicate a recognition of the intangible offensive outlined in Stalin's basic operations plan. Even those twenty-five words, mentioning psychological warfare in passing, indicate no actual preparations whatever against the unrecognized danger.[4]

Only on pages 270–71, in the fine and vigorous report of the Chief of Staff of the U.S. Air Force to the Secretary of the Air Force, did we find a section that would remotely indicate our concept of defense and the manner in which we go about defending ourselves. It may be useful as a bizarre comparative study to pit the concept of the Bolshevik revolutionary offensive against the doctrine of the democratic military defense, if only to show up the alarming discrepancy between the two, and our failure to understand the essence of the offensive against which we are called upon to defend the four freedoms.

General Hoyt S. Vandenberg's prudently worded report is entitled "Air Defense." It is a most security-minded digest of our "plans for the use and deployment of the Air Force, the Army, and the Navy on any future M-Day . . . in the form of a *Joint Doctrine for the Air Defense of the United States.*" [5]

In "Air Defense" our military leaders express the pivotal idea of the American defense doctrine. "In this age of the atomic bomb, guided missiles, aircraft of supersonic speed, and submarines of virtually unlimited range," the Defense Secretary told the President, "time and space are no longer formidable barriers between us and the rest of the world."

From what little our government was willing or able to tell us on the state of our air defense, we gathered that we are not too well defended. The responsibility for this, it seems, rests with Congress rather than with the Air Force or the National Military Establishment. It appears that "early in fiscal year 1949," which means rather late in the cold war, we recognized that "a delay in [the] initiation [of the defense of the United States from air attack] involves great risks." Obviously! The truism of this conclusion was stated by General Spaatz even on June 30, 1948, when he wrote:

"The tremendous multiplication of destructive power that the atomic bomb gives to aircraft, together with the constant shrinkage the globe is undergoing with each increase in the ranges and speeds of aircraft, lends an urgency to the solution of the defense problem that the United States has never before known in time of peace." [6]

But how urgent is urgent?

Nothing appeared to be done on this score throughout 1948, when the cold war was rapidly increasing in intensity; and there were indications that nothing would be done in 1949 either. But then suddenly, in apparent haste, our Air Force prepared a plan called "Interim Program for Aircraft Control and Warning Systems in the United States and Alaska."

On February 10, 1949, the late General Muir S. Fairchild of the Air Force went to Capitol Hill to plead with Congress for appropriations for the "Interim Program." In this case, it seemed, there would be no time wasted on empty Congressional talk. The urgency of the Air Force's request was recognized by all. Patriotic statements were issued to press and radio, endorsing the program and supporting its aims.

Shortly afterward an authorization bill was introduced into the House; the bill was quickly passed by both Houses of Congress; and on March 30 it was signed by the President—a world record for legislative speed.

One would now think that nothing was left in the way of implementation to make at least a hesitant first step to avoid another Pearl Harbor. But no! In the restrained but poignant language of General Vandenberg: *"Funds necessary for the construction of the aircraft control and warning system were not provided."* No funds, no defense. This seems to be in line with the principle, enunciated by the Secretary of Defense, when he said that we must be "always on the alert and resort to every means at our command to keep ourselves as well protected as possible,..." but: "we must do this economically and judiciously, without expending an excessive portion of our national income or otherwise impairing the national economy." [7]

The 1949 budget of the National Military Establishment did not seem to reflect such a solicitous preoccupation with the national pocketbook. As we may well recall it, the unprecedented sum of $15 billion was appropriated in 1949 for national defense proper, apparently not enough to build an aircraft control and warning system against the kind of attack, the sole kind of attack, that is likely to hit the United States.

It may be that such a system would represent a prohibitive economic burden on our taxpayers, although we cannot well see how such a consideration can ever interfere with what an anonymous high-ranking officer of our armed forces once called "minimum defensive measures." [8] On closer scrutiny it develops that the system of control and warning against missiles and aircraft requires 250 separate radar installations with an operating crew of 50,000 men. The whole establishment would cost $375 million—or only 2½ per cent of our defense budget, "obviously not a prohibitively large undertaking," as Ansley J. Coale found it in his study on *The Problem of Reducing Vulnerability to Atomic Bombs.*[9]

Considering all factors of the case, one is inclined to withhold sympathy as well as, perhaps, full confidence, from the National Military Establishment in the face of its failure to spend 2½ per cent of its budget on defenses against what is an 89 per cent likelihood of the only physical attack against the territory of the United States.

On the basis of General Vandenberg's melancholy report and the disappointing results of "Blackjack II," [10] a maneuver in which the efficiency of a makeshift warning system was tested, we may say with regret that the United States is ill defended against that "unannounced air attack" of "unpredictable fury" that might hit us "at any time" from the opposite hemisphere.

A trained intelligence analyst in an opponent's camp can make out quite a bit from clues like the ones provided by General Vandenberg's candid plaint. They enable him to piece together part of the picture of our defense philosophy and the state of our preparedness, much as a paleontologist is capable of reconstructing an antediluvian monster from its broken buck tooth found in some prehistoric mud. The work of that mythical intelligence officer or foreign spy is made remarkably simple in the United States. He can acquire a host of invaluable military data—indeed, the entire blueprint of our defense theories—from just a few indiscreet publications available through the United States Government Printing Office and the document offices of the Senate and House. So explicit and revealing are these publications that one hesitates even to list them despite the fact that they are in the public domain.

Some of them were issued by the Atomic Energy Commission, others by the Joint Committee on Atomic Energy of Congress; a most important set was published by the Committee on Armed Services of the House; and still another by the House Committee on Expenditures in the Executive Departments. In addition there are releases on the hour and "leaks" every day throughout Washington, adding more and more stones to the mosaic of our defenses, in theory as well as in practice. And significantly enough, one or another member on the staff of the Soviet Union's official Tass News Agency is usually among the first to pick up a copy or to procure a volume on what in his native Russia would be the highest state secret whose revelation to an American would be punishable with death.

And yet there seems to be less danger in these revelations than meets the eye. The fact is, and this is not written facetiously, that when the diligent intelligence officer or foreign spy finishes his homework with these documents, he gains but one supersecret from all this immense documentation. This secret is that we do not seem to have a comprehensive military or an equally adequate nonmilitary counterplan to the Russian blueprint. He will find that our war theories are either hopelessly vague or as yet altogether unformulated, due to the prolonged and vituperous debate between our Navy and Air Force. He will find that some of our definitive war plans, such as the establishment of overseas bases, are hampered by foreign political considerations, such as our relations with Spain and the countries of the Middle East.

He will also find that we like to express security in the deceptive terms of dollars and cents. In his budget message to Congress of January 3, 1950, President Truman wrote: "Our expenditures for national defense continue to be the largest item in the Budget. Under current world circumstances, in which the strength of the United States is making such a vital contribution toward world peace, we must continue to make the expenditures necessary to maintain a position of relative military readiness. At the same time, we must plan our expenditures for national defense so that we will achieve our purpose at reasonable cost, well within our capacity to sustain over a period of years." The inner contradiction of this paragraph is too evident to require comment. It is obvious that an all-out defense cannot be mounted with such limited budgetary philosophy, however important the former would be and however proper and prudent the latter actually is.

More important, however, is the finding that our method of expressing our basic defenses, both philosophy and installation, in the eloquent terms of hard cash further deceives us as to the efficiency of our preparedness and security. The foreign spy will not be deceived by the dollar sign standing as a symbol for cannon as well as the A-bomb, for all the immense equipment needed in a military establishment. He knows that purchasing price does not necessarily denote quantity, that we are vastly overpaying for our military purchases, and that the huge sum of $13 billion, represented as our expenditure on national defense, buys in reality only about $7 8/10 billion in actual defense.

Thus it appears that in the military field as well our counter-plans are deficient at best—if one can discover at all an explicit and tangible American counterplan.

It is, therefore, quite astonishing that any informed observer of the international scene should speak of an explicit American plan, allegedly designed in sinister toil by some diplomatic and military plotters in Washington, "to take over the world."

And yet this is exactly the charge preferred against the United States by Konni Zilliacus in a book called *I Choose Peace*. Published at 2s 6d (thirty cents) by Penguin Books in England, Mr. Zilliacus's husky little volume of more than 500 pages is a remarkable and effective weapon of the cold war. In it is collected all the evidence used day after day by Soviet propaganda to indict the U.S. before the world.

Mr. Zilliacus is, of course, the ex-member of the Labor party whose pro-Soviet sympathies had gained for him nothing but repudiation at the hands of his party and his constituents. Yet, we must not dismiss him. He commands an intellectual strength and integrity that other Soviet propagandists usually lack. His arguments are convincing when read with uncritical eyes. And even when read critically, they are frequently difficult to refute.

In a chapter called "The U.S. Prepares for War," Mr. Zilliacus speaks of a mysterious American plan designated by the familiar and popular letter of the alphabet most often applied to such non-existent plans.

"The American press," he wrote, "has been quite frank about it that late in 1947 or early in 1948 an organization, the so-called 'Plan X,' was actually set up, much on the lines demanded by Mr. John Foster Dulles, one of the chief architects and agents of the present 'bi-partisan' foreign policy of the United States. Addressing the Bond Club at the Waldorf Astoria Hotel, New

York, in May 1948, Mr. Dulles called for a 'non-military defense organisation' in Europe, headed by a special American Government officer and acting in effect as a branch of the E.C.A., for which the West European nations receiving aid under E.C.A. should be called upon to pay. Mr. Dulles's brother Alan, who was a high official in the Office of Strategic Services during the war, was then sent to Europe to organize 'Plan X.'" [11] Mr. Zilliacus continued the tale by quoting from *United States News and World Report* that "strong arm squads would be formed under American guidance" and the "assassination of key Communists would be encouraged" under this same X-plan.

Looking quite desperately for an American plan in the wrong places, under the bed rather than in our statute books, Mr. Zilliacus must have been misled by the promiscuous use of the letter "X" in the designation of plans, plannings, and planners. His confusion may be traced to the fact that there was in actual existence something resembling an American plan, popularly referred to as "the plan of X." It was a plan developed during the closing days of the war by a brilliant American career diplomat stationed at our embassy in Moscow.

Disturbed by the callousness of the Kremlin and the rapid deterioration of Russo-American relations, this diplomat prepared a long essay, called "Political Report," in State Department parlance, for his superiors in Washington. In it he outlined "the sources of Soviet conduct." His paper did attract some attention in wartime Washington. It was circulated to key men in the administration, on Capitol Hill, in the Pentagon. It was read perfunctorily by many and carefully by some, that latter including Senator Arthur H. Vandenberg on whom, at least, it made a profound impression. But on the whole it nevertheless failed to make the general impression its author hoped it would create.

The American diplomat who penned this report was, of course, George F. Kennan. He is an interesting and intriguing representative of the new career men who now dominate the foreign service of the United States. Their diplomacy is a happy and invigorating mixture of erudition and buccaneering. They take their diplomacy most seriously, work exceptionally hard at it, and develop, like the hucksters of the advertising trade, gastric ulcers in the process. Kennan's ulcers, so they say at Foggy

Bottom, are an important instrument of our international policy.

George Kennan for one was quite convinced of the importance of his paper in the face of rapidly mounting evidence of reckless Soviet expansionism. And he met influential friends in Washington and New York who shared this conviction. When it was found that its restricted distribution had failed to yield the desired results, plans were made to confide the Kennan Plan to the people of America. Thus it happened that a somewhat watered-down version of the original political report was published under the romantic pseudonym "X" in the July, 1947, issue of *Foreign Affairs* amid unmistakable signs of a fanfare prearranged by a group of "diplomatic activists" in our National War College, our own top-ranking geopolitical institute, and in the State Department. They were supported by kindred spirits, such as the Alsop brothers; the members of the Council on Foreign Relations; and the editors of *Time* and *Life*. Today Kennan is somewhat disillusioned, as evidenced by his more recent "plan" published as a signed article in the *Reader's Digest*. But the Alsops and *Time* and *Life* are not. They put up a last-ditch fight for "the plan of X." [12]

This particular "X-plan" was not aimed, as Mr. Zilliacus averred, at some key Communists in Europe. In the final analysis it was really aimed at James F. Byrnes, whose conciliatory foreign policy began to displease a growing segment of informed Americans. If the publication of the Kennan report was a "plot" at all, it succeeded remarkably well. It made its contribution to the eventual unseating of Mr. Byrnes. It skyrocketed Mr. Kennan to a diplomatic position of unprecedented importance in the State Department. Under Mr. Marshall he was made chief of a newly created policy-planning group whence he could mastermind and supervise the execution of more plans.

Here then was something that resembled a definitive plan. It was somewhat naïve and ebullient, to be sure, especially when it dragged in Providence for which it claimed "a certain gratitude" for "providing the American people with this implacable challenge" from the Kremlin. But this was due to the amateurish literary style rather than the diplomatic dilettantism of its author.

The salient premises and assumptions on which the Kennan Plan was based may be stated as follows:

(1) The United States cannot expect in the foreseeable future to enjoy political intimacy with the Soviet Union.

(2) It must be expected that Soviet policies will reflect no abstract love of peace and stability, no real faith in the possibility of a permanent happy coexistence of the socialist and capitalist worlds, but rather a cautious, persistent pressure toward the disruption and weakening of all rival influences and rival power.

(3) Russia, as opposed to the Western world in general, is by far the weaker party.

(4) Soviet society may contain certain deficiencies which will eventually weaken its own total potential.

(5) Soviet economic development, while it can list certain formidable achievements, has been precariously spotty and uneven.

(6) Soviet leadership is unstable. The transfer of "pre-eminent power" from Stalin to his successor may unleash, in Lenin's words, one of those "incredible swift transitions" from "delicate deceit" to "wild violence" which may shake Soviet power to its foundations.

The plan had one sole conclusion that was destined to make it, for many months in the postwar world, the major source of American conduct. According to Kennan, "the Soviet pressure against the free institutions of the Western world is something that can be contained by the adroit and vigilant application of counterforce at a series of constantly shifting geographical and political points, corresponding to the shifts and maneuvers of Soviet policy."

The recommendations based upon this conclusion were three: (1) The United States must regard the Soviet Union as a rival and not a partner in the political arena. (2) The United States must influence by its actions the internal developments both within Russia and throughout the international Communist movement. (3) The United States must enter upon a *"policy of firm containment"* designed to confront the Russians with unalterable counterforce at every point where they show signs of encroaching upon the interests of a peaceful and stable world.

Upon closer scrutiny the Kennan Plan was conspicuous chiefly for the negative nature of its recommendations. It proposed the famous theory of containment, a policy of indefinite stalemate incapable of diplomatic solution. By inference it advocated the war, which it was apparently designed to avoid, as the only solution to the problem.

It was a presumptuous and conceited plan, inevitably aggravating Russo-American relations if only by insulting the U.S.S.R., exceptionally touchy on this score. It is indeed presumptuous when one great power goes on record that it intends to "contain" another great power and that it expects the other great power to acquiesce without a countermove. Such policies may sound well behind the closed doors of a planning-group meeting. But when advertised publicly, with the fanfare they actually received, they are likely to defeat their purpose by their undiplomatic approach to elementary diplomacy. The fact is that the Kennan Plan became quite ineffective the moment it was made public in foreign affairs, a fact which, we understand, Mr. Kennan himself now acknowledges.

Walter Lippmann was among some voicing opposition to the "plan of X." In a series of twelve brilliant essays he warned America against the acceptance of the Kennan Plan. "Mr. X. has reached the conclusion," he wrote, "that all we can do is to 'contain' Russia until Russia changes, ceases to be our rival, and become our partner. . . . For a diplomat to think that a rival and unfriendly powers cannot be brought to a settlement is to forget what diplomacy is about. There would be little for diplomats to do if the world consisted of partners, enjoying political intimacy, and responding to common appeals." [13]

Lippmann's reservations may be summarized in five points:

(1) The method by which diplomacy deals with a world where there are rival powers is to organize a balance of power which deprives the rivals, however lacking in intimacy and however unresponsive to common appeals, of a good prospect of successful aggression.

(2) In our conflict with Russia a policy of settlement would aim to redress the balance of power, which is abnormal and dangerous, because the Red Army has met the British and American armies in the heart of Europe. No state in Western Europe

can be independent of the Kremlin as long as the Red Army is within it and all around it.

(3) A genuine policy would, therefore, have as its paramount objective a settlement that brought about the evacuation of Europe.

(4) Until a settlement which results in withdrawal is reached, the Red Army at the center of Europe will control Eastern Europe and will threaten Western Europe.

(5) In these circumstances American power must be available, not to "contain" the Russians at scattered points, but to hold the whole Russian military machine in check, and to exert a mounting pressure in support of a diplomatic policy which has as its concrete objective a settlement that means withdrawal.

It was evident at once that a fusion of the two designs, the Kennan Plan and the Lippmann Plan, could have placed the United States on the offensive instead of holding it back in a defensive which the application of the Kennan Plan inevitably meant. No such fusion was possible. In fact, the Kennan crowd regarded Lippmann's survey of their man's plan as an unwarranted interference, not with only a plan, but with American diplomacy as such. In the end, ballyhooed and oversold, the Kennan Plan prevailed. It did score some impressive tactical successes but led us and the world to the very stalemate Lippmann predicted, behind which looms the abyss of war.

22.

JAMES FORRESTAL
AND THE CONCEPT OF
POWER IN AMERICA

IT MAY seem both strange and unfortunate that in its greatest hour of history, the United States should be able to produce only a handful of political philosophers capable of developing broad and daring outlines for an effective American foreign policy. George Kennan and Walter Lippmann are two such men. One of them had the advantage of being inside the governmental machinery. He could thus utilize the vast apparatus of the state to translate his ideas into diplomatic action. The other had the advantage of being outside the government. He could enlist the aid of an immense audience, of the American élite, to gain acceptance for his proposals on official policy. This is how democracy works.

The influence of these two men has been very great. It exceeded even, in an abstract philosophical sense in which our diplomacy is weakest, the influence of some of our Secretaries of State. There have been a few others—Herbert Elliston, whose editorials in the *Washington Post* aided in the shaping of our foreign policies; Professor Bernard Brodie of Yale University, whose writings on "strategy as a science" pioneered a new approach to diplomacy and advocated its strategic orientation; James Reston of the *New York Times* whose diplomatic correspondence from Washington represented the sole reliable link between the high-level diplomacy of the nation and the nation at large; Hanson W. Baldwin, also of the *New York Times,* whose articles helped to restore a sense of proportion in our badly unbalanced views concerning the importance of armed forces in a cold war.[1]

This is a short list. But then we are still at the dawn of our destiny. The great challenge of the full day may yet produce great leaders to conduct us out of the wilderness of our present diplomacy.

The United States had such a man in its governmental organization—one whose evolution to leadership promised to meet eventually the high standards set by giants of continental diplomacy from Castlereagh to Briand.

Despite the important posts he had filled, his talents were wasted in our government. His energies were sorely tried. His patience abused, his integrity attacked, his genius doubted, he was—like Lord Castlereagh before him—driven into madness and suicide just when the nation needed his vision and brain most.

This man, of course, was James Forrestal.

He was an unassuming man, even shy, a self-effacing student of world affairs who failed to give the impression of greatness at first sight. And yet he was a great man. His greatness was in his understanding of the meaning of power. He alone among the political scientists and the war lords this era produced in such lavish abundance succeeded in discerning America's great need for a new concept of power. And more than that—he alone among them managed to develop such a concept.

Forrestal lived dangerously from the moment he decided to explore the problem of power in America. He was dealing with a bad five-letter word. Its connotation seemed forever discredited by Lord Acton's glib epigram: "All power corrupts, and absolute power corrupts absolutely."

Acton pitted the term "power" against the term "liberty," and blamed the former for the agonies of the latter.

"In every age," he said, "its progress has been beset by its natural enemies, by ignorance and superstition, by lust of conquest and by love of ease, by the strong man's craving for power, and the poor man's craving for food." [2]

"Yet power, as Machiavelli perceived, is the very stuff of politics," the practical student of modern politics answered angrily Acton's pious nonsense, "the deciding factor in public and international affairs. Existing in the nature of things, acquired or conserved by one country, squandered or lost by another, it is ever at work inexorably shaping events. What must settle the future of humanity is to whom it belongs and how it is used." [3]

We are reconstructing this imaginary discussion between men who, in fact, lived in different centuries, because we know that Forrestal studied them both in his search for an answer to his great dilemma. The silent argument of printed pages failed to resolve it. But battle did.

It happened on February 26, 1945. On that day, from the deck of a command ship of the U.S. Navy, in the company of Lieutenant-General Holland Smith of the Marines, he watched the climax of the battle of Iwo Jima. Wearing a steel helmet and the combat garb of a Marine private, he watched with his own eyes young Americans die by the hundreds despite the most painstaking material preparations and determination to cut human losses to a minimum.

When—a week or so later—he returned to the United States, James Forrestal spoke of his "tremendous admiration and reverence for the guy who walks up beaches and takes enemy positions with a rifle, grenade, or his bare hands." Concealed behind these words was an off-the-record psychological drama—the development of a new, hard core in a man's soul.

James Forrestal had always scorned war with the groping peace-mindedness of the average American. He held with James Thomson that war is man's corruption and disgrace. In the bloody battle for Iwo, his civilized dislike of war suddenly hardened into hatred. After this brutal shock, his mind was not again to be free of its effect. It even left physical marks upon him: a new brassy petulance in his eyes, deeper furrows on his brow, a forced jut to his chin, a tough, grim, gritty look to his face.

However powerful the experience, Iwo did not turn Forrestal into a pacifist. He was far too realistic to adopt such an overcharged emotional response even under immense provocation. He knew that in the modern world, conflicts are inevitable consequences of competition among nations. From his preoccupation with the great commentators on power, Hegel, Russel, Seillière, Marx, Hobbes, and Plato, he knew that war is usually the answer to what E. M. Winslow later so aptly called "the search for a formula." He determined to look deeper into the question and broaden his search for answers more adequate to his own quandary as a man of peace.

The outcome of this search was a philosophy of power.

Those who were close to Forrestal in those winter and spring days of 1945 found him somewhat moody, fretful, with a quiet, deeply buried wrath burning within him. It was obvious that he was groping for answers. When, a few months later, he found the solution to the great dilemma of a man who, hating war, must nonetheless bend every effort to it, his solution turned out to be far from original. The hypothesis had a long tradition in American history. It was first expressed by George Washington in 1790, but even he had borrowed the thought from Vegetius and Horace: "To be prepared for war is one of the most effectual means of preserving peace."

In the office of James Forrestal in the Pentagon, there was a printed card in a narrow black frame, proclaiming his policy and philosophy in the words of C. H. Van Tyne: *"We will never have universal peace until the strongest army and the strongest navy are in the hands of the most peaceful nation."*

Iwo was really only a catalyst in Mr. Forrestal's formalization of this idea. His long study of power had presented him much earlier with the intellectual challenge to evolve his own philosophy, to base it on a firm theoretical foundation and provide for it a sound scientific scaffolding.

The history of this intellectual evolution can be traced back to some time after the fall of France. Forrestal, then Under-Secretary of the Navy, was almost completely occupied with procurement problems.

His evenings and nights were devoted to a new interest—geopolitics. A close personal friend, Professor Robert Strausz-Hupé, wrote the first book in the U.S. on General Haushofer's ambiguous theories, and Forrestal was led by it to study this science further. From Haushofer, he went back to the original Mackinder and the Kjellen schools of geopolitics. But he failed to find answers to the questions his mind was constantly and impatiently posing. He concluded that neither German, British, nor Swedish geopolitical theories were adaptable to American problems. A functional, realistic common-sense, democratic American geopolitics would, he felt, have to be created from scratch rather than developed from alien prototypes.

Therefore, in 1943–44, he invited some of America's outstanding political scientists and historians to Washington. They were told the problem and given the fullest academic freedom to develop the system according to their own beliefs.

The permanent product of the project was the book, *Foundations of National Power*. Its theme was this extract from Carl Becker's then-current book, *How New Will the Better World Be*.[4]

"The simple fact is that politics is inseparable from power. States and governments exist to exert power, for the maintenance of order, the administration of justice, the defense of the community against aggression—in theory always and solely for these good ends. But the power, much or little, is always there, and will be used for some end, good, bad, or indifferent. ... Even those who deplore great political power because it is inherently dangerous ... recognize that a 'new and better world' cannot be made without it."

The popularization of this thesis on the eve of America's greatest moment in history may, we believe, be recorded as a major achievement of Forrestal.

The project stands even today as the only American effort at coming to grips intellectually with the major dilemma of the postwar United States: the *use of power* commensurate with the country's international responsibilities.

It is a truism that the desire for power, in the words of Thomas Hobbes "... is a general inclination of all mankind, a perpetual and restless desire of Power after power, that ceaseth only in Death."

The central idea of James Forrestal's political philosophy was a far more intricate development of this power principle. In his position as Secretary of Defense, he had many opportunities to apply his theories. Probably the first such demonstration came on July 21, 1945, in a letter to Senator Tom Connally, then as today chairman of the Senate Foreign Relations Committee, expressing determination to keep the strategic islands wrested from Japan during the war. This policy, in direct contradiction to Mr. Truman's moralistic declaration in Potsdam, later became the cornerstone of the United States policy within the United Nations.

Forrestal again was motivated by his new philosophy of power when less than two weeks after VJ-day, he called for a naval force consisting of 400 warships and 8,000 aircraft.[5]

But Forrestal's philosophy was never more clearly demonstrated than on September 30, 1946. Employing the old moralistic approach to American interests abroad, Congressmen, the press, and a considerable portion of the articulate public attacked the maintenance of U.S. naval forces in the Mediterranean. Forrestal's answer documented once and for all his philosophy of power:

"Today the U.S. Navy is continuing to maintain forces in the eastern Atlantic and the Mediterranean Sea for the following specific purposes:

"First, to support the Allied occupation forces and the Allied Military Government in the discharge of their responsibilities to the occupied areas of Europe.

"Second, to protect U.S. interests and support U.S. policies in the area." [6]

It is not generally known that President Roosevelt, toward the end of his life, had come to convictions similar to those that induced Forrestal to embark upon his power studies. In conversations with intimates during his last days, the late President said that, after the war, the United States would have to measure up to its international obligations and would therefore have to think in terms of *power politics* rather than in terms of what he called "the *welfare politics* advocated by Henry Wallace."

Roosevelt was not granted time either to elaborate upon or to share with the nation his new philosophy of power. Neither was Forrestal. The brutal realities of power remain to be glossed over by the diplomatic moralists of Washington. Characteristic of their moralism is their favorite after-dinner cliché that "world leadership has been thrust upon our country" and the new Fourth-of-July phrase that "the United States became a world power against its will." The theory of power has its own determinism. Power is not won in sweepstakes or gained in surrogate courts. It is achieved in hard toil and trouble by the fittest among the contestants.

The United States fought two world wars in one generation. It fought them well and in a good cause. If now, in the wake of those victories, it finds itself in the possession of the victor's supreme spoil—power—it must remember Disraeli's words that all power is but a trust and that its holder is accountable for its exercise.

Thus the meaning of power may as yet gain a new definition that is stripped of the term's old Machiavellian vulgarism and Actonian hypocrisy. But one wonders if Forrestal's departure from the scene did not remove from our midst the only man who was capable of devising this new definition and explaining it to our Washingtonians.

23. } THE GREAT WASHINGTON DILEMMA

To get the whole world out of bed
  And washed, and dressed, and warmed, and fed
To work, and back to bed again,
  Believe me, Saul, costs worlds of pain.
      JOHN MASEFIELD in The Everlasting Mercy

ONE FINE Indian summer day in 1949, Washington found itself suddenly confronted with the greatest dilemma growing out of America's new position of paramount power. For years it looked hesitantly to this day, when it would learn that Russia, long suspected of possessing the secrets of atomic energy, had actually exploded an A-bomb on one of its atomic proving grounds. There were several estimates floating around Washington as to the most likely date of such an explosion. The Air Force, excitable as its young people usually are, expected it to happen momentarily. The Navy, conservative and reserved, put down 1956 as the year. The Army, with admirable placidity, stayed noncommittal on the subject but when pressed for an estimate mentioned 1954 as the most likely date. A similar long-range view was taken by the men who should have known better, including General Leslie R. Groves and Dr. Vannevar Bush, our chief scientific planner. Dr. Bush's important book, *Modern Arms and Free Men,* almost went to press with the prediction that the Russians would not have an A-bomb for some time to come.

But then, in the early fall of 1949, the news was in. It reached the United States from a variety of sources, including a certain French source the disclosure of which would startle the world. The information was conveyed promptly to the White House by Rear Admiral Sidney W. Souers, then executive secretary of the National Security Council. Admiral Souers told the President that the Council regarded the evidence of Russian possession of the A-bomb as fully conclusive. The questions were (1) whether or not to share the information with the American people, (2) how to break the news, and (3) how to tell it to the people of the world.

If the Defense Department had prevailed the news would have remained in that category of classification that tops Top Secret. Then it would have reached the nation, we presume, in leaks or gossip, rumor or revelation by news commentators between two singing commercials. Fortunately the Department's views were not allowed to prevail. Mr. Truman decided to share the secret with the people.

The inherent menace of his decision weighed most heavily on all minds in the White House. It caused two sleepless nights to the President himself. He was most apprehensive that an injudicious statement would turn loose panic and hysteria throughout the land, a run on the banks, and an exodus from the cities.

Washington took a deep breath and on September 23, 1949, the President told the world about that Soviet A-bomb.[1] It was going on toward Friday afternoon, the people of America slowing down to their usual week-end standby. The weather was fine. Life was beautiful. The nation was in the midst of an epic World Series, the Yankees and Dodgers blacking out the news from Russia. So when the flash was out, the American people responded to the immense headlines with an impressive shrug of their collective shoulders: "So what?"

No one will ever know for certain what really motivated this response—whether it was the circumspect handling of the news, or the nation's preoccupation with its favorite pastime, or the adult intelligence of the American people, or simply apathy and psychic inertia that made the news go down so well, without excitement, panic, or hysteria.

Up to this point the event was handled masterfully by two responsible Americans—Truman and Souers—who have an innate affinity with the little people of this country. But there the achievement ended. From then on the news was shamefully mishandled by the notorious Washington information mill. Within the hour of the President's announcement, Pentagon public relations tried to disavow their Commander-in-Chief. Leaving a Cabinet meeting, Secretary Johnson told the press that "I wouldn't jump to conclusions if I were you, boys." In off-the-record statements the impression was peddled that it was not even an A-bomb that exploded somewhere in Russia; that our military experts refused to believe that the Russians had anything even resembling an A-bomb; and that the President was ill advised when he rushed to the people with the news.[2]

The White House became intimidated. Probably influenced by the secret-mongers of Washington, it failed to top the excellence of its initial handling of the news with an appropriate followup. The people were left suspended in air, not really knowing what to make of the secret they shared and how to react to a reality that is likely to influence their future and their lives.

Preoccupied as he was with the "domestic angle," President Truman, too, neglected to consider the international implications of this enormous new reality. Somehow he failed to look beyond the millions of his fellow Americans, to the hundreds of millions in the uneasy democratic world to whom the A-bomb posed a set of vexatious new questions. They looked to Washington for the answers and when they did not find them in their newspapers or hear them on their radios they grew restive and dubious. The Russians, on their part, were in no hurry to provide answers. In fact they kept uncannily quiet about the whole affair, in a calculated psychological effort to deepen the mystery and aggravate uncertainty. They are usually correct in gauging the minds of the peoples in Europe and Asia.

To those millions overseas the Russian A-bomb is no academic matter. It is one thing, they say, to live behind an oceanic barrier of 3,000 miles and another to live next door to the airfields from which A-bomb carriers can take off for short hops. The average European never cherished the idea of a Russo-American war in his back yard. The prospect of a Russo-American *atomic* war is repulsive to him. He is not particularly impressed when told that new American ultrafortresses are capable of delivering the

A-bomb, or anything, to Magnitogorsk or Irkutsk or Vladivostok or Murmansk, when they expect retaliation to hit, not Detroit or Houston or San Francisco or New York, but Paris and Oslo and Rome and Amsterdam. The Russians keep quiet but they never discourage these kinds of speculations.

Even if President Truman wanted to, he would not have found it an easy task to explain the meaning of the Russian A-bomb to the peoples of our world. For the plain truth is that the secret and unseen bomb of Russia demolished the very premise on which our war theories and security philosophies were built. First, it dealt a fatal blow to the concept of the "Atomic Blitz," or what Admiral Radford described as the "mass bombing of urban areas"; [3] and, second, it exposed the North Atlantic Pact as an ineffective means of our security.

Until that day in September, 1949, our military planners banked heavily on our exclusive possession of the atomic weapon. First they assumed that its sheer possession would be sufficient to keep the Russians from attacking us. Most of our operational plans revolved around the bomb, envisaging as they did a transcontinental war in which huge planes would take off from the scattered fields of our Strategic Bomber Command in the U.S., carry A-bombs to carefully chosen targets in Russia, return to the United States, and report to General LeMay, "Mission accomplished, sir, the war is won!" It was frequently painful and distressing to listen to young Air Force generals expounding and defending this theory, apparently convinced that it was a good one and that it would work.

We are not going to relive the odious B-36 controversy on these pages. Neither are we going to bat for the Navy's argument that carrier-borne planes are more effective than long-range land-based planes to execute such a fantastic mission. It was not the plane that was wrong but the theory of war revolving around it.

There is, however, one important point that needs to be made. In the realm of weapon development the term "bigger" does not necessarily denote "better" arms. On the contrary it is usually indicative of stagnant imagination whenever our ordnance experts come up with bigger versions of old weapons. For a while battleships were the apple of the eyes of all navies. They, too, went through the development from better to bigger. At first they displaced only a few thousand tons, but ended up with monsters like the German *Tirpitz* and the Japanese *Yamato*, whose immense tonnage was in excess of anything afloat but whose usefulness was nil.[4] Indeed one is not too far off base with the statement, which should be foremost in the minds of our military planners, that the bigger a conventional weapon becomes in the course of its development the more obsolete it is likely to turn out.

It is alarming, indeed, in this connection that our designers should not be able to improve upon our aircraft carriers and planes beyond suggesting bigger versions of old models. In an age in which the military planner is confronted with the unique problems of absolute weapons he cannot depend on the implements of yesterday's wars. He needs new weapons and has to build his new tactics around them.

The Molotov cocktail, that can be made and handled even by a child, proved often more effective than the intricate contraptions and traps built against tanks. Even today there are new vessels of gunboat size in many navies, which pack the fire power of modern cruisers and have the mobility of latest-type destroyers, combining the two basic elements of modern tactics in a manner of unprecedented efficiency in the smallest of space. Bacteria are unquestionably the most minuscule weapon ever devised and yet they are likely to become the most effective in any future war.

Hitler's strange military genius recognized a mounting revolution in military science but he failed since he acted upon the recognition too late. According to the official *German War Diary*, the Fuehrer urged his professional military and naval advisers to "forget about old weapons" and to "think up new ones," radical new inventions that would revolutionize the battlefield.[5] The professional military mind soaked in textbook tradition failed to respond to the stimulus. The German generals and admirals failed, for example, to develop atomic energy for military purposes.[6] But they succeeded in some other fields, as, for example, in the development of new underwater weapons, jet propulsion, and guided missiles. Stalin, too, belongs to the nonprofessional class of astute military thinkers. He is on record with the idea that future wars cannot be waged and won with old weapons. His scientists are working feverishly on the development of unorthodox arms, not in the abstract and fantastic atmosphere created by Hitler's mystic mind, but along practical lines influenced by Stalin's supreme realism. That uncomplicated simple mind produced the *Katyusha* which turned the tide of the Stalingrad battle.[7]

We must never indulge in the smug self-delusion that Americans are the best and most unorthodox weapon developers in the world. Somehow our imagination was a bit tardy in World War II when it came to the development of the great electronic miracles which Mr. Churchill properly and early foresaw would help win the war. Only a few of the great new developments of World War II were the product of native American imagination. Radar was first developed in Britain. Jet propulsion was developed in Britain and Germany. Guided missiles were developed in Germany. Rockets were developed in Russia. The breather or Schnorkel for protracted underwater cruising of submarines was invented in Holland and developed in Germany. The contact fuse, as decisive a piece as any developed during the war, was invented in Canada.

Even the development of the atomic bomb needed foreign prodding and encouragement. The hypothesis of fission was first announced and its experimental confirmation first obtained in 1939. But it was left to a "group of foreign-born physicists centering on L. Szilard and including E. Wigner, E. Teller, V. F. Weisskop, and E. Fermi," and to their foreign-born sponsor Dr. Alechsander Sachs, to stimulate reluctant American support for its use for military purposes.[8]

The obvious conclusion is that, neither unorthodox new weapons, nor such orthodox old ones as the B-36's, or Navy planes launched from the deck of even the biggest new carrier could decide the war with a strategic assault on the first day of the conflict. We must not forget that the A-bomb, that is supposed to have defeated Japan, was used, not at the beginning, but at the end of a long war of attrition. Napoleon, the Kaiser, and Hitler lost their wars against Russia because they failed to take into consideration the immense land and human masses of that incredible country. No matter how little Stalin seems to think of the wisdom of Clausewitz, he could gain reassurance from these words which the great Prussian military philosopher wrote "on the character of modern war":

> Since all methods formerly usual were upset by Buonaparte's luck and boldness, and first-rate Powers almost wiped out at a blow; since the Spaniards by their stubborn resistance have shown what the general arming of a nation and insurgent measures on a great scale can effect, in spite of weakness and porousness of individual parts; since Russia, by the campaign of 1812 has taught us, first, that an Empire of great dimensions is not to be conquered (which might have been easily known before), secondly, that the probability of final success does not in all cases diminish in the same measure as battles, capitals, and provinces are lost (which was formerly an incontrovertible principle with all diplomatists, and therefore made them always ready to enter at once into some bad temporary peace), but that a nation is often strongest in the heart of its country, if the enemy's offensive power has exhausted itself, and with what enormous force the defensive then springs over to the offensive; further, since Prussia (1813) has shown that sudden efforts may add to an Army sixfold by means of the militia, and that this militia is just as fit for service abroad as in its own country;—since all these events have shown what an enormous factor the heart and sentiments of a Nation may be in the product of its political and military strength, in fine, since governments have found out all these additional aids, it is not to be expected that they will let them lie idle in future Wars, whether it be that danger threatens their own existence, or that restless ambition drives them on.[9]

Visualize, then, even fleets of huge B-36's with hundreds of A-bombs in their bays, scattered in the immense air-ocean of the Soviet Commonwealth, tiny specks high above the clouds, with little men in them staring intently into bomb sights, trying to pinpoint the solar plexus of the Bolsheviks in an area covering 12,873,000 square miles, from Vladivostok to the Oder River.

THE NORTH ATLANTIC PACT

Our hapless theory of war was closely associated with our new philosophy of security that rests on a system of largely sentimental alliances: the North Atlantic Pact, the Military Aid Program to Turkey and Greece, the American Defense Compact; and on such bilateral arrangements as those existing with Iran, Southern Korea, and others.

The military commitments of the United States are unprecedented indeed in their dispersion, which is contrary to the basic military theory that concentration at focal points is the basic criterion of strategic strength. "The best strategy is *always to be very strong*," Clausewitz wrote in this connection, "first generally then at the decisive point. Therefore, apart from the energy which creates the army, a work which is not always done by the general, there is no more imperative and no simpler law for strategy than to *keep the forces concentrated*." [10] This basic law of "assembly of forces in space" is incomprehensibly violated by our acceptance of widely separated commitments. Out of it develops the fallacious assumption that we would be capable of defending the whole democratic world simultaneously and everywhere.

The center of gravity of our military concept is, of course, the North Atlantic Defense Alliance. "In our quest for peace and security," Secretary Johnson said, "we do not march alone. Beside us are the eleven resolute nations which have been banded together with us under the North Atlantic Treaty, as well as other liberty-loving countries which have received friendship, inspiration, and material aid from us. This treaty was an epochal event and should enhance our own security and the collective security of all free nations." [11]

One can but wonder about the purpose of such a presentation of the North Atlantic Pact. The fact is that our allies, however resolute they may be (and we doubt that they are), are also weak and impoverished, suffer from all the consequences of a devastating war, are beset with all kinds of economic and social troubles. Above all they view war with distaste and personal horror.

Washington had many memorable opportunities in 1949 to remind itself of its glamorous new role as the capital of the democratic world, but none was more memorable than April 4, the day of the signing of the North Atlantic Treaty. To some of us who dislike this kind of synthetic pageantry, the setting of the signing looked like an imitation of those glittering diplomatic spectacles Mussolini and Hitler used to stage whenever they lassoed still another hapless satellite. Of course the comparison ends right there. On our part it is not a question of selfish aggrandizement but a sincere desire to aid ourselves by aiding our allies.

For days the Protocol Division of the State Department was looking for a hall spacious enough to accommodate this pageant. When they eventually found one, the quiet and simple auditorium of the Interior Department, they decorated it with flags and potted palms. On the platform were four rows of chairs for their excellencies the foreign ministers and ambassadors of the signatories. Admission was by embossed invitation. Only the cream of Washington was expected to attend. Somehow, watching the morning-coated procession of guests, one had the feeling that the people were not invited and not really wanted at the spectacle. This was a *diplomatic* affair.

While the distinguished guests were waiting for their excellencies, a band was entertaining them. Its selection was by no means designed to provide musical themes for the occasion. Yet it was a curious coincidence that one of the tunes played was George Gershwin's "It Ain't Necessarily So," from the opera *Porgy and Bess.*

Even as their excellencies rolled off their polished speeches, signed the instrument of incorporation one after another with celebrated fountain pens, an event took place about 3,000 miles from the potted palms of the Interior auditorium that showed up the inconsistencies of our whole defense philosophy in frightening detail. Italy's own foreign minister was among the signers of the North Atlantic Pact. Bravely he said: "This pact is a complex and articulate instrument in which the will prevails to discourage, through our unity, any aggressive move...." [12] Melancholy words! Virtually in that same hour we moved to disband and demolish one of the important elements of our democratic strength. While Count Sforza was sailing west to the signing of the Pact, one third of the Italian Fleet was sailing east to join the Red Fleet as spoils of war. One is inclined to ask: is this the concrete way in which we propose to discourage aggression, by handing over, on a silver platter, the means of aggression to a potential aggressor? On the one side we agreed to arm

Italy so that she could defend herself against Russian aggression. On the other we stripped her of the best means of her defense, her useful and valiant fleet that joined us in 1943, at great risk, of her own accord.[13]

This event by itself has canceled out in one sweep much of the strain and toil that went into the making of the North Atlantic Treaty. Until that day in the spring of 1949, Russia had no means of contesting our control of the Mediterranean or putting, in the form of a strong Black Sea Fleet, physical pressure on the Dardanelles. But then, with a stroke of our pen, we endowed her with unexpected strength and made her into a substantial seapower in the Eastern Mediterranean. We gave only scrap iron to Japan and it is a long process before scrap can be made into battleships. To Russia we were giving the battleships.

In the same April when we thus increased Russia's naval power, Secretary of Defense Johnson ordered that the Navy's 63,000-ton supercarrier *United States* be scrapped forthwith. In the same month there was plenty of hot action in the cold war. Communist batteries on the north bank of the Yangtze shelled the British cruiser *London,* the destroyer *Consort,* and the sloops *Amethyst* and *Black Swan,* killing forty-two British seamen. In that same month the Communists of China conquered Nanking; the Communists of the Philippines ambushed and killed the widow and daughter of the republic's first president and ten members of their entourage; the Communists of Rumania kicked out two non-Communist members of their so-called coalition government; the Communists of Bulgaria hanged one of their own, Vice-Premier Traicho Kostov. In Paris the Communists were holding a world congress of their Partisans of World Peace, as an answer to the Washington signing of the North Atlantic Pact. Paul Robeson, head of the American delegation, declared that the Negroes of America would never fight against the U.S.S.R. Clearly, despite the pageantry in Washington and the nonsense of Robeson's declaration, the Bolsheviks had the initiative and were on the offensive.

The administration of Mr. Truman is fully committed to its own philosophy of security, which has the foreign-aid program for its cornerstone. This aid extends from political and cultural to economic and military fields. In the fiscal years of 1948–51 it cost us $22 billion.[14] (By comparison, we spent only $19 million on foreign aid in 1939.) This is an expensive means of maintaining the stability of allies and bolstering their military potential—of preserving, indeed, this uneven coalition that we deem essential for success in the cold war and indispensable for victory in the hot one.

This foreign-aid program had to be sold to the people of America and Congress. No one can deny that the Truman administration did a reputable selling job. But it also acquired a dilemma which it is incapable of solving without the danger of sacrificing the whole project. The dilemma is whether or not to tell the American people and their Congress the truth about the state of Europe, the truth about the value of this system of alliances, especially in the light of certain conversations some of the foreign and defense ministers of the North Atlantic Pact countries had with our own diplomatic and military officials.

The fact is that only two of the North Atlantic Pact countries, Great Britain and Norway, accept without qualifications the role we assigned to them as bulwarks against Russia. The high officials of Britain and Norway assured the United States in no uncertain terms that they meant every bit of it when they affixed their signatures to the various North Atlantic pacts and that they intended to live up to the letter and spirit of the Pact. Others offered certain qualifications which, in fact, made the ultimate value of the whole Pact as a means of American security somewhat illusory. France, especially, cautioned the State and Defense Departments not to expect too much from her in the event of premeditated Soviet aggression. She admonished our leaders to soft pedal the tone of their utterances when dealing with Russia. "Do not provoke war," they said in effect, "because we could not fulfill our obligations should we ever be called upon to carry them out." [15]

This is the kind of dormant bankruptcy that becomes evident promptly when the bills become due. There is more to the cynical Washington quip that defined the North Atlantic Alliance as a pact "obligating Luxembourg to come to the aid of the United States when attacked by Honduras" than meets the eye.

And yet one cannot blame our uneasy European allies for

refusing to rush headlong into war and annihilation. The pompous and, in some cases hypocritical, speeches delivered at the signing of the North Atlantic Pact represented merely the façade of the system, concealing developments within the edifice. When the defense chiefs of the North Atlantic countries were first acquainted with the ideas we had for their defense they threw up their hands in astonishment and despair. The general idea was to allow the Russians to overrun Europe while we delivered our grandiloquent strategic assault against the U.S.S.R. proper, the hinterland of the continental war. Then everyone was supposed to settle down to a stalemate or a phony war and look on while the United States rolled up its sleeves and started pouring out all that Secretary Johnson likes to call "hardware," the military equipment needed for the counteroffensive. "Do not worry," we told our European friends. "Even though you might be occupied for a year or so, we shall return and redeem you from bondage."

Commander Rodolfo Pacciardi represented Italy at the military phase of these conferences. He had no reason to be timid or inhibited by the memories of Mussolini's sins against the democracies. He was a gallant enemy of the defunct Duce, fighting against him on many battlefields. As Italy's minister of defense, he brought professional knowledge and common sense, as well as wholesome Italian sophistication to these negotiations, in addition to a courage to speak up in the presence of our Joint Chiefs. He told them in so many words that their plan would not work, if only because there would be precious little left of those Western European countries after one- or two-year occupation by the Russians, and whatever would be left would hardly be worth the effort of reconquest.

The Russians arrive in conquered lands with a highly perfected system of extermination and co-ordination. They come with blacklists and execution squads. They do not need a whole year to round up all who may at any future time organize undergrounds against them, or spy on them, or keep the home fires burning while America prepares for war. The Soviet system was tested in Eastern Europe and perfected there. Three nights of anarchy and terror are sufficient to reduce an occupied country to abject subservience, to purge it of its democratic leaders, and to emasculate it in blind fury, even as A-bombs might be dropping on Russian cities. The American plan had to be changed and redrafted along more realistic lines.

Another question was the distribution of weapons and the kind of arms to be made available for the defense of those countries. In this, one fears, our European partners show little judicious restraint. They submit long lists, ask for anything from battleships to embossed buttons for dress uniforms of admirals. Most of the weapons they are asking for are offensive arms par excellence, useful for aggression but useless for defense. This is the traditional blind spot of the professional military men in small countries whose chauvinistic pride deprives them of a sense of proportion and realism. Anyone who has ever watched military parades of little nations was always impressed with the array of their weapons displayed on parade grounds and in maneuvers. There were the heavy tanks, both of them, the self-propelled heavy guns, four or five, and big bombers flying overhead, half a squadron. A small country, or a weak one, usually refuses to admit to the facts of its smallness and weakness, and insists on aping the big and strong in the assortment of its arsenal.

What our little allies now need are *defensive* weapons: antitank guns instead of tanks, antiaircraft guns instead of bombers, the less spectacular but far more effective light arms to knock out the big enemy's vast war machine. The bazooka should be the symbol of the small nation in its present-day predicament. The experience of the recent war, it seems, taught us no lesson in this respect. Were we not told that Holland would foil a German attack because it had a small but effective army and dikes that could be opened with a master switch? But Holland was lost in three days. Even France succumbed, because her arsenals were building offensive weapons when it was defensive arms she needed.

There is still another point a frank review of which is essential to place this whole problem of arms in a better perspective. Arms valued at $645 million are to be sent abroad to equip members of the North Atlantic defense alliance. On paper this is quite a sum, especially when viewed against the national budgets of the recipients. But the arms go to eleven countries, with less than $65 million worth of equipment going to each on an average. Then again, dollars and cents can never express the quantitative and qualitative value of arms. Paying the highest prices for military equipment of any country, we get, of course, less for our dollar than foreign countries where production is cheaper and where arms are manufactured by nonprofitmaking nationalized industries.

A comparison between the price of weapons in the U.S. and foreign countries reveals that arms are 40 per cent cheaper in Europe than in the U.S. On this basis, the arms-aid program provides approximately 40 per cent less in actual value than the price would indicate it is providing on paper. Thus, in the final analysis, the material aid we are able to give to our hard-pressed allies in Europe is just a drop in the bucket. It will take a long haul to get them up to the point of military efficiency necessary to defend themselves—if this kind of dispersed aid will ever succeed in achieving that goal.

It is not pleasant to contemplate the European war with the armies which our allies will have ready even by 1956 and with the plans we are preparing for them. All this lacks the realism that was the chief attribute of our planning developed in the course of World War II. The only difference is that next time we shall hardly be allowed time to develop realism on an "as-you-go" basis. A little quip our Secretary of Defense made, offhand, to his fellow alumni of University of Virginia went far to show the whole dangerous inadequacy of our defense philosophy. He assured his audience that "if Russia should start something at four A.M. we would be on the job at five A.M." Our experience at Pearl Harbor should have taught us the lesson that we must be on the job at three o'clock if we want to meet a possible enemy attack at four. The one hour which Mr. Johnson is apparently willing to grant his military establishment to get ready for the "job" is eternity, indeed, in the age of modern war.

Now these are the facts of life which our solicitous government is trying to keep from us children. And therein lies the insoluble dilemma of the Truman administration. Should the administration tell the people and Congress that we are buying no definite assurances and security for the vast sums of money we are pouring into Europe and some parts of Asia, and that we are likely to face a "China situation" in Europe should it ever come to a showdown, the entire foreign-aid program might be placed in jeopardy. Congress would be most likely to withhold appropriations and bring the whole program down somewhat with the gesture of the biblical giant who perished himself under the ruins of the house he destroyed in his blindness and fury. And the people would probably drift quietly back to isolationism in the conviction that we are still secure behind our oceanic defenses as long as we are minding our own business.

The administration believes itself to be obligated to cover up the realities of Western Europe, to conceal the inherent weakness of our allies, and gloss over the precarious state of our advanced defense lines that extend to innumerable fronts all over the world against an opponent who holds the inner line. In 1950, the dilemma was bearing down most heavily on Secretary of State Dean G. Acheson, who did not create the problems which were vexing him most. In addition he also had to defend himself against charges of pro-Russian sentiments and suspicions of appeasement. He had to satisfy three masters: the President, the people and Congress, and his foreign friends. Thus our Secretary of State had to walk the thin tightrope of American diplomacy without the aid of a safety net. His personal tragedy accrued from the basic deficiency of the Truman administration that fails to recognize that the people of America are grown up and fully able to understand the problems and pains of internationalism. A heavy pale of secrecy has again descended on the diplomacy of the world. Still today, in our own democracy, vital decisions affecting the future of our peoples are made by men of limited responsibility behind the tightly closed doors of diplomatic drawing rooms and military headquarters.

Our chief partners in the cold war, Britain and France, are old-fashioned practitioners of continental diplomacy who find it difficult, after centuries of secret diplomacy, to open their books, as well as their hearts, to their peoples. The Russians regard secrecy as a vital element of their strength and security. Foreign Minister Andrei Y. Vishinsky boasted of the totality of Soviet secrecy and said that it is Russia's first line of defense against a hostile world.

In a genuine and truly popular democracy like ours, the only such republic in the whole modern world, secrecy must have a clearly defined meaning and place. In the final analysis it is the gravest challenge to the institution of democracy itself. Who is entitled to keep what from the people? And how can the people's influence be sustained on the intentions and decisions of their government if vital information and explanations are deliberately withheld from them? Can a democracy survive as a democracy in an atmosphere and mood of secrecy?

Because of the spread of official secrecy through our administration, there is no intimate link between the people of America and their own security apparatus. In this twilight our people develop a feeling of insecurity—chiefly because they have no means of ascertaining how secure they really are. They have to take Mr. Truman's, or Mr. Johnson's, or Mr. Acheson's word that they are secure indeed and that the best of care is being taken of their safety. But those among us who do remember Pearl Harbor and recall how safe we were then, demand more tangible evidence than mere administrative assurances that have been found woefully wanting in our recent past.

A need to take the people of America into the confidence of their government is keenly, sincerely, and instinctively felt by President Truman. Unfortunately he but rarely practices the commands of this wholesome instinct and virtually never *explains* our own and our opponent's moves on the international checkerboard, the meaning of current history.[16]

From time to time, hand-picked representatives of press and radio, of industry and finance, of labor and the arts are invited to Washington with gestures of condescending confidence to attend "briefings" or "orientations" staged by various hush-hush branches of the government. An elaborate, and frequently ludicrous, show of secrecy is maintained at these events punctuated with joyrides and cocktail parties in the best public-relations tradition. But what those chosen people learn as top-secret information usually resembles much of the news that the *New York Times* had seen fit to print some time before. Those meetings of the "élite" with the "initiated" merely serve to emphasize the decay of our official information policies.

Thus, when in 1949–50 the cold war was entering its decisive stage, the American public seemed to be getting from their government fewer "confidential tips" than ever before. No policy statements were forthcoming unless they were issued to justify *past* policies. Queries were met with monotonous "no comments," with facetious subterfuges, with diplomatic double talk, with contradictory "clarifications."

Perhaps we would be more charitable and complacent about our government's major failure to take the American people into its confidence were we convinced that it is due merely to a justifiable concept of exaggerated secrecy in a real emergency. Unfortunately we are not satisfied that this is the case. We have reason to fear that frequently secrecy is motivated by a desire to cover up gropings and ignorance, to conceal the absence of clear-cut ideas and imagination, to gloss over the lack of policy, to hide timidity and opportunism, or, the worst of them all, to conceal evidences of blunders.

It goes without saying that such practice merely adds to the confusion and bewilderment of the American people—a state of mind that has its inevitable repercussions, in a truly vicious circle, on the actions of the government as well.

What are we being told? Within one single week in the spring of 1950, our three highest-ranking executives revealed complete satisfaction with the order of things under their control. Mr. Truman told us that the U.S. was in the finest shape it ever had been in any comparable period of its history following any war ever fought by the country—and took full credit for this fine state of affairs. Secretary of Defense Johnson declared that his Military Establishment of the United States was in the best shape of preparedness in any peacetime period in the history of the United States. And Secretary of State Dean Acheson stated that the State Department was never better, or more efficient than today.

In situations like this, Alfred E. Smith liked to say: "And now let us look at the record." No one can deny that the United States achieved remarkable successes in vital spots of its global ministrations to the outpatients of the world's democratic wards. The Marshall Plan, especially, yielded gratifying results, but how far it has been responsible for keeping Western Europe out of the Red camp is one of those moot questions that not even history will ever be able to settle to everybody's satisfaction. There is, in fact, no evidence whatever that the Russians were ready to take over France and Italy at this time. So there can be no evidence that we succeeded in preventing them from doing what they did not intend to do. The fact is that the numerical strength of the Communists and their sympathizers in Italy and France did not diminish materially, even though their influence had been curtailed. As long as one third of a nation stays in the Communist camp that nation remains on the critical list. The symptoms of the illness may be gone but the illness itself remains uncured.

On the other side of the ledger is the sad record of the many defeats we suffered in the cold war. A catalogue of these defeats was provided by Secretary Johnson himself, almost in the same breath in which he assured the nation that everything was in the finest of shape. Appearing before the House Committee on Appropriations to plead for additional funds for some more "hardware," he conceded that our perfect defenses needed some improvement, after all, "in the light of recent events."

"The events to which I allude," Secretary Johnson said, "include the Soviet atomic explosion (somewhat in advance of the date we had anticipated), the fall of China, the serious situations in Southeast Asia, the break in diplomatic relations with Bulgaria and deteriorating relations with other satellite countries, the Soviet assumption of control over the armed forces of Poland, Soviet naval expansion, the increased Soviet pressure in Germany, the recent attack on naval aircraft in the Baltic, and the recent Soviet demands to Trieste." [17]

It is an immensely and alarmingly impressive list. It was further amplified by Mr. Acheson who, a few days before, mentioned renewed Soviet demands for special rights in the Dardanelles and the action of the Communist-controlled satellite governments against the U.S. as contributions to the seriousness of the tense world situation.

Reading such a candid list one must ask: Did all these defeats find our government unprepared? Was none of them anticipated? Was nothing done to prevent them from coming to pass? What are some of the answers?

(1) *The atomic bomb*. No matter what Washington now says, we did not expect the Russians to have a workable A-bomb for another two to eight years. So we thought we had time

enough to adapt our strategic and tactical concepts to the reality
of a Soviet A-bomb. In the meantime we went ahead with the
development of strategic and tactical ideas which failed to take
Soviet possession of the A-bomb into consideration. According to
Mr. Johnson, the National Security Council and the Joint Chiefs
of Staff "began their re-evaluation of the world situation, and its
relation to American defense requirements, immediately *after*
[sic] President Truman announced that there had been an
atomic explosion in the Soviet Union." But even seven months
after that announcement, and almost a year and a half *after*
what we believe was the first explosion, he had to add: "I would
not like to leave the impression that these studies are completed." Thus the fact emerges from Mr. Johnson's remarkable
confession that our defense policies are, at the time of this
writing, not adjusted to atomic realities and that we are not
properly prepared to wage an atomic war.

(2) *The fall of China.* Could the fall of China have been prevented with a more dynamic foreign policy? We think that we
had an excellent opportunity to do just that. The opportunity
for this arose with General Marshall's mission to China. His report of January 7, 1947, was remarkable for its wisdom and
frankness. However, our publicists focused our attention on its
negative elements. A powerful Kuomintang lobby persuaded us
not to recognize or heed its positive recommendations.

A man of General Marshall's insight, integrity, power of observation, and objectivity could not fail to recognize the material
corruption of the right wing of the Kuomintang and the political corruption of the left wing of the Communists. But he
discovered a potent third force in China and suggested that we
make it the center of our considerations and plans.

"The salvation of the situation, as I see it, would be the assumption of leadership by the liberals in the Government and
in the minority parties, a splendid group of men, but who as yet
lack the political power to exercise a controlling influence,"
General Marshall wrote. "Successful action on their part under
the leadership of Generalissimo Chiang Kai-shek would, I believe, lead to unity through good government." [18]

Nothing was done to implement this recommendation. The
adroit manipulations of the Kuomintang lobby on which

Chiang's corrupt henchmen spent hundreds of thousands of American taxpayer dollars managed to conceal from us the truly democratic elements in China.

Militarily, too, we could have created a kind of third force to stop and frustrate the Communist offensive. Today it is known that the combat strength of the Communists rarely exceeded 20,000 officers and men in any single campaign, against which the Kuomintang could oppose hundreds of thousands of troops. Colonel Curt Conrad Arnade, an ex-officer of the German General Staff who served as one of Chiang's advisers on strategy with the well-known Falkenhausen Mission, told us quite seriously that he could have stopped the Communists and turned the tide of civil war in China with an army not exceeding the numerical and material strength of New York's metropolitan police.·

There was an obscure effort made in this country to create a military third force under Feng Yu-hsiang, the "Christian General," who received such bad notices in Vincent Sheean's *Personal History*. Feng had been driven out of Peking in March, 1926, by Chang Tso-lin, and had gone to Moscow for a year. Then he suddenly reappeared in Mongolia with an army, as the savior of the Kuomintang.

"Everything he possessed from his army to the shirt on his back, he owed to the Russians," Sheean wrote, "and it never seems to have occurred to them that he would forget." But Feng did. He made a deal with Chiang against the Russians, in the manner not unusual among the war lords of China, just as it was not unexpected to see Feng leave Chiang's camp again and turn to us, as well as to the Russians behind our back, in search of another deal.[19]

But in 1948, Feng appeared a reformed war lord, his ethics and allegiance to the cause-of-single-purpose bolstered by a prolonged stay in the United States. Then one day in the summer of 1948, he disappeared from the U.S. and was discovered aboard a Russian vessel approaching the Soviet Union, en route to China, ostensibly to organize resistance to both the Communists and the nationalists. His movement seemed to have strong dissident roots in both camps. Rumor placed Chiang's Vice-President Li Tsung-jen, General Chang Chih-chung, and others in his group.

Feng's schemes were obscure indeed. No one knows what

promises and how much support he had from the Russians or from us. But the idea behind the abortive Feng mission (he burned to death when some movie films caught fire in his cabin) showed the way to organize such a third force and how to support it with all the might of the United States, in money and arms. If we had produced, in 1947–48, such a political and military third force, we could have gained for it both recognition and victory, while in its absence, we had to continue our support of the Chiang regime, maneuvering us into a predicament from which the State Department proved incapable of extricating the United States.

The antics of the Truman diplomacy in the dead-end street of China were remarkable indeed. On the one side, the State Department issued the bulky White Paper on U.S. relations with China. In it Mr. Acheson stated over his own signature that further aid to the Kuomintang people had become impossible because "they had sunk into corruption, into scramble for place and power, and into reliance on the United States to win the war for them and to preserve their own domestic supremacy." [20] Another administration spokesman, Senator Connally, described the Kuomintang as a cabal of unprincipled men unworthy of American aid and sympathy. But then, almost in the same breath, the Truman administration decided to support a Kuomintang campaign in the United Nations trying to win the war—inevitably lost in China—on the floor of the General Assembly in Flushing Meadows. The discrepancy between the State Department's words and actions, the grave cause of many of our defeats in the cold war, was never more evident than during those days in the summer and early fall of 1949, when the State Department was pulled hither and yon, between distaste and sympathy for the Kuomintang, between recognition and nonrecognition of the new dominant Communist regime.

It was no secret in Washington that Mr. Acheson, urged by the British, was most eager to recognize the Mao regime, firmly established in Peking, and that the White Paper was published to pave the way for recognition by closing the books on an ignoble era of the past. But then the Kuomintang lobby, an infinitesimal group of high-pressure public-relations men supported by huge sums of money, aroused apparent popular opposition to the plan.²¹ The State Department failed to take the American people into its confidence and say frankly that it would have liked to recognize the Peking regime. In failing to do so the Department violated its own basic diplomatic principle that nonrecognition is a negative approach to diplomacy and contrary to the working designs in the conduct of American foreign relations. The Department is quick in reasserting this policy whenever it is confronted with the question of recognizing a Latin American Junta or an Arab principality created in the sinister toil of some plotting militarists. But it was too slow in applying it to China where its application may represent the difference between eventual success and certain failure of America's Asian policy as a whole. This is an outstanding example of domestic politics interfering with the conduct of our foreign relations.

(3) *The appointment of Rokossovsky*. The first intelligence report describing in authentic detail Marshal Rokossovsky's impending mission to Poland reached us in the United States in August, 1949. His appointment was announced by the Russians three months later in November. The announcement itself was probably motivated by the realization that the news of Rokossovsky's transfer had leaked to the Western world and that his *séjour* in Warsaw could no longer be kept under cover. The Russians do not feel bound to announce such transfers. At present several Soviet marshals are serving with satellite armies and defense ministries, but only the mission of Konstantin Rokossovsky was given the limelight of publicity.

We should have acted immediately upon the information received about the impending transfer in the summer of 1949. Here was an opportunity for propaganda to join action in the cold war and to score one of its rare tangible triumphs. We realize that tradition-bound forces in the chancelleries of the world frown upon the use by propaganda of highly classified intelligence material. But propaganda can be a useful implement of the cold war only when and if it is fed material not generally found in the public domain and acquired, through daring or skill on the vast international battlefields of espionage, by operatives or *bona fide* informants. It was the work of such an informant, in communicating to us at once the Kremlin's decision to bring the Polish Army into Soviet bondage, that demanded a dexterous propaganda exploitation. The moment the news reached us we should have advertised it with all the means at our disposal, on the "Voice of America" beamed to the satellite world and in newspaper articles written on the basis of data given out to trustworthy correspondents. We should have warned Poland of the impending event and drawn the lesson of such a mission for the benefit of other satellites as well. We could have, with such a propaganda campaign, intimidated the Kremlin and frightened the Poles, and, indeed, thwarted Rokossovsky's mission to Warsaw. We would have given ammunition to the Gomulka group of Communist-nationalist dissidents within Poland, who could have pointed to the fact that the news of the Rokossovsky mission was already known to us in support of their plea to cancel the mission altogether. And, eventually, we should have kept the issue alive, through appeals to the United Nations, to the Hague Court of International Justice, and other international tribunals, and above all, through appeals to the Polish and satellite peoples over the heads of their government. The fact that virtually nothing was done, or is being done, that the Rokossovsky mission was treated as a one-day news item with no material for follow-up stories, helped the Russians to the very victory that Secretary Johnson now lists and regrets.

(4) *Deterioration of relations with the satellites.* It was in the form of another intelligence report, received from similar sources in 1947, that we first learned of an all-out campaign of diplomatic vilification that the satellites planned to wage against the United States and the United Kingdom. The report described in detail and quoted verbatim from a secret communication Foreign Minister (then Deputy Foreign Minister) Andrei Y. Vishinsky sent to all satellite foreign offices, in the summer of 1947. His note was drafted in the wake of a series of defections in Hungarian, Rumanian, Bulgarian, and Czechoslovakian diplomatic missions throughout the world. The Vishinsky document was designed not only to warn the satellites against the consequences of such defections, but also to let them know how the repetition of such incidents could be avoided in the future.

The document instructed the satellites to withdraw from their diplomatic missions all "unreliable elements whose allegiance to the Communist sections of the respective governments was in doubt." Simultaneously it directed them to reduce their diplomatic missions to the barest minimum and to prepare for a complete, but gradual, elimination of formal representations abroad. "Sooner or later," Vishinsky told the satellites, "your representation will be assumed by the diplomatic agencies of the U.S.S.R." In view of such drastic curtailment of their own diplomatic sovereignty, the satellites had no reason to resist the *pièce de résistance* of Mr. Vishinsky's ukase that instructed them in so many words to assume a belligerent and uncompromising, indeed insolent, attitude toward the Western world in all their diplomatic intercourse. He assured them that they would enjoy the fullest backing of the Soviet Government in staving off all probable unpleasant consequences of such a stand. Vishinsky also predicted that the West would not retaliate but, on the contrary, would accept humiliation without strong countermeasures.

Thus the so-called deterioration of satellite relations with the Western world is but part of a grandiose plan prepared in advance in the Kremlin and given ready-made to the satellites for "action." It is a deliberate campaign of humiliation, shrewdly assigned to some of Hitler's former allies, to increase the pain of its sting. We can blame only ourselves when and if we fall into the trap thus prepared for us in the Kremlin and when we continue to tolerate the henchmen of Moscow in our midst, in diplomatic guise, who are under orders to insult us. We can blame only ourselves if the campaign succeeds despite the fact that its contours were known to us long in advance. A copy of the Vishinsky communication—this can be stated without equivocation—was transmitted to one of our highest ranking intelligence agencies by a former member of the Hungarian Legation in Washington who obtained it, after his departure from the "orbit," through a contact in Budapest. It seems—and the action of our own government on the highest echelon seems to indicate this most strongly—that the document has never reached our top policy makers, or otherwise they would have adjusted their own

attitudes on the satellites to the situation created by the Vishinsky ukase.

In the face of these and similar defeats in the cold war we are
inclined to pose the crucial question: Are we really prepared to
wage the cold war with all our means fully mobilized, with our
intelligence services working at highest efficiency, and with our
propaganda going full blast? Or are we, as the Russians claim
we are, "completely befuddled" by the dilemma confronting us
and ready to be challenged, not merely in the arena of the cold
war, but even on the battlefields of a shooting war? However
erroneous Soviet calculations may be on this score, they bring
the shooting war into the realm of possibilities, and necessitate
in turn an objective analysis of the relative strengths and weaknesses of both major contestants. Such a balance sheet is presented in the next chapter.

Part Six

CONCLUSIONS AND RECOMMENDATIONS

24.

BALANCE
SHEET OF
DISASTER

IT IS with infinite hesitation that we undertake at this serious moment of history the discouraging task of counting the relative political, economic, and military forces of the allies of yesterday in a possible war of tomorrow. A few years ago, only the Nazis and Fascists would have dared to hope that within a few months after VE-day the Western democracies and the U.S.S.R. would be sharply divided by distrust and that thoughts of another armed conflict would be voiced by a considerable number of serious-minded people.

However, there are solutions to the problems now confronting us. In the interest of peace, a frank examination of the potentialities of both sides should be made, for there are too many people who believe that in case of a war between the two giants of our time—the United States and the U.S.S.R.—the other peoples of the world would make their choice easily. Supporters of the United States assume that they would go automatically with the Western democracies. The adherents of the U.S.S.R. assume that the bulk of the world's population would assist them. Many people are under the impression that a war would consist chiefly of a few air excursions with atomic bombs. At the same time many in the U.S.S.R. assume that the opponent regimes would crumble under the impact of revolutionary strife.

In the April, 1947, issue of the magazine *United Nations World* we examined the relative power potentials of the two colossi. At that time, the appraisal attracted considerable attention in the highest political and diplomatic circles of the world. We received numerous communications including some from heads of states and the ministers of defense in Western European countries, endorsing our views, and expressing agreement with the power potentials of the individual contestants.[1]

In the meantime the cold war developed on a grand scale in both sound and fury. And yet, the basic contentions of our earlier analysis survives almost unchanged.

The truth is that any war other than a concerted action by the United Nations against an aggressor would, under present conditions of technical development, end in disaster for humanity. The prospect is that such a war would be the longest war in history; that it would result in the complete destruction of vast parts of the inhabited earth. Humanity is deeply divided, and in case of such a conflict hundreds of millions of people would be unable to decide with whom to align themselves. It would be the most ruthless atomic, biological, bacteriological, rocket, and genocide war that humanity has ever experienced.

THE LINE-UP IN CASE OF WAR

It can be safely assumed that if the war begins outside of the United Nations framework, it will be almost impossible to establish the real aggressor. Each side will contend that it is fighting for the highest ideals—the Western world will proclaim that it is fighting for the establishment of democracy everywhere in the world while Russia will say that it is fighting for the establishment of universal socialism. Under these slogans, the line-up in case of war would probably follow present trends but there are quite likely to be many surprises in the line-up of certain nations when confronted with the realities of war.

In case of a conflict—starting outside of the United Nations Organization—the Western bloc would have 447 millions on its side. The Eastern bloc would have 734 millions on its side if the 441 million Chinese should really cast their lot with the Russians. Fourteen million Europeans would be neutral at the start of the war, and so also would India's 388 million, plus another 166 million who are doubtful, all over the world. More than 200 million would be involved in civil war.

Of course, these alignments representing the peoples involved are only one of the elements to be considered in trying to evaluate the various assets of the potential opponents. However, as humanitarians, we have a duty to consider this numerical factor as extremely important for, after all, unless we let ourselves be guided by savage passions, we cannot fail to think of the majority of humans and their aspirations.

The most tragic aspect of this situation is the tremendous number of people who will try everything within their feeble power to remain neutral in such a war either as a country or in their own conscience. We had hoped after the war of 1939–45 that the very notion of neutrality would disappear and that an international society would be guided by the general concepts of international law. In principle, there should be no neutrality, and all peace-loving and just peoples should participate in punitive action against an aggressor. Antineutral sentiment was very strong when the war ended. Former neutral democracies made every effort to be admitted into the United Nations and to shake off the stigma of neutrality which has ceased to be an attitude of which people can be proud. And yet, there are again hundreds of millions of people—some among them representing the oldest civilization on earth—who feel that they cannot take sides. This in itself is the gravest condemnation of belligerency on both sides.[2]

During the two world wars, the peoples of the earth were told by the Allied governments that a new world based on law and order would emerge out of the victory of the anti-Axis forces. During the Dumbarton Oaks days, in San Francisco, London, and New York, people were led to believe that military action would be justified only if a country committed an act of aggression in violation of the Charter of the United Nations. Only under such circumstances could the resources of the whole of mankind be mobilized by the United Nations to crush the aggressor in the same way as the resources of a state are used against crime. The people were given to understand that any war outside the framework of the United Nations would be a war of aggression.

THE MAJOR REGIMES ARE STABLE

In continuing with this discouraging balance sheet, we have to consider the stability of the respective regimes. There again, the more ruthless elements on each side display their illusions when they imagine that the government machinery of their opponents will break down early in the war. In the Western world the system of parliamentary democracy is accepted by the majority of the people—and it is hoped that these regimes, including those in France and Italy, will have behind them in case of war the majority of their citizenry. The same applies to the Soviet regime in the U.S.S.R. since the people believe that the Communist system constitutes a great progressive step over the former Tsarist regime. The revolutionary wars they fought are chapters of glory and objects of admiration for almost all of their citizens. Therefore, one can say that the stability of the regimes on both sides is very strong and that no major military consequence can be expected from the weakening of either.

As far as economic resources are concerned, there is no doubt that the Western world would have the advantage of industrialization, of highly skilled labor, and a vast industrial potential which can be transferred almost overnight into a war potential. The West would also have at its disposal the necessary raw materials for a prolonged war.

The Eastern bloc, while not having the advantage of industrialization in the initial stages, would have, however, a vast reserve of raw materials. But these would have to go through a stage of intensive development before becoming available to them. The Eastern group would have a standard of living sufficiently low to make every sacrifice dictated by war acceptable. It would have vast spaces into which to retreat, in line with the strategic concept that triumphed in the last war. Above all, the East could overrun the whole of Europe within a few weeks, extending their influence as far as the English Channel. As of today, no serious strategist in Europe can doubt that immediately after the outbreak of a war the Russian armies, with the support of revolutionary forces in the respective countries, would take over the whole of Europe. Let us hope that the plans we are now making for the defense of Western and Southern Europe and the Middle East will change this power situation.

It is again with trepidation that one thinks of the tragic consequences of such a situation, for it would force the United States to accept unnatural and distasteful alliances.

THE ELEVENTH HOUR

It is the *eleventh* hour. A show of force has begun, and while we have no doubt that the last thing the government of the United States wants is war, we must not forget the lessons of history. Even in modern times most governments and their military staffs are never really ready for war. Except for the totalitarians, governments have never boldly accepted the fact that war is likely to come. The fateful summer of 1914 is a typical example of this unrealistic attitude. In 1939, the allies were not ready. And yet war came, as war will always come when there are vital unsettled issues and great standing armies, navies, and air forces, propaganda organizations, and absolute weapons. This is particularly true in this age of A- and H-bombs when fears are generated by the existence of these terrible weapons and there is lacking a positive peace policy backed by a *strong* international organization.

The United Nations Organization is facing a permanent crisis through lack of confidence. Low morale in the Security Council, the lost confidence in the Atomic Energy Commission, and the atmosphere in the Economic and Social Council, where long-range plans for rebuilding the world on new and better foundations seem almost unreal in the growing atmosphere of international tensions, are causing even among the best elements anxiety as to the future of the United Nations.

The way out is a return to the principles and policies which made the Allied victory possible; to the programs on which the Allies have agreed; to the fulfillment of the principles of the United Nations Charter which the legislative bodies of all the United Nations have ratified.

Despite the gravity of the hour, we firmly believe that the governments of the United Nations and their peoples, when they realize the full impact of the present trend and its possible consequences, will become alert once more—as the Western democracies did in 1939—and conscientiously undertake the task of laying the true foundations of international peace. In that peace, Western powers and the Soviets must live peacefully under international law and open the way for the establishment of a free federation of the peoples of the earth.

But before this can be accomplished, a series of major diplomatic steps must be taken in order to call a halt to the present dangerous trend. It is with peace rather than war in mind that we make an attempt at drafting an action program of the eleventh hour. It is an alternate plan to an operations plan in which militant measures are advocated to save humanity from annihilation. For we agree with Theodore Roosevelt, who said in 1899:

"Far better it is to dare mighty things, to win glorious triumphs, even though checkered by failure, than to take rank with those poor spirits who neither enjoy much nor suffer much, because they live in the gray twilight that knows not victory nor defeat." [3]

25. AN ACTION PROGRAM FOR PEACE

*Let us have the courage to act if it benefits
    humanity.
What's brave, what's noble—let's do it.
Then we should be proud to be called the
    children of God.*
        SHAKESPEARE in Anthony and Cleopatra

YEARS HAVE passed since those summer weeks
of 1945 when President Truman and Generalissimo Stalin met
in Potsdam. Their meeting occurred during the closing days of
World War II and on the eve of the atomic age. On the concluding day of that conference, Mr. Truman spoke of the value
of such meetings and expressed the hope that the next conference would be held in Washington.

"God willing," Stalin said—but they have never met again.[1]

President Truman, with understandable truculence born of
disillusionment and despair, refused to leave the United States
to meet Stalin in a man-to-man conference on the highest possible diplomatic level. And Stalin is pleading ill health and the
impediments of old age when he refuses to make the long journey to the United States.[2]

The Generalissimo is past seventy, a man of great though
somewhat subdued vitality and quiet vigor. He suffers from a
heart ailment which his doctors, carefully selected specialists
attached to the exclusive Kremlin hospital, diagnosed as serious.
Stalin may die any minute and then again he may live to be a

hundred years old, as it is, indeed, not unusual for Stalin's
Georgian-Ostian stock to reach the biblical age of Methuselah.[3]

The Soviet Union takes no chances in assuring the prolongation of Stalin's life. In an unprecedented action, his two doctors
presented their diagnosis to the Politburo together with recommendations. A special session of the Politburo was thereupon
summoned to act upon the findings of the physicians. A resolution was passed relieving Stalin of the heavier burdens of states-
manship and instructing him to spend considerable parts of the
year in quiet seclusion far away from the turmoil of the Kremlin.

Stalin respects the orders of his Politburo. He follows the
strict rules of his doctors with as much discipline and obedience
as he expects Communists to follow the Party line.[4]

But even if Stalin should die, his successor is certain to follow
in the Stalinist tradition—at least for the next few crucial years
of the cold war. Stalin learned the lessons of Lenin's failure to
leave behind an organized apparatus. He is determined to leave
behind a Soviet state that is strong and well consolidated; a Communist party that is firmly entrenched in domestic power and
world leadership; and a successor or successors who will continue
the Stalinist program of "evolutionary socialism" without the
interruptions necessitated by fighting first for recognition and
their own personal power. He fears that such a fight, coupled
with the cold war, would wreck communism in Russia, and
Soviet power in Russia's commonwealth.

Anxious to avoid the chaos, uncertainty, and fratricidal strife
that grew out of Lenin's ambiguous testament (in which he,
indeed, warned against the appointment of Stalin as his successor), Stalin is now working on a book to be published as the last
volume of his *Collected Works,* entitled *Socialism in the
U.S.S.R. in War, Peace and Revolutionary Crisis.* It is a detailed
guide for his successor on all matters of Party and State, domestic
and foreign policies.

Who most likely will be this successor? On the basis of what
we regard as the most authentic information available on this
score, and analyses prepared by the best students of Russian
affairs, we expect Molotov and/or Malenkov to succeed Stalin.
Molotov's succession seems as good as assured by his great loyalty
to Stalin and the length of his service in the Party, in some of its

highest posts. Stalin likes to joke about that long and faithful
service. When a satellite Bolshevik assured him in an audience
that he was not a recent but a life-long Communist, Stalin
answered: "So is Molotov." It is this slight condescending jocular attitude that characterizes Stalin's relations with Molotov
that sometimes fills us with doubt as to the question of his succession. But if it is not to be Molotov it is certain to be Malenkov, the most powerful young man of the Bolshevik hierarchy.

There is an immense difference, both immediate and potential, between the two men. In the event of Molotov's appearance
at the apex of the Bolshevik hierarchy, there will be no percep-
tible change in Soviet policies, domestic or foreign. Molotov has
been so closely associated with Stalin for so long a period of time
and followed so closely all Stalinist gyrations of the past thirty
years that the process of assimilation and mimicry became complete in his case. This is a second reason why we expect no stability in a Molotov regime. The dynamism of the change over,
well described by Kennan in his *Foreign Affairs* article on the
sources of Soviet conduct, from one pre-eminent leader to another requires actual changes in policies and not merely in personalities. Only men capable of bringing about such tactical
changes without deviating from the strategic lines of Russian
bolshevism can hope to establish themselves firmly in power and
to survive in it as long as Stalin did after Lenin's death.

This is why we expect Malenkov and not Molotov to succeed
Stalin and to entrench himself as the number-one man of bolshevism, even though Molotov might enjoy the glory of a short
séjour in the Generalissimo's orphaned shoes. Malenkov, too,
is in a better position to seize pre-eminent power should it not
be passed on to him automatically by Stalin's testament or the
Politburo's decision. He is top-ranking Party secretary and chief
of the Central Committee's most important administrative
branch, the Administration of Cadres, the highest personnel and
placement bureau of bolshevism. He controls the personnel
bureaus of all Communist organizations throughout the Bolshevik world and has his own men in key posts everywhere, both
within and without Russia. Should his succession be ever contested and Malenkov obliged to fight for power, he can count

upon his men in key posts, whose own survival depends on his success to support his fight and help him to triumph.

In so far as foreign policies are concerned, Molotov's succession to power would bring about no changes whatever and the present policy line, intransigent and persistent, would continue in an even aggravated form. The cold war would then mount rapidly in intensity and the world soon could be embroiled in a shooting war. But Malenkov would bring about changes that could prevent the outbreak of a shooting war and could, indeed, result in a gradual alleviation of the cold-war tension. Malenkov is a young man. His life was not spent in Siberian prisons. He did not have to flee from Tsarist persecution. He was not compelled to live a dark underground existence of conspiracy, prior to emerging into the open, only to seize power unexpectedly and without warning. He was raised in a Bolshevik world and groomed for power. Therefore he has little left in him of the conspiratorial traits which became, in the case of Lenin and Stalin and their fellows, ingrained until they dominated their thinking processes and actions.

It is this conspiratorial character structure of the Soviet leaders that confronts us with the seemingly insoluble Soviet enigma. We are appalled and repelled by its manifestations, and inevitably fail in our relations with the U.S.S.R., because we are incapable of adjusting our mental world to the thinking processes of the Bolshevik leaders.

There are two men in the Politburo who do not fit this category of permanent conspirators. One is Kosygin, a technician, in charge of the electronic and precision industries which became so essential for victory in World War II. The other is Malenkov. At present Malenkov deliberately refrains from intercourse with foreigners. In an elaborate and calculated show, he remains in the background as one of Stalin's lieutenants. But when Stalin is no longer around, Malenkov will step forward to claim his place in the sun, and to take and hold it. In Malenkov we shall find the first conciliatory Soviet leader. In him, too, we shall find the return of the European mind to the Kremlin replacing the Asiatic mind of Stalin. In him, too, the U.S.S.R. will gain a new symbol—a third-generation Bolshevik leader to whom power is no longer a matter of wonderment but a matter of hard reality. To men like Voroshilov and Mikoyan and Kaganovich, the chief subject of conversation is the miracle of their own career. To Malenkov it is not. He was, so to speak, born into a Bolshevik land where every Russian boy has as much right to dream of ending up in the Kremlin as American boys in the White House.

Whoever is the head of the Bolshevik hierarchy during the next few months and years, Stalin or Molotov or Malenkov, he will be the dominant factor in the settlement of the cold war or in its aggravation into a hot one. Strategic controversies in which totalitarian states are involved cannot be settled on tactical levels. Only a meeting between the chiefs of states, between Generalissimo Stalin and President Truman or whoever the principal protagonists may be, can settle the grave controversies between the U.S.S.R. and the U.S.

A MEETING OF THE CHIEFS OF STATES

If, therefore, we recommend that such a meeting be held at the earliest practicable date we frankly accept a pragmatic short cut to the settlement of the cold war, an intellectual bout in which complete victory cannot be gained by either side. It is a recommendation that envisages peace rather than war, conciliation rather than continued antagonisms and hostilities. It is born of the conviction that men of all nations desire peace above everything else and that peace is still possible at this eleventh hour. It is born of the conviction that the peoples of the world —in America, in Asia, in Europe, everywhere—are sound. They are tired of the miseries and hardships, of the inequities and injustices of war. They are even disillusioned about victory.

Peace is indivisible and, like liberty, it requires eternal vigilance. It is given only to men and nations who know how to fight for it, how to gain it, and how to preserve it. But even today Americans, among the most peace-minded nations of the world, look at peace with quizzical eyes. They weigh it in the balance of their national existence whether or not it is worth the trouble of preservation.

On the issues of war or peace, Washington fails to provide the leadership American public opinion now sorely needs. During the unique presidential campaign of 1948, Mr. Truman was conducting a vigorous but highly personalized peace crusade of his own. Accurately gauging the essentially pacific mood of the American people, the President emphasized in all his campaign speeches the possibility, probability, and, indeed, desirability of continued peace. He in fact assured his nationwide audiences that he would rather have peace than be President.

His peace campaign reached a climax with the decision to send Chief Justice Vinson to Moscow, for a clear-the-air, man-to-man talk with Generalissimo Stalin. The decision was communicated to the Pentagon as well as the State Department, the two government strongholds where the President's widely expected defeat was not regarded either with regret or apprehension. It did not take long for the presidential decision to leak to the press. The editorial uproar that followed, whipping mercilessly the President, whose political fortune then seemed to be at its lowest ebb, killed the plan at once. It is regrettable that Mr. Truman allowed himself to be swayed by the artificial uproar that greeted his initial decision. Public-opinion polls conducted confidentially and in an atmosphere of nonpartisan objectivity revealed that the editorials opposing the idea of the Vinson mission did not reflect public opinion.

Even so, the President's commendable idea caused damage, if only by the manner in which it was developed and then squashed. Foreigners, on whose good will we depend as long as our international relations are based on a system of alliances, cannot very well follow the gyrations and vacillations of four foreign policies. An astute American observer who happened to be in Stockholm when the news of the Chief Justice's impending mission was flashed to the world, told us about the reaction in the Swedish capital. Those were days of soul searching and debate in Sweden, of efforts to resolve the question whether or not to join the U.S. in the cold war against the U.S.S.R. Those souls were sorely tried by the news from Washington. The shock was best expressed by Dr. Ivar Andersen, editor of the influential *Svenska Dagbladet*, in a conversation with our American informant.

"What is American policy vis-à-vis Russia?" he asked. "On the one side you are trying to involve Sweden in an anti-Russian alliance that would jeopardize our national security. On the other side you are trying to negotiate what amounts to a separate peace in the cold war, leaving us all to hold the bag. Why don't you make up your mind?"

Mr. Truman did make up his mind. The uproar that killed Mr. Vinson's mission to Moscow also changed the tune of Mr. Truman's campaign. When the time for his inaugural address came he was as belligerent as any of his subordinates. Those who recalled the peace plank of the 1948 democratic platform, the apparently sincere pacifism of Mr. Truman's campaign speeches, and his off-the-cuff overtures to Russian leaders in Washington press conferences and in Kansas City (the so-called Eddie Jacobson *démarche*) asked themselves as they listened to the blistering words of the inaugural address: "Is peace only one of those campaign promises?"

It is regrettable that Mr. Truman decided, after his election, to discontinue his efforts to seek peace in direct negotiation with his opponent. Whatever reasons he may have had for this decision, political or psychological, national or personal, they must seem petty in the light of the issues involved. We have searched Mr. Truman's pronouncements on peace, on war, on Russia, on Stalin, and on the problem of direct negotiations with Stalin. He was explicit and frank on all in his long talk with Arthur Krock of the *New York Times*. To Mr. Krock the President said that he remembered with what good will toward the Russian people and their rulers he went to Potsdam. There he planned to offer help for reconstruction of Russia as well as the rest of the world, on a very large scale. He remembered with pride and sympathy how Russians had smashed the German armies in the East, and he believed their assistance was necessary to win the war against Japan. But he found that all Stalin wanted to talk about was the abrupt cessation of Lend-Lease, hence the atmosphere was unfavorable to what Mr. Truman had in mind.

"The agreement the Russians made at Yalta to enter the war against Japan was the only one they ever kept out of nearly forty. He has no hope they will keep any which now it would be good policy to seek . . .

"If a campaign had not been in progress in 1948 he would have sent Chief Justice Fred M. Vinson to try to straighten out

Stalin and the other Russian leaders on this and on our real intentions. Maybe that will be the thing to do some time. But in nothing must we show any sign of weakness, because there is none in our attitude." [5]

There is some truculence in this attitude that is, even under the hammer blows of the cold war's many disappointments, not fully justified by the traditional realities of international intercourse. Above all, it is not a positive or constructive attitude the situation requires. This attitude was reflected in several of Mr. Truman's off-the-record remarks in meetings with some of his fellow citizens of elevated standing (but, unfortunately, not in direct intercourse with the people at large), and in statements of his Secretary of State. Both seem to regard further negotiations with Russia as useless and humiliating.[6]

There is indeed an ambivalence in Mr. Truman's attitude. All his political past, in Missouri and in the United States Senate, failed to teach him the lesson that political compromise must be applied to international relations as well. In the foreign field he is essentially a man of peace. But he does not seem to be a man of alternatives. All he would have to do is to apply some of his not inconsiderable domestic political experience to his conduct of foreign relations and he would improve America's position in the cold war and the chances of peace in the world. Whenever he encounters Russian obstructions, chicanery, and insults, he should view foreign relations in the light of his political experiences at home. There are indeed many sweeping similarities between the domestic cold war Mr. Truman is waging with consummate skill against a vociferous and vituperative Republican minority, and the cold war in which he has to fight against an equally vociferous and vituperative foreign opponent for vastly higher stakes. Mr. Truman, for example, uses his own veto power against a Congressional majority with as much reckless effectiveness as the Russians are using theirs in their efforts against the United Nations majority. The man who accepts his struggle with Congress in the best American tradition fails to apply the same standards of political conduct to his struggle with his foreign opponents.

Most frequently the futility of the Yalta and Potsdam conferences is cited as proof against the usefulness of another Truman-

Stalin meeting. But all that we can learn from those mistakes is that we must not repeat them. In Teheran and Yalta, Roosevelt and Churchill met with Stalin under the pressure of war when expediencies ruled all decisions and where the difficulties of the road ahead made searches for short cuts imperative.[7] The Potsdam Conference was held in the shadow of Roosevelt's death, Japan's imminent defeat, the use of the atomic bomb, termination of Lend-Lease, Russian participation in the Pacific war, and, above all else, in the shadow of Mr. Truman's own woeful inexperience at that time.

The abrupt and arbitrary abolition of Lend-Lease was a blunder whose magnitude could not be appreciated then and is still not weighed in the true perspective of its consequences. The circumstances of the decision are obscure. It was, it seems, born of the impulse of the moment, fathered by Mr. Truman's burning desire to return to normalcy. It is certain, no matter what the Russians might say or think, that it was no act deliberately aimed at the U.S.S.R. Indeed, Mr. Truman thought that he owed it to the American people to take the greatest single economic burden off their back as soon as our foreign allies no longer needed Lend-Lease aid for their actual survival.

Whatever it was, the decision to abolish Lend-Lease disregarded the fact that the tired and devastated Allied world needed aid for peacetime reconstruction at least as much as it needed it for the efficient prosecution of the war. The abolition of Lend-Lease led to most of the ills of the postwar world, to the near-bankruptcy of England, to the rapid deterioration of political conditions in the Western world. In the final analysis the Marshall Plan itself was merely the belated recognition of those mistakes and the restoration of Lend-Lease under a different name and slogan.

In our relations with Russia the abolition of Lend-Lease resulted in a rapid alienation of Soviet affections. This was acknowledged by Mr. Truman himself when he told Arthur Krock: " 'To abolish lend-lease at the time was a mistake.' But he was 'new' then; the papers had been prepared for Roosevelt, and represented a Government decision. He felt there was nothing else he could do but sign. He had no staff and no Cabinet of his own. Now he has both."

It is impossible to exaggerate the impact of the decision on Stalin's own mind. During his second meeting with Harry Hopkins on May 17, 1945, he mentioned it specifically as one of five examples of the apparent cooling of American attitudes toward the Soviet Union. The following is Mr. Hopkins's transcript of Stalin's words on this issue:

"He said that if the United States was unable to supply the Soviet Union further under Lend-Lease that was one thing but that the manner in which it had been done had been unfortunate and even brutal. For example, certain ships had been unloaded and while it was true that this order had been canceled the whole manner in which it had been done had caused concern to the Soviet Government. If the refusal to continue Lend-Lease was designed as pressure on the Russians in order to soften them up then it was a fundamental mistake. He said he must tell Mr. Hopkins frankly that if the Russians were approached frankly on a friendly basis much could be done but that reprisals in any form would bring about the exact opposite effect." [8]

While thus surveying some of the American inhibitions which interfere with the badly needed catharsis of another Truman-Stalin meeting, we do not overlook the heavy road blocks which the U.S.S.R. is placing in the path of peace. But ingenuity and diplomatic skill on our part, and greater good will on the part of the Russians, would be capable of removing at least some of them. For it is our contention that before any radical steps should be undertaken on our part to defend ourselves against the cold war and a shooting war that is certain to follow in its wake, we must make a last determined effort to seek peace in direct negotiations with the Russians, on the highest diplomatic level.

Both statesmen must go into such a conference with a detailed agenda prepared and fully accepted in advance. Questions not included in the agenda in advance must not be introduced. Past conferences failed over endless discussions of the agenda and over Soviet attempts to introduce problems for which the agenda provided no time and for which our negotiators appeared materially and psychologically unprepared.

The conference should accept as its basic premise the total

breakdown of Russo-American collaboration and the undeniable fact that the Yalta and Potsdam agreements have ceased to be valid yardsticks of the postwar conduct of their signatories. Both parties must frankly concede that the Yalta and Potsdam agreements became invalidated by their divergent interpretations.

Then the whole complex of international co-operation should be reviewed and solutions sought for better collaboration without regard for the delusive amity that our wartime co-operation seemed to generate.

The conference should then draft a treaty of nonaggression for presentation to the Congress of the United States and the Supreme Soviet of the U.S.S.R., to cover a period of at least five but preferably ten years, appointing the United Nations as the supreme arbiter of all disputes between the two countries.[9]

The treaty should (a) provide clear-cut explanations for those provisions of the Yalta and Potsdam agreements, which in the past were subject to divergent interpretations by the U.S. and the U.S.S.R., and (b) demarcate in explicit political and geographical terms the boundary lines of all U.S. and U.S.S.R. interests in territories which they regard as being in their respective orbits. The treaty must state explicitly that crossings of those boundary lines would lead to immediate countermeasures under Article 51 of the Charter of the United Nations.

The treaty should include special provisions for the consummate settlement by bilateral arrangements of such outstanding issues as the international control of atomic energy, the establishment of an international police force, regulation of armaments, peace treaties with Austria and Japan, etc., to facilitate the eventual solution of these problems within the framework of the United Nations.

By making these recommendations we do not propose that the United States should abandon its efforts now aimed at the strengthening of the country for its role in world leadership. On the contrary, we firmly believe that a continued effort on the part of the U.S. Government and the American people can have only salutary effects, since both Stalin and the U.S.S.R. respect strength and determination far more than mere diplomatic shadow boxing and the window dressing of military power.

But while continuing our efforts and maintaining our forces in a high state of preparedness, and developing our strength to match our international commitments, we should make it crystal clear, to our own people, to the peoples of the world, and especially to the people of the U.S.S.R. that we have no aggressive designs or warlike intentions whatsoever. Such an assurance was indeed included in the note General Smith prepared for Mr. Molotov after their conversations of May 4, 1948. It should be given on the highest level to reassure Stalin and the U.S.S.R. that American strength is designed solely for the preservation of this nation's great liberal institutions and for the maintenance of peace and tranquillity in the world.

There will be, by the very necessity of diplomatic *quid pro quo,* some retreats necessary from the present rather intransigent American position that expects Russia to make all the concessions and gain none in return. This kind of attitude to international intercourse denies and, indeed, defies the basic law of diplomacy and overlooks completely the simplest rule by which human relations are guided. Mr. Truman once remarked, probably only as a jocular aside, that only an unconditional surrender of Russia could terminate the cold war. He expressed the hope that at some time in the not too distant future he expected the Soviet Union to surrender, indeed, unconditionally. The havoc that such seemingly innocuous remarks can wreak in Russian fears and sentiments is difficult to express. With his statement Mr. Truman aligned himself with Arnold Toynbee and others who expect the cold war to continue indefinitely. But a policy that envisages the indefinite prolongation of the cold war is worse than no policy at all. First of all it is fraught with the dangers of a shooting war which, history shows, usually develops at a climactic stage of diplomatic and military tension. Second, it demands an enormous toll from all peoples, and especially the American people, in psychological and economic sacrifice. It stretches nervous tension throughout the world beyond what psychiatrists regard as the breaking point of human endurance. Contrarywise, it decreases appropriations of the nation's funds for purposes more constructive than the mere sustenance of armed truce. Even in prosperity, nations might become impoverished if they fail, over years, to devote their funds to such useful developments as housing, scientific research for health, the building of roads, and others.

It is in these concrete terms rather than in the abstract speculations about the psychological damage that the dangers inherent in an indefinite prolongation of the cold war can best be demonstrated. Take a perfunctory look at the American budget. In the fiscal year 1939, our expenditures amounted to a total of $9 billion. In the period between 1948–51, our total expenditures amounted to the staggering average of $40 billion per year, a total of $160 billion in four years. Of these sums, in 1939, we spent just a little over $1 1/10 billion on national defense and on the conduct of our international relations. But in 1948–51 we spent an annual average of $18 billion on the same purposes. In the 1951 budget more than 71 per cent of all federal expenditures had to be devoted to meeting the remaining burdens of the last war and to the prosecution of the cold war.

By contrast, in 1939, we were spending $3 9/10 billion on social welfare, health, and social security, while the 1948–51 annual average amounted to only about $2 billion, a tragic cut indeed in an essential field by a nation that is riding the crest of the wave of prosperity. Other expenditures show some qualified growth in comparison with 1939, but their increases are by no means commensurate with actual needs in such vital fields as housing, education, general research, the development of our natural resources, agriculture, transportation, and communications.

It should be evident to all that such an unbalanced spending and such economic and psychological strain cannot continue indefinitely. And since it is caused by the cold war, it should be just as evident that the cold war cannot be prolonged indefinitely without causing irreparable damage to the nation's economic and mental health. We must therefore do everything, and soon, to abandon our present national policy of indefinite stalemate and shadow boxing. We must insist upon a positive policy of operative action that would end the cold war at the earliest possible date without sacrificing our national interests. This can be achieved either by agreement or by a determined campaign of an all-out offensive short of a shooting war.

The Truman-Stalin meeting should be regarded as a last

effort to end the cold war through negotiations—but also as the acid test. We must anticipate Russian truculence and, indeed, Soviet determination to seek even armed showdown in the belief that we are weak and impotent to prevent a Soviet victory. The Russians, ill informed and prejudiced as they are, might regard our very willingness to enter into direct negotiations as evidence of such weakness and impotence.

The possible and probable failure of the Truman-Stalin meeting should then provide for us the proof positive that collaboration with the U.S.S.R. along established patterns of honorable diplomacy is impossible. It should prove to us that the Russians are determined to press their advantages; that they want the cold war to develop to the breaking point; and that they have taken into account this calculated risk. It must reveal to us the inner thoughts and basic designs of Russian diplomacy and imperialism. It should then induce us to hoist the danger signal at once and to do all in our power to mobilize this nation and the world in earnest for action to avert the war the Russians are apparently seeking. Far from causing it, we are firmly convinced that such an *all-out* mobilization of *all* democratic resources would prevent the outbreak of a shooting war and would, in fact, lead to the termination of the cold war itself.

It is obvious to all serious students of international affairs that the extent and efficiency of our present mobilization is insufficient, even for an efficient prosecution of the cold war. It is woefully inadequate to meet aggression or even the threat of aggression. While it would be both presumptuous and, indeed, beyond the limited power of a few to draw up an effective action program that could solve all the ills of a sick world, we may be allowed here, at the conclusion of this secret history of the cold war, to outline a few of our own ideas which we think could, if translated into action, strengthen our side and weaken the camp of our opponents. The measures suggested below are essentially defensive. We feel very strongly about them, since we are convinced that unless a radical change is made in the methods, forces, and orientation of our foreign policy, our weaknesses will continue to show themselves in mounting blunders and defeats. They in turn will provoke an unscrupulous and ambitious foe to exploit them in a cold war and unleash a shooting war with relative impunity.

TEN-POINT PROGRAM FOR PEACE

This, then, is an operations plan for democratic peace, a ten-point program for effective international action to prevent the outbreak of the shooting war.

(1) *The conduct of our foreign relations must undergo basic reorganization.* At present our foreign policies are made haphazardly, in an improvised manner, with one eye on domestic conditions, another on party political needs. The White House has but qualified control over the conduct of our international relations, due chiefly to the President's lifelong preoccupation with native American politics and unfamiliarity with diplomatic history and international geopolitics. In another important field, national economics, Mr. Truman was the first to concede his unfamiliarity and, in the Employment Act of 1946, to call for the appointment of a Council of Economic Advisers "to assist the President in the preparation of his Economic Reports to Congress and to advise him on developments within the national economy and on what the government should do to keep it strong and prosperous."

In a similar manner, a Council of Foreign Political Advisers should be appointed forthwith, to consist of three full-time councilors and an appropriate professional staff, to assist the President in his constitutional duties in so far as they concern the conduct of our foreign relations. The President should be required to submit to Congress at regular intervals Foreign Political Reports containing in full an overall review and forecast of diplomatic trends and international conditions. There should be established within the Congress itself a Joint Committee on the Foreign Policy Report, which should study all findings sent to it by the President, and which should submit to the Senate and the House its own recommendations. Specific reports on individual issues of immediate topical interest should be prepared by the President and sent to the Congress in the form of White Papers, outlining *in advance* the course the administration proposes to follow in the handling and settlement of such issues. This is a system followed traditionally and with great success by the British Government, leading to a closer and more efficient collaboration between the executive and legislative branches of the government.

From such White Papers and from the periodic reports on foreign policy this nation in particular and the peoples of the world in general would learn the diplomatic ideas and intentions of the U.S. Government. There would no longer be any doubt in the minds of our friends or foes as to the foreign policies of the United States. We would not be suffering from a schizophrenic conduct of our foreign relations, some of it done in the Pentagon, some of it in the State Department, some of it in the Congress, and so forth, without a single unifying force or agency to present, not a bipartisan but a nonpartisan foreign-policy front to the outside world. From such reports the people of this nation and the world would learn the issues involved and would become effective participants in the execution of our plans and policies.

It should be evident to everyone concerned with international affairs that we must have a well-integrated and effective intelligence organization which we do not have today, in order to keep ourselves informed of what is going on around the world. This is necessary first, to prevent us from being surprised unpleasantly, and second, to enable us to take preventive measures when necessary. Most important is to have a proper allocation of the function of evaluation if we are to avoid the many mistakes we have made in the past.[10]

In order to have a suitable propaganda agency, all international information activities must be removed from the State Department in order to avoid the embarrassment incident to the maintenance of an undiplomatic agency within our chief diplomatic establishment, and to give it the independence, material, and technique necessary to be effective. As long as our propaganda activity remains in our diplomatic establishment, our diplomacy is likely to be influenced by our propaganda, and our propaganda by our diplomacy, to the detriment of both.[11]

(2) *Our economic security must be assured through realistic collaboration between government on the one side, and private industry and business on the other.* The Russians anticipate progressive crises to engulf the United States and expect an even-

tual economic collapse to usher in favorable preconditions for a Soviet war against the Western world. It is evident that we must do everything in our power as a nation to prevent recession from developing into depression, and depression from developing into economic catastrophe. In this effort labor and management, producers and consumers, government and private industry must collaborate. The chief danger to continued prosperity, as we see it, is an unhealthy attitude on profits in the calculations of our big business. It is an exaggerated anxiety, somewhat justifying the remarks of a prominent British economist who told us in effect: "The Russians and certain non-Communist Europeans, traditionally and viciously anti-American, are wrong in describing American big business as 'power mad.' In fact we in Britain sometimes wish Wall Street had a better understanding of the meaning of power and would make a better use of its influence when it comes to foreign affairs. American big business, as seen from the continent, has little power. Take the Spanish situation, for instance. One of the biggest American corporations and the world's biggest bank joined forces to champion Generalissimo Franco's cause and to promote his admission to the United Nations. But did they either have or exert the power to gain acceptance, not by the United Nations, but by their own government, of the project they advocated? They did not! They failed to gain the support of the State Department and of the American delegation to UN, where it was Mrs. Roosevelt's negative views on Franco rather than the views of American Tel & Tel and the Chase Bank that prevailed.

"But while your Big Business is far from being 'power mad,' it is, indeed, 'profit mad.' It may be prudence rather than a mercenary trait that suggests such a course to your corporation executives. But whatever it is, it may be in the long run, detrimental not merely to America's own future prosperity but to the continued well-being of the democratic world as well."

There must be, indeed, a fair and equitable review of the profit problem, and big business must wholeheartedly co-operate in the development of a new profit policy, for its own good, to preserve American prosperity within sound economic limits. This may be an oversimplification of a crucial issue, but we are not surveying here the whole complex in exhaustive detail. The

facts of our economic life as they are presenting themselves to us
even today tend to support not merely the contentions of our
British friend, but even some of the calculations of the Russians.
While there are a series of excellent means on our statutes to
cushion the worst features of any depression, we must, nevertheless, face certain unassailable facts that indicate a steady deterioration in our economic structure. The 1939 dollar is now
worth only fifty-seven cents. While wages and salaries have increased only about 40 per cent since 1939, the purchasing power
of the dollar, at face value, decreased about 42 per cent, food
prices (amounting to more than one third of the nation's expenditures) increased 110 per cent, clothing prices increased 92
per cent. Even today, the Bureau of Labor Statistics reports that
in population centers like Houston, Detroit, and Denver, the
people of the United States are spending in excess of their incomes, and that any expenditures beyond the barest essentials
must come from savings or borrowings.[12]

In so far as unemployment is concerned, Leon H. Keyserling,
one of the President's economic advisers, stated in July, 1949:
"For rough purposes of discussion we might say that a situation
in the United States could not be called one of substantial depression at any time when unemployment has not exceeded six
million for at least a year, although the national policy of continuous maximum employment to which we are committed
under the Employment Act of 1946, propels us to strive at all
times toward holding unemployment well below the current
level of above 3 million." Conversely this means that when unemployment figures soar to a figure exceeding six million, we
are on the way to depression. According to the calculations of
the *New York Times*, unemployment figures are bound to reach
the staggering total of twelve million by 1954, even if our prosperity remains at its present high state, by the sheer failure to
increase our ability to absorb the new labor supplies provided
by the natural growth of this nation. The *Times* figure of twelve
million sounds very much like the Varga figure presented to
Stalin in the economic estimate of the situation which we outlined on page 28. We feel that we must do more than what we
are doing now if we want to prevent this factor of our economic

well being from becoming a source of Soviet strength by our default.

A new and more realistic policy must also be introduced to prevent still another Soviet expectation from coming to pass. It concerns the whole economic structure of our home-financing program with a somewhat sounder mortgage policy, on the parts of builders, the banks, and the public. This is largely an educational program. Once the public is told of the possible consequences of its state of "mortgage happiness," and frankly advised of the true price structure of its homes acquired since 1942, it might show greater restraint and a more economical attitude, and prevent the change in incomes from exerting a disastrous influence on the mortgage market, leading to a wiping out of middle-class savings, and resulting in the mass bankruptcy of mortgage holders. As in every sphere of our economic existence, collaboration between government and private interests is essential, even though such collaboration must not lead to an undue increase of government influence on private interests.

(3) *National unity must be preserved by the enlightened elimination of all unnecessary friction, selfish partisanship.* At the present time the only major threat to our unity is presented by the issue of communism in America. It is exploited for the purposes of selfish partisanship by all the subversive forces that traditionally breed on the prejudices of any nation, by the lunatic fringe, and by irresponsible partisans in both political parties in selfish, headline-hunting pursuits. We have no reason in fact to fear the advent of bolshevism in the United States. First of all, we have an excellent psychological system that helped us in the past to immunize ourselves against all kinds of foreign isms, fascism as well as nazism, and which is now helping us, by means of prophylaxis, to prevent the influx of bolshevism.

Second, the United States is safe from a Stalinist ideological assault, simply because Stalin himself never intended to bolshevize the U.S. This statement is made on the authority of an old Bolshevik, one of Lenin's closest friends, a hero of the October Revolution who enjoyed Stalin's respect though not his affection. He was Ivan Ivanovich Petrovsky whom the Bolshevik Revolution rewarded with an ambassadorial post in Persia. Lingering on in the spacious compound of his embassy in

Teheran, Petrovsky was dying of an incurable disease of his kidney, tormented by perpetual physical pain that made him completely unafraid of the threats of the Cheka. He said so in so many words when his listeners wondered at the reckless courage of his frequent anti-Stalinist statements.

Petrovsky assured his foreign friends—capitalists all—that the United States had nothing to fear of Stalin's fury and nothing to expect of his favors. "There are two or three countries in the world," he said, "which Stalin would never allow to go Communist. One is Germany; the other is Britain; the third is the United States. Should in any one of these countries communism triumph, they would wrest leadership from us backward Russians—especially the U.S., where communism would certainly be 'bigger and better.' Stalin would never abandon Russian leadership to a foreign section. No, my friends, you have nothing to fear from our Soso. *He* is living in panicky fear of you!"

The danger to our national unity comes from within. At the time of this writing the nation is subjected to vicious and groundless attacks against the integrity of the government. Foreign lobbies try to influence public opinion and enlist our aid to serve selfish interests abroad. Since most of the attacks come from ex-Communists who profess to have changed, we suspect that at least in some cases the change is feigned and that the man or woman is under instructions from Moscow to undermine national unity through baseless accusations and to detract attention from current espionage by concentrating on its past cases.

In the words of Frederick H. Osborn, former deputy U.S. representative on the UN Atomic Energy Commission, unity on American foreign policy is essential to avert another war. "We must be sure our foreign policy is one on which we can appear united," he said. "Dictators are badly informed on public opinion, they always think that divided opinions are a sign of weakness." [13]

(4) *Our national strength must be bolstered by a more equitable and realistic program within the military establishment.* Even as these lines are written, the great debate about the merits and demerits of the Defense Department rages unabated. It is far beyond the scope of these brief recommendations to outline

in detail all that needs to be done to guarantee this nation's physical security against aggression from abroad and to secure our victory, first, in the military phases of the cold war, and second, in a shooting war when and if it comes. It is important to mention but a few measures. We must review and remedy the fraudulent and delusive features of our great armed-forces unification project, to create efficiency in unity rather than inefficiency in continued disunity. A genuine unification of effort can be maintained by leaving measures of independence within the branches whose material efficiency depends on such intangible morale forces as tradition, *esprit de corps,* and pride in their own achievements. In this age of air power and absolute weapons—bacteriological, biological, and climatological weapons which surpass even the atomic bomb in destructiveness and are capable of wiping out humanity—we must come to have a full appreciation of seapower and its two vital components—Naval Aviation and the Marine Corps. Every nation in history that has lost the concept of seapower has gone down to defeat, and it could happen to us.

Under the present law, the Department of the Navy, as it should be, consists of two separate services entirely co-ordinated —the Navy and the Marine Corps. It must remain that way to be effective. The Navy, with its Naval Aviation, is the one defense today against a surprise attack over either ocean if it is allowed to keep the tools with which to work. The Marine Corps represents a powerful striking force in readiness at all times. Any attempt to substitute something for either of these could well spell disaster for us.

As the head of one of these vital components, the Commandant of the Marine Corps should have a place on the Joint Chiefs of Staff along with the Chief of Naval Operations. It so happens that as a member of that body, the Commandant of the Marine Corps would be the only one with a full knowledge of the service schools of the other branches.

(5) *A new system of effective alliances must replace an alignment of weak and dependent nations.* We should abandon the concept of blanket alliances and rid ourselves of weak allies whose very weakness dilutes our own strength. During World War I, General von Falkenhayn, when told of Italy's decision to

join the Allies despite her treaty with Austria-Hungary, said: "What difference does it make? As long as she was our ally, we needed ten divisions to protect her. Now, as our enemy, we need the same ten divisions to defeat her." This is only too true in the case of many of our present allies. Their weakness pins down and immobilizes much of our existing strength.

The question of security should also be an important consideration. During World War II, we hesitated to accept General de Gaulle's Free French forces as full-fledged allies, partly for mistaken political reasons, but partly for fear that certain irresponsible and unreliable elements within their ranks would communicate our innermost military secrets to the enemy. In the White Paper on China, Mr. Acheson stated that there was a similarly grave risk that secret information transmitted to the nationalist capital of Chungking would become available to the Japanese almost immediately. An alliance with as broad a base as that of the North Atlantic pact and with as many defense departments as are involved in its implementation cannot provide for the air-tight security we need in this age of spies and saboteurs. The security risk involved in advertising our own plans and intentions to scores of allies is far greater than the physical risk we incur in ridding ourselves of some of them. Collective security, as we understand it, is a diplomatic term and should have diplomatic and economic implementation. A system of military alliances must retain consideration for the basic security needs of individual countries.[14]

Instead of continuing the present system of ephemeral alliances with all their detrimental influences on our own security, we should develop at once, in the form of bilateral treaties, within existing frameworks, a system of interdependent alliances with a few key countries. We suggest that such bilateral alliances be concluded with Britain, France, Turkey, Israel, and Transjordan, and the Philippines.

(6) *Britain must be restored to power and influence.* It is our best interest to preserve the remarkable alliance that exists between this country and Britain and to deepen the ties by all means at our disposal. Britain is not only our strongest and most trustworthy ally, but she is also the cradle of our civilization that continues to exert invigorating influence on our own cul-

ture. Britain shows few of the symptoms of decadence and decay her enemies are so fond of attributing to her. It would be, indeed, the major tragedy of modern times and probably the beginning of the end of our own civilization should the ties which now bind us to England ever be allowed to loosen. On the contrary, we must do everything to strengthen those ties. Above all, we must aid in the restoration of Britain to its codominant power position in the world. A continued existence in the shadows of economic plight is a precarious existence indeed for a nation that aspires for leadership in the democratic world. Prolonged existence under such condition is likely to undermine the very foundations of a truly democratic Britain.

Haphazard, occasional, and condition-bound aid will not be enough. We must grant Britain a loan of at least $10 billion in cash and with no strings attached, to enable her to repurchase her economic position in the world which she was compelled to sell out to meet the immense obligations that accrued during World War II. A Britain that tries to remain in the running by peddling small motorcars to overseas buyers and which hopes to increase her dollar reserves with such pathetic gestures as Queen Mary's decision to sell her embroidery on the American market is a dubious ally in the moment of our own greatest need. But a Britain which is again a successful and respected world trader, with holdings in many lands, and influence on the trade of others, is an equal ally—and alliances are useful only when and if they are concluded between equals.

(7) *Restoration of France to dominant position on the Continent.* While thus we would be restoring Britain to economic preponderance, we should do everything to restore France to political preponderance on the Continent. This step is dictated by an elementary requirement of our military predicament. There is a tendency now to regard Germany as our most important potential ally should war ever break out between the West and the East. The fallacy of such a speculation is evident in the history of this generation that found itself betrayed twice by Germany. Even today, a guilty nation shows no signs of remorse or a desire to reform. It remains a scheming and truculent nation that may be expected to snap out of its feigned lethargy the moment it perceives an opportunity to stage power-political

comeback. It is also an opportunistic nation that will join the highest bidder. Germany must never be taken into account as an ally. We must do but a minimum to sustain her beyond her own efforts at rehabilitation.

On the other hand we must make France strong, if only to maintain a constant check on the unreliable Germans and to secure for ourselves a beachhead in a Europe that might, at any time, again be overrun by totalitarian forces. Instead of aiding France with piecemeal equipment enough for individual regiments, we must conclude a military alliance with her that would create a new army there as rapidly as we succeeded in creating one here in this country under the pressure of war. We must also do everything to help France to lay the economic foundations for a political stability, by binding ourselves, body and soul, to France as our chief continental ally.

(8) *Alliances should be concluded with Turkey, Israel, and Transjordan.* These would be purely strategic alliances designed frankly for military purposes. Most important among them is the alliance with Transjordan. Anyone who looks at the map of European Russia will readily recognize that the Soviet Union's warmaking capacity depends on unhampered control over a relatively small area in the south. Indeed, the region represents the soft underbelly of Russia. What makes it so decisive is the fact that it is the location of her major oil fields around the Caspian Sea. If the flow of oil is interrupted, Russia is incapable of any aggressive moves. Transjordan is the geographical point whence such a strategic blow could be delivered. And Transjordan is the country whose integration into a major system of interdependent alliances, and whose development into our *major* air overseas base could create a military *fait accompli* in which Russian aggressive designs could be effectively checkmated. We need not elaborate here on this plan. It had been submitted in detail to Mr. Forrestal and he was considering it in all seriousness when tragic illness forced him to resign. He approved it wholeheartedly. Israel's and Turkey's participation in the alliance is essential as auxiliary to the basic scheme to provide for the forefield of the major base, and for unobstructed, unhampered approaches to it from the sea.

(9) *Attitude toward Soviet satellites, and our treaty relations*

with the U.S.S.R. must undergo complete revision. Part of what we believe needs to be done has already been outlined in earlier passages of this chapter. But we must go far beyond the mere revision of our wartime and postwar agreements. We must, indeed, take under review the very agreements concluded between President Roosevelt and Foreign Commissar Litvinov in 1933 and examine them for possible violations. We should then, in the light of this painstaking study, suggest to the U.S.S.R. that new agreements be drafted in the light of new realities. We must not recognize the Soviet right to the establishment of a satellite empire as growing out of the treaties to which we ourselves were signatories. We must not recognize the U.S.S.R. as the overlord of Eastern Europe, or its right to drag down sovereign nations to its own level of economic bondage and political oppression. We must, on the contrary, do everything in our power to eliminate the U.S.S.R. from the position it is now holding beyond its own natural boundaries. First, we must conclude peace treaties with Austria and Japan, with or without Soviet acquiescence or cooperation. Second, we must insist upon the withdrawal of Soviet forces from Hungary, Bulgaria, Poland, and Eastern Germany. In other words, we must demand a demilitarization of Europe and an effective international control over this demilitarization. It goes without saying that we must then withdraw our forces from Europe and restore to Europe genuine peace and self-determination that can be the sole guarantors of political stability and economic prosperity.

Russia's chief desire is to isolate herself from the rest of the world. In this isolation she expects to find security and happiness. We are not arguing here with this strange concept of national endurance in a world that depends on mutual trust and international collaboration for its own survival. But in the face of the offensive suspiciousness and insulting diplomacy of the Soviet Union, we should promote this desire of isolation. We should cut our ties with the Soviet Union to a practicable minimum. We should withdraw our newspaper correspondents from the Soviet capital and allow no space in our newspapers to advertise Soviet intentions or achievements. We should withhold from Russia information about ourselves, about our intentions and achievements in a similar manner. Let her then taste the bitter fruits of isolation and suffer all its consequences as our own country did in an unenlightened period of our own history.

Our relations with the Soviet satellites are closely tied to our relations with the U.S.S.R. The same policy of quarantine that we plan to apply to Russia should be applied to Poland and Czechoslovakia. But a different policy must be applied to Rumania, Hungary, Albania, and Bulgaria. With these countries we have peace treaties whose violation must not be tolerated under any and all circumstances. But the plain truth is that such violations did occur and are occurring right now, in virtually every single provision of those treaties. Most of the violations are doubly detrimental to us. First of all, they reduce faith in the sanctity of treaties and create an evil precedent, undermining the effectiveness of international intercourse. Second, most of the violations are in the military sphere and are directed physically against our own security.

It is suggested, therefore, that the President and Congress in joint action abrogate the peace treaties between this country and Rumania, Bulgaria, and Hungary and restore into force the armistice agreements that existed previous to the signing and ratification of the peace compacts. The whole complex of this country's relations with Russia's satellites must then be revised in the new light created by the American action. If the return of military control over them becomes necessary, we should not hesitate to impose such a control, to prevent them from an execution of aggressive designs.

(10) *The United Nations must be strengthened by a greater American reliance upon its political agencies as arbiters of international disputes and comptrollers of international agreements.* In its present form, the UN is unable now to function in the role we would like to assign to it. Means must therefore be found to invoke the appropriate provisions of the Charter and bring about a change, whereby the General Assembly, where the veto does not prevail, gains power and influence, and the Security Council, where the veto stifles effective action, loses some of its own. The United States should turn to the United Nations with all its complaints against its opponents, however major or minor they may be, and utilize the forum of the United Nations as a tribunal before which its case is being tried. In the past, the

United States violated its own allegiance to the UN by detouring it and circumventing it in many instances, and actually sabotaging it in some. Lip service is being paid in generous abundance to the UN but the service it could do to humanity beyond the ties of sovereignty and national interests is fully disregarded.

All we need to do today is to reread the lofty preamble of the Charter, and Chapter I, with its Articles 1 and 2, which describe the purposes and principles of the UN, to see for ourselves how many and how serious are the violations we have ourselves committed, if not against the letter, then against the spirit of that document.

According to the Preamble, the United Nations is the product of a resolution, not of the governments, but of the peoples of the world. They have combined their efforts "to save succeeding generations from the scourge of war ... to reaffirm faith in fundamental human rights ... to establish conditions under which justice and respect for the obligations arising from treaties and other sources of international law can be maintained ... to promote social progress and better standards of life in larger freedom." The peoples then instructed their governments to establish the United Nations, and to administer it in trust.

The United Nations should be looked upon as a spiritual force rather than a physical power. It should be the living challenge to the moral values within us rather than to the instincts of interest within our states. It should be the ultimate guarantor of peace, by the strength of its own ethical structure and by the determination of the people conjoined in it.

But in the winter of 1950 that goal seemed to recede farther in time and space than at any other time in current history. In the winter of 1950 the forces of war seemed rampant in the world and the forces of peace lay prostrate in the empty halls of Lake Success. In the winter of 1950 we were ourselves confronted with the horrorful realities of our times, in the personal tragedy of a single man whose fate reflected the plight of mankind.

EPILOGUE

It was a winter morning early in 1950, when a tall white-haired man stepped from a train in New York's Grand Central Station. Hatless, his burly frame in the thinnest overcoat, he wore a white shirt under a rumpled black suit, the only suit he had. In one hand he carried a battered gray suitcase of pressed cardboard. In his other hand he carried a bundle of books, including the Stepanov translation of Marx's *Das Kapital,* published by Skirmunt of Moscow.

His fellow passengers hurried by with brisk and eager steps, and left him to lag behind, as he walked hesitantly toward the exit. The big man was in no hurry to arrive.

As he stepped into the huge marble hall of the terminal, he was stopped by a peculiar feeling of pagan reverence. The rays of an unseasonable sun swept down in bundles through the tall glass corridors to the east. Someone was playing soft music on an invisible organ. The people seemed to tiptoe across the hall in the strange quiet of a nebulous world. For a moment he thought he had lost his way. Then he remembered—he was in America.

On the registration card at a small hotel, he called himself Paul F. Balin. But when he was born they named him Pavel for an uncle on his mother's side and Fedor after his father, Pavel Fedorovich Byalitnisko, son of a teacher of languages in a lyceum for the daughters of nobility. That was 69 years before, in St. Petersburg, the year Tsar Alexander II was blown to bits by the Nihilists. Born into heroic times, Pavel Fedorovich aspired not to the role of the hero in the mold of Carlyle. But he had Turgenev's temerity to believe in nothing and to pray for miracles. So he sought for himself a place in front of the barricades.

In 1905, young Byalitnisko marched with the workers against the Winter Palace in the abortive rebellion for civil rights. The Okhrana arrested him frequently thereafter and the judges of St. Petersburg sent him into a succession of Tsarist jails.

It was a busy and invigorating experience, those imprisonments under the Tsar. One met so many interesting people. In an Archangelsk jail he played chess with a gawky adolescent—a sullen rebel named Skriabin, a slow-thinking, stammering boy who pondered almost endlessly before he moved a pawn on the board. A few years later, at the Smolny in Petrograd, Pavel met him again. By then they called him Molotov.

In a Batum prison his samovar was stolen by a pock-marked Georgian then known as Koba. He confessed the theft in laughter through a set of dark decaying teeth when Balin saw him next, with Lenin and Trotsky, in the late summer of 1917. By then they called him Stalin.

The October Revolution of 1917 was won. The Military Revolutionary Committee of the Petrograd Soviet proclaimed: "The Provisional Government is deposed! The State Power has passed into the hands of the organ of the Petrograd Soviet... that cause for which the people were fighting—that cause is securely achieved."

Pavel Fedorovich Byalitnisko was a Menshevik. He tried hard to adjust himself to this new world he himself had helped the Bolsheviks to create. A few years before in Siberia all had seemed so simple as he read in Dostoevski: "Man is a pliable animal, a being who gets accustomed to everything." But all that his Dostoevski could tell him now was: "Consolation is not what you need. Weep and be not consoled, but weep."

A few months later he made his way to Riga in Estonia, then to Berlin. He was an exile again. He had changed his name to Paul F. Balin. Behind the protective shield of the Weimar Republic's confused tolerance, he settled down to middle-class comfort to study "purist Marxism," as he called the theory that had failed in his own Russia. His life made him a historian.

Then in 1933 he had to flee again. He went to Amsterdam. In 1940, again a fugitive, he went to Paris. In 1942, another flight, this time to Oran. By then the Russians, recent allies of Hitler, were fighting on the side of Britain and America. His refugee camp in North Africa was honeycombed with Soviet spies and *agents provocateurs*. He sensed another danger. This time he determined to go far—far beyond the reach of Hitler's Gestapo and Stalin's NKVD. In 1946, he finally reached Shanghai, China. For three years he rested.

Then one morning in 1949, General Chen's Communist soldiers came sauntering down the Bund. Pavel Fedorovich had to move on. He has grown old in flight. Arrivals and departures no longer thrill him, and now he looks at the United States with frightened skeptical eyes. When we listened to his story, he asked us: "Will this be my last refuge?"

In Pavel Fedorovich Byalitnisko's harassed life is reflected the hectic biography of search for "freedom in our time." In March,

1917, his Holy Russia was still a monarchy. Then in April, the obscure Bolshevik Ulyanov—soon to be known as Lenin—arrived in a sealed train, sent by Imperial Germany to make trouble for Prince Lvov's shaky provisional government and to hasten a separate peace with the Reich in the confusion of the revolution.

On November 7, of that same year, in an insurrection of remarkable efficiency, a handful of Bolsheviki established themselves as the government of Russia. We still remember the headlines in the *Times* and the shrug of many shoulders with which the news was received.

The world gave Lenin-Ulyanov's victory the traditional 100 days. Captain Gomberg, secretary of the Mensheviks' military section, shrugged his shoulders, too, and said to John Reed: "Well, perhaps the Bolsheviki can seize powers, but they won't be able to hold it more than three days. They haven't the men to run a government. Perhaps it's a good thing to let them try— that will finish them."

The conversation, at the deserted corner of the Morskaya in Petrograd on the day of the October Revolution, occurred more than thirty years ago. Three days became thirty years!

The world should have known better. Lenin never concealed his aims. The morning after the insurrection, he proclaimed: *"Final victory is possible only on a world-wide scale and through the united efforts of workers in all countries."*

A month later, in December, 1917, the Soviet Government sent the first 2,000,000 rubles to its representatives abroad "for the need of the revolutionary internationalist movement."

Only fourteen months later, in March, 1919, the Communist International was formed with Moscow as headquarters. The campaign was on. But Lenin had no illusions. "Having started as a spectacular success in one country," he said, "our revolution may have to go through periods of trial. . . . Our task is to exercise tact and caution; we must maneuver and retreat until reinforcements come to our aid."

For years they maneuvered. Then in 1945 their retreats ceased. Now tact and caution could be thrown to the wind. On November 7, 1917, the Bolsheviki held a precarious sway only over the 1,400,000 inhabitants of stunned and paralyzed Petrograd. As the second half of the twentieth century was ushered in by the thoughtless revelers of the West, the Bolsheviki ruled nearly 800,000,000 peoples in 12,873,000 square miles of the inhabited earth. One third of the earth has come under their heel in one third of a century. This is the most phenomenal career of revolution mankind has ever seen.

There is nothing gained by turning our faces away from the fact that bolshevism is the dominant force in the world of today, the greatest empire the world has ever known since that day in antiquity when Alexander wept when told that there were no more worlds to conquer.

The Soviet Empire extends from the Sea of Japan to the Oder River in one unbroken geographical continuity. It is the dreaded heartland that dominates the world. Although still expanding, it already exceeds the British Empire on the day of its greatest glory. It is an empire of darkness over which the sun never rises. It is an empire that has swollen in the cold sweat of the cold war, whose victories are as mysterious as are its defeats.

We have an obligation to Pavel Fedorovich Byalitnisko and to the Byalitniskos throughout the world. When they raise their eyes in skeptical quest and ask us, "Is America our last refuge?" we must answer in the firm voice of Thomas Jefferson. "May it be to the world, what I believe it will be (to some parts sooner, to others later, but finally to all) the signal of arousing men to burst the chains . . . ," he wrote in memory of American Independence on its fiftieth anniversary, "and to assume the blessings and security of self-government. That form which we have substituted restores the free right to the unbounded exercise of reason and freedom of opinion. All eyes are opened, or opening, to the rights of men. The general spread of the light of science has already laid open to every view the palpable truth that the mass of mankind has not been born with saddles on their backs, nor a favored few booted and spurred, ready to ride them legitimately, by the grace of God.

"These are grounds of hope for others."

Sources

Chapter 1

1. In the preparation of this book, we made use of all bona fide intelligence sources available to persons no longer in government service. We employed the examination of documents, the interrogation of travelers, discussions with statesmen, diplomats, high-ranking officers. We conducted extensive research into so-called secondary sources in the public domain and studied and analyzed newspapers, books, radio intercepts, etc.

Attracted by our interest in and understanding for their problems, a great variety of foreign sources favored us with their confidence and allowed us access to information of immense value otherwise not easily available to individuals outside of the official intelligence organizations of governments. Among these sources were 237 refugees from behind the iron curtain who submitted to interrogation either by us or by our assistants and contacts, both in the United States and abroad. These refugees represented the cream of a generous crop. Among them were senior officers of the Red Army and Navy, atomic scientists, outstanding economists, diplomats, and officials from virtually every branch of the Soviet bureaucracy.

In the course of this study, we have amassed what appears to be valuable data on the true state of the world from what we regard as trustworthy sources—data and sources which are available to probably no other private persons in the United States. This book was written to share this information with the American public; we look upon this book as a lengthy intelligence report, with no strings of false security classification attached to it.

It is impossible to record, even in an extensive bibliography, all the sources upon which we have drawn in the preparation of this report. The following will guide the reader to some of those sources and will acknowledge at least part of the debt of gratitude we owe to our informants both here and abroad.

2. Second Report of the Secretary of Defense. Washington: U.S. Government Printing Office, 1950, p. 6.

3. Lieutenant General Walter Bedell Smith, *My Three Years in Moscow*. Philadelphia: J. B. Lippincott Company, 1950, p. 307.

4. In his address on "Implementing Peace in the World," at Columbia University, March 23, 1950.

5. *Cf.* articles by Erno Gero, Luigi Longo, Victor Michaut, and others, in *For a Lasting Peace, for a People's Democracy*, official journal of the Cominform, published weekly in several languages, in Bucharest, Rumania.

6. See Stalin's remarks on May 6, 1929, to the American Commission of the Comintern, *Bolshevik*, January 15, 1930, p. 8.

7. In conversation with correspondents, as reported by the Associated Press.

8. Including such high-ranking Soviet diplomats as Andrey A. Gromyko, Semyon K. Tserepkin, Professor Boris Stein, Arkady A. Sobolev, and officers like Major General Ilia M. Sarayev, Lieutenant General A. F. Vasiliev, Rear Admiral Semyen S. Rameshvily, Rear Admiral V. L. Bogdenko, and, in former years, Maxim M. Litvinov.

9. See *United Nations World*, Vol. III, No. 1, January, 1949.

10. Walter Bedell Smith, *op. cit.*, p. 304. Quoted by permission.

11. See *United Nations World*, June, July, August, 1949, on Gromyko's protracted talks with business and industrial leaders in the United States; also articles by Thomas J. Hamilton and A. A. Rosenthal, in the *New York Times*, June 5 and 6, 1949.

12. We could not establish in Washington whether or not Stalin's letter was ever actually received in the White House. To several inquiries, White House spokesmen on middle echelons responded with noncommital answers, but refused to convey the query to higher echelons.

13. As a matter of fact, Stalin himself elaborated his theory in a letter, dated February 23, 1946, he wrote to Colonel E. Razin, professor of military history at the Voroshilov Supreme Military Academy, clarifying his own deviations from Lenin's well-known military theories based on Clausewitz's philosophy of war.

14. Secretary Johnson's 1950 report, p. 6.

15. Harrisburg, 1949, especially Chapters 13, 14, and 15. While writing his book, Colonel Ely was chief of intelligence division, Intelligence Section, Army Field Forces. He bases his information on the interrogation of "thousands of members of the Red Army who have left the Soviet forces to take up life in the Western world."

16. For a detailed survey of Stalin's attitude toward the United States, see Chapter 20. His true designs on America were most frankly stated in conversations with American Communist leaders, on September 9, 1927, May 6, 1929, and more recently, especially in 1947 when William Z. Foster called upon him in the Kremlin.

17. *Cf.* Joseph Stalin, *Leninism,* Vol. I, pp. 74–75, 76–80, 235–36, 299–300; also his "Strategy and Tactics of the Russian Communists," *Pravda,* 1923, No. 56. Lenin, *Collected Works,* Russian ed., Vol. X, pp. 80–81; Vol. XXVII, pp. 69–70, 271, etc.

18. Non-Russian geologists dispute the validity of this Soviet hypothesis.

19. *Cf.* the unpublished record of Soviet talks with a Franco-British delegation in Moscow, in the summer of 1939; Molotov's talks with Hitler and Ribbentrop, on November 12 and 13, 1940, in Berlin; the draft of a Russo-German secret agreement, dated November 25, 1940, No. 2362 of communications sent by German Embassy in Moscow to the German Foreign Office, and captured by the 9th Division of the U.S. Army, at Degenershausen in the Hartz Mountains, in April, 1945.

Chapter 2

1. President Truman announced on September 23, 1949, that "an atomic explosion" had occurred somewhere in the U.S.S.R., but the Russians, in a series of obscure pronouncements by Molotov and Vishinsky, claimed that such an explosion had already taken place in 1947. According to information at our disposal the Soviet Union came into the possession of all atomic secrets in 1947, exploded its first A-bomb in October, 1948, and conducted a second explosion under scientifically controlled circumstances in the summer of 1949. It was this second explosion that formed the basis of the Truman announcement.

2. For background of the Russo-Yugoslav rift, see *Pravda,* September 9, 1948, and *Borba,* official organ of the Yugoslav Communist party, October 2, 3, 4, 1948. Also the lengthy report of Politburo member Mikhail Suslov to the November, 1949, meeting of the Cominform.

3. For a detailed account of the Rokossovsky appointment, see page 180. Much of our information on Rokossovsky came from Colonel Kyril D. Kalinov, formerly of the Red Army General Staff and an associate of the Colonel "Khralov," who is the source of these data.

4. *New York Times,* November 29, 1949.
5. Khralov is not his real name. The names of all our Russian informants had to be changed throughout this book.
6. In *Gulliver's Travels,* Book I, Chap. IV.
7. For the significant role Soviet military leaders play in the formulation of policies, and the intellectual preparedness they bring to that role, see Lion Feuchtwanger, *Moscow 1937,* London, 1937, pp. 110–113. Most of the officers whose participation at these Politburo meetings was reported to us are members of the Academy of Military Science, an institution of the highest scientific standing, devoted to the study of strategy in the light of Marxism-Leninism. Its president is Marshal Vasilevsky, himself the outstanding protagonist of a new Marxist military school.

Chapter 3

1. Stalin, *Leninism,* Vol. II, p. 255. See also his report to the Seventeenth Congress of the CPSU (B), on January 26, 1934, Part One of which was entitled: "The Continuing Crisis of World Capitalism and the Position of the Soviet Union in International Affairs." Pitted against a savage exposition of his favorite crisis theory was a mellow presentation of "the continued progress of the national economy and the internal situation in the U.S.S.R."
2. Soviet preoccupation with such data is reflected in articles on abstract economic subjects regularly published in *Bolshevik,* the Russian Communist party's chief theoretical organ, but also in a conference held at the Jefferson School of Social Science in New York, on May 14 and 15, 1949, in the wake of the Kremlin's decision described in this chapter. See *The Economic Crisis and the Cold War,* New York, 1949, especially pp. 67–99.
3. *Program of the Communist International,* Part II, Sec. 1, elaborated upon by J. Stalin, in *Leninism,* Vol. II, pp. 254–255.
4. J. Stalin, *Foundation of Leninism,* Sec. 3, Chap. 3.
5. Stalin was described to us by various refugee officers of the Red Army as "a brilliant strategist and a master tactician." His autodidactic knowledge of the art and science of war was responsible for many successes in the Russo-German conflict of 1941–45.
6. G. Zinoviev and N. Lenin, *Socialism and War,* written in Geneva in August, 1915, reprinted in V. I. Lenin, *Collected Works,* Eng. ed., New York, 1930, Vol. XVIII, p. 219.
7. See Lenin's secret directive to Soviet delegates departing for The Hague to attend the International Congress of Co-Operatives

and Trade Unions. In his *Selected Works*, Eng. ed., Vol. X, p. 317. Also his short note to "Members of the Politburo," *ibid.*, p. 315.

Chapter 4

1. Ralph Ingersoll, *Top Secret*, New York, 1946, p. 104. The highest security classification was "For Eyes Only," meaning the eyes of the addressee. The British liked to add the instruction: "Burn after reading." This gave rise to the quip popular in Allied intelligence circles that several highly classified reports failed to influence the course of history because they were burned *before* being read, by overzealous, security-conscious officers.

2. Winston S. Churchill, *The World Crisis*, New York, 1942, pp. 338–339.

3. Hitherto unpublished intelligence sources reported to us by B. Gisevius and K. H. Abshagen, former high officials of the Abwehr, Germany's strategic intelligence organization during the recent war.

4. This incident was described to us in melodramatic detail by a famous old Bolshevik who helped in the drafting of the lectures and accompanied Stalin to Sverdlov University.

5. J. Stalin, *Foundations of Leninism*, New York, 1934. Reprinted by Committee on Foreign Affairs, Eightieth Congress, Second Session, House Document No. 619.

6. *Ibid.*, p. 102.

7. This is a telescoped presentation of the operations plan, drawn from sections (B) and (D) of the seventh lecture. *Ibid.*, pp. 103–104.

8. *Ibid.*, p. 103.

9. V. I. Lenin in *Sotsial Demokrat*, No. 35, December 12, 1914.

10. J. Stalin, *The Great Patriotic War of the Soviet Union*, New York, 1945, especially p. 15.

11. See Stalin's statement on the "proper attitude toward peoples of foreign countries" in the light of his definition of "Soviet patriotism," as quoted in "Against the Bourgeois Ideology of Cosmopolitanism," *Voprosy Filosofii*, No. 2, 1948.

12. The following quotations from Stalin's well-known writings are presented in the form of an imaginary interview to facilitate understanding of the passage. His "answers" are literal transcripts of the Russian original.

13. J. Stalin, "Tactics of the Russian Communists," *The October Revolution*, pp. 122–129. His statements are elaborations upon

the broad principles Lenin stated in Chapter VII of his *Proletarian Revolution and Renegade Kautsky,* and in "The United States of Europe Slogan," *Collected Works,* Eng. ed., Vol. XVIII.

Chapter 5

1. The former Soviet diplomat here called Zhelezhnyakov, on whose detailed report this chapter is partly based, now lives in Western Europe. We established contact with him while he was still with Colonel Rogoshin in Austria.
2. Report of the German Ambassador in the U.S.S.R. to the Berlin Foreign Office, dated Moscow, April 13, 1941, reprinted in *Nazi Soviet Relations 1939–41,* New York, 1948, p. 324.
3. A careful and persistent reading of *New Times* provides an excellent opportunity to reconstruct Soviet intentions in the foreign field and establish the order of the "priority areas" which we are describing here. The magazine is published in several languages by Trud, the Central Administration of Trade Unions, whose Foreign Affairs department, rather than the Cominform, is the *de facto* foreign ministry of the world revolution.
4. Actual wording in Molotov's top secret draft for a Russo-German treaty, dated November 26, 1940. Reprinted in *Nazi-Soviet Relations,* pp. 259, 268, 284.
5. *Ibid.,* p. 259.
6. *Program of the Communist International,* Parts I and II, "Theses of the Sixth Congress of the Comintern," International Press Correspondence, No. 83, 1928; Resolutions on the Report of Ercoli, *Seventh World Congress of the Comintern,* 1935, pp. 40–45.

Chapter 6

1. Walter Lippmann, *U.S. War Aims,* Boston, 1944, p. 194.
2. *Ibid.,* pp. 208–209.
3. In interview given to Roy Howard on March 1, 1936, and in conversations with Wendell Willkie, Elliott Roosevelt, Harold L. Stassen, and many others.
4. Eleanor Roosevelt, *This I Remember,* New York, 1949, p. 361.
5. *Documents on American Foreign Relations,* Vol. VII, Princeton, 1946, pp. 892–894. Also Arthur Bliss Lane, *I Saw Poland Betrayed,* Indianapolis, 1948, pp. 75–76.
6. *United Nations World,* January, 1949.
7. At the time of this writing, the grand narrative of Mr. Churchill's *Second World War* covers only the period up to January, 1942.

8. These statements are borne out by the record of the official transcripts of the Teheran, Cairo, and Crimea conferences.

9. Robert E. Sherwood, *Roosevelt and Hopkins,* New York, 1948, pp. 850–870; James F. Byrnes, *Speaking Frankly,* New York, 1947, pp. 21–45; Edward R. Stettinius, Jr., *Roosevelt and the Russians,* New York, 1949. Also various private reports to us from several participants in these conferences.

10. For a complete account of the conflicting intelligence reports, see *United Nations World,* January, 1949, pp. 17–19.

11. *Christian Science Monitor,* January 2, 1945.

12. Department of State, *Bulletin,* XII, p. 213; Senate Document No. 8, Seventy-ninth Congress, First Session. For supplementary (secret) agreements not included in the report of February 11, 1945, see Department of State, *Bulletin,* XIV, p. 282; *Ibid.,* XII, p. 394; *Executive Agreement Series* No. 505; *New York Times,* March 1, 1945.

13. This view was widely held in what was then (1946–47) the Central Intelligence Group, including its Czechoslovak desk.

14. *United Nations World,* March, 1947, p. 15.

15. V. I. Lenin, "Against Boycott," *Collected Works,* Russian ed., XII, pp. 20–22.

16. *Washington Evening Star,* November 27, 1949.

Chapter 7

1. James F. Byrnes, *op. cit.,* p. 49.

2. *Corps Diplomatique,* I, June 15, 1946, p. 7. Also see William Nelson, *From the Crocodile's Mouth,* New York, 1950.

3. Byrnes, *op. cit.,* p. 60.

4. *Ibid.,* p. 63. Also Sherwood, *op. cit,* p. 899.

5. V. M. Molotov, *Problems of Foreign Policy,* Moscow, 1949, pp. 13–20, 26–36.

6. *Report to the President in the Results of the San Francisco Conference,* Department of State Publication 2349, Conference Series 71, June 26, 1945, pp. 20–31. Also *Postwar Foreign Policy Preparation,* Department of State Publication 3580, General Foreign Policy Series 15, February, 1950, pp. 7–434.

7. E. M. Zacharias, *Secret Missions,* New York, 1946, p. 332.

8. Department of State, *Bulletin,* XIII, p. 15. *Congressional Record,* XCI, p. 7216.

9. New York, 1939, pp. 68–86.

10. *Washington Post,* May 21, 1946.

11. Information related to us by eye witnesses of the great White House drama.

12. John C. Campbell, *The United States in World Affairs, 1945–47*, New York, 1948, p. 157.

13. This episode was described to us by the embarrassed magazine editor who had raised the question.

14. The second phase of the incident was related by a State Department aide who witnessed it.

15. Based on personal observations and on information obtained from several "working newspapermen" assigned to the State Department Press Room.

16. Walter Lippmann, "A Year of Peacemaking," *Atlantic Monthly*, CLXXIII, December, 1946, pp. 35–40; Harold Nicolson, "Peacemaking at Paris," *Foreign Affairs*, XXV, January, 1947, pp. 190–203.

17. Department of State, *U.S.–U.N.* Series 6, 1946. Also Senate, Hearings before the Committee on Foreign Relations, July 9–13, 1945; Senate Executive Report No. 8, July 16, 1945.

18. Byrnes, *op. cit.*, pp. 138–158. Also his "Report on the Paris Peace Conference," October 18, 1946, Department of State Publication 2682, Conference Series 90.

19. Sumner Welles, *Where Are We Heading?*, New York, 1946, pp. 2–3, 6–18. For text of the Charter, see James W. Gantenbein, *Documentary Background of World War II*, New York, 1948, pp. 1033–1034.

20. Speech of June 4, 1946, also Campbell, *op. cit.*, pp. 191–194.

21. E. J. Dillon, *The Inside Story of the Peace Conference*, New York, 1920, pp. 464–468.

22. Department of State, *Executive Agreement Series* 437, 490, 457. Also *Foreign Policy Reports*, XXII, August, 1946, pp. 118–127, XXII, April, 1947, pp. 22–32.

23. Department of State Publication 2682, Conference Series 90.

24. *Washington Post,* June 5, 1946.

25. Joseph and Stewart Alsop, in *New York Herald Tribune* (Paris ed.), May 28, 1946.

26. Speech at Stuttgart, on September 6, 1946, Department of State Publication 2616, European Series 13, 15.

27. Campbell, *op. cit.*, pp. 447–448. Byrnes, *op. cit.*, pp. 239–243. Also information privately communicated to us by some of the protagonists, on both sides, of the Wallace incident.

28. This important diplomatic report reached us through a member

of the Polish delegation to the United Nations, whose identity cannot be revealed since he is still behind the iron curtain.

29. We have no reason to doubt the accuracy or authenticity of this information from our Polish contact, even though it would indicate that the Kremlin itself remained in the dark in so far as atomic developments were concerned despite the espionage activities of such highly placed scientists as Dr. Allan Nunn May and Dr. Klaus Fuchs. It seems that information of such highly technical nature was not communicated to the Kremlin by General Kuznetsov of the Military Intelligence Directorate.

30. This information was obtained from an American business leader who gained it in prolonged conversations with Andrei A. Gromyko in New York.

31. In conversations with various informants, including the foreign ministers of satellite countries.

32. Byrnes, *op. cit.*, p. 44.

33. *Ibid.*, p. 36.

34. *Ibid.*, p. 37.

35. In an interview with Roy Howard, March 1, 1936.

36. For a detailed description of the "conspiracy" see Ferenc Nagy, *The Struggle Behind the Iron Curtain*, New York, 1948, pp. 311–386.

37. Speech of April 20, 1946.

38. House Report No. 1920, Eightieth Congress, Second Session, 1948, p. 114.

39. Nagy, *op. cit.*, pp. 409–425; *New York Times,* July 21, 1947.

40. Information supplied by George M. Dimitrov, former secretary general of the Bulgarian Agrarian party, and Petkov's closest collaborator.

41. The account of the Rumanian coup was told us in great detail by King Michael himself during his visit to the U.S. in the early spring of 1948. Additional data were supplied by the late Dr. Ernest Bianu, chief of the King's own personal security police force in the palace, concealed behind a curtain in the King's study during Vishinsky's dramatic call.

42. A brilliant exposé of the Prague coup was prepared by an anonymous author for the House Committee on Foreign Affairs, Eighty-first Congress, First Session, House Document No. 154. Additional data were gained from the memoirs (published in the U.S.) of Dr. Hubert Ripka, minister of the ousted Cabinet, and from similar sources among Czechoslovakia's democratic refugees in the U.S.

Chapter 8

1. For some time these schools employed non-Communist Americans as teachers. They were thus given unprecedented insight into the workings of Soviet nepotism. An English teacher, the wife of a prominent American editor, was severely reprimanded when she gave bad marks to the child of a high-ranking Soviet official.

2. There was some disagreement even among these refugee Russians as to the true merit of the case. Thus the role of Victor Kravchenko, described in an uninhibited communiqué by himself, was criticized by several leading members of the Russian colony in New York, including some of Mme Kasenkina's hosts.

3. The propaganda exploitation of the incident was described by George V. Allen, then Assistant Secretary of State, *cf.* Hearings, Department of State Appropriation Bill for 1950, Washington, 1949.

4. Smith, *op. cit.,* pp. 74–75, 180–181.

5. Department of State, *Bulletin,* XVIII, p. 928.

6. For the description of a typical Soviet network of spies see the Report of the Royal Commission, June 27, 1947, Ottawa, pp. 11–96; and Alexander Foote, *Handbook for Spies,* New York, 1949, pp. 61–91.

7. At the time of the Kasenkina incident, the U.S. maintained two Foreign Service officers (the consul general and a vice consul) in Vladivostok, in addition to a small nonconsular staff.

8. Department of State, *The Berlin Crisis,* European and Commonwealth Series 1, 1948; Great Britain. *Germany: An Account of Events Leading up to a Reference of the Berlin Question to the United Nations,* London, Command Paper 7534, 1948; *The Soviet Union and the Berlin Question* [a collection of documents], Foreign Ministry, Moscow, 1948; *New Times,* supplement, No. 27, June 30, 1948; Department of State, *Bulletin,* XVIII, pp. 807–810.

9. Smith, *op. cit.,* p. 251.

10. *Ibid.,* pp. 248–249

11. Byrnes, *op. cit.,* pp. 121–122.

Chapter 9

1. K. Marx and F. Engels, *Manifesto of the Communist Party,* Moscow, 1948, pp. 70–72.

2. J. Stalin, "The October Revolution and the Tactics of the Russian Communists," from the preface to the book *On the Road to*

October, reprinted in *Leninism,* Selected Writings, New York, 1942, pp. 9–35. Also John Reed, *Ten Days That Shook the World,* appended notes to Chapter II of the Modern Library edition, New York, 1934, pp. 326–329.

3. Curzio Malaparte, *Coup d'Etat,* New York, 1932, pp. 13–56.
4. Revolutionary alias of Finnish Communist leader Tuure Valdemar Lehen. His other known alias is Tuure Lehti.
5. Alfred Lange, *The Road to Victory,* Chap. VI.
6. A copy of this secret textbook was smuggled out of Budapest in 1948 by one of our informants.
7. Sec. 3 of the English text.
8. Eightieth Congress, Second Session, House Report No. 1920, 1948, pp. 62–64. Also Hearings before Special Committee on Un-American Activities, Vol. IX, November 30, 1939.
9. It is located at 5 Akadémia Utca in the center of Budapest, across the street from the ancient Academy of Sciences into whose building it overflows.
10. Hearings, etc., Vol. IX, pp. 6984–7025.
11. A comprehensive report was presented to us in the fall of 1949 by a young Hungarian who had graduated from the famous school in that same year.
12. House Report No. 1920, p. 71, testimony of W. O. Nowell.
13. Malaparte, *op. cit.,* pp. 38–41. The functions of the Red Guard were described in the official "Struggle Against Imperialist War and the Tasks of the Communists," an account of the Seventh Congress of the Comintern, p. 48.

Chapter 10

1. Constantine Brown, in the *Washington Evening Star,* December 9, 1947. Mr. Brown is known to have excellent contacts with some of our top intelligence organizations and is remarkable for the accuracy of his revelations. Our estimate is based on reports directly from Italy to us.
2. Eightieth Congress, Second Session, 1949, House Document No. 707, p. 75.
3. *Ibid.,* p. 71.
4. *Washington Post,* citing "a secret U.S. Army intelligence report," September 8, 1947.
5. Martin Ebon, *World Communism Today,* New York, 1948, pp. 236–238.
6. *New York Times,* November 14, 1947, a typical example of innumerable reports on direct action by the Italian Red Guards.

7. *New York Times,* February 15, 1950, *L'Unita,* of the same day.
8. *New York Times,* November 16, 1947.
9. Unpublished report on the Partisan movement within the Italian Communist party, prepared specifically for us by a contact in the Emilia region, January, 1949.
10. André Marty, *La revolt de la mer noir,* Paris, 1929.
11. *New York World Telegram,* February 27, 1950.
12. Maurice Thorez, *France Today and Tomorrow,* 1945. Also A. Rossi, *A Communist Party in Action,* New Haven, 1949, pp. 133–141, 166–179, 180–183.
13. *For Lasting Peace for People's Democracy,* February 3, 1950.
14. V. I. Lenin, *Collected Works,* Eng. ed., XVIII, pp. 149, 197–202, 234.
15. *New York Times,* February 15, 1950, printed this item under the headline "French Guided Missiles To Be Tested in Sahara," thus unfortunately misplacing the emphasis and giving the impression of French strength instead of weakness. Since Americans like to stop reading such news items with the last letter of the headline, many of us never learned what really happened in Nice.
16. Lenin, *op. cit.,* p. 278.
17. J. Stalin, *Replies to Questions of the Sverdlov Students,* 1930.

Chapter *11*
1. V. I. Lenin, *Collected Works,* Russian ed., XXIV. Also L. Trotsky, *Problems of the Chinese Revolution,* 1932, pp. 73–79.
2. J. Stalin, *Foundations of Leninism,* Chap. 3, Sec. 3.
3. *New York Times,* April 28, 1927.
4. Mao Tse-tung, *Red China,* New York, 1934.
5. Edgar Snow, *Red Star over China,* New York, 1944, pp. 121–134.
6. *United States Relations with China,* pp. 230–233.
7. *Ibid.,* pp. 313–314.
8. *Ibid.,* pp. 315–323.
9. Mao Tse-tung, *The Fight for a New China,* New York, 1945.
10. By missionaries of the American Friends Service Committee scattered throughout China.
11. *New York Times,* March 7, 1950.
12. For a description of the Polish pattern, see Jan Ciechanowski, *Defeat in Victory,* New York, 1947, pp. 158–173.
13. Information supplied by Chinese Communist contacts of substantial standing.

14. Private reports to us from Nanking and Canton, by trustworthy contacts on the spot.
15. *Time,* March 17, 1949.
16. For the full text of the treaty, see *For Lasting Peace for People's Democracy,* February 23, 1950.
17. Information from authoritative Chinese sources via India.
18. Information provided by one of America's outstanding "China hands," formerly General Wedemeyer's chief political aide in Asia.
19. Foster Haley, *One Half of Two Worlds,* New York, 1950.
20. Harold Isaacs, *No Peace for Asia,* New York, 1947.
21. Information gained from authoritative private sources.
22. G. D. H. Cole, *World in Transition,* New York, 1949, pp. 510ff.
23. *Ibid.,* pp. 525–526.

Chapter 12
1. Throughout the months of the Berlin blockade, a Soviet contact in New York advised us to concentrate our attention on China rather than on Berlin.
2. *U.S. Relations with China,* pp. 230–278.
3. House Document No. 154, Vol. II, pp. 8–12.
4. J. T. Shotwell and F. Deak, *Turkey at the Straits,* New York, 1940.
5. *Cf.* K. S. Papazian, *Patriotism Perverted,* Boston, 1934.
6. E. Lengyel, *Turkey,* New York, 1941. R. P. Arnot, *Soviet Russia and Her Neighbors,* 1927.
7. Quoted by Albert Rhys Williams, *The Soviets,* New York, 1937, p. 485.
8. H. N. Howard, "The United States and the Problem of the Turkish Straits," *Middle East Journal,* I, 1, January, 1947, pp. 59–73. Also Department of State, Near Eastern Series 5, 1947 (Documents).
9. Hitherto unpublished information obtained through authoritative private sources.
10. *Nazi-Soviet Relations,* p. 127.
11. *Ibid.,* p. 132.
12. *Ibid.,* p. 168.
13. *Ibid.,* p. 171.
14. *Ibid.,* pp. 173–177.
15. Esmer, A. S., "The Straits," *Foreign Affairs,* XXV, 1, January, 1947, pp. 290–302.

16. The intelligence data on which this narrative is based were supplied by a former lieutenant colonel of the Red Army Military Intelligence Directorate. Confirmation was gained from authoritative Turkish sources in Washington and New York.

17. Information supplied by a top-ranking German ex-Communist who occupied high position in the Soviet-controlled government of Saxony.

18. G. Tongas, *La Turquie, centre de gravité des Balkans et du Proche orient*, Paris, 1939, pp. 272–276.

19. Sir W. Martin Conway's *No Man's Land*, Cambridge, 1906, is still the best available history of the region, from the earliest time to 1902. For more recent developments, V. Pantenburg, *Russlands Griff um Nordeuropa*, Leipzig, 1938.

20. Store Norske Spitsbergen Kulkompani aided in the collection of these data during a trip to the Far North of Norway in the fall of 1948.

21. Based on a release of U.S. Air Force, October, 1948.

22. Private information gained from reliable observers on the spot. *Cf. United Nations World*, December, 1948; January, 1949.

Chapter 13

1. H. P. Hall, "American Interests in the Middle East," *Foreign Policy Association, Headline Series,* 1948. Also *United Nations World,* May, 1948, "The Inside Story of the Palestine Fiasco."

2. *United Nations World,* August, 1948, pp. 18–19.

3. House Document No. 154, Vol. II, 1949, pp. 33–36.

4. He is described by authoritative sources as "the most important Communist leader in the area, president of the Lebanese Federation of Trade Unions, who visited Moscow in May, 1947."

5. House Document No. 154, Vol. II, p. 2.

6. Directive issues to the All-Union Lecture Bureau, Ministry of Higher Education, July 17, 1946.

7. Directives issued on July 6 and August 13, 1946. Also see V. Mayev's article in *Izvestia,* May 30, 1946. "Mayev" is the pseudonym of Ivan Maisky.

8. Department of Defense transcript, dated April 10, 1950.

Chapter 14

1. D. Hinshaw, *Sweden, Champion of Peace,* New York, 1949, pp. 8–46, 88–104, 130–190.

2. Isabel de Palencia, *Alexandra Kollontay,* New York, 1947, pp. 51–78, 186ff.

3. D. M. Strashunsky, *Shvetsiya (Sweden)*, Moscow, 1940. Also, E. Thermaenius, *Riksdagspartierna*, Stockholm, 1935.

4. V. Törnblom, *Utrikespolitisk Passivitet eller Aktiv Fredspolitik*, Stockholm, 1935. Most of the data were gained in personal surveys on the spot in 1934, 1948, 1950.

5. A. F. Rickman, *Swedish Iron Ore*, London, 1939.

6. House Document No. 707, pp. 109–110.

7. Resolutions on the Report of Ercoli, *op. cit.*, pp. 40–45.

8. *Ibid.*, Sec. 15 (a).

9. J. H. Jackson, "Finland since the Armistice," *International Affairs*, XXIV, October, 1948, pp. 505–514; also A. Enckell, *Democratic Finland*, London, 1948. The issue is discussed from the Russian point of view by P. Romanov in his *Finlyandiya i Yeye Armiya*, Moscow, 1938, and in *War and Peace in Finland*, New York, 1940, A. Brody, ed.

10. House Report No. 1920, pp. 62–64.

Chapter 15

1. Much of the material contained in this chapter was gained from private sources.

2. House Document No. 154, Vol. I, 5.

3. *Ibid*, Appendix C, p. 24.

4. The end product of this intelligence exploit appeared in the world press on May 25, 1946.

5. Great emphasis was placed upon the activities of a few young American intelligence officers working overtly in Rumania and Hungary while the U.S. was still actively participating in the control of those defeated Axis satellites. Our failure to resist Soviet offensive, shrewdly designed to destroy our primitive intelligence network behind the iron curtain, resulted in a serious defeat of our intelligence organization.

6. Nagy, *op. cit.*, pp. 397–404.

7. This seems to be a recurrent complaint, voiced by many of our more enterprising intelligence officers and agents.

8. Skillful British participation in the frantic intelligence attack upon the iron curtain is recorded in virtually every one of the satellite trials, staged with deterring regularity in Prague.

9. J. Stalin, *Foundations of Leninism*, Chap. III, Sec. 3.

10. K. Zilliacus, *I Choose Peace*, London, 1949, pp. 126–127.

11. Hansard, November 3, 1945.

12. Part II, Sec. I.

13. *Washington Post*, April 4, 1950.

14. Zilliacus, *op. cit.*, p. 87, "on the authority of a Labor M.P. who was then an officer serving in Greece and to whom this remark was made."

15. *Life,* April 19, 1947.

16. Leland Stowe in *The New Republic,* September 15, 1947.

17. See the periodic reports of the President to Congress on *Assistance to Greece and Turkey,* Department of State Publications 2957, 3035, 3647, etc.

18. Private information from a source extremely close to Markos.

19. UN General Assembly. Report of the Special Committee on the Balkans. UN Document A/574, June, 1948, and UN Document A/644, September 16, 1948.

20. From Soviet sources in Paris and New York.

21. J. Stalin, speech delivered to Central Committee of Communist party, reprinted in *Leninism,* pp. 88*ff.*

22. *Ibid.,* pp. 132–133.

23. R. West in the *New York Herald Tribune,* August 8, 1948.

24. *Times,* London, September 7, 1947.

25. *Ibid.,* September 8. 1947.

26. Based on information supplied by authoritative Yugoslav sources close to Marshal Tito.

27. Royal Institute of International Affairs, *The Soviet-Yugoslav Dispute,* London, 1948.

28. Communist party of Yugoslavia, *Report to Fifth Congress,* Belgrade, 1948.

29. *United Nations World,* August, September, December, 1948.

30. Yudin is a crack administrator rather than a political zealot. During World War II he was in charge of important phases of war production. M. Suslov and D. Manuilsky are the political supervisors of the Cominform, occupying the position A. A. Zhdanov held until his death in 1948.

31. The material which follows was placed at our disposal by *actual participants* of the meeting, siding with Tito against the Kremlin.

32. Our informant has recently been "liquidated."

33. Information from Tito's circle.

34. *United Nations World,* August, 1948.

35. Byrnes, *op. cit.,* p. 88.

36. *Ibid.,* pp. 89–90.

Chapter 16

1. *Information Bulletin,* U.S.S.R. Embassy, Washington, D.C., November, 1949.

2. Abundant material is available from intelligence sources of exceptionally high reliability and probability rating to support these statements. Among our informants were such early stalwarts of the Russian-sponsored neo-German military movements as Lt. Heinrich Count von Einsiedel, great-grandson of Bismarck, and Captain von Puttkamer, of the German Navy. The State Department's belated protest to the Russians, in the late spring of 1950, and its accompanying release describing the organization of this dangerous new force in Eastern Germany, were both outdated and inaccurate, apparently based on old or inadequate intelligence sources. The General Zeisser mentioned in the release—the notorious "Gomez" well-known from the Spanish Civil War—is no longer with the phantom army. His place has been taken by "real Germans" like Mueller and Korfes.

3. According to the Cominform journal of March 31, 1950, the number of so-called peace committees in Rumania alone "now totals 17,204." On February 3, 1950, the journal reported that "the Permanent Peace Committee maintains contact with 76 countries. During the past year [1949], National Peace Congresses and Conferences were held in 26 countries, International Peace Day was observed in 60 countries."

4. Compare with the Ercoli Resolution of 1935, printed in full in the special 1935 issue of the *Communist International,* devoted to the Seventh World Congress of the Comintern.

5. S. Mikolayczyk, *The Rape of Poland,* New York, 1948.

6. General Damyanov has been "kicked upstairs" since this writing. He was named vice premier, with no influence over matters of "defense," to allow complete control to the Soviet's delegate at the head of the Bulgarian armed forces. (See Department of State Publications 2743, European Series 21, 1948, pp. 4–6, Sec. I–II, Articles 9–19, for pertinent passages of the Bulgarian Peace Treaty.)

7. House Report No. 1920, 1948, p. 108.

8. *New York Times,* October 2, 1946.

9. Smith, *op. cit.,* 82.

10. A. M. Pankratova, *A History of the U.S.S.R.,* Moscow, 1948, Vol. III, p. 417.

11. J. von Puttkamer, *Ich war ein Vorzugsgefangener in Russland,* Zofingen, 1949.

12. The first such group was established in 1943, northwest of Moscow, in Zone 3, Camp 23, of the network of prisoner-of-war "cages" the Russians maintained for their "privileged captives" from Field Marshal Paulus's Sixth Army. Later GHQ of what amounted to a clandestine German General Staff-in-Exile was established in the Antifa (anti-Fascist) School at Krasnoyarsk.

Chapter 17

1. Frunze, M. V., *Selected Works,* Mcscow, 1934.

2. *The Struggle against Imperialist War, etc.,* Moscow, 1935, pp. 40–41, 135.

3. Lange, *op. cit.,* Chap. VI.

4. For its role in the Bolshevik order of things, see M. V. Frunze, *Uniform Military Training and the Red Army,* Moscow, 1941; *Military-Political Training of the Red Army,* Moscow, 1934; and *Reorganization of the Red Army,* Moscow, 1934.

5. Sea Treaties of Peace with Bulgaria, Hungary, and Roumania, Eng. version, Washington, 1948.

6. Estimate based on testimony of ex-colonel of Hungarian General Staff, now an exile in London.

7. For the inside story of the Pálffy case, see Col. V. Kruchina, "A Szovjet karhatalma Magyarországon," *Hontalan Magyarok Naplója,* July-September, 1948. Col. Kruchina was Pálffy's deputy from the first day of Soviet occupation to January 17, 1947.

8. K. Marx, *Der 18. Brumaire des Louis Bonaparte,* New York, 1852.

9. V. I. Lenin, *Selected Works,* Vol. VI, pp. 263–264.

Chapter 18

1. J. Stalin, *On the Great Patriotic War, etc.,* Moscow, 1946, p. 41.

2. Parkratova, *op. cit.,* Vol. III, p. 404.

3. *Bolshevik,* 1947, pp. 3, 6–8.

4. For a translation of the Bolshevik article, see *Military Affairs,* XIII, 2, pp. 75–78.

5. Typical literary example of the infiltration of Tsarist traditions into the Red Army is a book by General A. Krivitsky, entitled "Traditions of the Russians Officers Corps," published in Moscow during World War II, and still enjoying immense popularity and, what is more, official support.

6. This figure was computed for us by Ellsworth L. Raymond (q.v.) on the basis of data revealed in the so-called Military Vote in the 1950 Soviet elections.

7. These figures were brought out during a press conference in the Pentagon held by the Chief of Staff of the U.S. Army on April 10, 1950.

8. Data on the Red Air Force were supplied in abundance by several senior officers who somehow found their way to the West; and by a civilian official of the Ministry of Foreign Trade who, at one time in the recent past, was chief of procurement for General Tupolev. According to figures released in the House of Commons, the Red Army maintains 500 regiments, with 30–35 aircraft assigned to each. British intelligence sources estimate that Russia has 15,000–17,000 planes for tactical co-operation with ground forces; 2,000 planes with the Red Fleet; 14,000 front-line planes for strategic purposes; and 10,000 planes in reserve. Annual production is said to be amounting to 1,500 to 1,800 heavy bombers, 3,000 to 4,000 light bombers, 5,000 to 6,000 fighters (half of which are supposed to be jets), 1,200 to 1,400 transport planes, 3,000 to 4,000 trainers. Hansard, 472, 13, pp. 1808–1809, 1860, March 3, 1950.

9. Data concerning the Red Fleet are based on extensive interrogation of former personnel of the various Soviet naval units, including some of its senior officers. A preliminary report of our special investigation was prepared by us for *Corps Diplomatique,* I, 2, May 15, 1946, pp. 7, 13.

10. British intelligence sources estimate that the Red Fleet now has 360 front-line submarines, some of them capable of 20-knot underwater speed. Under a Five-Year Plan, the U.S.S.R. hopes to build 1,000 submarines by 1954. In 1948–49, 100 new submarines were added to the Red Fleet, some of them built in German yards.

11. *Bolshevik,* 1947, pp. 3, 8.

12. *Military Affairs,* XIII, 2, Summer, 1949, p. 75.

13. J. V. Stalin, *Three Peculiarities of the Red Army,* Moscow, 1941.

14. B. Shaposhnikov, *Brain of the Army,* Moscow, 1927, pp. 184–199.

15. *Military Thought,* September, 1946.

16. *Ibid.,* May, 1946.

17. *Communist International,* October, 1935.

18. Material for these paragraphs is derived from the vast investigations we conducted into the principles and techniques, development and organization of the Soviet propaganda machine.

A total of 1,167 individual references were read, translated, and abstracted under this research project.

19. AP dispatch from Moscow, April 1, 1949. According to private sources, the Central Committee now has a super-Agitprop within the Marx-Engels-Lenin Institute for the conduct of the cold war political warfare, in charge of Central Committee member Peter Nikolayevich Pospelov.

20. *Cf.* V. P. Potenkim (ed.), *Diplomatic History* (Russian), Moscow, 1946, 1947.

21. This is evident from a comparative study of the so-called Blue and White Books on foreign diplomatic personnel, compiled and published by the State Department. The Blue Book contains the names of those who are covered by diplomatic immunity. The White Book lists additional personnel not so covered. In one single issue of the White Book we found 243 listings under Great Britain, and 63 under the U.S.S.R. Fifteen of the latter were butlers, maids, and chauffeurs in the Soviet ambassador's household.

22. Speech at the Tenth Congress of the Russian Communist party, March 10, 1921.

Chapter 19

1. E. Ashby, *Scientist in Russia*, London, 1947, pp. 196–201.

2. A detailed report on these developments was prepared by us immediately following the White House announcement and disseminated to hundreds of newspapers throughout the world, on October 1, 2, 3, 1949.

3. Based on information provided by the seismograph department of Fordham University.

4. W. H. Laurence, *Dawn over Zero*, New York, 1946, pp. 187–195.

5. In the fall of 1945, at Georgetown University, Washington, D.C.

6. *Atomic Energy Development, 1947–48*, U.S. Atomic Energy Commission, pp. 17, 28.

7. U.S. Atomic Energy Commission, *Fourth Semiannual Report*, July, 1948, Proving Ground Operations, pp. 1–5. Large scale additional tests are expected momentarily at the time of this writing.

8. *Report of the Royal Commission*, Ottawa, 1946, pp. 447–458.

9. *New York Times*, August 13, 1946.

10. "Written at the request of Maj. Gen. L. R. Groves, U.S.A.," Princeton, 1945, 264 p.

11. The description of this strange "bomb," supplied by one of

Russia's refugee scientists, suggests some groping in the direction of the H-bomb.

12. Others included Prof. Max Steenbeck, Dr. Karl Bernhardt, Dr. Kurt Mie, Dr. Robert Loepel. They were invited to the U.S.S.R. in June, 1945, *prior to the Alamogordo test,* and worked, first, in the Crimea, and then in the Urals.

13. V. Veksler, L. Gromov, N. Dobrotin, *Experimental Methods in Nuclear Physics* (Russian), Moscow, 1940.

14. G. Oster, "Research on Atomic Energy in the U.S.S.R.," *American Review on the Soviet Union,* VII, 2, February, 1946, pp. 47–48.

15. This is a biblical setting in Transcaucasia, the Alagos (14,440 feet) and the Ararat, volcanoes of the tertiary period, remembered as the scene of Noah's escape.

16. According to information available at UNESCO, communicated to us privately.

17. Ashby, *op. cit.,* p. 203. See also Turin, *The U.S.S.R.—an Economic and Social Survey,* London, 1944.

18. United Nations Document AEC/7, June 24, 1946. Also Document AEC/18, December 30, 1946; Document AEC/21, March 26, 1947; Document AEC/31, Rev. 1, June 27, 1948. On October 26, 1946, Stalin declared emphatically that the U.S.S.R. did not possess A-bombs. In 1947, however, in statements remarkable for their calculated obscurity, both Molotov and Vishinsky hinted that Stalin's disclaimer was obsolete.

19. L. Jomini, *Life of Napoleon,* Eng. ed., Washington, 1863, Vol. II, pp. 244–354.

20. *Ibid.,* pp. 249–50.

21. *Ibid.,* p. 252.

22 *"Die deutsche Wehrmacht muss darauf vorbereitet sein, auch vor Beendigung des Krieges gegen England, Sowjetrussland in einem schnellen Feldzug niederzuwerfen (Fall Barbarossa)."* See article "Deutsche Geheimdokumente, Der Fall Barbarossa," *Suedd. Sonntagspost,* 1949, pp. 10, 22–28.

23. L. Lochner, *The Goebbels Diaries,* New York, 1948, p. 117.

24. *Ibid.,* p. 460.

25. Jomini, *op. cit.,* pp. 337–339.

26. K. Assmann, "The Battle for Moscow, Turning Point of the War," *Foreign Affairs* XXVIII, 2, January, 1950, pp. 308–326.

27. See Harry Schwartz in *New York Times,* March 26, 1950. According to ingenious computations based on Malenkov's speech (*q.v.*), in 1949, quarterly production of steel in Russia amounted

to 6,200,000 metric tons; of coal to 62,500,000 metric tons; of petroleum to 8,990,000 metric tons. A total of 78 billion kilowatt hours of electric power was generated in 1949. Dr. Schwartz concludes: "American observers studying Mr. Malenkov's data note that they indicate a mixed pattern of fulfillment for the current fourth five year plan, similar to that of earlier plans in the Nineteen Thirties. Output of basic industrial raw materials and many types of heavy industrial machinery this year will apparently equal or exceed the plan's goals, but many important consumer goods will be produced in volume below that projected and perhaps even below that of 1940 when the Soviet Union had a smaller population than now."

Chapter 20

1. Quoted by Albert Rhys Williams, *op. cit.*, p. 101.
2. *Bolshevik*, 1930, No. 2, January 15, p. 8.
3. V. I. Lenin, *A Letter to American Workers*, New York, 1934.
4. A Fineberg (ed.), *Soviet Union 1936*, London, n.d., p. 56.
5. *New York Times*, September 25, 1946. Also see *Trends in Russian Foreign Policy*, Legislative Reference Library, Library of Congress, 1947, pp. 60–61.
6. *Look*, February 4, 1947, p. 22.
7. House Document No. 619, 1948, pp. 149–152.
8. *Voprosy*, 9th ed., 1932, pp. 280, 287.
9. "Historicus," "Stalin on Revolution," *Foreign Affairs*, XXVII, 1, January, 1949, pp. 39–40.
10. House Document No. 619, pp. 140–141.
11. Byrnes, *op. cit.*, pp. 63–64.
12. For a typical incident of Anglo-American rivalry, see *The Memoirs of Cordell Hull*, New York, 1948, Vol. II, pp. 1498–1527, especially pp. 1514–1516. Also K. Hutchinson, *Rival Partners*, New York, 1946, pp. 143–210.
13. The value of the satellites to Russia, in material terms, was well described in House Document No. 154, Vol. I, pp. 13–14.
14. See various pertinent articles in Prof. Varga's *World Politics and World Economy*, now defunct, also in the *Bulletin* of his institute, a branch of the academy.
15. House Document No. 619, pp. 184–207, transcript of Vishinsky's speech at the UN, on September 18, 1947, described as "a landmark in public appreciation of the sharp differences in point of view between the Communists and their former allies."
16. Especially significant are data concerning the Soviet Union's

preparations in the industrial sphere, convincingly presented by
E. L. Raymond on the basis of prodigious research, in his *Soviet
War Potential,* unpublished manuscript. The order of battle
here mentioned was prepared on the basis of information provided by interrogated refugees from the Red Army and Navy.

Chapter 21

1. In the inaugural address, January 20, 1949.
2. *The Military Assistance Program,* Department of State Publication 3563, General Foreign Policy Series 13, July, 1949, p. 1.
3. *Ibid.,* p. 41.
4. Secretary Johnson, *op. cit.,* p. 179.
5. Gen. H. S. Vandenberg, *Annual Report,* Fiscal Year 1949, p. 270.
6. Gen. C. Spaatz, *Final Report,* Fiscal Year 1948, June 30, 1948.
7. Vandenberg, *op. cit.,* p. 270.
8. H. W. Baldwin, *The Price of Power,* New York, 1947, p. 152.
9. Princeton, 1947.
10. A two-month maneuver, jointly held by the Air Force, the Navy,
    the Civil Aeronautics Administration, and the Army as an ob-
    server, during May and June, 1949. It proved the vulnerability
    of the U.S. to aerial sneak attack.
11. Zilliacus, *op. cit.,* pp. 211–212.
12. Especially *Life,* XXVIII, 9, February 27, 1950, devoted to the
    theme, "War can come, will we be ready?" pp. 19–81.
13. W. Lippmann, *The Cold War, A Study in U.S. Foreign Policy,*
    New York, 1947, pp. 60–62.

Chapter 22

1. See his brilliant *The Price of Power,* which should be read as a
   source book by all interested in the vital subject of our defenses.
2. Lord Acton in speech on May 28, 1877 at Bridgnorth, reprinted
   in *The History of Freedom and Other Essays,* London, 1907.
3. Lionel M. Gelber, *Peace by Power,* London, 1942, p. 10.
4. Princeton, 1946.
5. *New York Times,* August 27, 1945.
6. October 1, 1946.

Chapter 23

1. See the tersely worded White House release, *New York Times,*
   September 24, 1949.
2. Both Hanson Baldwin and the Alsop brothers protested this
   attitude, revealing in detail the campaign described here.
3. Hearings, House of Representatives, Committee on Armed Serv-

ices, *The National Defense Program—Unification and Strategy,*
October 6–21, 1949, p. 51.

4. Brodie, B. *A Guide to Naval Strategy,* Princeton, 1944, pp. 20, 22–23.

5. *Geheimes Kriegstagebuch, Oberkommando der Kriegsmarine,* a daily record of World War II, from August 1, 1939 (!), on, kept by the German Naval High Command, and captured by us intact at Tannbach, in the spring of 1945.

6. S. A. Goudsmit, *Alsos,* New York, 1947, pp. 140–159, 232–246.

7. According to information supplied by Col. Kalinov, the *Katyusha,* a multibarreled rocket-firing mortar, was invented by Lt. Gen. A. Kostikov "when he read the story of Joseph Fieschi's infernal machine used in 1835 in an attempt to assassinate King Louis-Philippe of France."

8. Smyth, *op. cit.,* pp. 47–49.

9. Clausewitz, *On War,* 4th ed., London, 1940, pp. 230–231.

10. *Ibid.,* pp. 207–208.

11. Secretary Johnson, *op. cit.,* p. 6.

12. *New York Times,* April 5, 1949.

13. For the diplomatic phase of this surrender, including documents, see *American Journal of International Law,* XI, 1, 1946, pp. 11–20.

14. *The Federal Budget in Brief,* Bureau of the Budget, January, 1950, pp. 10–14.

15. The President's so-called nonpolitical trip in the spring of 1950 failed to correct this impression. Although he was in intimate touch with the people and did a lot of talking, he failed to provide explanations in the familiar manner of Roosevelt.

16. Information from diplomatic sources, supported by the significant but widely neglected dispatches of Harold Callender to the *New York Times* from Paris.

17. *New York Herald Tribune,* April 5, 1950.

18. U.S. Relations with China, *op. cit.,* p. 688.

19. V. Sheean, *Personal History,* New York, 1934, p. 239. Other data based on intelligence supplied by Chinese sources on both sides through contacts in the U.S.

20. U.S. Relations with China, *op. cit.,* Vol. VII.

21. *New York Times,* April 30, 1950, Part IV.

Chapter 24

1. Including Mr. Ramadier, then premier and later defense minister of France, and Herr Karl Renner, president of Austria.

2. We discussed the question of neutrality with former French Premier Reynaud, and some of these notes are based on the ideas he expressed.
3. Speech on April 10, 1899, before Hamilton Club, Chicago.

Chapter 25

1. Byrnes, *op. cit.*, p. 86.
2. In his interview with W. Kingsbury-Smith, chief European correspondent of the International News Service.
3. The material concerning Stalin's health was provided by a prominent physician-exile, long associated with Prof. Levine, head of the cardiac division of the Kremlin Hospital, chief of Stalin's attending doctors. Levine's articles in the bulletin of the Kremlin Hospital provided additional clues.
4. Upon his return from Moscow, Secretary General Trygve Lie of the United Nations attested the excellence of Stalin's current health, at least in so far as appearances go.
5. *New York Times,* February 15, 1950.
6. See Secretary Acheson's speech at Portland, Ore., March 17, 1950.
7. For a balanced journalistic account of those conferences, and Roosevelt's role in them, see J. Gunther, *Roosevelt in Retrospect,* New York, 1950.
8. Sherwood, *op. cit.*, p. 894.
9. Trygve Lie suggested that such a treaty be drafted to cover a period of twenty years, to allow the UN time to develop into an effective force for the preservation of peace.
10. H. W. Baldwin, *op. cit.*, pp. 203–219, 323–324.
11. For an exposition of the American propaganda effort, see L. Markel, *Public Opinion and Foreign Policy,* New York, 1949, a study prepared for the Council on Foreign Relations. Of course, the suggestion to remove this activity from the State Department is ours. It would probably be opposed by the contributors to Mr. Markel's study.
12. A report prepared by the Bureau of Labor Statistics, in December, 1949. Already, in 1948, "the average net deficit was $202 for Detroit families, $50 for Denver, and $306 for Houston families." *Monthly Labor Review,* December, 1949.
13. Unpublished manuscript of his address.
14. *New York Times,* April 5, 1950, in a dispatch from London in the wake of the controversy over the suitability of John Strachey as British secretary of war.

Index

Index

Index

Index

Index